Adventures in
Public Relations

Adventures in Public Relations

Case Studies and Critical Thinking

David W. Guth
University of Kansas

Charles Marsh
University of Kansas

Boston • New York • San Francisco

Mexico City • Montreal • Toronto • London • Madrid • Munich • Paris

Hong Kong • Singapore • Tokyo • Cape Town • Sydney

Series Editor: Molly Taylor
Series Editorial Assistant: Michael Kish
Marketing Manager: Mandee Eckersley
Editorial-Production Service: Omegatype Typography, Inc.
Manufacturing Buyer: JoAnne Sweeney
Composition Buyer: Linda Cox
Cover Administrator: Joel Gendron
Electronic Composition: Omegatype Typography, Inc.

For related titles and support materials, visit our online catalog at www.ablongman.com.

Between the time Web site information is gathered and then published, it is not unusual for some sites to have closed. Also, the transcription of URLs can result in typographical errors. The publisher would appreciate notification where these errors occur so that they may be corrected in subsequent editions.

Many of the designations used by manufacturers and sellers to distinguish their products are claimed as trademarks. Where those designations appear in this book, and Allyn and Bacon was aware of a trademark claim, the designations have been printed in initial or all caps.

Library of Congress Cataloging-in-Publication Data

Guth, David.
   Adventures in public relations : case studies and critical thinking / David W. Guth, Charles Marsh.
     p. cm.
   Includes bibliographical references and index.
   ISBN 0-205-40570-3
    1. Public relations. 2. Public relations—United States—Case studies. I. Marsh, Charles, 1955– II. Title.

HM1221.G86 2005
659.2'0973—dc22

                                                   2004051070

Printed in the United States of America

10 9 8 7 6 5 4   09 08 07

Contents

Preface

When it comes to the focus of this book, there should be no mystery: The title tells it all.

Adventures in Public Relations: Case Studies and Critical Thinking reveals three major elements of this text: adventure, case studies, and critical thinking. Let's look at each more closely:

- **Adventure**—The word implies excitement, passion, drama, and uncertainty. What better way to convey a true sense of a dynamic profession? Public relations builds mutually beneficial relationships—even in the most trying times. It accepts and overcomes challenges. And it sometimes confronts the consequences of failing to act in an honest and/or strategic manner. In this book, the authors seek to share a sense of the adventure of public relations.

- **Case studies**—Educators and professionals agree on the value case studies bring to the practice of public relations. Each case allows us to learn from its successes and failures. A guiding principle in the writing of this book was to present a real-world portrait of the profession. At times, practitioners succeed in achieving their goals. Other times, they fail. And still other times, the outcome lies somewhere between success and failure. Not every public relations campaign wins awards or involves a prominent global organization. Public relations exists everywhere, including the frontlines of everyday living. The selection of cases for this book reflects this diversity.

- **Critical thinking**—Developing thinking skills is one of the true values of a college education. Certainly, students must master the rote learning of facts and figures. However, only well-rounded individuals—critical thinkers—can give that knowledge a sense of meaning and purpose. You need only look at the front page of this morning's newspaper to know that our world faces significant challenges. We need problem solvers—the very essence of what a public relations practitioner is supposed to be. Life doesn't provide easy answers, and neither do the case studies in this book.

An underlying theme of *Adventures in Public Relations: Case Studies and Critical Thinking* is an unwavering belief in the role of values in public relations. The identification of and adherence to values provides meaningful guidance in a world that is neither black nor white. One of the many benefits of case studies is that they help readers identify, refine, and test their own values systems. Just as important, case studies can open minds to the existence of alternative values.

This book is divided into four major sections: Foundations, Internal Communication, External Communication, and The Social Environment. The Foundations section defines the profession of public relations in a social and theoretical context. It also provides guidance for the evaluation of public relations campaigns, and it introduces an eight-step process for analyzing case studies: RECAP.

The book's remaining three sections contain chapters on traditional areas such as employee relations and media relations. However, those sections also include emerging topics that have profound influence on the profession, including business-to-business relations and cyber-relations.

With the exception of chapters in the Foundations section, each chapter contains three case studies. Because of the cross-disciplinary nature of public relations, the decision to place individual cases in specific chapters was difficult. Rarely is a case *just* a consumer relations case or *just* a crisis communications case. In reading this book, you'll find that each of its 36 cases could easily have been placed in a different chapter. For that reason, we invite educators to assign these cases based on their own needs and not on the organizational rationale of the authors.

An ACT File—using an acronym for Advanced Critical Thinking—appears at the conclusion of each chapter. Each ACT File introduces a critical thinking process that students can use in evaluating—and creating—public relations campaigns. Again, because of the dynamic nature of public relations, the processes described in each ACT File are not restricted to just the cases in the relevant chapter. Instructors are encouraged to use these critical thinking processes when, where, and how they wish.

This book represents countless hours of labor among a group of dedicated people, the great majority of whom do not have their names listed on the cover. Although writing is most often thought of as an individual activity, book publishing is a team effort. The authors wish to acknowledge the determination, talents, and critical thinking skills of those who turned an idea into the reality you now hold in your hands.

For the authors of this book, public relations is more than a profession. It is a calling. We salute the educators and practitioners who inspire us to transform their experiences into tales of adventure. We especially treasure the love and support of our wives and children, without whom our personal adventures would be meaningless.

D. W. G.
C. M.

Adventures in
Public Relations

CHAPTER 1

The World of Public Relations

M y, how things have changed.
In its earliest days, it operated in the shadows. Although its roots date back to the dawn of recorded history, its formal practice did not begin until the Industrial Revolution of the late 19th century. Not until the publication of *Crystallizing Public Opinion* by Edward L. Bernays in 1923 was this calling given its name: **public relations.** Newspapers viewed the emerging profession as an economic threat and ran antipublicity campaigns to counter its effects. During the period just before and during World War II, public relations was unfairly branded as a form of propaganda that had been used to justify the enslavement and murder of millions of people. Even today, some people still use *public relations* in a sentence as if it were a pejorative term.[1]

Just look at it now. Public relations practitioners, as well as the fruits of their labors, are everywhere you look. They have become a major force in the Information Age. This is a time of **globalization,** a period of economic interdependence resulting from technological advances and increasing world trade. We also live in a very complex world with diffused special interests. In this environment, public relations has become a catalyst for compromise and change. Through public relations, individuals and organizations get their voices heard in the great marketplace of ideas. By creating targeted messages, practitioners help these voices rise above the ever-increasing cacophony of media competing for our attention. While keeping a professional distance, many journalists now view public relations practitioners as important sources in news gathering. Most significant, public relations has taken an important role in the post–Cold War world by helping previously totalitarian nations make the sometimes difficult transition toward democracy.

At its very best, the profession encourages social consensus and tolerance. At its worst, it creates divisions that promote conflict. And at all times, it reflects the complexity of an interconnected global society.

Welcome to the adventure of 21st century public relations!

Defining Public Relations

So what, exactly, is this hot career that attracts so much interest? Before we attempt to define *public relations,* let's define another word: *ubiquitous*—an adjective that means "existing or being everywhere."[2] Air is ubiquitous. Think of what would happen if someone came up to you and asked, "What is air?" Of course you *know* what air is—you use it all the time! However, as you soon discover, giving a precise definition is more problematic. Do you discuss the various gasses that make up our atmosphere? Do you describe the climatological factors that drive our weather? Or are we talking about what happens when a basketball player takes a running jump from the foul line and slams the ball through the hoop? What at first may seem a simple task suddenly becomes very complicated.

That is the challenge we face when defining public relations. It is ubiquitous. The public relations efforts of total strangers probably influence an untold number of decisions you make every day. This can involve the food you eat, the clothes you wear, the radio station you listen to, the car you drive, the television program you watch, the politician you elect—and even the school you attend. It affects the way you feel about things. That your view of one company may be favorable while that of another is negative is often the result of good—or bad—public relations. In hundreds of ways—some obvious and many not—public relations is a major force in your life.

Because of its ubiquitous nature, a definition is hard to pin down. Try this experiment: Ask a dozen of your friends to define public relations. There is a good chance that you will get a dozen different answers.

In this book, we define public relations as "the values-driven management of relationships between an organization and the publics that can affect its success."[3] While a 17-word description may seem a bit brief for such a ubiquitous profession, the authors of this book think it does the job quite well.

Let's look at the five-word phrase at the heart of that definition: "values-driven management of relationships." When you think of it, that's pretty powerful stuff. "Values-driven" implies that public relations is activity guided by personal, organizational, professional, and societal values. In turn, that implies honorable and ethical activity. "Management" suggests that public relations is part of the discipline of organizational leadership. In leadership roles, managers monitor the pulse of their organization and the pulses of the publics critical to their success through an ongoing program of research, planning, communication, and evaluation. The final word in the phrase, "relationships," stresses the long-term nature of this activity. A successful relationship requires dialogue, empathy, and mutual respect. In short, even with a concise definition of this dynamic and far-reaching profession, you have still said a mouthful.

The Public Relations Process

As with its definition, the process of conducting public relations has been described many ways under a variety of titles. But here, at least, some consensus exists: Most agree that public relations follows a four-step process.

1. Research—This is the information-gathering phase. Through formal and informal research methods, practitioners gather data on the client, the environment in which it operates, and its **stakeholders,** the people who can affect or are affected by the organization's ability to achieve desired results. Practitioners identify the problems and opportunities facing the client and determine what, if any, action is appropriate.

2. Planning—In the planning process, practitioners decide on a future course of action. They may create ad-hoc, or limited-purpose, plans to address a short-term situation, or standing and contingency plans that have a longer shelf life. Whatever path they follow, these plans should all be values-driven. When they are, consensus is reached not only on desired **goals,** but also on the **objectives** that will be followed to achieve those goals and the specific **tactics** needed to execute those objectives.

3. Communication—In the communication phase, the plan is transformed into action. The availability of key resources, such as budget, staffing, and time, will influence the process. Under ideal circumstances, practitioners send their messages to individual publics using media (channels of communication) that those publics prefer.

4. Evaluation—In the evaluation phase, practitioners determine what they did right, what they could have done better, and what the next step should be. Many organizations weigh success according to profits and losses. With the focus of public relations on the building and maintenance of relationships, such measurement can be very challenging. Practitioners must be ready to demonstrate in tangible ways their contributions to the organization's bottom line.

Let us add a cautionary note: We do not mean to imply that this four-step process follows a straight and narrow path. Public relations is a dynamic process in which one may engage in each of these steps at any time. For example, while conducting research, it makes sense to think about evaluation and how you will determine whether the plan succeeded. And during the communication phase, it may be necessary to evaluate incoming data, conduct new research, and revise the plan. (See Figure 1.1.)

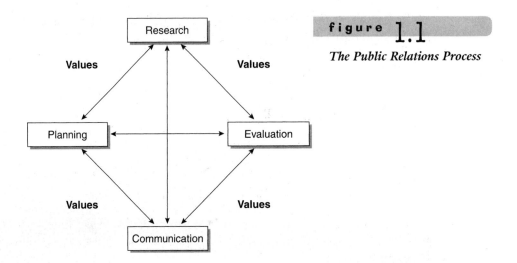

figure 1.1

The Public Relations Process

Public relations is targeted communication. While an organization's values and goals may remain constant, it tailors messages to individual audiences using language they understand and appeals they find relevant. It is critical that communicators have a thorough understanding of their target audiences. Public relations is most successful when practitioners are able to identify shared values and interests.

You can see an example of this principle in action at your own college or university. Although there are times—such as during final exams—that it may seem as if school is the only thing that matters, you only have to look around to see that it is just one piece in a complex social puzzle. Your college has to nurture relationships with the community in which it is located. It has to respond to the needs of donors, politicians, business and industry, fellow educators, and the news media. Each of these publics has its own values and interests. As your college seeks to achieve its goals, such as increased financial support, it may remind these stakeholders of the values they all hold in common, such as the community's social, cultural, and economic health. The challenge—the adventure—of 21st century public relations is to explore this common ground.

Another 21st century challenge comes in selecting the most appropriate channels to reach the target. At home, in the office, and everywhere in between, people are bombarded by thousands of messages every day. The communicator's challenge is to have a particular message heard by a desired listener. This involves the selection of channels the target finds convenient and credible. These can be **controlled channels,** such as advertising, in which the practitioner determines the form, timing, and placement of the message—often at considerable expense. Or they can be **uncontrolled channels,** such as publicity, in which the delivery of the message is in the hands of someone else, such as a newspaper editor. While the first approach has the obvious advantage of control, the second brings with it **third-party endorsement,** the credibility that results from positive statements made by others about your organization. In an ideal situation, you would use both. But as

Public relations tactics range from the traditional to the unusual. At its 2003 rally near the Augusta National Golf Club, the National Council of Women's Organizations protested the exclusion of women members. (See Case 6.3.) (Courtesy of Ralph Estes)

we know, this is not always an ideal world. These are some of the hard choices today's practitioner must face.

The Profession at a Glance

Who Does Public Relations?

Public relations professionals perform a wide variety of tasks in an equally varied range of settings. Why? Because everyone needs public relations. Try to name one organization that does not need to maintain good relations with others who wield influence over whether it achieves its goals. Not many come to mind.

In general, public relations is practiced in five job settings: agencies, corporations/businesses, nonprofits/associations, governments, and independent consultants. Because the profession is not licensed within the United States and its job descriptions and titles are so varied, it is difficult to determine the precise number of practitioners. The U.S. government estimated that 227,000 people were employed in public relations jobs in 2002. However, that does not take into account so-called marketing and promotions jobs that involve the discipline of public relations.[4]

The real number of practitioners in the United States may be somewhere around 400,000. And in terms of the global practice of public relations, that number is anyone's guess!

In a most basic sense, public relations professionals help organizations and individuals find their voice. They are communications consultants who help identify the most appropriate messages and channels for reaching important **publics.** In a public relations context, a public is any group of people who share a common interest, value, or values in a particular situation. They also listen to the concerns of those same publics and communicate them back to their organizations.

They are also **managers.** While everyone reacts to things from time to time, the best public relations practitioners plan and try to dictate the course of events. They are able to do this because they have done their research and have an intimate knowledge of their organization, the people important to its success, and the environment in which it operates. And while they may not be their organization's ultimate decision makers, they are valued counsels to those who are. As we will soon discuss, the public relations function can vary from one setting to the next. But at the very core of every public relations activity is the management of important relationships.

As noted, the specific tasks these practitioners perform are as varied as their job settings. Most use writing skills to communicate with a variety of publics. They often prepare news releases and executive speeches for **external publics,** those outside of the organization. They also create employee newsletters or personnel

NASA Administrator Sean O'Keefe has used public relations to maintain support for the space agency following the 2003 *Columbia* disaster. (See Case 13.1.) (Courtesy of David Guth)

benefits brochures for **internal publics,** those with direct ties to the organization. In recent years, practitioners have used the Internet as their organization's front door to the world. Knowledge of video and audio production is useful, as is knowledge of graphics design and desktop publishing.

One of the most valued—and often unappreciated—skills a practitioner can develop is the ability to interpret and translate changes in the environment. By this, we mean recognizing the significance of seemingly irrelevant or unconnected events and communicating that information to management. This is known as **issues management,** the process of identifying issues as they emerge and preparing a timely response to address them. Many refer to this as "getting ahead of the curve." And in today's 24-hour high-pressure news cycle, it is better to go out and greet the future than wait for it to show up on the doorstep.

Theory versus Reality

For the past few pages, we have attempted to describe public relations as it should be. However, the risk of defining anything—especially a profession as dynamic and complex as public relations—is that theory often runs head-on into reality. Human beings are unique and have their own motivations. That translates into a world with infinite variables and an unpredictable environment.

With that in mind, let's discuss the reality of public relations. As noted, others may choose to define public relations differently than we have. And they often do that through the actions they take. The conduct of the public relations function can vary widely from one organization to another. The reasons for these discrepancies vary. Sometimes they reflect management philosophy. Often they are reactions to events outside the organization's control. And other times, they are just the way things evolved over time.

Researchers Todd Hunt and James Grunig have written that the practice of public relations typically falls into one of four models.[5]

1. The press agentry/publicity model—In this role, practitioners focus on media relations. They tend to be tacticians—as opposed to strategists—interested in short-term gains. Often, their focus is on promoting the organization, and they believe that the generation of publicity is their primary purpose.

2. The public information model—In this role, practitioners act like reporters within their own organizations. Their focus is on the dissemination of objective and accurate information. These individuals tend to be more tacticians than they are counselors.

3. The two-way asymmetrical model—In this role, practitioners actively engage in persuasion. Their goal is to bring target publics around to a certain way of thinking through advocacy.

4. The two-way symmetrical model—In this role, practitioners serve as the catalyst for conflict resolution and consensus. Their goal is to encourage two-way communication that leads to mutual understanding and cooperation.

Which approach is preferred? Hunt and Grunig wrote that the two-way symmetrical model is most consistent with public relations' stated goal of building strong relationships.[6] However, the reality is that individual management styles and operating environments determine how organizations practice public relations. That different people engage in public relations in so many different ways is one reason the authors wrote this book.

Gender and Ethnic Diversity

If you are a student sitting in a public relations classroom, you only need to look around to see one of the most important changes that has occurred in the profession during the past generation: women.

"Among the most significant demographic trends of the past 25 years has been the rising participation of women in the labor force, which greatly increased the productive capacity of the nation," wrote Jeffrey Humphreys, director of the Selig Center for Economic Growth at the University of Georgia. "As women became more career-oriented, they delayed marriage and childbearing, which lowered birth rates and altered the age distribution of the population."[7]

In the United States, public relations has evolved from a profession that was once a male-dominated domain into one in which women now hold nearly seven out of ten jobs. Elizabeth Toth of Syracuse University has studied this transition for nearly two decades and cites a variety of reasons for this gender shift.

"Public relations doesn't put up the barriers to women found in many occupations," Toth said. "It's a very flexible field in which women can balance family and marriage. Organizations seem to prefer women in public relations roles because they think they are better communicators, more nurturing and willing to listen and collaborate."[8] Toth also credits equal-opportunity laws and a migration of men to more lucrative careers for this feminization of public relations.

Another thing you may have noticed in your look around the classroom is a lack of ethnic diversity. While comprehensive employment figures for public relations do not exist, current data suggest a pressing need to recruit more people of color into the profession. According to the Bureau of Labor Statistics, only 7.4 percent of those employed in what was classified as "management and public relations services" in 2001 were black, and only 3.0 percent were of Hispanic origin.[9] To place those numbers into context, persons of Hispanic origin constituted 13 percent and black or African Americans made up 12.3 percent of the nation's population in the 2000 Census.[10]

While much work remains to be done, steps are being taken to increase diversity within the ranks of public relations practitioners. Among the objectives listed in the Public Relations Society of America's *2001–2004 Strategic Plan* are efforts to "attract more international and intercultural members" and to "create greater understanding about communicating to international and intercultural audiences."[11] The Public Relations Society of America also launched a National Diversity Program to "reach out to African American, Hispanic, Asian and other minority PR firms and practitioners" and to develop minority internship and mentoring programs.[12]

"In order to deal with local, national, and global diversity, cross-cultural teamwork and a diverse professional staff become essential in a firm's business success," said 2002 PRSA President Joann E. Killeen in an address to the annual conference of the Black National Public Relations Society. "If we, as public relations executives, are to function effectively and productively, we must learn to see our differences as assets rather than as liabilities."[13]

Humphreys wrote in *American Demographics* that the move to a more inclusive society is inevitable. "As African Americans, Asians, Native Americans and Hispanics increase in number and purchasing power, their growing share of the U.S. consumer market will continue to reshape the commercial and political landscape of America," he concluded. "I have no doubt that these groups increasingly will share in the economic success of the U.S. and will wield formidable economic clout."[14]

Salaries

And now the answer to the BIG question: How much does this job pay? The two largest public relations professional associations, PRSA and the International Association of Business Communicators, released an extensive survey of member salaries in 2000. It provides students interested in a public relations career an indication of what they may expect to one day earn.

According to the *PRSA/IABC Salary Survey 2000,* the average practitioner earned $53,000 per year in 1999. Salaries among the two organizations ranged from $28,000 to $147,000. The average annual salaries of accredited members of the professional associations were more than $21,000 higher than those of non-accredited members. The highest average annual salaries were paid in corporations ($70,000), followed by those in agencies ($52,000) and nonprofits ($40,000). The survey said that the highest average annual salaries were paid in the metals/mining industry ($147,000), and the lowest ($32,000) were paid to those in the hotels/lodgings industry. In general, higher salaries were paid to practitioners living along the coasts of the United States ($52,000–$65,000) than to those in the Midwest ($48,000). The survey also exposed a gender gap: The median annual salary for men was $65,000, and only $50,000 for women.[15] (See Table 1.1.)

As useful as the survey is, one should remember that PRSA's and IABC's membership represents a small fraction of the people who work in public relations. It is also likely that PRSA and IABC members are better paid, making it more likely that they can afford (or that their company will pay) membership dues. In other words, these figures may be a bit on the high side of reality.

The U.S. Department of Labor's Bureau of Labor Statistics provides another window into the world of compensation. According to the *Occupational Outlook Handbook, 2004–05 Edition,* the median annual earnings for salaried public relations specialists, those who do not hold managerial positions, was $41,710 in 2002. In contrast, median annual earnings for public relations managers was $60,640 that

table 1.1   *PRSA/IABC Salary Survey 2000*

	All	*Men*	*Women*	*Firms*	*Corporations*	*Nonprofits*
Up to $30,000	6.6	3.5	9.1	5.6	6.5	16.5
$30,001–$50,000	31.3	22.3	35.7	32.5	15.3	44.3
$50,001–$70,000	24.7	24.2	24.9	26.2	18.3	22.2
Over $70,000	27.3	40.8	21.0	27.0	42.6	10.8

Note: Percentages do not include nonrespondents.

Source: Data from *Public Relations Society of America. PRSA/IABC Salary Survey 2000.* Public Relations Society of America and the International Association of Business Communicators. Online: www.prsa.org.

year. The BLS reports that "salary levels vary substantially, depending upon the level of managerial responsibility, length of service, education, firm size, location and industry." It also predicts that the demand for jobs in public relations will grow at or above the average for all occupations through 2010. "Keen competition will likely continue for entry-level jobs as the number of qualified applicants is expected to exceed the number of job openings."[16]

The Value of Case Studies

Public relations case studies are like a certain breakfast cereal we have seen advertised on television in that they are both good for you and taste good, too! (Before you start gnawing on the cover, be advised that we are using *taste* in a figurative sense.)

The Commission on Public Relations Education—a panel comprising educators and professionals—recommended in 1999 that case studies should be an integral part of a public relations education. Its recommendations also included courses that focused on public relations research, planning, and writing combined with a strong traditional liberal arts and social science education.[17]

In the strictest sense, the value of case studies is that they link classroom theory to everyday experience. Through the study of the actions of others, we learn that success and failure are often linked to the application of—or the failure to apply—basic principles. At the same time, these cases remind us there are no cookie-cutter approaches to public relations; what works in one situation may not apply to another. By examining the actions of practitioners operating under a wide range of environmental influences, we hone our own decision-making skills. We become better problem solvers. This is what is known as **critical thinking.**

That's a term we know you've heard bandied about. A reasonable person—a critical thinker—may ask the obvious question, "What *is* critical thinking?" Like public relations, it is a term with many definitions. Here are just two:

1. Michael Scriven and Richard Paul of the National Council for Excellence in Critical Thinking define it as "the intellectually disciplined process of actively and skillfully conceptualizing, applying, analyzing, synthesizing, and/or evaluating information gathered from, or generated by, observation, experience, reflection, reasoning, or communication, as a guide to belief and action."[18]

2. The American Philosophical Association reported, "The ideal critical thinker is habitually inquisitive, well-informed, trustful of reason, open-minded, flexible, fair-minded in evaluation, honest in facing personal biases, prudent in making judgments, willing to reconsider, clear about issues, orderly in complex matters, diligent in seeking relevant information, reasonable in the selection of criteria, focused in inquiry, and persistent in seeking results which are as precise as the subject and the circumstances of inquiry permit."[19]

While thorough, both definitions are also inordinately long. For the sake of brevity, we define critical thinking as reasoned judgment and problem solving driven by research, analysis, and evaluation. Critical thinking is about making good decisions following a systematic examination of all of the facts. Rather than basing actions on hunches, feelings, or "vibes," critical thinkers take a reflective look at their world and act following careful deliberation. Do they ever make mistakes? Sure they do. But they are less likely to err than when they act impulsively.

That is what this book is about: helping emerging public relations practitioners develop critical thinking skills that will serve them throughout their professional lives.

In short, case studies provide emerging practitioners with a glimpse of the real world. They get to see their future career path through someone else's eyes and learn from the successes and failures of others. In a book such as this, with dozens of case studies covering a wide array of topics, emerging professionals view the practice of public relations in a variety of settings. That is why we call it an adventure.

Discussion Questions

1. How does the ubiquitous nature of public relations complicate matters for its practitioners?

2. In what way is public relations a dynamic process?

3. Where does the theory of public relations come into conflict with reality? What models represent the reality of the practice of public relations?

4. Does the profession of public relations reflect the diversity of society? Please cite specific examples to support your answer.

5. How do emerging public relations professionals benefit from reading and discussing case studies?

Key Terms   • • • • • • • • • • • • • • • •

communication, p. 3
controlled channels, p. 4
critical thinking, p. 10
evaluation, p. 3
external publics, p. 6
goals, p. 3
globalization, p. 1

internal publics, p. 7
issues management, p. 7
managers, p. 6
objectives, p. 3
planning, p. 3
publics, p. 6
public relations, p. 1

research, p. 3
stakeholders, p. 3
tactics, p. 3
third-party endorsement, p. 4
uncontrolled channels, p. 4

Endnotes   • • • • • • • • • • • • • • • •

1. For a comprehensive look at the evolution of public relations, the authors recommend *Public Relations: The Unseen Power, A History,* by the late Scott M. Cutlip (Hillsdale, NJ: Lawrence Erlbaum Associates, 1994).

2. *New Webster's Dictionary and Roget's Thesaurus* (New York: Book Essentials, 1992), 409.

3. The authors present a more detailed explanation of the genesis of this definition in another book, *Public Relations: A Values-Driven Approach,* 2nd ed. (Boston: Allyn & Bacon, 2003), 1–22.

4. *Occupational Outlook Handbook, 2004–05 Edition.* U.S. Department of Labor, Bureau of Labor Statistics. Online: www.bls.gov.

5. Todd Hunt and James E. Grunig, *Public Relations Techniques* (Fort Worth, TX: Harcourt Brace College, 1994), 8–9.

6. Hunt and Grunig, 8–9.

7. "Demographic Diamonds," *American Demographics,* April 1, 2002. Online: www.inside.com.

8. Gary Pallassino, "Research Report: Tracking the Gender Switch in Public Relations," *Syracuse University Magazine,* Spring 2003, Vol. 20, No. 1. Online: http://sumagazine.syr.edu.

9. "Household Data Annual Averages, Table 18: Employed Persons by Detailed Industry, Sex, Race, and Hispanic Origin." U.S. Department of Labor, Bureau of Labor Statistics. Online: www.bls.gov.

10. "Census 2000 Shows America's Diversity." U.S. Department of Commerce news release, March 12, 2001.

11. *PRSA 2001–2004 Strategic Plan.* Public Relations Society of America. Online: www.prsa.org.

12. Remarks of Joann E. Killeen at the Annual Conference of the National Black Public Relations Society. October 4, 2002. Washington, DC: Public Relations Society of America. Online: www.prsa.org.

13. Remarks of Joann E. Killeen.

14. "Demographic Diamonds."

15. *PRSA/IABC Salary Survey 2000.* Public Relations Society of America and the International Association of Business Communicators. Online: www. prsa.org.

16. *Occupational Outlook Handbook, 2004–05 Edition. Occupational Outlook Handbook, 2002–03 Edition.* U.S. Department of Labor, Bureau of Labor Statistics. Online: www.bls.gov.

17. Commission on Public Relations Education, *Public Relations Education for the 21st Century—A Port of Entry* (New York: Public Relations Society of America, 1999).

18. Michael Scriven and Richard Paul, National Council for Excellence in Critical Thinking Web site, www.criticalthinking.org.

19. Peter A. Facione, *The Delphi Report—Critical Thinking: A Statement of Expert Consensus for Purposes of Educational Assessment and Instruction* (Millbrae, CA: California Academic Press, 1990), 2. Online: www. insightassessment.com/dex.html.

ACT file # 1 ·················

Platonic Dialectic

Critical thinking killed its first practitioner. (Now *there's* a recommendation.)

In Athens in 399 B.C., Socrates received a death sentence for, in his words, being found guilty of the charge that "he inquires into things below the earth and in the sky, and makes the weaker argument defeat the stronger, and teaches others to follow his example."

Socrates did inquire into things, and he did so in a way that was goal-oriented, comprehensive, and systematic—not a bad definition of critical thinking. If he seemed to make the weaker argument defeat the stronger, that probably reflected the opinion of powerful opponents who didn't enjoy having their beliefs challenged. In one heated debate, Callicles, provoked beyond endurance by Socrates' surgical dissection of a flawed argument, actually forecast Socrates' trial: "It quite strikes me, Socrates, that you believe . . . [you] could never be dragged into a law court by some perhaps utterly paltry rascal."

Socrates responded, "It would be no marvel if I were put to death."[1]

Plato, Socrates' famed student, recorded and perhaps embellished many of Socrates' debates. In those dialogues, Plato used Socrates' own term for critical thinking: *dialectic.* Professor Winifred Horner of Texas Christian University defines Platonic dialectic as "a method of searching for truth through dialogue."[2] Today, we use the term *Socratic method* to describe a pattern of probing questions and answers.

Just as it takes two to argue, it takes at least two to create a dialectic. You certainly can and should conduct an internal dialectic, challenging your own beliefs through question and answer, but true Platonic dialectic requires at least two people who seek knowledge.

Platonic dialectic comprises four essential steps: definition, analysis, synthesis, and conclusion.[3]

1. Definition: Clarify the existing situation, particularly the definitions of key terms. For example, if you apply dialectic to a relationship, your colleague might say, "Well, we have a good, productive relationship with that public. I'm satisfied." As a dialectical partner, you would respond by asking what your colleague meant by the words *good, productive, public,* and *satisfied*—and maybe even *relationship.* You might discover that you're not all that sure who the public is and that you're not really satisfied.

2. Analysis: Break the situation down into its simplest, most elemental facts. (*Analysis* comes from a Greek word meaning "to loosen throughout.") To return to your dialectic with your colleague, what things make the relationship good and productive? What things make your colleague satisfied? Are those things real? Can they be proven?

3. Synthesis: Bring together the elements that survived your analysis—the true, provable facts. (*Synthesis* comes from a Greek word meaning "to put together.") Using the facts from your analysis, work with your dialectical colleague toward agreement on a new view of the situation—or, perhaps, a solidly confirmed view of your original belief.

4. Conclusion: Restate the situation in light of what your dialectic has revealed. Does this conclusion seem fair to both you and your colleague? In dialectic, a conclusion often becomes the new situation—and the process of testing it through question and answer begins again.

Somewhat like the public relations process of research, planning, communication, and evaluation, the dialectical process is dynamic. While it's hard to skip forward—to conclude before synthesis, for example—you may find it necessary to move backward and conduct additional definition, analysis, and synthesis before concluding.

It's not too dramatic to say that Socrates sacrificed his life to give us the gift of dialectic, of critical thinking—and that he believed the price to be fair. "Now it is time that we were going," he said at the end of his trial, "I to die and you to live, but which of us has the happier prospect is unknown to anyone but God."[4]

Discussion Questions · · · · · · · · · · · · · · · · · · ·

1. What is the difference between analysis and synthesis?

2. How is Platonic dialectic similar to the four-step public relations process? How is it different?

3. How does dialectic differ from a simple argument?

4. As you read case studies in the chapters that lie ahead, how might you apply Platonic dialectic in them?

Endnotes · · · · · · · · · · · · · · · · · · ·

1. Plato, "Gorgias," trans. W. R. M. Lamb, in *The Rhetorical Tradition*, eds. Patricia Bizzell and Bruce Herzberg (Boston: Bedford Books, 1990).

2. Winifred Bryan Horner, *Rhetoric in the Classical Tradition* (New York: St. Martin's Press, 1988), 443.

3. James L. Golden, "Plato Revisited: A Theory of Discourse for All Seasons," in *Essays on Classical Rhetoric and Modern Discourse*, eds. Robert J. Connors, Lisa S. Ede, and Andrea A. Lunsford (Carbondale, IL: Southern Illinois University Press, 1984).

4. Plato, "Apology," trans. Hugh Tredennick, in *Plato: Collected Dialogues*, eds. Edith Hamilton and Huntington Cairns (Princeton, NJ: Princeton University Press, 1989).

CHAPTER 2

Analyzing Case Studies

Have you ever gone to the movies with your friends, only to discover that you've all come away from the theater with entirely different impressions of the film? One person may have thought that the movie was great because of the actor playing the lead character. Another may have liked the actor but felt the story line was weak. Yet another may have judged the film on the quality of its special effects. All saw the same movie but judged it by different standards.

That experience sums up the challenge in analyzing the performance of public relations practitioners. Before one can declare something to be good, bad, or somewhere in between, the criteria for making such a judgment must first be established. Those criteria are developed through an understanding of the profession, one's personal experiences, and observation of challenges faced by other practitioners. When those challenges are committed to paper and reported in detail, including behind-the-scenes information not necessarily apparent to casual observers, they are known as case studies. As noted in the first chapter, these case studies can help fill gaps in our personal experiences by helping us learn from the actions of others. The more we study the good, the bad, and the in-between, the better prepared we are to make our own informed judgments.

Let's go back to movies for a minute. Film critics enter the theater with their own set of standards. Because they are knowledgeable about the movie industry, actors, producers, and writers, they have developed their own set of criteria for judging movies. Even as the opening credits begin to roll, these cinematic analysts have a checklist of things they want to examine before giving a movie a "thumbs up" or "thumbs down." Of course, different critics have different standards and may disagree with one another—just like you and your friends. But what often distinguishes their approach from those of you and your friends is their expertise.

Credibility is at the heart of any profession—especially public relations. We tend to believe trustworthy, knowledgeable people. Case study analysis is an excellent way to develop your own expertise. But that takes us back to the original question: What constitutes good public relations practice?

Measuring Success

There are many ways to measure the success of public relations practices. We will focus on four common approaches: the measurement of **inputs, outputs, outcomes,** and **relationships.** Each approach, in and of itself, does not provide a complete picture of a public relations program or campaign. However, when used in concert, they encompass the entire public relations process of research, planning, communication, and evaluation. Rarely are public relations campaigns complete successes or failures. Through a systematic study of the entire public relations process—through critical thinking—we can uncover the various factors that led toward or away from success.

The concept of inputs and outputs comes from what management experts call **systems theory,** in which management views an organization as a system of interrelated parts interacting with one another and with a larger outside world. While each system has boundaries that separate it from its environment, those boundaries have become increasingly flexible in recent years.[1] Public relations management expert Mark P. McElreath has written that systems theory is particularly useful in examining public relations and its **boundary-spanning role,** where practitioners serve as a bridge or liaison between an organization and its stakeholders. "It is precisely this role of helping an organization's members recognize and facilitate important relationships that constitutes the core responsibility of the public relations manager," he said.[2]

We will first examine each of these four approaches to measuring public relations success. Then we will introduce a case analysis process that incorporates all of them into a simple, eight-step process that we call RECAP.

Inputs

Under the systems approach, inputs are the "raw materials, money, labor, and energy . . . that organizations acquire, transform into products or services, and then provide as outputs to the external environment."[3] In terms of public relations practice, inputs represent the time, energy, and resources that go into developing strategies and tactics. They represent the decision-making process up to and including the creation of tactics. In a sense, they are products of the research and planning steps of the public relations process. While inputs, in and of themselves, are not measures of a plan's success, they lay the foundation. Actions taken—or not taken—go a long way toward determining outcomes.

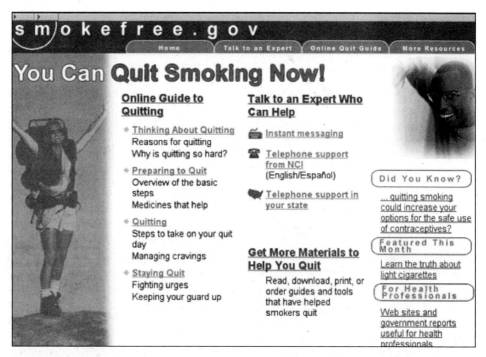

The number of hits on smokefree.gov can tell how many people visited this antismoking Web site, but it can't provide a measure of outcomes: the number of people who actually quit smoking. (See Case 12.3.) (Courtesy U.S. Department of Health and Human Services)

When analyzing inputs, you should ask:

• **Were the public relations objectives and tactics based on solid research?** What kinds of research methods were employed? How accurately did the research reflect the problems and opportunities confronting the client? Did practitioners have a thorough understanding of the client? Was there an understanding of all of the stakeholders—the various groups and individuals with direct or indirect interests that could inhibit or promote the achievement of our goals? Were there steps not taken that could have provided a clearer understanding of the situation facing the client? Was the analysis of the research thorough and did it result in appropriate conclusions?

• **What kind of plan was developed?** Is it an **ad hoc plan**—a one-time-only plan for a specific purpose? Is it a **contingency plan**—a plan that outlines different actions for a variety of anticipated situations? Or is it a **standing plan**—an ongoing and long-term plan to nurture a relationship?

• **What was the quality of the planning?** Was there evidence of a planning structure? Did the plan address the critical challenges facing the client? Did it take into account all of the stakeholders with a direct interest in its outcome? Did it also take into account those who may not have a direct interest in the outcome but wield influence over those who do? Perhaps most important, was the plan consistent with the stated values and goals of the client?

• **How well were the tactics targeted?** Did the tactics match the medium and message to the purpose and public? Did the tactics use channels of communication preferred by each of those publics? Were the various publics reached by more than one medium?

• **Did the plan include methods for evaluating success and determining future courses of action?** How was success defined? Was it an all-or-nothing proposition? Were there multiple measures of success? Were the quality and success of the inputs measured?

• **Was there consensus?** To use a metaphor, did everyone sing from the same sheet of music? Was there a common understanding among practitioners and managers for what would transpire during the communication step of the public relations process? (For example, did the client know you planned to change the logo the company had used for the past 50 years?) Did everyone have the same definition of success? (For example, was it enough that everyone was talking about your campaign? Or did management expect to see increased sales?) These may seem like obvious questions. However, plans can and do fall apart because practitioners overlook these issues.

Answers to these questions about inputs help public relations case analysts determine the quality of the decision-making process leading to outputs, the next measure of success.

Outputs

In systems theory, outputs are the "products or services" that an organization delivers to the external environment.[4] For practitioners, outputs are the specific actions taken during the execution of a public relations plan. As researchers Linda Childers Hon and James Grunig have noted, "More often than not, they represent what is readily apparent to the eye. They measure how well an organization presents itself to others, the amount of attention or exposure that the organization receives."[5] The quality of outputs alone does not indicate the overall success of a plan. However, without successful outputs, a plan cannot succeed.

Questions that should be asked when examining outputs are:

• **Were the messages clear and on-strategy?** Were the messages delivered via those channels unambiguous and consistent with the client's values, goals, and objectives? Did those messages address each public's self-interests? What was the underlying purpose behind each message, and was that purpose met? And were messages in one medium consistent with those delivered in all media?

- **Were there any forces that inhibited the delivery or understanding of those messages?** Good plans often run smack into reality. Events beyond one's control can derail the best-laid plans of mice and men. Such disruptions can take the form of events that distract public attention or focus it upon something negative. In communication theory, this is known as **noise.** However, there could be other reasons the message didn't get through. One reason could be a process failure—as simple as someone not doing his or her job or doing it poorly. Another reason could be a relationship failure—when people outside the organization inhibit your ability to achieve stated goals. And it could be a management failure—when the remedies you have prescribed are inappropriate and cannot achieve the desired outcome.

- **Did the quality of the tactics satisfy the expectations of the client and the target publics?** Did the actual tactics meet the specifications of the plan? Was each tactic implemented? If not, why not?

- **Were resources managed wisely?** It is possible to be efficient but not effective. The reverse is also true. Either can kill a public relations plan. In an ideal situation, you want both efficiency and effectiveness. To put it another way, you want the biggest bang for the bucks. However, it is important to remember that resources include more than budget, facilities, equipment, and staffing. They include relationships with key publics. For example, an industry may provide a community with jobs and products in return for fair regulation and a quality workforce. How one manages these critical relationships can make the difference in whether the key resources others have are available to us.

You should not minimize the value of analyzing inputs and outputs. This examination can provide valuable lessons for the future. However, while this analysis helps us understand how a race was run, the story isn't complete until we determine the results at the finish line. Those results are known as the outcomes. For many managers, this is the most important measure of success. And in the world of public relations, it can also be the most difficult to express in tangible terms.

Outcomes

According to Hon and Grunig, "Outcomes measure whether target audience groups actually received the messages directed at them . . . paid attention to them . . . understood the messages . . . and retained those messages in any shape or form. They also measure whether the communications materials and messages that were disseminated have resulted in any opinion, attitude and/or behavior changes on the part of those targeted publics to whom the messages were directed."[6]

While the concept behind outcomes is easy to understand, the challenge often comes in measuring them. The difficulty is directly related to the purpose of the campaign. The difficulty often boils down to the difference between quantitative and nonquantitative research. Quantitative research involves the use of scientific methods that yield hard and reliable numbers. If the goal of a public relations

Effective public relations helped introduce purple ketchup to an eager target market. (See Case 8.1.) (Courtesy of H. J. Heinz Company and Jack Horner Communications Inc.)

plan is expressed in tangible terms, such as increasing sales or winning an election, the results are easily quantifiable.

It becomes more difficult to come up with these hard numbers when the purposes driving the campaign are less specific, such as increasing brand awareness or trying to influence people to engage in a healthier lifestyle. Obtaining quantitative results through the use of surveys or experiments can be time-consuming and expensive. For those reasons, organizations often use nonquantitative methods to measure outcomes. Because they do not use scientific methodology designed for accurate measurement, nonquantitative data cannot be viewed as an accurate picture of reality. However, they can be seen as an indicator of reality. And the more indicators suggesting the same outcome, the more likely they are accurate.

The questions that analysts should ask when measuring outcomes include:

- **Did the objectives and tactics achieve the stated goals?** Was this a situation where partial success was acceptable, or was it "all or nothing"? What were the client's priorities, and were they achieved?

- **Were appropriate measures used to determine success?** Measuring inputs and outputs gives only a partial picture. At the same time, the use of inappropriate indicators can lead to a false reading of the results. One example is equating the number of people who attend a campaign rally with the number of people who actually vote. The attendees may have been more interested in the free hot dogs at the rally than in voting for the candidate.

- **Were there unintended effects?** Were there any unanticipated outcomes, either positive or negative? For example, did messages received by untargeted publics generate a reaction? Did the solution to one problem create another?

- **How did the actions affect relationships with key stakeholders?** Hon and Grunig have noted that most outcome measures tend to have a short-term focus.[7] And because case studies, by their very nature, tend to focus on a specific program, the effect of actions on long-term relationships is often overlooked.

- **Do the outcomes suggest a future course of action?** The end of one campaign often marks the start of another. As with other aspects of life, our failures are often more instructive than our successes. Were there lessons from which we can discern immediate remedies or from which we can identify future opportunities?

Relationships

While case study analysis does not easily lend itself to the measurement of the value of long-term relationships, such relationships should not be ignored. That belief is a mantra among those who ascribe to the systems theory of management. "If a public relations person is working to affect changes in any system, big or small, simple or complex, the facts remain: it is the set of relationships that defines the system," wrote McElreath, a public relations management expert. "Change these relationships and the system changes." He cites as proof the success that small, little-known grass-roots organizations have had in forcing major corporations to change their policies by focusing on vulnerable relationships, such as those with stockholders, customers, and regulators.[8]

Let's revisit our definition of public relations: the values-driven management of relationships between an organization and the publics that can affect its success. Our definition rests on the realization that we cannot achieve our goals without the assistance of others. **Resource dependency theory** is based on the idea that no individual or organization is entirely self-sufficient. Each party relies on the goodwill and/or resources of others.[9] The idea that no person—or organization—is an island may appear to be a no-brainer. However, that was not always the case. The earliest management theories focused exclusively on the internal environment of organizations, ignoring the importance of external influences.[10] However, in recent decades, reality has finally sunk in. In a world in which actions taken on the opposite side of the globe can directly affect our health and well-being, we need one another.

The measurement of relationships—the conduits of resources—is especially important to public relations practitioners. Hon and Grunig, pioneers in the area of relationship measurement, wrote, "In order to answer the much broader question—'How can PR practitioners begin to pinpoint and document for senior management the overall value of public relations to the organization as a whole?'—different tools and techniques are needed."[11]

The method they propose, the **PR Relationship Measurement Scale,** involves an extensive questionnaire that measures the strength or health of relationships based on six components:

1. **Control mutuality**—The degree to which parties agree on who has the rightful power to influence one another. While some imbalance is normal, Hon and Grunig believe stable relationships require that each party have some control over the other.
2. **Trust**—Each party's level of confidence in and willingness to open up to the other party. This confidence is based on belief in each other's integrity, dependability, and competence.
3. **Satisfaction**—The extent to which each party feels the relationship is one in which the benefits outweigh the costs.
4. **Commitment**—The extent to which each party believes and feels that the relationship is worth maintaining and promoting.
5. **Exchange relationship**—The extent to which one party gives benefits to the other only because the other has provided benefits in the past or is expected to do so in the future.
6. **Communal relationship**—The extent to which both parties provide benefits to the other because they are concerned for the welfare of the other—even when they get nothing in return.[12]

Even if one does not choose to develop hard numbers to quantify relationships, there is still benefit to understanding the components of relationships. Identifying the nature of each key public's relationship with the client during research makes it easier to understand each public's motivations. That, in turn, has a direct effect on planning. For example, if trust has become a sticking point within a relationship, the public relations plan needs objectives and tactics that address that issue. Failing to do so could undermine the best of intentions. While relationships are often difficult to measure, the effects they have on public relations outcomes are quite powerful.

Case Study Analysis

By now you probably have come to the realization that there's a lot to analyzing public relations cases. The challenge boils down to one critical question: Where do I begin? The answer to this mystery is elementary, my dear Watson. We recommend that you begin at the end.

The authors of this book suggest you follow a process similar to what is known as reverse engineering. It is a concept well known to designers and mechanics—as well as spies and any typical three-year-old. It involves selecting a finished product and taking it apart to see what makes it tick. Quality control specialists often use reverse engineering techniques to spot and correct faults in manufactured products. It is also a way one can learn from—OK, steal from—a competitor. (We are not advocating industrial espionage, but it *does* happen.)

The Reverse Engineering Case Analysis Process (RECAP)

We propose that you use what we call RECAP, the Reverse Engineering Case Analysis Process, to analyze case studies. RECAP follows the four steps of the public relations process: research, planning, communication, and evaluation. In short, we suggest that you figure out how each campaign achieved its outcomes by retracing the public relations process the practitioner followed. It is a clean, simple, and structured eight-step process—a critical thinking process—that allows you to answer the many questions we have raised about inputs, outputs, outcomes, and relationships. It also creates an appreciation for the public relations process itself.

To use RECAP when evaluating the effectiveness of a public relations event or campaign, follow these steps:

1. What research was used to identify problems, opportunities, solutions, and values? Is there evidence of formal or informal research? Were the methods appropriate for the situations? Could more effective research methods have been used? Was there a clear understanding of the client, the challenges it faced, and the social, political, legal, cultural, and ethical environment in which it operated? Did the practitioners consider the evaluation of results when developing the plan?

2. Did research identify key publics? These publics are considered stakeholders, groups that can affect or are affected by the course of events. Did research identify **primary publics,** those in a position to make crucial decisions that determine success or failure? Did it target any **intervening publics,** those with whom we communicate to influence the primary publics? Were there any publics, primary or intervening, overlooked or ignored?

3. Did research identify each public's stake? What were each public's self-interests that came into play during the time period being studied? Some publics may have been unaware that their interests were at stake. What was the nature of the relationship between the client and each public? What were identified as each public's most powerful motivations? Did the plan identify—or ignore—common interests between the client and each public?

4. Did the plan clearly articulate desired outcomes? Did the plan clearly state its goals? Were they explicit or implicit? How measurable were these outcomes?

5. Did the plan clearly articulate targeted messages? Were these messages directed to specific publics, both primary and, if necessary, intervening? Did these messages both promote the client's goal while addressing each public's stake? Could more effective messages have been used? Were they clear and unambiguous? Did the messages overlook or ignore key interests of some of the targeted publics? Was there any noise in the environment that inhibited the delivery of messages?

6. During communication, were appropriate media and tactics used? Did the client use media preferred by and more credible to each public? Were multiple media used? Were messages consistent across media? Were the messages clear, explicit, and unambiguous? Was each medium used to its greatest effect? Did the client/organization miss any opportunities to communicate? Were executions within budgetary and time restrictions?

7. Were campaign actions and messages consistent with previously identified values? Did all actions reflect existing mission statements, values statements, and codes of ethics? Were any laws, regulations, or policies broken? Were any actions taken that were not consistent with the professional values of public relations? Did the client or organization act in the public interest?

8. To what degree was the campaign successful? How was success or failure evaluated? Is there a middle ground between complete success and complete failure? Were forces at play that influenced the outcome? Did the plan anticipate those forces? Were sufficient resources brought to bear? What lessons were learned? Do the results suggest future actions?

Ideally, you should answer the RECAP questions in a neutral and unemotional manner. Adopt an analytical tone. Inexperienced case analysts have a tendency to be judgmental and use absolutes. The trouble with this is that most situations are rarely black or white. Sometimes good people with good intentions fail. The opposite is also true. The purpose of this exercise is to gain a better understanding of events, their outcomes, and the forces that shaped them. The criticism and/or praise of practitioners may be a by-product of RECAP, but neither is its focus.

The challenge is to harness the power of detached objectivity, a key quality of critical thinking. Let the facts speak for themselves. They require no embellishments. And when it is appropriate to offer an opinion, support it by providing evidence. In short, when you use RECAP, we want you to be fearless but fair.

Public relations is a dynamic profession. That is why a public relations career can be so exciting and fulfilling. But it can also be very challenging. Some practitioners and their plans are very successful. Others are not. And the consequences of success or failure can be enormous. In the pages that follow, you will read how people very much like you made critical decisions affecting many others.

While some of the cases in this book focus on big-name companies and widely publicized campaigns, many do not. Instead, the authors have chosen to examine "public relations in the trenches"—often featuring local and regional campaigns that may not have caught the eye of the national news media but were nevertheless important to the stakeholders involved. These are real-life adventures in public relations, more like those you will face during your career.

Let the adventure begin!

Discussion Questions

1. What four common approaches to measuring public relations success are discussed in this chapter? Briefly describe each.

2. What are the three kinds of plans described in this chapter? Briefly describe each.

3. What are Hon and Grunig's six components of relationships? Briefly describe each.

4. What is resource dependency theory?

5. What are the steps of the RECAP process?

Key Terms

ad hoc plan, p. 17
boundary-spanning role, p. 16
commitment, p. 22
communal relationship, p. 22
contingency plan, p. 17
control mutuality, p. 22
exchange relationship, p. 22

inputs, p. 16
intervening publics, p. 24
noise, p. 19
outcomes, p. 16
outputs, p. 16
primary publics, p. 24
PR Relationship Measurement Scale, p. 22

relationships, p. 16
resource dependency theory, p. 22
satisfaction, p. 22
standing plan, p. 17
systems theory, p. 16
trust, p. 22

Endnotes

1. James A. F. Stoner, *Management,* 2nd ed. (Englewood Cliffs, NJ: Prentice-Hall, 1982), 52–53.
2. Mark P. McElreath, *Managing Systematic and Ethical Public Relations* (Madison, WI: Brown & Benchmark, 1993), 14.
3. Stoner, 61.
4. Stoner, 61.
5. Linda Childers Hon and James E. Grunig, *Guidelines for Measuring Relationships in Public Relations* (Gainesville, FL: Institute for Public Relations, 1999), 2. Online: www.instituteforpr.com.
6. Hon and Grunig, 2.
7. Hon and Grunig, 2.

8. McElreath, 15.
9. David W. Guth and Charles Marsh, *Public Relations: A Values-Driven Approach,* 2nd ed. (Boston: Allyn & Bacon, 2003), 92–93.
10. Stoner, 60.
11. Hon and Grunig, 2.
12. Hon and Grunig, 3. The methodology used in developing this scale is detailed in this publication of the Institute for Public Relations' Commission on PR Evaluation and Measurement. It is available through the institute, located at the University of Florida, or on its Web site, www.institutefor.pr.com.

ACT file # 2 . . . .

The Planning Grid

A planning grid is a goals-driven approach to planning that embraces a two-way symmetrical model of public relations. Simply put, it is a step-by-step process that targets message and media to specific stakeholders. A variety of planning grid models exists. For example, the Public Relations Society of America uses a three-tiered, 12-step model in its accreditation process. While there are other variations of the planning grid, each with its own special features, our eight-step model has the advantage of simplicity. To demonstrate the planning grid in action, let's assume you represent a mythical company seeking tax breaks from city government. You believe that these tax breaks will eventually lead to higher profits, more jobs, and, ultimately, increased tax revenues to pay for city services.

1. Identify the goal. A goal is a statement of the desired outcome. A public relations plan could involve more than one goal—which would require a separate grid for each goal.

2. Identify the publics most critical to achieving the goal. Decision makers, stakeholders whose actions will determine the success of your plan, are considered primary publics. Stakeholders who wield influence over decision makers are considered intervening publics. The reason for distinguishing between primary and intervening publics will soon become evident.

3. Identify each public's stake. Stake is defined as a statement of each public's self-interests. In any given scenario, there could be multiple statements of self-interest. You are looking for the most persuasive statement of each public's self-interest that most closely addresses the goal.

4. Identify the messages that you want to deliver to the targeted publics. These messages are statements designed to motivate specific publics to take a desired action. They should address both your goal and the public's stake. To put it another way, you are trying to craft a message that creates a "win–win" situation for all parties.

- *For primary publics:* The message is always structured along these lines: "You should help me achieve my goal because it addresses your stake."
- *For intervening publics:* A different message structure is necessary because these are not the decision makers and, therefore, do not have the power to determine your success or failure. Their power rests in the influence they have with the primary public. For that reason, the message is always structured along these lines: "Influence the primary public to help me achieve my goal because it addresses your stake."

Goal: "To gain city government approval of tax breaks for our company"

Publics	Stake	Message	Media	Timetable	Monitor	Budget
City Council (primary)	It needs tax revenues to pay for city services.	"You should support tax breaks for our company because they will lead to increased tax revenues to pay for city services."	A meeting with city officials.	Must be accomplished before the council votes on the tax breaks next month.	Was the meeting held? Did all of the council members attend? Did they commit their support to the tax breaks?	Nominal. Costs limited to preparation of meeting materials.
Business leaders (intervening)	They desire a healthy local economy.	"Influence the City Council to support tax breaks for our company because it will lead to a healthy local economy."	A letter from the company CEO asking them to contact the City Council in support of the tax breaks.	The letters should be sent immediately in advance of the CEO's meeting with the City Council.	How many letters of support were sent to the City Council?	Nominal. Costs limited to letter preparation and postage.

5. Identify appropriate media. You should use channels of communication—ideally more than one—that are preferred by each public. Your choices will involve the use of controlled media, uncontrolled media, or a combination of both. That choice depends on time, money, and other considerations.

6. Determine the timetable. One of the things you should learn during research is the time frame in which things must be accomplished.

7. Determine how you will monitor the progress of your plan. This is the evaluation phase of the public relations process. It is important to know what constitutes success before launching a plan.

8. Determine the budget. Both efficiency and effectiveness should be the prime goals of budgeting.

Discussion Questions

1. What are some of the benefits and drawbacks of using planning grids when creating a public relations campaign?

2. How can messages differ between those directed at primary publics and those directed at intervening publics?

3. When using a planning grid, what is the most important consideration in selecting a medium?

4. In the example shown, a mythical company seeks tax breaks from city government. You represent a public interest group that opposes the tax breaks. How would you fill out the planning grid using the same publics?

CHAPTER 3

Employee Relations

"Somewhere along the line," says employee relations consultant Maril MacDonald, "management teams have begun to actually believe that their people are their greatest asset."[1]

That's good news for **employee relations,** the division of public relations that builds productive relationships with an organization's employees. But until management beliefs translate into action, the "greatest asset" may be the business world's greatest untapped opportunity for growth.

The Disconnect

Recent research in employee relations has revealed a disconnect between what managers and employees believe about organizational communication. While 71 percent of managers rate businesses as being truthful, only 53 percent of employees agree.[2] While 83 percent of managers say they discuss organizational goals with their staffs, only 68 percent of employees say those discussions occurred.[3] Fewer than half of employees surveyed say they know what actions their companies are taking to achieve business goals.[4] While 70 percent of employees say they wanted financial information about their organizations, only 54 percent of managers say they believe that's important.[5] And while a whopping 46 percent of employees say they first learned about important company information through office gossip— the so-called grapevine—only 17 percent of managers say they believe the grapevine is that powerful.[6]

The results of poor or deceptive employee relations can be dramatic. Recalling media coverage of tearful Enron employees leaving the bankrupt company's headquarters, employee relations specialist David Narsavage said:

> Employee relations took a hard slap upside the head from the media last summer [2002]. The signature image was of people stumbling out of their office buildings, clutching boxes filled with coffee mugs, Dilbert desk calendars, and framed grip-and-grin photographs.
>
> They had the dazed and hollow look of ambush victims. They never saw it coming. "Sorry about all that 'happy news' we've been giving you," they were told. "We're actually going down the tubes. You have to leave now."[7]

The disconnect between management and employee evaluations of internal communication involves more than unpleasant television images. A 2002 employee loyalty survey conducted by Aon Consulting found the lowest levels of employee commitment to employers since 1997, the year the survey began.[8] And only slightly more than half believed that their own company tells them the truth.[9]

"These results reveal a worrisome employer–employee dynamic that should be a wake-up call to any senior executives who will need to communicate with employees," said Mark Schumann of management consulting firm Towers Perrin. "Regardless of the topic, an organization will find it difficult to motivate, engage, and retain its most talented employees if its messages are not believed."[10]

A 2003 Towers Perrin survey titled "Enhancing Corporate Credibility" found that employees believe company managers communicate more honestly with stockholders and the news media than with employees.[11] This awareness of communication with other publics makes a case for bringing employee relations into an organization's public relations department, which might better coordinate communication with employees, stockholders, and the news media. However, in many organizations, employee relations exists within a human resources or personnel department.

"This is one reason why PR and corporate communications is emerging as the rational home for employee relations, elbowing aside former rivals like human resources, according to many in the industry," reported *PR Week*.

"You can leave it up to employees to interpret [the news] for themselves, or you can help them understand it," Monica Oliver, formerly of AOL Time Warner, told *PR Week*. "This was one of the biggest challenges we had in the early days of AOL Time Warner. Things would come out, and employees knew nothing about it until they had read the paper that morning."[12]

ROI: Return on Investment

If poor employee relations practices are disastrous, the opposite also is true: Excellent employee relations significantly benefits organizations, including the bottom line.

A 2003 survey conducted by Watson Wyatt Worldwide, an international human resources firm, found that companies with effective employee relations re-

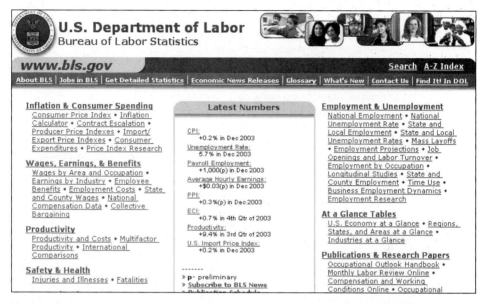

The Web site of the Bureau of Labor Statistics provides a wealth of information on employee publics in the United States. (Courtesy of the U.S. Bureau of Labor Statistics)

turned three times more value to stockholders than companies with ineffective employee relations.

"The bottom line is that employee communication is no longer a 'soft' function but rather a business function that drives performance and contributes to a company's financial success," said Kathryn Yates of Watson Wyatt.[13]

The Watson Wyatt study also determined that effective employee relations reduces employee turnover, which reduces recruiting and training costs.[14] Other 2003 survey research established that 83 percent of employees who say their supervisors are excellent communicators report that workplace morale is good or excellent.[15]

Employee Publics

Who are these employees who exert so much influence over an organization's success? A key descriptive term is *diverse*. With 147 million Americans in the civilian workforce at the beginning of 2004, employee publics are as diverse as the nation itself.[16]

Treating this wide-ranging public as one homogenous group would be a recipe for failure. Yet employee publics do have common values. Survey research shows that more than two-thirds of the nation's employees say that family is their top priority. Fortunately, only 10 percent say that family matters distract them at work.[17] Employees say job security is the most important element in job satisfaction, followed closely by **benefits** packages, which traditionally include health insurance, vacation, and retirement policies.[18]

A variety of publics exist within the broad employee public. A single organization's employee public might be segmented by geography and, possibly, language, job duties, management level, and seniority. Each of those publics might have unique values and concerns. (See Table 3.1.)

Employee age and longevity with a company are among the most important areas of diversity within employee publics. Almost 70 percent of employees age 35 and under believe that their companies communicate honestly. That compares with only 44 percent of employees 50 and older who hold that belief. Almost two-thirds of employees who have five or fewer years at a company believe in the integrity of the organization's communications. Slightly fewer than half of employees with more than five years of service hold that same belief.[19] Younger employees value continuing education and training more than do older employees. They also value flexible work schedules more than their older co-workers.[20]

Annual salaries appear to influence employees' degree of trust in their leaders. Almost 60 percent of employees who earn more than $100,000 per year—which no doubt puts most of them in management ranks—believe their organizations have trustworthy employee communications. However, only 44 percent of employees

table 3.1 *And the Survey Says . . .*

National survey research supplies these additional facts about employee publics:

- 32 percent of employees believe their organizations communicate effectively with employees.
- 45 percent of employees have confidence in the effectiveness of their organization's senior management.
- 51 percent of employees believe that their organizations try too hard to "spin" the truth.
- 35 percent of employees see a clear connection between job performance and salary.
- 49 percent of employees are satisfied with their benefits: 74 percent of employees at large organizations are satisfied; 60 percent at mid-sized organizations; and 47 percent at small organizations.
- One-third of female employees are interested and engaged in their work; one-fourth of males report such commitment. Only 11 percent of female employees feel disconnected; 17 percent of males feel disconnected. Almost 40 percent of female employees would recommend their company as a great place to work; almost 30 percent of males would do the same.

Sources: Towers Perrin Web site, www.towersperrin.com; Watson Wyatt Worldwide Web site, www.watsonwyatt.com; Society for Human Resource Management Web site, www.shrm.org; the Gallup Organization Web site, www.gallup.com.

earning less than $50,000 per year—usually the rank and file of an organization—share that faith.[21]

By this point, you may have guessed that in employee relations, there's a national survey for almost everything. Some recent surveys even suggest that, because of the uncertain economy of the early 21st century, employees are so grateful for their jobs that employee morale is high. A national survey by the Society for Human Resource Management in 2003 found that 76 percent of U.S. employees are basically satisfied with their jobs. Although surveys may paint an accurate picture of overall employee values and beliefs, good critical thinking demands that practitioners study employees within their own organizations. National research can be a valuable indicator of possible organizational trends, but it should not be the sole foundation for an employee relations program.

Achieving Effective Employee Communications

Fortunately, research also indicates that excellent employee relations can solve problems of trust and sagging profits.[22] A 2003 Watson Wyatt study found "nine communications practices" in employee relations that increase a company's financial value.[23] In order of importance, they are:

1. Drive supervisory/managerial behavior: Commitment to excellent employee relations must be a true, pervasive company value that starts at the top.
2. Follow a formal process: Employee relations must be a planned activity.
3. Create employee line of sight: Employees must understand the connection between their actions and organizational goals.
4. Facilitate change: Employee communications must do more than report; they must help create needed change.
5. Focus on continuous improvement: Employees want to do their jobs with greater effectiveness and efficiency; organizational communications can show them how.
6. Connect to the business strategy: Employee communication tactics must openly address how they relate to specific organizational goals.
7. Use employee feedback: Employee communications should solicit, acknowledge, and report the results of employee feedback.
8. Integrate total rewards: Employee communications should report the rewards for feedback, productivity, and attaining organizational goals.
9. Leverage technology: Employee communications should use company technology to reach employees in a variety of ways, particularly those favored by employees.[24]

Soliciting employee feedback on communications efforts and company policies can be particularly beneficial. A study by Randstad North America, a worldwide employment services agency, found that 78 percent of employees in companies that emphasize and honor feedback report that their morale is excellent or good.[25]

Employee Relations Tactics

Ideally, research and planning precede the tactics of any public relations campaign. Because employee communication programs rarely begin from scratch, one research tool that can provide direction for an employee communications campaign is a **communication audit** (see ACT File #3). It measures how well an organization's communications are fulfilling their stated goals. A communication audit is a critical thinking tool that can help you identify the most effective tactics for communicating with your organization's employees.

Traditional employee relations tactics include:

• **Face-to-face meetings with immediate supervisors:** Employee relations studies generally rank this tactic first in effectiveness. Some 75 percent of employees who learn about company policies from their supervisors say that company morale is excellent or good.[26]

• **Newsletters and magazines:** Frequent periodicals can reach employees in their homes as well as the workplace. Print can give a message longevity, allowing multiple readings.

• **E-mail:** Studies show that e-mail is the most-used employee communications tactic. However, employees often see it as a poor substitute for face-to-face communication, one that frequently delivers bad news.[27] And important messages can get lost in an avalanche of unwanted personal messages and spam.

• **Videos:** Often used for employee training or orientation, videos are ideal for demonstrating technical processes and procedures. Some large, widespread organizations have television networks to communicate with employees in multiple locations.

• **Intranets:** Not to be confused with the Internet, an **intranet** is a controlled-access Web site available only to members of an organization. An intranet can store policy and procedure documents, report breaking news, and host chat rooms on important company topics.

• **Special events:** Special events are—well, special. They're planned, out-of-the-ordinary occurrences that draw attention to a particular message. For example, a food products company might organize a picnic to introduce a new line of products to employees.

Additional employee relations tactics may also serve an organization's particular communication needs: old-fashioned bulletin boards, speeches, instant messaging, office memos, and more.

Sharing Values and Vision

Employee relations may be the secret advantage that organizations seek in a competitive marketplace. Effective employee communication improves morale, enhances employee retention, and increases the financial value of the organization.

"Today, most companies recognize that employees are one of their more important publics, often the most essential to success," says Gordon Lindsey, associate information manager for the J.C. Penney Company.[28]

But if employees are to help their companies succeed, that success must mean something to them. Employee relations practitioners must share the vision and the values that unite the organization and shape its goals. In the barrage of surveys cited in this chapter, employees have spoken clearly: They want to trust their organizations, they want to communicate with their supervisors, and they want to be part of the team. They want to help create success.

At least one employee relations specialist doesn't think you'll need a Ph.D. in critical thinking to get the job done.

"This isn't rocket science," says David Narsavage. "Tell employees the truth, tell them often, and tell them what they want to know."[29]

Discussion Questions

1. Given the survey research cited in this chapter, how would you characterize the mood of employee publics in the United States?

2. Why, in your opinion, does the disconnect between management and employee beliefs about communication exist?

3. Why, in your opinion, does improved employee communication improve company profits?

4. Are you an employee of any organization? Does your experience reflect the national research findings cited in this chapter?

5. The professors at your college or university constitute an employee public. How might that public be divided into smaller publics?

Key Terms

benefits, p. 34
communication audit, p. 36
employee relations, p. 31
intranet, p. 36

Endnotes

1. Paul Cordasco, "Employee Communications: Windows of Opportunity," *PR Week,* August 11, 2003. Online: Lexis-Nexis.

2. "New Year's Resolution for the Boss," Randstad news release, December 20, 2003. Online: www.randstad.com.

3. "New Year's Resolution for the Boss."

4. "Growing Confusion about Corporate Goals Complicates Recovery," Watson Wyatt Worldwide news release, September 9, 2002. Online: www.watsonwyatt.com.

5. "National Survey Finds Workers Starved for Information," Randstad news release, May 14, 2002. Online: www.randstad.com.

6. "Workplace Grapevine Is Like Kudzu," a Randstad news release, June 17, 2003. Online: www.randstad.com.

7. David Narsavage, "Full Communication Will Help the Staff Feel Like a Family," *PR Week,* January 13, 2003. Online: Lexis-Nexis.

8. Narsavage.

9. "Towers Perrin Survey Finds Almost Half of American Workers Doubt the Credibility of Employer Communications," Towers Perrin news release, January 8, 2004. Online: www.towersperrin.com.

10. "Towers Perrin Survey Finds Almost Half of American Workers Doubt the Credibility of Employer Communications."

11. "Towers Perrin Survey Finds Almost Half of American Workers Doubt the Credibility of Employer Communications."

12. Cordasco.

13. "Effective Employee Communication Linked to Greater Shareholder Returns," a Watson Wyatt Worldwide news release, 3 November 2003, online: www.watsonwyatt.com.

14. "Effective Employee Communication Linked to Greater Shareholder Returns."

15. "New Year's Resolution for the Boss."

16. U.S. Bureau of Labor Statistics Web site, www.bls.gov.

17. "National Survey Finds Workers Starved for Information."

18. "SHRM/CNNfn Job Satisfaction Survey Says More Employees Satisfied with Benefits at Large Or-ganizations versus Small," Society for Human Resource Management news release, December 4, 2003. Online: www.shrm.org.

19. "Towers Perrin Survey Finds Almost Half of American Workers Doubt the Credibility of Employer Communications."

20. "SHRM/CNNfn Job Satisfaction Survey Says More Employees Satisfied with Benefits at Large Organizations versus Small."

21. "Towers Perrin Survey Finds Almost Half of American Workers Doubt the Credibility of Employer Communications."

22. "New Year's Resolutions for the Boss."

23. "Effective Employee Communication Linked to Greater Shareholder Returns."

24. "Effective Employee Communication Linked to Greater Shareholder Returns."

25. "New Year's Resolutions for the Boss."

26. "Workplace Grapevine Is Like Kudzu."

27. "The Lure of E-Mail May Be Deceiving," Watson Wyatt Worldwide news release, July 26, 1999. Online: www.watsonwyatt.com.

28. David W. Guth and Charles Marsh, *Public Relations: A Values-Driven Approach* (Boston: Allyn & Bacon, 2003), 125.

29. Narsavage.

case **3.1**

Apparent Success

Wachovia Pleases Moms and Dads with Award-Winning Employee Relations

Reporter Elizabeth Stieber of Philadelphia's *Northeast Times* knew she had a good story. A Wachovia Corp. employee named Janine had set aside her work for a moment, left her desk, and tiptoed into a darkened room—and Stieber knew why.

Embezzlement? Computer crime? Smoking in the restroom?

None of the above. Janine was visiting her infant daughter in a Wachovia child-care center.

"I think it's wonderful," the new mother told Stieber. "To be just a couple of steps away makes the transition so much easier."

A mom visits her baby, and that's news? It is in corporate America, where fewer than 20 percent of companies offer comprehensive child-care services. Wachovia is a leader among companies that assist working parents through innovative employee relations programs.

"We are committed to creating a company that offers working parents an environment where they can be successful," says Wachovia Chairman and CEO Ken Thompson.

With assets of approximately $400 billion, Wachovia Corp. is the nation's fifth-largest bank holding company and third-largest full-service investment brokerage firm. Based in Charlotte, N.C., Wachovia provides financial services to more than 9 million households. The modern Wachovia began in 2001, when the former Wachovia Corp., which traces it origins to 1879, merged with First Union banks, founded in 1908. Wachovia is the Latin translation of Wachau, the German name of the North Carolina region where the banking giant began.

Boosting the Bottom Line

To learn what employees want in their relationships with the company, Wachovia goes to a well-informed source: the employees themselves. In the five-year span of 1999–2003, Wachovia conducted three in-depth employee surveys to gauge satisfaction and to identify emerging concerns.

"We constantly solicit and listen to employee feedback to ensure we are giving employees the resources and tools they need," says Paul George, Wachovia's human resources director.

Thompson believes that satisfied employees boost the bottom line by offering better customer service and being effective company ambassadors in Wachovia's communities. "In order for Wachovia to reach its true potential," he says, "we must continue to build an organization that values individual differences. Our focus is on creating an inclusive workplace where we value and retain employees and deliver our best service to customers and communities."

Jill Kirschenbaum, editor-in-chief of *Working Mother* magazine, agrees. *Working Mother* has researched employee relations programs since its founding in 1979. "When an employee's personal life runs smoothly, her productivity continues uninterrupted," Kirschenbaum says. Of child-care programs, she adds, "These programs markedly cut absenteeism."

When Wachovia and First Union merged, Thompson created a Diversity Due Diligence Project to unite the two companies in a continuing commitment to innovative, inclusive employee relations programs.

"In bringing together these two companies," he said, "we focused on providing superior workplace and career opportunities for every employee and on continuing the work–life legacy of two strong organizations."

The report of Wachovia's due diligence/diversity team became the platform for an award-winning, family-friendly employee relations program.

"Creating an Inclusive Workplace"

A central goal of Wachovia's employee relations program is to help employees coordinate the competing demands of their personal and professional lives.

"Introducing and sustaining programs that help Wachovia's employees balance work and life is a priority for us," says George, Wachovia's human resources director. "Respecting and valuing the individual is one of our company values."

The report from Wachovia's diversity team helped establish objectives toward the fulfillment of that goal. Of particular importance to working parents are these:

- We will continue the diversity commitment focused on valuing differences and creating an inclusive workplace.
- We will build on the best of what has been developed around diversity in each legacy organization (First Union and the former Wachovia Corp.) in the new company.
- We will work to ensure that all employees feel the positive impact of our diversity commitment.

Thompson himself launched the first tactic in pursuit of those objectives by creating the Corporate Diversity Council, which he chairs. He also directed each business unit in the company to form its own diversity council and diversity plan. "Senior leaders will chair the business unit councils and have specific accountabilities for diversity in their business units," he added.

Child-care services at Wachovia include seven centers at three different locations, plus access to two other centers prepared to serve as backup providers. Wachovia also sponsors contingency child-care programs for parents who unexpectedly need to bring their children to work. *Working Mother* magazine estimates that only 18 percent of companies nationwide offer "child-care resource and referral services."

Employee Benefits

Working Mother magazine provides these national statistics regarding United States–based companies and child care:

- 55 percent provide flexible schedules for parents and other employees.
- 18 percent provide child-care resource and referral services.
- 7 percent provide sick-child care.
- 4 percent provide before- and after-school child care.

Source: Working Mother magazine, www.workingmother.com.

"It's excellent," employee Kathleen Ruppert told the *Northeast Times* about Wachovia's care of her 6-year-old son. "I can check on him. We go out to lunch. . . . He loves it, and there's no TV, which is the best part. He's always playing games and making things."

Wachovia also offers employees its Flexible Work Options program, which allows them adjustable work schedules and opportunities to work from their homes—to telecommute. *Working Mother* magazine estimates that 55 percent of U.S. companies offer flexible schedules.

Lee Ann Lopez works a four-day week at Wachovia, spending the fifth day with her preschool child. "They've been so willing to work with me on this," she says.

Wachovia employee Donna Schultz, who also uses company child-care options, works a nontraditional 8 a.m. to 3 p.m. schedule at Wachovia.

"I can get home and pick up my kids and not be so rushed at night," Schultz told the *Northeast Times*. "That way, we can have quality time before dinner. . . . I'm so grateful Wachovia has these programs for working moms."

In praising Wachovia, Schultz also echoes Thompson's belief that a family-friendly employee relations program strengthens the company. "The quality time at home makes me a better person and a better mom, which makes me a better employee," she said.

Another family-friendly offering from Wachovia is its Time Away from Work for Community Service policy. Both Schultz and Ruppert have spent traditional work hours away from the office serving as parent volunteers on their children's school field trips.

"It allows us to be involved in our kids' school life," Schultz said.

Wachovia honored its pledge to "build on the best of what has been developed around diversity" in part by expanding the number of private rooms it provides for nursing mothers. In 2002, the company increased the number of such rooms from 17 to 25.

Heidi and Roy Detweiler used Wachovia's policy of Adoption Leave and Family Care Time to travel to China to adopt a daughter and spend extra time at home with her. Both husband and wife work for Wachovia, and the company allowed them to carry over leave time from one year to the next. Wachovia also assisted with adoption costs.

"It obviously made decisions easier for my husband and me to adopt," Heidi Detweiler said.

Wachovia offers women's-issues programs to all female employees, not just working moms. For example, "Smart Women Finish Rich" attracted 600 employees. The company also opened its customer-focused "Women and Retirement" series to its own employees. More than 6,000 women attended the series launch, 17 percent of whom were Wachovia employees.

Wachovia's Triple Play

Evaluative research reveals the impact of Wachovia's family-friendly employee relations tactics. In 2002,

- 2,178 Wachovia managers were trained on work/life issues.
- 2,083 managers received flexible-schedule training.
- 7,200 employees used Wachovia's employee assistance program.

In 2003, for the second year in a row, Wachovia earned a spot on *Working Mother* magazine's annual "100 Best Companies for Working Mothers." In doing so, however, the company scored a rare triple play. *Working Mother* named Wachovia a "Top 10" company as well as "Best in Class" for family-friendly corporate cultures and "Best in Industry" among financial and professional services companies.

"Wachovia is all about understanding work-life benefits and why they matter," editor-in-chief Kirschenbaum said on NBC's *Today* show.

"This recognition from *Working Mother* is an honor," said Thompson.

Wachovia's commitment to employee relations programs that strengthen diversity has earned additional honors. *DiversityInc* magazine has named Wachovia one of the nation's "Top 50 Companies for Diversity," citing company achievements such as linking managers' compensation and promotion to success in achieving diversity objectives. *Latina Style* magazine ranks Wachovia in the Top 50 U.S. companies for Hispanic women, praising the company's mentoring programs, tuition assistance, and work–life programs. *Black Collegian* magazine includes Wachovia in its "Top 100 Employers Survey."

As for the *Working Mother* award, Wachovia employee Chris Harris also might want to put in a word for working dads. Harris' two children accompany him to work at Wachovia, where he reports to the computer programming department and his children go next door to a company child-care center. "If they were in a day care, say 15 minutes away, I'd have to drive over there, check on the girls, drive back," he said. "Here, I just pop down, check it out, and I'm back to work."

Sources

NBC *Today* show, September 23, 2003. Online: Lexis-Nexis.

Margie Peterson, "Family-Friendly Companies Are Smart Business," *The Morning Call,* September 25, 2003. Online: www.mcall.com/news/columnists.

Elizabeth Stieber, "Banking on a Family Affair," *Northeast Times,* October 9, 2003. Online: www.northeasttimes.com.

Wachovia Corp. Web site, www.wachovia.com.

"Wachovia Named One of '100 Best Companies for Working Mothers,' "Wachovia news release, September 24, 2002. Online: www.wachovia.com.

"Wachovia Named One of the Top Ten Companies for Working Mothers," Wachovia news release, September 23, 2003. Online: www.wachovia.com.

Working Mother magazine Web site, www.workingmother.com.

"Work/Life Benefits Survive Economic Hard Times," *Working Mother* news release, September 23, 2003. Online: www.workingwoman.com.

Gold Medals and Golden Arches

case **3.2**

McDonald's Showcases Its Employees at the 2002 Winter Olympics

As it descended through winter skies over France, the airplane carried an unusual cargo to uncommon recipients. The shipment? A plane-full of McDonald's hamburgers. The beneficiaries? Members of the 1968 U.S. Winter Olympics team, whose homesickness for McDonald's hamburgers had sparked international headlines. So began the association of the world's best-known restaurant chain with the Olympic Games.

Eight years later, McDonald's made it official, becoming an Olympics sponsor. By the time athletes lit the torch at the 2002 Winter Games in Salt Lake City, McDonald's had become the official restaurant of the Olympics. And McDonald's wanted the 2002 Winter Games—set in the United States with international attention on world-class athletes—to be a showcase for its own world-class employees.

For help in creating an employee relations plan worthy of its own gold medal, the world's largest restaurant group turned to one of the world's largest public relations agencies: Burson-Marsteller. And McDonald's wanted something more than a super-sized program: It wanted an Olympic-sized idea for honoring and motivating its restaurant crews.

"The spirit of friendship and fun, the thrill of competition, and the goal to be the best are values that McDonald's shares closely with the Olympic movement," explained McDonald's USA President Mike Roberts.

"Would You Like Millions of Fries with That?"

Commitment to effective employee incentive programs was nothing new under the Golden Arches. "McDonald's Corp. has been running motivation programs that recognize the best employees and crews for years," declared *Promo* magazine in 2002. Burson-Marsteller focused its research, therefore, on past employee relations efforts at McDonald's, particularly those involving the Olympics. The agency also conducted a content analysis study of media coverage of McDonald's previous Olympic promotions and examined the company's satisfaction with earlier coverage.

A situation analysis of McDonald's participation in the upcoming 2002 Winter Games reinforced the need for an Olympic-sized promotion. McDonald's would be the official restaurant of the Athletes Village and the Main Press Center. Company projections showed that in just the few weeks of the Winter Games, McDonald's would serve an average of 5,000 hamburgers a day—a total of 1.8 million meat patties, 22,000 pounds of lettuce, and 60 tons of potatoes.

Stung by a *Chicago Tribune* newspaper report that questioned the company's commitment to customer service, McDonald's and Burson-Marsteller created a lofty goal for the new employee relations program: to elevate an employee rewards/recognition program to international Olympic stature. Research showed that to achieve that goal, they needed one clear idea that focused on three target publics: employees, consumers, and the news media.

The Best Served by the Best

To create an employee incentive program of Olympic proportions, Burson-Marsteller and McDonald's developed three objectives:

1. Establish McDonald's as a top worldwide employer, one that recognizes and rewards employees' hard work
2. Showcase internally and externally employee value as well as employee satisfaction
3. Generate positive media coverage of the company's commitment to innovative employee incentive programs

To avoid diluting media attention, McDonald's and Burson-Marsteller created one big idea for the plan: the "McDonald's World Champion Crew." To staff its Olympic restaurants, McDonald's would need 400 employees from its 1.3 million restaurant workers in its 29,000 restaurants in 121 countries. With Burson-Marsteller's advice, the company decided to hold its own internal Olympics to pick its very best employees worldwide to work at the Winter Games. To develop judging standards for a competition on excellent service, McDonald's turned to its own Hamburger University in Oak Brook, Ill.

Coordinating a contest among 29,000 restaurants worldwide presented obvious logistics problems. Burson-Marsteller helped McDonald's implement a comprehensive, frequent communications program that included conference calls to worldwide locales, simple and clear contest guidelines, and news releases that each location could customize and distribute. And so, during the autumn before the Winter Games, the games under the golden arches began.

"This is an opportunity for McDonald's to reward employees who work hard to do a good job," said Allison Sindelir, a McDonald's training consultant in Raleigh, N.C. "The crews, who even have their own team cheers, are judged on correct procedures, teamwork, friendliness, and precision with personality. It has been really exciting to see the teams come together. This is a great morale builder."

"This is wonderful," said Katherine Wells, an employee of 10 years from Fayetteville, N.C. "The team spirit is great, and I love to see everybody clapping for everybody else."

Local, national, and international news releases kept the competitions on the news media's agenda. Major releases noted such events as a competition in Illinois near McDonald's worldwide headquarters. The company distributed the stories through PR Newswire and Business Wire; it also posted them on McDonald's Web site.

One hundred days before the beginning of the Winter Games, McDonald's announced its 400 worldwide winners with another international news release. The winners came from five continents and more than 40 countries, including the United States, Australia, Malaysia, Russia, Brazil, Egypt, Hungary, Spain, South Korea, and the United Kingdom. To celebrate the winners, McDonald's also named its gold medal winners in a full-page ad in *USA Today*.

"Our crew is the heart and soul of who we are," said McDonald's CEO Jack Greenberg. "So it's fitting that the world's best athletes will be served their favorite McDonald's food by the world's best crew."

"Being selected as a member of the crew that will serve the best athletes in the world is a real honor," said Lad Hudac of Springfield, Ohio. "I look forward to making my country proud at the Olympic Winter Games."

In late December, just more than a month from the lighting of the torch in Salt Lake City, McDonald's launched a worldwide television commercial called, appropriately, "World." The spot showed the McDonald's World Champion Crew preparing for its own Olympic experience.

"We're proud to salute the accomplishments of our crew in our new Olympic ad campaign," said Neil Golden, McDonald's USA's vice president of marketing. "These individuals bring to life the same Olympic ideals and spirit that have always been part of McDonald's."

Newsroom

Press Releases
< Return to the Listing of All Press Releases

1/24/2002

McDonald's® Celebrates Grand Opening of 2002 Olympic Village Restaurant in Salt Lake City

Olympian Lincoln Dewitt to Enjoy "First Burger of the Games" Served by McDonald's Salt Lake City World Champion Crew Member

The Salt Lake City World Champion Crew posing with Ronald McDonald and Olympian Lincoln Dewitt

Olympian Lincoln DeWitt Enjoyed The "First Burger of the Games" Served By McDonald's Salt Lake City World Champion Crew Member, Tusiga "T" Lealaogata

Mike Perry, Olympian Lincoln DeWitt, and O/O Chuck Sparrer, posing with Ronald at the opening of the Olympic Village Restaurant

WHO:	• **Lincoln DeWitt**, the first American to win the overall World Cup skeleton title and Park City resident • **Tusiga "T" Lealaogata**, McDonald's World Champion Crew Member, Salt Lake City, Utah
WHAT:	Presentation of "the first Big Mac® Sandwich" of the Salt Lake Games to **Lincoln DeWitt** during the Grand Opening of McDonald's special restaurant in the Olympic Village. McDonald's also invites media to a menu-tasting at its Olympic Village restaurant. "T" is a member of McDonald's World Champion Crew - one of 400 crew chosen through worldwide competitions among McDonald's 1.3 million crew around the globe.
WHEN:	**Saturday, January 26, 2002** • 9 a.m. - 4 p.m. - Olympic Village and McDonald's Village Restaurant Open House • **11 a.m. - Lincoln DeWitt Served First Big Mac Sandwich**
WHERE:	**McDonald's Olympic Village Restaurant** Douglas Dining in Residential Zone, University of Utah Campus

McDonald's Corp. used its Web site to help distribute a news release and photographs praising the accomplishments of its World Champion Crew. (Courtesy of McDonald's Corp.)

Around the world, McDonald's used tray liners in its restaurants to celebrate regional winners serving on the company's World Champion Crew.

Once in Salt Lake City, the elite 400-member crew celebrated in a huge rally that included a competitive Big Mac Building Exhibition. McDonald's officials invited members of the news media, broadcast the competition live on the company Web site, filmed the event for a video news release and issued a standard news release announcing the winners. Crew members were less competitive at another party, this one at a mountaintop resort where festivities included dinner and dancing.

"This is what you get when you work for McDonald's," said Peter Wilhelmsson of Sweden as he surveyed his dancing teammates, all of whom had arrived at the restaurant via cable-borne gondolas.

Mindful of media relations, Burson-Marsteller executives helped coach crew members on working with reporters. With McDonald's executives, they organized orientation meetings that included distribution of briefing books containing key media messages. They staged mock interviews to test message delivery. One key message was the comparison of McDonald's top employees to the world's top athletes.

The athletes and the World Champion Crew finally met when employee Tusiga Lealaogata, of Salt Lake City, served the first burger of the Games to U.S. athlete Lincoln Dewitt from nearby Park City, Utah. McDonald's used a media advisory to invite the news media, and Ronald McDonald even showed up to pose with athletes and employees. McDonald's sent its own photographer and posted photos in the media relations portion of its Web site.

Burson-Marsteller and McDonald's also issued news releases for special events, such as the World Champion Crew's visit to the dedication of a nearby Ronald McDonald house, a haven for families whose children face extended hospital stays.

McDonald's and Burson-Marsteller budgeted $400,000 for the World Champion Crew campaign.

"Love under the Arches"

Around the world, McDonald's World Champion Crew campaign motivated employees and won media attention. Crews from more than 50 nations participated in the competition; more than 40 nations sent winners to Salt Lake City. More than 100 mentions of the campaign appeared in national and international broadcast media, including, in the United States, the four major networks plus CNN, ESPN, and even *The Tonight Show with Jay Leno*. Internationally, stories on the crew appeared in Russia, China, Canada, the Netherlands, and the United Kingdom.

The campaign also generated more than 100 local-media stories in the United States alone. Local headlines ran from the standard—"Local McDonald's Team Wins Trip to 2002 Winter Olympics"—to the clever: "McDonald's Workers Flip for the Chance to Serve Olympians."

"You can go as far as you want to at McDonald's," employee Gloria Greene told reporters in Palm Beach, Fla. "There are people who have made a good career at McDonald's."

Enthusiasm on the World Champion Crew itself was so powerful that McDonald's created a videotape of testimonials about employees' spirit and opportunities at the company. "It really is the best serving the best," said crew member Lad Hudac. "I saw so many smiles from people. The reception from the customers was tremendous."

Promo magazine, which earlier had praised McDonald's commitment to employee incentive programs, concluded that the company "upped the ante" with its World Champion Crew campaign.

The efforts of Burson-Marsteller and McDonald's even impressed marketers for the International Olympic Committee. "The McDonald's brand exemplifies best in class," said Richard Pound, chairman of the IOC Marketing Commission.

Ricky Wade isn't a member of the International Olympic Committee. Instead, he owns seven McDonald's franchises in Florida. But his comments to reporters about opportunities under the Golden Arches were every bit as memorable as praise from the IOC's top marketer.

"It's a good steppingstone for teaching kids responsibility," he told reporters as he prepared his employees for the World Champion Crew competition. "You work with a diverse group of people, a mixture of age and tenure. And we don't hold people back who want to advance their careers."

And then he added the clincher: Working for McDonald's might just advance your life in other areas. As a McDonald's employee, Wade met another employee named Lisette; they're now husband and wife. Before turning his attention back to his crew, Wade described that ultimate employee relations program: "It was love under the arches."

Sources

Mary Anderson, "Local McDonald's Team Wins Trip to 2002 Winter Olympics in Utah," *The* (Asheboro, N.C.) *Courier-Tribune,* no date. Online: www.courier-tribune.com.

Matthew Kinsman, "The Secretarial Prize Pool: Incentive Programs Are Now Used to Inspire All Sorts of Productivity," *PROMO* magazine, April 2002. Online: www. promotions.it/promonews/trends_005.asp.

"McDonald's Celebrates Grand Opening of 2002 Olympic Village Restaurant in Salt Lake City," media advisory, January 24, 2002. Online: www.media.mcdonalds.com.

"McDonald's Gears Up to Serve the World's Athletes at 2002 Winter Games in Salt Lake City," McDonald's news release, February 6, 2001. Online: www.media.mcdonalds.com.

"McDonald's Kicks Off All-American Crew Competition," McDonald's news release, September 22, 2001. Online: www.media.mcdonalds.com.

"McDonald's Names Olympic-Bound Crew from Worldwide Restaurant Staff," McDonald's news release, October 29, 2001. Online: www.media.mcdonalds.com.

"McDonald's New Olympic Ad Salutes World Champion Crew," McDonald's news release, December 20, 2001. Online: www.media.mcdonalds.com.

"McDonald's USA 2002 Olympic Winter Games." Online: www.mcdonalds.com.

"Olympic Greats Mike Eruzione and Johann Olav Koss Join McDonald's World Champion Crew for Dedication of New Salt Lake City Ronald McDonald House," McDonald's news release, February 18, 2002. Online: www.media.mcdonalds.com.

Tim O'Meila, "McDonald's Workers Flip for the Chance to Serve Olympians," *Palm Beach* (Fla.) *Post,* August 31, 2001. Online: Lexis-Nexis.

Taking a Stand

SBC Unleashes the Power of Its Employees

If telecommunications giant SBC Communications had been an old-fashioned board game a decade ago, it would have been *Monopoly*. For most of its life, the company enjoyed the exclusive right to provide local telephone service to customers in its markets. But with the deregulation of the telecommunications industry, the company may have felt more like a game of *Dungeons and Dragons*. In the turbulent first years of the 21st century, SBC customers switched to competing companies. By the summer of 2002, SBC had lost more than 1 million phone lines in its Midwest region.

As one of the top 30 companies in the *Fortune* 500, SBC remained a major player in its markets, but it couldn't afford to continue losing business. To reverse the trend in its Midwestern region, SBC turned to a longtime partner in a different profession: public relations agency Fleishman-Hillard.

Problem as Solution

SBC management suspected that some of the problem and much of the solution lay with its employees. Fleishman-Hillard's research quickly confirmed the first half of that belief: A survey of more than 2,000 of SBC Midwest's 60,000 employees revealed that more than a third didn't wholly understand the threat posed by customer loss. Almost half the employees didn't know about new competitively priced SBC services, and more than one-third didn't really know what they could do to help the company succeed in the new economic environment.

"We've got the experience, the people, and the technology to deliver outstanding service to our customers," said Cindie Bucks, general manager of SBC network services in Michigan. Fleishman-Hillard and SBC management agreed that if they could inform employees and show them how to help market SBC's array of new offerings, customers would stay—and others might even return.

The target public for the plan clearly was SBC Midwest employees. Within that large group, however, Fleishman-Hillard identified three particular publics whose cooperation would be essential to success:

1. Senior leaders, who had to deliver a consistent message and lead by example
2. Front-line supervisors, who could serve as coaches and information sources for employees who dealt directly with customers
3. Network technicians, who as a group had 30,000 daily contacts with customers—but never before had engaged in sales efforts

Fleishman-Hillard and SBC knew the goal: retain and attract customers by turning employees into ambassadors. They knew the target publics. It was time to plan.

Good Things Come in Threes

To inform and motivate employees, Fleishman-Hillard helped SBC create a three-part plan that came to be known by its slogan: Take a Stand. Phase One would be Take a Stand: Our Future Is on the Line. The initial phase would inform employees of the new economic realities and challenges. Phase Two would be Take a Stand: Deliver Infinite Service. The second phase would focus on strengthening customer service. Phase Three would be Take a Stand: Supervisor Workshops. The final phase would show supervisors how to build on the success of the earlier phases.

To provide direction for the plan, budgeted at $600,000, Fleishman-Hillard helped bring together leaders from all units of SBC Midwest. Together, the executives established three objectives:

1. Reverse the trend of customer losses by the end of 2002 by improving the level of service that employees provide to customers
2. Increase awareness of the competitive environment and impact on SBC's bottom line to more than 75 percent of employees
3. Motivate employees to personally commit to retain and win back customers, family, and friends through referrals

The planning team realized that unless Phase One succeeded—unless employees understood the significance of the challenge—Phases Two and Three were pointless. Therefore, SBC communicated the new economic realities in a variety of ways. Every SBC Midwest employee received a mailing that explained new service options and the importance of their success. The same information was conveyed through an intranet site and through meetings between employees and supervisors.

To help turn service technicians into ambassadors and sales staff, each technician received laminated descriptions of new services as well as handouts that he or she could discuss and leave with current customers.

"We were very candid with employees and shared a lot of numbers that people had not seen before," said Fleishman-Hillard Account Supervisor Christine Drab told *PR News* magazine. "We did not set out to scare anyone, but we wanted them to realize the seriousness of the situation."

Phase Two built on employees' new knowledge of the marketplace and SBC's new services. To inspire employees to deliver even higher levels of customer service, senior leaders at SBC held 28 regional rallies in just two weeks. Supervisors then held smaller follow-up pep talks for every employee and delivered the same message: Superior service increases customer loyalty and attracts new customers. In addition to the rallies, SBC created a toll-free number that employees could call for on-the-spot solutions to possible delays in customer service.

Phase Three launched as the success of Phases One and Two began to register. If employees viewed the Take a Stand campaign as a passing fancy, the momentum in customer service and customer retention would fade. The purpose of

Phase Three was to integrate that momentum into SBC Midwest's corporate culture, particularly through continuing use of the toll-free number. SBC senior management held workshops for supervisors to show enduring commitment from the top and to brainstorm ways of keeping employees at all levels informed and motivated. Top SBC management instructed unit leaders to regularly submit reports on their units' campaign plans and progress.

Phase Value

Evaluation of the plan began even before Fleishman-Hillard and SBC had fully implemented the three phases. Early research showed that the crucial initial, educational phase succeeded dramatically: The number of employees who strongly agreed that new competition presented a substantial threat to SBC soared to 79 percent, exceeding the 75 percent objective. The number of employees who understood SBC's new services jumped to 83 percent. Perhaps most important, the number of employees who believed they now knew how to help SBC compete in the new marketplace grew to 82 percent.

"We did not just say, 'Competition is out there,'" Drab told *PR News*. "We said, 'It is out there, and look at the difference in our business.' Because if employees do not understand what is happening, then why should they act?"

Follow-up surveys proved that employees did understand—and further evaluation showed that they acted on that knowledge. Employees phoned the toll-free number thousands of times, and the numbers spiked to almost 200 calls a day during the two weeks of the regional rallies. Almost two-thirds of employees reported discussing SBC's new offerings with friends and family members, and nearly half reported they had referred existing or returning customers to SBC marketers for additional services.

Sales and customer satisfaction measures jumped to levels not seen in almost three years. For the first time in more than a year, the rate of customer loss decreased. In Michigan, service and satisfaction measures far exceeded new levels established by the state Public Service Commission. For example, technicians fixed out-of-service problems in less than half the time required by the state. Customer trouble reports were half the allowed level, and technicians installed 98.9 percent of new services within five days, beating the mandated standard of 90 percent.

SBC Michigan technicians even drew praise for a small touch: In winter months, they began wearing clean "booties" into customers home to prevent tracking in snow and slush.

"Delivering excellent service is what our customers expect and what a competitive marketplace demands," said Bucks of SBC Michigan.

Despite the success of the Take a Stand campaign, Fleishman-Hillard's Drab told *PR News* that the evaluation process revealed things she would have done differently. With only six weeks to help plan and launch the campaign, she lacked as much time as she wanted to talk with SBC unit managers. "It would have been good

NEWS

Federal Communications Commission
445 12th Street, S.W.
Washington, D.C. 20554News media information 202 / 418-0500
Fax-On-Demand 202 / 418-2830
Internet: http://www.fcc.gov
TTY: 202/418-2555

This is an unofficial announcement of Commission action. Release of the full text
of a Commission order constitutes official action. See MCI v. FCC. 515 F 2d 385
(D.C. Circ 1974).

FOR IMMEDIATE RELEASE
September 15, 1999 NEWS MEDIA CONTACT
Mike Balmoris (202) 418-0253

FCC PROMOTES LOCAL TELECOMMUNICATIONS COMPETITION

Adopts Rules on Unbundling of Network Elements

Washington, D.C. -- The Federal Communications Commission
(FCC) adopted rules today that specify the portions of the nation's
local telephone networks that incumbent local telephone
companies must make available to competitors seeking to provide
competitive local telephone service. This FCC decision removes a
major uncertainty surrounding the unbundling obligations of the
Telecommunications Act of 1996 and is expected to accelerate the
development of competitive choices in local services for
consumers. Unbundling allows competitors to lease portions of the
incumbent's network to provide telecommunications services.

-more-

The Telecommunications Act of 1996 increased competition among phone companies,
leading SBC to turn to its employees for a competitive advantage. (Courtesy of the U.S.
Federal Communications Commission)

to try to involve some of those people even earlier so that they could be developing more things that would help support this among their employees," she said.

For its efforts in helping SBC Midwest reposition itself in a ferociously competitive market, Fleishman-Hillard earned a 2003 Silver Anvil from the Public Relations Society of America, the organization's highest campaigns award.

Standing Firm

Like its SBC Midwest division, SBC Communications faces continued challenges in the highly competitive telecommunications marketplace. In announcing second-quarter profits in 2003, SBC chief executive officer Ed Whitacre praised company performance and sounded the very themes that brought success to Take a Stand: "Superior execution, aggressive product bundling and excellent customer service highlighted our second-quarter results," he reported. "We changed the competitive landscape . . . by introducing highly attractive rates and innovative product bundles that have delivered outstanding results in terms of new sales, customer retention and improved stability in our core business."

Sources

Fleishman-Hillard Inc. Web site, www.fleishman.com.

"How Telecom Company Calls on Employees to Boost Bottom Line," *PR News,* June 23, 2003. Online: Lexis-Nexis.

Public Relations Society of America Web site, www.prsa.org.

Todd Rosenbluth, "Time to Hang Up on SBC," *Business Week Online,* June 27, 2003. Online: Lexis-Nexis.

"SBC Communications Reports Second Quarter Diluted EPS of $0.42," SBC news release, July 24, 2003. Online: www.sbc.com.

"SBC Michigan Delivers Outstanding Service," an SBC news release, July 31, 2003. Online: www.sbc.com.

"SBC Reports Income Fell in 2nd Quarter," *San Antonio* (Texas) *Express-News,* July 25, 2003. Online: Lexis-Nexis.

ACT file # 3 ....

The Communication Audit

If you think you're tight with a dollar right now, wait until you're a public relations manager. It's a rare manager who has all the funds necessary for relationship-building programs. And money isn't the only scarce resource: You'll be scrambling for talented employees, high-quality equipment—and time. There's never enough time.

In other words, you won't tolerate wasted resources.

Preventing such waste is one reason for conducting a communication audit. A communication audit usually measures how well an organization's communications are fulfilling the stated goals. As such, it often is part of the evaluation phase of the public relations process. In a communication audit, we often focus on one target public at a time, and we measure communication success from that public's standpoint—not just from ours.

Besides ensuring the wise use of resources, communication audits also help prevent the consequences of poor communication. "Lack of communication can have disastrous results leading to decreased performance, decreased productivity, problems with safety and morale, and (in some industries) regulatory and statutory violations," say public relations practitioners Dean Kazoleas and Alan Wright.[1]

A basic communication audit seeks answers to five questions:

1. What are our communications goals with a particular target public?
2. What specific communications are we using to reach those goals?
3. Which communications are effective in fulfilling those goals, in the opinions of both the target public and ourselves?
4. Which communications are ineffective in fulfilling those goals, in the opinions of both the target public and ourselves?
5. Given our answers to the above questions, what recommendations do we have for future communications?

To answer these questions, we generally use surveys (questionnaires) and in-depth interviews with members of the target public. We also conduct content analysis of our communications, which means that we examine each communications tactic—a newsletter, for example—to see if it contains key messages that we believe will help fulfill our communications goal.

Communication audits don't always focus on communications with particular publics. For example, we may wish to audit our communications to see if they reflect our diversity goals. Or we may wish to examine the effectiveness of a particular communications effort—a Web site, for example.

Because communication audits can enter sensitive diplomatic territory—who wants to be told that his media kits are ineffective?—organizations often hire outside consultants to conduct them. After all, a good working relationship with your colleagues is another resource you can't afford to squander.

Endnote

1. Dean Kazoleas and Alan Wright, "Improving Corporate and Organizational Communications: A New Look at Developing and Implementing the Communication Audit," in *Handbook of Public Relations,* ed. Robert Heath (Thousand Oaks, CA: Sage, 2001), 472.

4

Member Relations

Typical day. In the words of the old Beatles song, "A Day in the Life."
You trudge off to your morning classes, but only after programming your roommate's VCR to record *The Young and the Restless:* You've got to know what really happened when Neil and Dru jetted to Japan. Between classes, you meet a friend who wants help promoting the new season of University Theater plays; she knows you love both public relations and the stage. During lunch at the deli, you see a poster for a Public Relations Student Society of America meeting, and you write the date in your calendar.

Classes over. Back to the apartment to dress for work—another big night of waiting tables. You gulp down some mac-and-cheese and watch your soap opera. Sliding into your 1999 Saturn SL, you crank up a Lenny Kravitz song and head for the pizzeria. If you're lucky, you'll be awake enough to read your case studies book after work.

Typical day. And it makes you invaluable to different associations in the United States and around the world.

If you can sing every word to "A Day in the Life," maybe you belong to the Strawberry Fields Beatles Fan Club, based in Florida. If Lenny Kravitz is more your style, you may be a member of Lenny Kravitz's Official Fan Club, based in San Francisco. Still don't know what happened to Neil and Dru? You can join other members of *The Young and the Restless* Fan Club in an online chat room. You're already a member of PRSSA, and maybe your theater friend has persuaded you to join the Association for Theatre in Higher Education. Love your Saturn? You might belong to an area Saturn Car Club. Frustrated by your job? You may have sent dues to the Waiters Association, based in Tigard, Oregon.

You get the picture.

A Nation of Joiners

Ninety percent of U.S. adults belong to at least one association, and 25 percent belong to at least four. Like the publics in employee relations, member publics are almost as diverse as the U.S. population itself. Approximately 150,000 associations exist in the United States alone. Almost 2,500 international associations have their headquarters here. New associations form at the rate of 1,000 per year.[1] That's a lot of associations, a lot of members—and a lot of jobs in **member relations,** the part of public relations that builds relationships among leaders and members of an organization.

In 2004, the five largest associations in the United States had a combined membership of 109 million:

1. American Automobile Association: 43 million
2. AARP, formerly known by its full name, the American Association of Retired Persons: 33 million
3. YMCA of the United States: 17 million
4. National Geographic Society: 9.5 million
5. National Congress of Parents and Teachers: 6.5 million[2]

Important early steps in critical thinking, you'll recall, are definition and analysis. In the typical day described above, the potential associations in your life could be separated and defined by categories: fan clubs, professional organizations, trade associations, and hobby groups. The *Encyclopedia of Organizations,* which annually publishes information on associations throughout the world, groups organizations into 18 broad categories:

1. Trade, business, and commercial
2. Environmental and agricultural
3. Legal, governmental, public administration, and military
4. Engineering, technological, and natural or social sciences
5. Educational
6. Cultural
7. Social welfare
8. Health and medical
9. Public affairs
10. Fraternal, nationality, and ethnic
11. Religious
12. Veterans', hereditary, and patriotic
13. Hobby and avocational
14. Athletic and sports
15. Labor unions, associations, and federations
16. Chambers of commerce, trade, and tourism
17. Greek-letter and related organizations
18. Fan clubs[3]

The multivolume *Encyclopedia* contains information on more than 22,000 national associations in the United States; more than 116,000 local, state, and regional associations in the United States; and more than 20,000 associations based outside the United States—including, of course, the Tattoo Club of Great Britain.[4]

Association Finances

Joining an association usually involves nothing more than completing an application and paying dues. Membership dues constitute the largest source of income for associations in the United States, totaling almost 30 percent of the average association's financial resources. Other important sources of income include conventions, continuing education programs, and publication sales.[5]

In some organizations, membership dues are not enough. Prospective members may have to meet certain age, occupation, residency, or income requirements to qualify for membership. However, these requirements are not always obvious. For example, one does not have to be retired to be a member of AARP. And many fathers are members of the Girl Scouts. When targeting an association as a special public, you should research its membership policies.

The great majority of associations are **nonprofit organizations,** a status that can provide reduced taxation. However, if an organization engages in **lobbying** activities in the United States—that is, if it tries to influence governmental legislative processes—it must pay taxes on its lobbying expenses. Almost a third of national associations engage in lobbying in addition to their other functions. These organizations would be seen as special interest groups. (See Chapter 12.) The remaining organizations provide educational, professional, and charitable services—but no lobbying. As a result, they have a different tax status. Nonprofit associations must annually file a federal Form 990 to declare and verify the nature of their activities.[6]

Most members of associations are individuals. However, companies often join associations, particularly trade associations such as the National Association of Manufacturers. Whether members are individuals or organizations, so-called **association management companies** provide administrative support for more than 3,000 associations in the United States, Canada, and Europe. Association management companies are hired managers, supervising several associations from a central location. These companies organize and host almost 4,000 meetings and conventions annually.[7]

Association Purposes

"Associations serve their members in many ways, but, above all, they do for the membership that which individual members cannot do for themselves," declares the *Encyclopedia of Associations.*

The *Encyclopedia* specifies several purposes for organizations, including

- Educating members and other key publics
- Setting professional standards, such as ethics codes

- Motivating and organizing volunteers
- Creating forums for networking and communication
- Exercising a unified voice in political and social issues[8]

The mission of an association may dictate where it chooses to locate its head-quarters. Many business associations have selected New York, arguably the world's financial capital, as their headquarters. Trade and business associations interested in influencing public policies have offices in the seats of government power: Washington, D.C.; Ottawa, Canada; or various state and provincial capitals. Look for energy-business associations in Houston and Dallas. Agricultural interests have headquarters in Midwestern cities such as Chicago and St. Louis. Interested in the entertainment industry? Look to Los Angeles.

Some associations created for honorary purposes have evolved into philan-thropic organizations. The Honorable Order of Kentucky Colonels began in 1932 as a loose association of people recognized by gubernatorial proclamation for their contributions to the Bluegrass State. In response to floods in 1937 that left thou-sands homeless, the association began a Good Works Program. Since then, the Kentucky Colonels have taken seriously their commission to be "Kentucky's am-bassador of good will and fellowship around the world."[9] The organization con-tributed $1.3 million to charity in 2003.

Other associations serve as umbrella organizations that bring together simi-lar groups in a coalition of common interests. For example, the North-American Interfraternity Conference is a grouping of 66 member organizations with 550 chapters located on 800 campuses in the United States and Canada. The NIC ad-vocates on behalf of its member fraternities and sororities. It also serves as a forum and information clearinghouse for issues such as binge drinking, hazing, academic achievement, and Greek housing issues.[10] The National Council of Women's Or-ganizations in Case 6.3 is another example of an umbrella organization.

There are also associations based largely on emotional ties. You may be a member of your high school's alumni association. Your college or university will certainly solicit you after graduation to become a member of its alumni association. Professional athletes and various branches of the military services have alumni as-sociations. The missions of these associations often focus on strengthening the organization or institution their members hold close to their hearts.

Many associations offer health insurance policies to their members. More than 8 million Americans have health insurance through an association, generat-ing almost $6 billion in annual premiums.[11] Other benefits may include travel dis-counts, association publications, and special purchasing opportunities.

Association members expect such benefits. "There has been little academic study surrounding the management of memberships," say the authors of a recent study of why and how members commit to associations. But their research does point to one solid conclusion: "Membership increasingly is becoming short-term focused and espouses an attitude of 'what have you done for me lately?'"[12]

Kimberly Griffiths, associate editor of *Industrial Distribution,* a trade magazine, says, "The concern for association managers is that they must continue to provide a valuable and active service for their members."[13]

Member Relations Tactics

The key to good member communication is maintaining a constant flow of accurate and relevant information. The size and complexity of an organization can complicate this flow; however. For example, communicating with members of an elementary school parent–teacher association or with residents of a neighborhood association may be easy. In those instances, communication usually flows unimpeded between leadership and members. However, consider how difficult member relations may be for an organization such as the Public Relations Society of America, which has approximately 20,000 members in 10 regional districts and 116 chapters. PRSA members can also be affiliated with one or more of the organization's 18 Professional Interest Sections or its College of Fellows. PRSA also sponsors the Public Relations Student Society of America, with more than 7,000 members on 227 campuses.[14] Although some communications flow directly from PRSA's New York headquarters to individual members, much communication is channeled through district offices, local chapters, and interest sections. And each of these units has its own communication needs. This complexity demonstrates why practitioners should turn to research to gain a thorough understanding of an association's organization and governance structures.

Public relations practitioners communicate the benefits of an association to its members—and they relay member attitudes back to the association's managers. In doing so, they conduct research and deploy many of the tactics used in employee relations (see Chapter 3), including newsletters, magazines, and other publications; e-mail; and videos. However, in member relations, two relationship-building tactics have paramount importance: interactive Web sites and conventions.

Association Web Sites

One recent study of associations found that 86 percent have an interactive Web site, with member relations being its top function. (See Table 4.1.) More than half of the associations also believed that selling additional services, such as educational materials, was an important activity for their site. Special access to an association's

table 4.1 *Associations Online*

- Associations recruit 4 percent of their members through the Internet.
- Associations say that communicating with members is the chief purpose of their Web sites, followed by selling products and offering continuing education.
- Fifty-four percent of associations believe that revenue generation is an important Web site function.
- Web sites generate a median 2 percent of associations' income. Eighty-two percent of associations expect that figure to increase.

Source: American Society of Association Executives Web site, www.asaenet.org.

Web site can also be viewed as a membership benefit. Through password-protected Web sites, members gain exclusive access to membership lists, current research, and publication archives. In addition to providing benefits and generating revenue, Web sites help cut costs. "Many organizations are already reporting a decrease in costs for activities like publishing," the study reported. It also found that, because of small staffs, 68 percent of associations **outsource** their Web sites, paying someone outside the association to create and maintain them.[15]

Association Conventions

Association conventions are big business. "The highest participation level is for our annual convention and trade show," says Georgia Foley, executive director of the Specialty Tools and Fasteners Distributors Association. "We've consistently attracted more than 4,200 people since 2000."[16]

Associations spend more than $56 billion annually on conventions and major meetings, which total more than 375,000 a year.[17]

The International Association of Business Communicators, for example, holds its annual convention every June, attracting members throughout the world. "I treasure my IABC friendships," says Sharon Bond, president of Insight Inc. of Park Ridge, Ill. "Getting to know people from all over the world has enriched my life immeasurably, both personally and professionally."[18]

Association Profile: IABC

Founded in 1970, IABC includes many public relations practitioners among its 13,000 worldwide members. IABC research shows that 11 percent of its members specialize in independent communication consulting; 10 percent specialize in public relations; and the remainder work in communication jobs in areas such as education and government. Like many associations, IABC surveys its members to measure satisfaction and identify areas for additional benefits. It knows, for example, that almost half its members—49 percent—work in corporations. Almost one-third—31 percent—engage in international communication. More than half—63 percent—began their communication careers before 1990. IABC has members in more than 60 nations, including the United States, Mexico, Peru, Zimbabwe, Thailand, and Slovenia.[19] The organization has 12 districts/regions and almost 100 chapters.

Of the association purposes noted earlier, IABC concentrates its efforts on creating forums for networking and communication, providing continuing education for its members, and setting professional standards. In addition to its annual convention, the international office in San Francisco sponsors several professional development seminars each year, and local IABC chapters hold monthly meetings. IABC publishes *Communication World* magazine as well as *CW Bulletin,* an

IABC Code of Ethics
for Professional Communicators

Preface

Because hundreds of thousands of business communicators worldwide engage in activities that affect the lives of millions of people, and because this power carries with it significant social responsibilities, the International Association of Business Communicators developed the Code of Ethics for Professional Communicators.

The Code is based on three different yet interrelated principles of professional communication that apply throughout the world.

These principles assume that just societies are governed by a profound respect for human rights and the rule of law; that ethics, the criteria for determining what is right and wrong, can be agreed upon by members of an organization; and, that understanding matters of taste requires sensitivity to cultural norms.

These principles are essential:

- Professional communication is legal.
- Professional communication is ethical.
- Professional communication is in good taste.

Recognizing these principles, members of IABC will:

- engage in communication that is not only legal but also ethical and sensitive to cultural values and beliefs;
- engage in truthful, accurate and fair communication that facilitates respect and mutual understanding; and,
- adhere to the following articles of the IABC Code of Ethics for Professional Communicators.

Because conditions in the world are constantly changing, members of IABC will work to improve their individual competence and to increase the body of knowledge in the field with research and education.

Articles

1. Professional communicators uphold the credibility and dignity of their profession by practicing honest, candid and timely communication and by fostering the free flow of essential information in accord with the public interest.

2. Professional communicators disseminate accurate information and promptly correct any erroneous communication for which they may be responsible.

3. Professional communicators understand and support the principles of free speech, freedom of assembly, and access to an open marketplace of ideas; and, act accordingly.

The ethics code of the International Association of Business Communicators unites IABC's 13,000 members from more than 60 countries in a quest for high professional standards. (Courtesy of the International Association of Business Communicators)

(continued)

2

4. Professional communicators are sensitive to cultural values and beliefs and engage in fair and balanced communication activities that foster and encourage mutual understanding.

5. Professional communicators refrain from taking part in any undertaking which the communicator considers to be unethical.

6. Professional communicators obey laws and public policies governing their professional activities and are sensitive to the spirit of all laws and regulations and, should any law or public policy be violated, for whatever reason, act promptly to correct the situation.

7. Professional communicators give credit for unique expressions borrowed from others and identify the sources and purposes of all information disseminated to the public.

8. Professional communicators protect confidential information and, at the same time, comply with all legal requirements for the disclosure of information affecting the welfare of others.

9. Professional communicators do not use confidential information gained as a result of professional activities for personal benefit and do not represent conflicting or competing interests without written consent of those involved.

10. Professional communicators do not accept undisclosed gifts or payments for professional services from anyone other than a client or employer.

11. Professional communicators do not guarantee results that are beyond the power of the practitioner to deliver.

12. Professional communicators are honest not only with others but also, and most importantly, with themselves as individuals; for a professional communicator seeks the truth and speaks that truth first to the self.

Enforcement and Communication of the IABC Code for Professional Communicators
IABC fosters compliance with its Code by engaging in global communication campaigns rather than through negative sanctions. However, in keeping with the sixth article of the IABC Code, members of IABC who are found guilty by an appropriate governmental agency or judicial body of violating laws and public policies governing their professional activities may have their membership terminated by the IABC executive board following procedures set forth in the association's bylaws.

IABC encourages the widest possible communication about its Code.

e-mail newsletter. Members can access additional professional development materials and how-to guides on IABC's Web site. The association also sponsors the IABC Research Foundation, which commissions and publishes communication studies. And IABC's Code of Ethics for Professional Communicators is one of the best-known ethics codes in the public relations profession.[20]

"What a source of strength and support IABC has been to me," says Bish Mukherjee, president of Mishna Network Australia, in Sydney. "I have acquired leadership and public speaking skills that have propelled me to a new level of professionalism and status that I could never have dreamed of before."[21]

Jobs in Member Relations

Public relations practitioners who specialize in member relations perform a wide variety of tasks. Most associations have a management team of fewer than 10 people: Median staff size is seven full-time employees. With such small staffs, member relations professionals generally have direct access to the association's top manager—but they also may help stuff envelopes and answer the phone. In 2004, median salary for member relations professionals was $42,720.[22]

Associations provide public relations professionals a grand opportunity to match their professional skills with their individual values and interests. National and international associations include the American Karaoke Society in Nashville, Tenn.; the American Scientific Glassblowers Society in Madison, N.C.; the British Isles Bee Breeders Association in Cogenhoe, England; and the Ghost Research Society in Oak Lawn, Ill.

And—this should come as no surprise—association managers have their own association: the American Society of Association Executives in Washington, D.C.

Discussion Questions

1. Do you belong to any associations? If so, why? What benefits do you derive?

2. What student associations exist at your college or university? What member relations tactics do they use?

3. Without consulting the *Encyclopedia of Associations,* can you name an association in each of its 18 categories?

4. Why have Web sites become such an important member relations tactic?

5. Why would a company join a trade association that includes competitors?

Key Terms

association management companies, p. 59

lobbying, p. 59
member relations, p. 58

nonprofit organizations, p. 59
outsource, p. 62

Endnotes

1. American Society of Association Executives Web site, www.asaenet.org.

2. American Society of Association Executives Web site.

3. *Encyclopedia of Associations,* ed. Alan Hedblad (Farmington Hills, MI: The Gale Group, 2003).

4. *Encyclopedia of Associations.*

5. "Net Profitability Down for Associations, According to New ASAE Study," American Society of Association Executives news release, December 17, 2003. Online: www.asaenet.org.

6. American Society of Association Executives Web site.

7. International Association of Association Management Companies Web site, www.iiamc.org.

8. *Encyclopedia of Associations.*

9. Honorable Order of Kentucky Colonels Web site, www.kycolonels.org.

10. North-American Interfraternity Council Web site, www.nicindy.org.

11. American Society of Association Executives Web site.

12. Thomas W. Gruen, John O. Summers, and Frank Acito, "Relationship Marketing Activities, Commitment, and Membership Behaviors in Professional Associations," *Journal of Marketing* (July 2000), 34, 44.

13. Kimberly Griffiths, "What Have You Done for Me Lately," *Industrial Distribution,* January 2004. Online: Lexis-Nexis.

14. Public Relations Society of America Web site, www.prsa.org.

15. American Society of Association Executives Web site.

16. Griffiths.

17. American Society of Association Executives Web site.

18. International Association of Business Communicators Web site, www.iabc.com.

19. International Association of Business Communicators Web site.

20. International Association of Business Communicators Web site.

21. International Association of Business Communicators Web site.

22. American Society of Association Executives Web site.

Water Hazard

A Coalition of Environmental Groups Takes on an Economic Superpower—and Wins

College traditions come and go, but the venerable road trip—in which several friends pile into a car and motor to points known or unknown—endures. If your next road trip leads to Austin, Texas, consider adding these attractions to your don't-miss list: Conan's Pizza, for its whole-wheat crust; the Oasis restaurant, for stunning views of Lake Travis; Esther's Follies, for the planet's funniest comedy troupe—and, of course, the vast, empty tract of land at the intersection of MoPac Expressway and Slaughter Lane.

A vacant lot on the itinerary? That's right: The rolling expanse of mesquite trees and limestone deposits marks the spot where, in 2003, a determined coalition of citizens groups squared off against one of the most powerful forces in the U.S. economy: Wal-Mart.

Geology 101 Meets Economics 101

The tract of land in question sprawls within the Edwards Aquifer, which extends from central to southern Texas. Maybe one of your road-trip companions will be a geology major who can explain that an aquifer is a region of underground rocks that gather and channel surface water into underground rivers or lakes, wells or outlet springs. To complicate matters, the Edwards Aquifer consists mostly of limestone, which doesn't filter pollutants from the water as well as do sandstone aquifers. Pollutants that enter a limestone aquifer with surface water thus can flow into sources of drinking water. The proposed building site for the new Wal-Mart SuperCenter sat squarely within a key part the Edwards Aquifer: the so-called recharge zone that gathers water for nearby Barton Springs.

Barton Springs might be another must-see attraction for an Austin road trip. Located within Zilker Park, only minutes from downtown Austin, the springs offer a beautiful, refreshing gathering spot. Just as important, they supply the major source of drinking water for almost 50,000 Austin-area residents.

Environmental groups in Austin oppose any aquifer developments that would put "impervious cover" in the Barton Springs recharge zone. Impervious cover—a paved parking lot is the most common example—gathers pollutants such as motor oil and gasoline, allows them to mix them with rain water, and then lets the mixture run off to the soil where it sinks into the aquifer. An Austin city ordinance mandates that only 15 percent of any recharge-zone development can contain impervious cover. However, the proposed Wal-Mart site came with a legal exemption that allowed 65 percent impervious cover. Wal-Mart planned for 51 percent.

"It is entirely up to Wal-Mart to make the right choice and locate the project elsewhere," said Austin Mayor Will Wynn, who opposed the project but noted that Wal-Mart had the legal right to build the SuperCenter. "The City of Austin must honor and abide by the agreements it makes."

Wal-Mart and the Endeavor Real Estate Group, its Austin-based partner in the project, planned to buy additional nearby land and leave it undeveloped to mitigate the damage of its impervious cover.

Different Values, One Mission

Leading a coalition of almost 20 Austin citizens groups was the Save Our Springs Alliance, acting in accordance with its mission statement: "Our mission is to protect the Edwards Aquifer, its springs and contributing streams, and the natural and cultural heritage of the Hill Country watersheds, with special emphasis on the Barton Springs Edwards Aquifer."

Other groups in the coalition acted on different values. Neighborhood associations, whose members lived near the proposed Wal-Mart site, objected to increased traffic that the 24-hour SuperCenter would bring to the area. The Sendera Homeowners Association, for example, surveyed more than 400 of its members. The resulting data revealed an additional concern: the impact of large trucks making deliveries to the new Wal-Mart.

The S.O.S Alliance helped unite the organizations into the No Big Box Coalition, named for the groups' opposition to warehouse-sized stores that both look like big boxes and often sell merchandise in big containers. "Diverse Detractors Duel with Wal-Mart" declared the headline of an *Austin American-Statesman* newspaper article about the coalition. Reporter Stephen Scheibal noted that other coalitions had opposed development proposals in Austin, "but seldom with so much unanimity."

With no legal way to stop the SuperCenter, an S.O.S. Alliance representative knew the only hope for success was for coalition members to stand united and make their voices heard. "Right now, it is in the court of public opinion," said Colin Clark, S.O.S. communications director. "Ultimately, Wal-Mart will have to respect what the people of this community want."

Key target publics for the coalition's communication efforts included coalition members, the news media, and officials at Wal-Mart and the Endeavor Real Estate Group.

"Wailing, Moaning, and Rending of Garments"

Clearly, the goal of the plan was to stop Wal-Mart from building the proposed SuperCenter in the Barton Springs recharge zone. Objectives included keeping coalition members united, creating newsworthy protest events, and communicating with Wal-Mart and Endeavor officials.

Perhaps the greatest tactic in the grass-roots campaign was the existence of the coalition itself. In addition to the S.O.S. Web site, several other sites grew out of the coalition, including SaveAustin.com and NoAquiferBigBox.com. The *Austin American-Statesman,* which had earlier noted the unusual cohesion of the coalition, concluded that "Wal-Mart's plans ignited a wall of opposition from groups that fought over Southwest Austin development through the 1990s."

In addition to sponsoring its own Web site and supporting others, S.O.S. communicated with members and supporters through broadcast e-mails, newsletters, and public meetings. So successful were the broadcast e-mails that a lawyer representing a different development project sent this message of protest to Austin city officials: "Please see attached from our friends at SOS. Approving a settlement is going to be another tough vote for the Council as SOS will make damn sure there is wailing, moaning, and rending of garments."

The coalition moved a public meeting from the Lady Bird Johnson Wildflower Center to Bowie High School when it became clear that the crowd would overflow the center. Coalition members, reporters, and representatives from Wal-Mart and Endeavor filled the high school's 500-seat auditorium. Environmentalists, homeowners, and even the mayor spoke in opposition to the new Wal-Mart.

"There are people who have very legitimate concerns. We always want that feedback," said a Wal-Mart representative. But when asked if Wal-Mart would consider another site, she responded with a single word: "No."

S.O.S. Alliance tactics to prevent a new Wal-Mart store in an environmentally sensitive area included protests outside the headquarters of Wal-Mart's local realty partner. (Courtesy of S.O.S. Alliance)

At the meeting, S.O.S. representatives gave coalition members contact information for officials at Wal-Mart and Endeavor. They also distributed preprinted protest postcards to make such communications even easier.

In its Fall 2003 newsletter, S.O.S. praised coalition members for "writing, faxing, calling, and e-mailing Wal-Mart and their local partner, Endeavor Realty, letting them know that their plans were completely unacceptable for water quality and quality of life reasons."

Two weeks after the public meeting, the coalition took the protest to Endeavor headquarters. As the *Austin American-Statesman* reported, "Commuters into downtown Austin were greeted by more than two dozen people protesting Endeavor Real Estate Group and its plans to sell environmentally sensitive land to Wal-Mart." The article noted that protesters represented a spectrum of groups from environmentalists to neighborhood associations. The *Austin Business Journal* later wrote of "the tremendous demonstrations in recent months from area residents against the development."

One coalition action became both a fund raiser and a communication tactic: The NoAquiferBigBox.com Web site sold anti-Wal-Mart T-shirts.

Another coalition fund raiser even drew media attention. When coalition member Save Barton Creek Association sold tickets for a showing of an anti-Wal-Mart documentary, the *Austin Business Journal* published an article on the tactic four days before the showing.

A Good Corporate Citizen

Through unity and coordinated actions, coalition members made their voices heard. "To call the reaction to the project mild would be an understatement," said a partner in the Endeavor Real Estate Group.

On Oct. 1, eight months after announcing their intent to build in the Barton Springs recharge zone, Wal-Mart and Endeavor canceled plans for the SuperCenter. "We recognize the unique and sensitive nature of this land located in the Barton Springs–Edwards Aquifer recharge zone," said a Wal-Mart representative. "We also recognize that pursuit of a store at this location was interfering with our efforts to better serve the entire Austin community."

Austin Mayor Will Wynn and members of the City Council were quick to praise Wal-Mart and Endeavor for surrendering their legal right to build the SuperCenter. "I think this decision by these two companies shows that they have been listening, and I applaud their decision," Wynn said. "Today, Wal-Mart and Endeavor Real Estate Group have done the right thing for Austin. Wal-Mart and Endeavor have set the example for good corporate citizenship with regard to their approach and ultimate decision on this site."

"This is a very responsible decision," added City Council member Betty Dunkerley.

As goodwill and praises for good citizenship filled City Hall, City Council member Daryl Slusher directed attention to the Austin citizens who, against the odds, had acted on their values and prevailed against an economic juggernaut. "This just shows what a determined coalition of citizens can accomplish," Slusher said. "I applaud Wal-Mart and Endeavor officials for acknowledging community values and withdrawing from the project."

Sources

"Barton Creek Group to Raise Funds for Wal-Mart Fight," *Austin Business Journal,* September 8, 2003. Online: www.bizjournals.com/austin.

Ann Hatchitt, "Neighbors Voice Concerns about Proposed Wal-Mart," *Austin Business Journal,* June 30, 2003. Online: www.bizjournals.com/austin.

Ann Hatchitt, "Wal-Mart Withdraws Plan for SW Austin Store," *Austin Business Journal,* September 29, 2003. Online: www.bizjournals.com/austin.

Shonda Novak, "Big Wal-Mart Planned for Aquifer Zone," *Austin American-Statesman,* March 26, 2003. Online: Lexis-Nexis.

Stephen Scheibal, "Diverse Detractors Duel with Wal-Mart," *Austin American-Statesman,* July 6, 2003. Online: Lexis-Nexis.

Stephen Scheibal, "Wal-Mart Dumps Plans for Southwest Austin Store," *Austin American-Statesman,* October 1, 2003. Online: Lexis-Nexis.

Stephen Scheibal, "Wal-Mart Retreats on MoPac Plans," *Austin American-Statesman,* October 2, 2003. Online: Lexis-Nexis.

S.O.S. Alliance Web site, www.sosalliance.org.

"Victory: Wal-Mart Abandons Aquifer Site!!" *S.O.S. Alliance Fall News,* Fall 2003. Online: www.sosalliance.org.

"Wal-Mart, Endeavor Withdrawing from Edwards Aquifer Site," city of Austin news release, October 1, 2003. Online: www.ci.austin.tx.

"Wal-Mart Foes Take to Streets," *Austin American-Statesman,* July 17, 2003. Online: Lexis-Nexis.

case 4.2

AARP's SOCO

To Placate Unhappy Members, AARP Develops a Strategic Overriding Communications Objective

The caller to CNN was irate. "Many members of AARP have been tearing up their cards," she told host Martin Savidge. "And rather than do that, I would suggest calling the 800 number on the back of the card, ask them to cancel your membership, and request a refund of the unused portion. Many of us are so angry that I'm sure it will hit them in the pocketbook, the way AARP has helped hit us in the pocketbook."

During Thanksgiving 2003, AARP may not have known whether to give thanks or curse fate. *Newsweek* magazine reported that the organization for older Americans was embroiled in "a public relations nightmare" that could "damage the organization's longstanding credibility."

What had gone wrong inside an organization that *Fortune* magazine ranks as one of the most powerful voices in shaping U.S. government policy? AARP had supported a Medicare expansion that even its own newsletter labeled as "bitterly controversial." Medicare is a government program that helps provide health care for older Americans, and the 2003 expansion included a multiyear $400 billion package to help senior citizens purchase expensive prescription drugs. But the price tag, the criteria for qualifying, and other details of the Congressional bill angered some AARP members.

AARP—once known as the American Association of Retired Persons—is a nonprofit organization that, in the words of its mission statement, is "dedicated to enhancing the quality of life for all as we age." The organization provides discounts, services, and issues-oriented publications for its members, and it lobbies legislators at all levels of government to ensure the enactment of policies favorable to older adults. In 1998, the organization decided to drop its full name and function simply as AARP, to acknowledge that many of its members still worked and had not retired.

Commitment and Backlash

After monitoring the Medicare bill's slow progress in Congress and lobbying successfully for changes, AARP threw its support behind the bill on Nov. 17, just a week before the decisive and contentious vote.

"To support its passage, we launched a campaign for our members and for Congress," said AARP President James Parkel, the organization's highest-ranking volunteer.

AARP's campaign partially succeeded. On Nov. 25, the Senate passed the bill, which the House had earlier approved, and sent the measure to the White House for the president's signature. But the campaign to persuade AARP members may have been less successful.

Both the Associated Press and *Newsweek* used the term "firestorm" to describe members' reception of AARP's support for the bill. Reuters news service reported, "Senior citizens angry over the AARP's endorsement of the Medicare bill are ripping up or burning their AARP cards." The *New York Daily News* charged, "AARP is awash in membership cancellations" and called AARP a "loser." In *Jack O'Dwyer's Newsletter,* a major public relations periodical, O'Dwyer himself wrote, "AARP's members' message board burned with rage last week after the group . . . announced support for the Republicans' new Medicare bill."

President George W. Bush signed Medicare reform legislation into law in December 2003 in a White House ceremony. Passage of the bill was assured when Bush won critical backing of the measure from AARP. (Courtesy of the White House)

On that message board, one member wrote, "Why! Why! Why! did you sell out your members? Our membership is canceled."

In Washington, D.C., AARP members burned their cards in front of the organization's headquarters.

Even AARP's newsletter, the *AARP Bulletin,* conceded that "AARP had to take its lumps from some of its own 35 million members. Within a week of the announcement, 15,000 members had cancelled their memberships."

But 15,000 members is far less than 1 percent of the organization's membership, and AARP had done its research regarding member opinions. In a prominent message on its Web site, AARP officials reminded members that before supporting the bill, "AARP gathered ideas and reactions from our members through surveys; town meetings; calls and letters; face-to-face meetings with groups of members; and other means. All of this information was presented to our all-volunteer Board of Directors, which reviewed it and voted to endorse the bill."

A year earlier, AARP had surveyed Americans 45 and older and learned that one-third of that public would be "very angry" if Congress failed to pass prescription drug benefits. During the final weeks of the 2003 debate, AARP surveyed its members and found that 75 percent wanted Congress to pass the new Medicare bill. However, the same survey revealed that 62 percent of members were "not very familiar or not familiar at all" with the bill's specific details.

"We develop positions and policies only after extensive study and consultation with our members and only with the approval of our all-volunteer-member board of directors," said AARP CEO Bill Novelli.

Fighting Back: AARP Creates a SOCO

The percentage of resigning members may have been low, but media attention was high and there were no guarantees that the resignations would subside. Led by Novelli, AARP created a plan to inform and retain members. Its goal was simple: AARP would tell its side of the story to its members.

"I expect there to be criticism," Novelli said. "What we have to do is explain our position."

AARP developed several objectives to help it tell its side of the story:

- It developed a so-called SOCO—a strategic overriding communications objective. In simple language, AARP developed one clear message to send to its members.
- It planned to deliver the SOCO through a variety of media.
- It planned to directly and forcefully counter inaccuracies and rumors about its position.
- It planned to prove the existence of broad support for its position.

In developing a SOCO and sending it through a variety of media, AARP was following the experience of its CEO, Bill Novelli. Novelli is a founder of Porter/Novelli, a well-known public relations agency. In describing his handling of the members' unrest, *Newsday* of New York called him "a master at public relations." *Newsweek* called him "a marketing guru."

Clearly, Novelli's staff believed in the power of public relations to turn the tide. "We use PR and communications as a way to advance the goals of the organization," said AARP Communications Director Lisa Davis.

AARP's SOCO was a single sentence, and one of its first appearances came in a news release also posted for members on the organization's Web site. "Though far from perfect," wrote AARP President Parkel, "the bill represents an historical breakthrough."

The "imperfect but acceptable beginning" SOCO soon appeared in virtually every AARP communiqué related to the debate.

- In a letter to members of Congress (placed on the AARP Web site for members), Novelli wrote, "We all know that this bill is not perfect; but on balance, it represents an important breakthrough. . . ."
- In an *AARP Bulletin* article, Novelli declared, "The bill isn't perfect, but millions of older Americans cannot afford to wait for perfect." In the same article, John Rother, AARP's director of policy, said, "There are things in this bill

we do not like. Nonetheless, we hope that our members will understand that on balance it brings substantial help."

- An AARP fact sheet on the proposed bill, posted on the Web site, contained this message: "It is true that the proposed legislation is not perfect, but our members cannot wait for the perfect bill. They need help now."
- In a *Newsweek* article, Novelli said, "It does a lot more good than it does harm. We need to get it into place now and then build on it." Reuters news service paraphrased Rother as saying that "the bill was not perfect, but it was a step forward."
- In full-page newspaper ads, AARP acknowledged that the bill it supported was "far from perfect."

Months before AARP unleashed its "imperfect" SOCO, *PR Week* magazine had noted a penchant for "one streamlined PR message" in its analysis of AARP's public relations operations.

AARP launched a variety of other tactics to fulfill its objectives. It sent representatives to protest meetings, sent mass mailings at the state level to members and sent state directors to local meetings—all to deliver the SOCO.

The organization also directly confronted what it perceived to be inaccuracies and unfounded rumors. For example, Novelli scoffed at rumors of an impending revolt of AARP members. "There's not going to be a revolt within AARP," he told *Newsweek*. "There's going to be a problem if Congress fails to pass this legislation."

Told by a *Newsweek* reporter that some critics believed that AARP had sold out to insurance and pharmaceutical companies, Novelli replied with a common barnyard epithet.

The avowedly nonpartisan AARP also denied a sudden tilt to the Republican Party. "While you may have heard from some media reports that AARP only met with Republicans, that's simply not true," officials declared on the organization's Web site.

When a story in *USA Today* implied that AARP could benefit financially from selling its own services under the new bill, Novelli fired off a letter to the newspaper, writing, "This legislation even could decrease the need for our current products. Nonetheless, this is the right thing to do."

AARP also cited the support of national opinion leaders in hopes of winning over its members. In one section of its Web site, the organization listed prominent national organizations, including the National Council on the Aging and the Alzheimer's Association, that supported the bill. In another section of the site titled "Highlights from Nationwide Opinion Pages," AARP cited the support of leading editorial writers.

Success and a Counter SOCO

The success of AARP's campaign might best be measured by silence. Within weeks of the bill's passage, the news media had moved on to other issues: AARP membership revolts no longer were front-page stories. By January 2004, resignations had risen to 45,000, but they still totaled well below 1 percent of overall membership. Because the Medicare bill features a gradual implementation, however, the success of the AARP SOCO could take years to determine.

For all the furor, Bill Novelli believes that, given its own research, AARP had no choice in the matter. "There are times when you have to take a stance," he said. "And we have done that on Medicare."

In an ironic postscript to the "imperfect but acceptable" campaign, AARP Communications Director Lisa Davis noted that many of the messages from angry members sounded alike—and she suspected an organized campaign. "We know some come from a concerted effort," she said, "because they all say the same thing."

Sounds as if AARP educated its rebellious members well. They fired back a SOCO of their own.

Sources

"AARP Loses Thousands over Medicare Law," Associated Press, January 17, 2004. Online: Lexis-Nexis.

AARP Web site, www.aarp.org.

"Angry Seniors Protest AARP's Support of Medicare Bill," *The Bulletin's Frontrunner,* November 28, 2003. Online: Lexis-Nexis.

Kenneth A. Bazinet, "Senate Passes Rx Bill," *The New York Daily News,* November 26, 2003. Online: Lexis-Nexis.

CNN, November 26, 2003. Online: Lexis-Nexis.

Saul Friedman, "If Medicare Withers, You Can 'Thank' AARP," *Newsday,* November 29, 2003. Online: Lexis-Nexis.

David Noonan and Mary Carmichael, "A New Age for AARP," *Newsweek,* December 1, 2003. Online: Lexis-Nexis.

Bill Novelli, "AARP Responds to Members Needs," letter in *USA Today,* November 28, 2003. Online: Lexis-Nexis.

Jack O'Dwyer, "Novelli Rapped for Medicare Stand," *Jack O'Dwyer's Newsletter,* November 26, 2003. Online: Lexis-Nexis.

Elaine S. Povich, "Boos for Bush's Medicare Plan," *Newsday,* December 3, 2003. Online: Lexis-Nexis.

Douglas Quenqua, "Case Study: AARP Fortifies Its Clout through Size and PR Synergy," *PR Week,* August 25, 2003. Online: Lexis-Nexis.

Douglas Quenqua, "Opponents of New Medicare Bill Mobilize Comms Effort against AARP," *PR Week,* December 1, 2003. Online: Lexis-Nexis.

Marilyn Rauber, "Split over Medicare Reform," *Richmond Times Dispatch,* November 27, 2003. Online: Lexis-Nexis.

Gary Rotstein, "Members Give AARP Earful," *Pittsburgh Post-Gazette,* November 19, 2003. Online: Lexis-Nexis.

Warren Wolfe, "AARP Members Quit in Medicare Protest," *Minneapolis Star Tribune,* November 27, 2003. Online: Lexis-Nexis.

Libraries, Underpants, and the First Amendment

The American Library Association Rallies Its Members to Fight Book Bannings

So the incredibly naughty cafeteria ladies from outer space forced the innocent school kids to eat freeze-dried worm guts, Boston baked boogers, and zombie-nerd milkshakes.

Big problem for the school kids.

Bigger problem for librarians. The above anecdote comes from author Dav Pilkey's book *Captain Underpants and the Invasion of the Incredibly Naughty Cafeteria Ladies from Outer Space (and the Subsequent Assault of the Equally Evil Lunchroom Zombie Nerds)*. Pilkey's book enjoys two national distinctions: It's hugely popular among elementary school kids in the United States; and it, with other books in the *Captain Underpants* series, is on the American Library Association's list of the most challenged books of recent years—meaning that some people want to ban it from libraries.

"Not everyone wants to read every book," says Dubuque, Iowa, librarian Betty Baule. "But we don't want anybody, any government official, telling us we can't read a certain book."

To focus public awareness on the issue of potential book bannings, the American Library Association helps sponsor a Banned Books Week every September. To publicize the week and the dangers it addresses, the association enlists the help of its members—librarians throughout the nation.

A First Amendment Issue

In bringing national attention to potential censorship, the American Library Association honors the values that unite it as an organization. Its Library Bill of Rights, adopted in 1948, begins with three statements of belief:

- Books and other library resources should be provided for the interest, information, and enlightenment of all people of the community the library serves. Materials should not be excluded because of origin, background, or views of those contributing to their creation.
- Libraries should provide materials and information presenting all points of view on current and historical issues. Materials should not be proscribed or removed because of partisan or doctrinal disapproval.
- Libraries should challenge censorship in the fulfillment of their responsibility to provide information and enlightenment.

"The ability to read, speak, think, and express ourselves freely is a core American value," says Judith Krug, director of ALA's Office for Intellectual Freedom. "We hope Banned Books Week helps to remind Americans of the importance of our freedom at a time when freedoms are being eroded in the United States. Now—more than ever—we must let freedom read."

To assist its members' advocacy efforts, the ALA has conducted extensive research into book challenges and book bannings. With research assistance from organizations such as the American Booksellers Association, ALA has learned the following:

- Since 1998, the most challenged books have been the *Harry Potter* series by J. K. Rowling.
- From 1990 to 2002, the ALA recorded more than 7,000 challenges (the organization's research shows that only one-fourth of challenges actually get reported).
- The top seven reasons for challenges are (1) sexual explicitness; (2) offensive language; (3) unsuitability to age group; (4) occult themes or Satanism; (5) violence; (6) homosexual themes; and (7) promotion of a particular religious viewpoint.
- Almost three-fourths of the challenges during the 1990s were to books in school libraries; the remaining one-fourth were to books in public libraries. In 2000, parents issued 60 percent of the challenges, library patrons issued 15 percent, and administrators issued 9 percent.

To fulfill the values of its Library Bill of Rights and promote Banned Books Week in 2003, ALA devised three objectives for communication with its members: to inform them of Banned Books Week; to provide an understanding of the underlying issues; and to provide tools for advocacy and action.

Huck Finn in Trouble Again

To inform members of the dates of Banned Books Week 2003, ALA used its many publications, including its flagship magazine, *American Libraries*. But the bulk of its Banned Books Week communication occurred through its Web site.

To help members understand the intricacies of potential book bannings, the ALA Web site featured a "Challenged and Banned Books" page that highlighted links to a host of specific topics:

- "Why Banned Books Week" included a history of Banned Books Week and a reminder of the values of the Library Bill of Rights and the First Amendment of the U.S. Constitution, with its pledge of freedom of speech and freedom of the press.
- "Challenges and Banned Books" described the differences between challenging (a protest) and banning (censorship through removal).
- "Why Books Are Challenged" reviewed the logic that leads people to seek a book's removal from a library.
- "Who Challenges Books" shared ALA's research regarding the demographics and psychographics of book challengers. The section included a memorable

$$\text{ALA}\quad\text{American Library Association}$$

Banned Books Week - Celebrating the Freedom to Read

Banned Books Week - Celebrating the Freedom to Read is observed during the last week of September each year. Observed since 1982, the annual event reminds Americans not to take this precious democratic freedom for granted.

Banned Books Week is sponsored by the American Booksellers Association, the American Booksellers Foundation for Free Expression, the American Library Association (ALA), the Association of American Publishers, the American Society of Journalists and Authors and the National Association of College Stores. It is endorsed by the Library of Congress Center for the Book.

Many bookstores and libraries across the nation join in the celebration with displays and readings of books that have been banned or threatened throughout history. These include works ranging from the Bible and "Little Red Riding Hood" to John Steinbeck's "Of Mice and Men."

Each year, the American Library Association's Office for Intellectual Freedom receives hundreds of reports on books and other materials that were "challenged" or asked to be removed from school or library shelves. The ALA estimates the number represents only about a quarter of the actual challenges. "Most Challenged" titles include the popular "Harry Potter" series of fantasy books for children by J.K. Rowling. The series drew complaints from parents and others who believe the books promote witchcraft to children.

The challenges reported reflect a continuing concern with a wide variety of themes. Other "Most Challenged" titles include "The Adventures of Huckleberry Finn" by Mark Twain, for its use of language, particularly references to race; "It's Perfectly Normal," a sex education book by Robie Harris, for being too explicit, especially for children; and "I Know Why the Caged Bird Sings" by Maya Angelou, for the description of rape she suffered as a child.

The date for Banned Books Week 2004 is:

September 25 - October 2.

For more information, contact the Office for Intellectual Freedom at 800-545-2433, ext. 4223, send e-mail to **oif@ala.org** or see the **Banned Books Week Web site**.

To help promote its annual Banned Books Week, the American Library Association posts a media kit on its Web site. Members can edit the documents—including this backgrounder—to highlight local issues and events. (Courtesy of American Library Association)

quote from a former *Los Angeles Times* editor: "Censorship is the strongest drive in human nature; sex is a weak second."

- "Dealing with Challenges" offered advice on how members could respond to threats of censorship at their own libraries.
- "The Top 100 Challenged Books" was just that: a list of the most-challenged books. The list included novels that many readers consider American classics,

among them *The Adventures of Huckleberry Finn* by Mark Twain and *I Know Why the Caged Bird Sings* by Maya Angelou.

ALA also used its Web site to suggest and provide promotional tactics for Banned Books Week. Chief among them was a Banned Books Week Kit—offered for sale—that included posters, bookmarks, lists of banned books, and banned-book pins. The site also included offers of Banned Books Week T-shirts and a book titled *The Banned Books Resource Book*. The site featured a link titled "Action Guide, Suggested Activities," which detailed special events to generate publicity and education.

To help members reach beyond the library walls, the ALA Web site included a Banned Books Week media kit that members could download, modify, and distribute. The site also included a sample newspaper editorial with these instructions: "Edit and adapt this opinion column for your local newspaper." The first paragraph of the sample editorial read:

> Throughout the country, most children are starting a new academic year. Teachers are sending out their lists of required readings, and parents are beginning to gather books. In some cases, classics like *The Adventures of Huckleberry Finn, The Catcher in the Rye,* and *To Kill a Mockingbird* may not be included in the curriculum or available in the school library due to challenges made by parents or administrators.

In addition to its Web site, ALA has a Chapter Relations Office that helps state chapters access the resources of the national organization. Besides its required individual memberships, ALA has a chapter in every state, as well as in the District of Columbia, Guam, and the U.S. Virgin Islands. Almost 50 percent of ALA members also belong to their state or territorial ALA chapter.

Grandma Speaks

Banned Book Week 2003 succeeded in generating more than 150 newspaper stories throughout the United States. Often, those stories focused on publicity efforts at local libraries:

- The New Port Richey Public Library in Tampa, Fla., sponsored a "What the First Amendment Means to Me" essay contest for high school students. Winner Crystal Buotte wrote, "The First Amendment is the most important amendment to me because it lets me be who I am today."
- The Carnegie-Stout Library in Dubuque, Iowa, held a Banned Books Read-a-Thon, in which library patrons signed up to read aloud from their favorite challenged book. During a reading at Campbell Library at Rowan University in Glassboro, N.J., one patron read (presumably more than the title) from *Captain Underpants and the Invasion of the Incredibly Naughty Cafeteria Ladies from Outer Space (and the Subsequent Assault of the Equally Evil Lunchroom Zombie Nerds)*.
- The San Bernardino Public Library in San Bernardino, Calif., hosted a reading from the author of one of ALA's most-challenged books: *Always Running:*

La Vida Loca—Gang Days in L.A., by Luis Rodriguez. "I realize the book is hard-core," said Rodriguez. "Maybe it's not for everybody. But when a community is standing up for a book, it should be available."

- The Ephrata Public Library in Ephrata, Pa., displayed books that its own patrons had challenged, including William Steig's *Shrek!*. "Most of the time, people are shocked to find out which books have been banned," said Penny Talbert, the library's community relations coordinator.
- The Ouachita Parish Public Library in Monroe, La., sponsored an intellectual freedom symposium, and the Bloomington Public Library in Bloomington, Ill., held a young-adults discussion of the *Harry Potter* books.
- At Tulare Western High School in Tulare, Calif., librarian Jerry Asher noted that "we have yet to have a parent ask that a book be banned"—but he put up ALA's Banned Books Week posters anyway.

ALA's busy Web site also included an unwelcome sign of success for Banned Books Week: Days before the event began, the organization regretfully announced to members that it had sold out of its Banned Books T-shirts.

One of the most gratifying signs of success, perhaps, came from a grandmother in Greenville, S.C. In a letter to her local newspaper, she indicated that ALA's value of the freedom to read had moved through its members and into the community:

> As a parent of seven children and a grandmother of 12, I buy books for them and encourage reading. I guess I do censor what I give to read, but I don't want the likes of a committee to say my child can't read a book. That must be the job of the parents.
> I encourage the ALA to keep people like me up to date on books for my banned book reading list. Thanks, librarians!

Sources

American Library Association Web site, www.ala.org.

Brandon Christol, "Challenging Reading: Numerous Events Planned for Banned Books Week," *The Pantagraph* (Bloomington, IL), September 18, 2003. Online: Lexis-Nexis.

Laura Dwight, "Ex-Gang Member Whose Book Was Challenged Will Lecture," *Press Enterprise* (Riverside, CA), September 23, 2003. Online: Lexis-Nexis.

"Ephrata Exhibit Exposes Censorship," *Sunday News* (Lancaster, PA), September 21, 2003. Online: Lexis-Nexis.

Jean Gordon, "Word Warrior," *News-Star* (Monroe, LA), April 13, 2003. Online: Lexis-Nexis.

Megan Hussey, "Teens Offer Thoughts on First Amendment," *Tampa* (FL) *Tribune,* November 8, 2003. Online: Lexis-Nexis.

"Letters," *Greenville* (SC) *News,* September 25, 2003. Online: Lexis-Nexis.

"Library Patrons Celebrate Freedom to Read," *Telegraph Herald* (Dubuque, IA), September 23, 2003. Online: Lexis-Nexis.

Marita Maccherone, "Readers Take a Stand during Banned Books Week at Rowan," *Courier-Post* (Cherry Hill, NJ), September 30, 2003. Online: Lexis-Nexis.

Anita Stackhouse-Hite, "Schools Plan to Educate Students about Banned Books Week," *Tulare* (CA) *Advance-Register,* September 6, 2003. Online: Lexis-Nexis.

ACT file # 4

Measuring Relationships

Talking about the importance of relationships is one thing. Actually measuring their value is different. It is like using hard numbers to describe images of ever-changing cloud patterns or the movements of the ocean. However, relationship management is an important function of public relations practitioners. They have a vested interest in describing the value of their work in tangible terms easily understood in the board room.

The PR Relationship Measurement Scale discussed in Chapter 2 was created for just this purpose. Public relations researchers Linda Hon and James Grunig created the scale in 1999. Based on a 52-question survey, it measures the intensity of relationships using six basic factors: control mutuality, trust, satisfaction, commitment, exchange relationship, and communal relationship.[1]

Each of the survey items is a rating-scale question, one that measures degree of intensity. Survey respondents are asked how much they agreed with each statement on 1-to-9 scale. Hon and Grunig developed a series of questions for each of the six relationship components. For example, one of the statements designed to measure trust is "This organization treats people like me fairly and justly." While each statement, in and of itself, offers a glimpse into the nature of a relationship, the entire body of work provides a clearer and fuller picture. The concept is not much different from the federal government's use of various economic indicators to chart the health of the nation's economy.

The answers to each of the questions are tabulated to create a hard number representing the current state of the relationship between the members of a public and the organization. If these procedures are repeated accurately, that figure serves as a benchmark for comparing the relationships among different publics or changes in relationships with a single public over time. These comparisons, in turn, serve as measures of the effectiveness of each organization's public relations efforts.

Approximately three years after the initial research, Grunig published a follow-up paper, "Qualitative Methods for Assessing Relationships between Organizations and Publics."[2] Maintaining that there are times when numbers alone are not enough, Grunig wrote that qualitative methods, such as in-depth interviews or focus groups, can provide more insight into the dynamics of a relationship. In short, the difference between the quantitative and qualitative approaches is a trade-off between generating hard numbers and providing intimate detail. Practitioners should choose the approach—or combination of approaches—that best suits their needs.

These studies provide a glimmer of hope for practitioners seeking tangible measures of the value of public relations to their organization. However, these methods of measuring relationships are not a magic solution. For many executives, the only numbers that really matter are those found at the bottom of a financial

Advanced Critical Thinking

statement. They would first have to accept the Hon–Grunig methodology to see it as relevant. CEOs who understand the value of relationship management are likely to be receptive to this "new math." However, those who are fixated on the bottom line may dismiss this as more "blue smoke and mirrors" from public relations.

Discussion Questions

1. Do you think the PR Relationship Measurement Scale is a valid measure of the relationship between an organization and its publics?

2. Why are stakeholder relationships important to organizations?

3. What are the benefits of placing tangible measurements, such as hard numbers, on a relationship?

4. What are some other ways an organization can measure the strength of the relationships it has with various publics?

Endnotes

1. The methodology used in developing this scale is detailed in "Guidelines for Measuring Relationships in Public Relations," a publication of the Institute for Public Relations' Commission on PR Evaluation and Measurement. It is available through the institute, located at the University of Florida, or on its Web site, www.institutefor.pr.com.

2. James E. Grunig, "Qualitative Methods for Assessing Relationships between Organizations and Publics," Commission on PR Evaluation and Measurement, Institute for Public Relations. Online: www.institutefor.pr.com.

CHAPTER 5

Investor Relations

Beset by corporate scandals, bewildered by its relationship to public relations, and besieged by those who would rename it, **investor relations** in the 21st century seems poised on the verge of important changes.

What is this profession that stirs so much controversy? The Canadian Investor Relations Institute offers a succinct definition:

> Investor relations is the strategic management responsibility that integrates the disciplines of finance, communications, and marketing to achieve an effective two-way flow of information between a public company and the investment community, in order to enable fair and efficient capital markets.[1]

A **public company,** as opposed to a private company, sells stock in itself. In other words, it sells shares of ownership to investors, known as **stockholders** or **shareholders.** That exchange relationship, to use a term from Chapter 1, necessitates communication, particularly about a public company's financial status and financial plans. Ideally, the process of communication builds relationships with publics in a broadly defined investment community—and the discipline that makes it all happen is called investor relations.

Like the United States–based National Investor Relations Institute, the Canadian Investor Relations Institute has a Code of Ethics that reveals much about the nature of investor relations. More concise than the similar NIRI code, the CIRI code contains eight brief sections (Case 5.2 includes portions of NIRI's Code of Ethics). In the CIRI code, a member pledges to

1. Practice investor relations within the highest legal, regulatory, and ethical standards.

2. Exercise independent professional judgment in the conduct of my duties and responsibilities.
3. Attempt to avoid even the appearance of professional impropriety in the conduct of my investor relations responsibilities.
4. Keep up to date regarding the affairs of my company/clients, as well as the laws, regulations, and principles affecting the practice of investor relations.
5. Maintain the confidentiality of information acquired in the normal course of business.
6. Not use confidential information acquired in the normal course of business for my personal advantage, nor for the advantage of others, except in the legitimate performance of my duties on behalf of my company/clients.
7. Report to company authorities, the board of directors, or appropriate securities regulators, if I suspect or recognize fraudulent or illegal acts.
8. Recognize that the integrity and credibility of the capital markets is based on complete, timely, and non-selective disclosure of financial and non-financial corporate information and, to the best of my ability and knowledge, work to ensure that my company or client communicates such information on a timely basis.

The ethics code of the National Institute of Investor Relations also begins by requiring adherence to "the highest legal and ethical standards."[2] Overseen in the United States primarily by the Securities and Exchange Commission, investor relations is the most regulated area of public relations. In the aftermath of the 1929 stock market crash, Congress created the SEC to "administer federal securities laws and issue rules and regulations to provide protection for investors and ensure that the securities markets are fair and honest."[3] Much of this chapter will address compliance with federal legislation.

From the CIRI and NIRI codes of ethics, you can deduce that an investor relations professional must be part lawyer, part financial specialist, and part communicator. Who are the publics in the investment community that demand such impressive expertise?

Publics in Investor Relations

You already know one obvious public in investor relations: stockholders—or potential stockholders. Other important publics in investor relations include institutional investors, mutual fund managers, securities analysts, financial news media, employees, and official regulators.

Individual Investors

Almost half the adults in the United States now own stock in public companies, so the investors public is almost as diverse as the nation itself.[4] (See Table 5.1.) Companies can segment their investor public using such variables as longevity of in-

t a b l e 5.1 *Investor Relations Fact Sheet*

At the end of the 20th century:

- 84 million Americans owned stock.
- 27 million Americans had purchased stock through mutual funds.
- 34 million Americans had purchased stock in individual companies.
- Approximately 20 percent of stockholders were under age 35.
- Approximately 13 percent of stockholders were over age 65.
- Approximately 40 percent of stockholders had family incomes of less than $50,000.
- Approximately 18 percent of stockholders had family incomes of more than $100,000.

Source: New York Stock Exchange Shareownership Study. Online: www.nyse.com.

vestment, size of investment, age of investor, and interest in company policies. Stockholders can vote on management issues at a public company's annual meeting, usually getting one vote per share of stock.

Institutional Investors

Large organizations, such as the California Public Employees Retirement System, that exist mainly to manage purchase stock for their members represent another important public. These so-called **institutional investors** often own large blocks of shares and thus wield both economic and voting power within a public company.

Mutual Fund Managers

Similar to institutional investors, **mutual fund managers** buy and sell large blocks of stock for individual investors. A mutual fund resembles an investment club. Individual investors can examine the stock holdings of different mutual funds and decide which one to buy into. The popularity of mutual funds has grown dramatically in the past two decades.

Securities Analysts

A **security** is a stock or a bond, and a **securities analyst** recommends buying, selling, watching, or avoiding particular securities. These individuals advise investors and serve as sources for the news media. Securities analysts are an important intervening public in any campaign to build relationships with investors.

Financial News Media

The financial news media are a key intervening public in communications with investors and advisors. Virtually every news medium—television, radio, newspapers,

Members of the financial news media, including Maria Bartiromo of CNBC, are a key target public for investor relations practitioners. (Courtesy of the U.S. Census Bureau)

magazines, and the Web—now features financial news. Some media, such as the *Wall Street Journal,* CNBC-TV, and ValueLine.com, focus almost exclusively on financial information.

Employees

Employees of public companies often participate in so-called ESOPs: employee stock-ownership plans. Employee retirement plans in public companies can involve ownership of company stock. Employee relations (Chapter 3) for public companies often involves aspects of investor relations.

Official Regulators

Investor relations practitioners help a company's legal team comply with **disclosure law** and stock-market rules. Disclosure law comprises regulations—many from the Securities and Exchange Commission—that govern how public companies must communicate with government agencies as well as the investment community. For example, investor relations professionals may help with a Form 10Q (a quarterly financial report) for the SEC; they also issue news releases to comply with an SEC mandate to inform investors of events that could affect company stock

prices. Stock exchanges, such as the New York Stock Exchange, have similar requirements that public companies must meet to qualify for membership.

Investor Relations Tactics

To communicate with the diverse publics in the investment community, investor
relations practitioners use a variety of tactics. Disclosure law mandates some tactics, such as annual meetings and annual reports, but many public companies strive
to exceed the legal minimum in order to build productive relationships with the investment community. Investor relations tactics include annual meetings, annual
reports, newsletters and magazines, personal letters, Web sites, Webcasts, conference calls, news releases, and media kits.

Annual Meetings and Annual Reports

By law, a public company must hold an **annual meeting** for its stockholders. At
such meetings, company officials discuss current financial status as well as plans
for the future. Stockholders vote on various issues, including election of company
officers. Compliance with disclosure law also requires the issuance of an **annual
report** before the annual meeting. Every stockholder receives the report, which,
like the annual meeting, discusses the company's current health and future plans.
Public companies also send their annual report to securities analysts and the financial news media.

Newsletters, Magazines, and Personal Letters

Investor relations practitioners use a variety of print media to communicate with
stockholders and other publics in the investment community. Like the annual report, these tactics often include charts and graphs to help clarify technical financial language. "Companies should help investors understand how a company
makes money," said NIRI President Louis Thompson in testimony before the SEC.
"That needs to be laid out in plain English. Much of disclosure today is impenetrable."[5] Unlike annual reports, these smaller print tactics can quickly respond to
issues of concern in the marketplace.

Web Sites, Webcasts, and Conference Calls

Public companies can post extensive financial information on their Web sites, including current stock prices, annual reports, news releases, executive speeches, and
SEC forms. **Webcasts** are streamed audiovisual feeds, often live, of meetings with
investment analysts. They have grown in popularity since the federal government,
through recent legislation discussed below, cracked down on some public companies' policy of sharing information with select securities analysts in hopes of gaining
gratitude and positive evaluations. That same logic has led companies to increase
the number of analysts included in telephone conference calls.

News Releases and Media Kits

Investor relations practitioners use news releases and media kits to deliver company information to the financial news media. By law, public companies must keep investors apprised of events that can influence the value of company stock. Communicating with investors through the intervening public of the news media helps companies achieve compliance with disclosure law. To comply with disclosure law, news releases and other communications regarding company performance are fact-laden and devoid of hyperbole. Financial news releases generally include a closing paragraph noting that they are "forward-looking statements" that contain information subject to change.

In addition to this array of communication tactics with investors, investor relations practitioners increasingly communicate with one another—through organizations such as NIRI and CIRI—as they strive to tackle significant challenges facing the modern profession.

Turbulence in Investor Relations

The volatility of the stock markets in recent years has brought turmoil and new challenges to investor relations. Significant among those challenges are corporate scandals and consequent legislation, a fractured relationship with traditional public relations, and the name of the profession itself.

New Legislation and Professional Guidelines

Investor relations practitioners have been under increased legal scrutiny since the 1960s, when U.S. courts and the SEC ruled in a complaint involving Texas Gulf Sulphur Company. In that matter, the courts found that the company had used a news release to mislead investors. The courts also ruled that company officials were guilty of **insider trading**—that is, purchasing securities using information not available to other investors. Soon afterward, PRSA tightened its Code of Ethics to further address those issues. And silence—a lack of news releases—won't pass muster. Under its updated Member Code of Ethics, adopted in 2000, PRSA tackles silence in this example of improper investor relations conduct: "Lying by omission: A practitioner for a corporation knowingly fails to release financial information, giving a misleading impression of the corporation's performance."

Accounting and investor relations scandals at companies such as Enron (Case 5.2) and WorldCom triggered new and powerful legislation in the first years of the 21st century: Regulation Fair Disclosure and the Sarbanes–Oxley Act. Combined, the new laws mandated increased communication, increased management evaluation of disclosure, and increased accountability:

- Public companies cannot selectively disclose financial information to favored analysts or journalists.

- Chief executive officers and chief financial officers must sign statements that they have reviewed key financial documents and found those documents to be accurate.
- Company officials cannot obstruct in any way the efforts of accounting companies hired to conduct mandatory independent audits of company finances.
- Disclosure of financial information to stockholders is subject to new, more stringent rules regarding frequency, conflicts of interest, and information on independent audits.

The Sarbanes–Oxley Act also specifies new, harsher penalties for leaders of public companies that fail to comply with the new legislation. "Federal regulators have imposed some 30 new rules, most of them tied to the landmark Sarbanes–Oxley Act, signed into law in mid-2002," NIRI reported in September 2003.[6]

Investor Relations and Public Relations

Is investor relations a subset of public relations, much like media relations? Or has the demand for advanced legal and financial knowledge—as well as the discipline's prestige—made it a separate profession? The answer may depend on whom you ask.

"The higher end functions (i.e., those that are best paid, most influential, and closest to top management) such as investor relations . . . are being lost to other functional areas within organizations [besides public relations]," said James Hutton, a marketing professor at Fairleigh Dickinson University. Those other functional areas, Hutton reported, fall within the jurisdiction of chief financial officers or treasurers—rather than public relations managers.[7]

Investor Relations Business magazine and Business Wire, a news release distribution service, recently found that 78 percent of almost 300 investor relations professionals surveyed believed that journalists and analysts respect them more than other public relations professionals.[8] Both the survey and the response indicate a growing awareness of a gulf between investor relations and public relations.

However, investor relations specialist Andrew Edson & Associates holds that "public relations is a broad field of practice encompassing several specific areas," among them "investor relations." In a primer on investor relations for non-U.S. companies, the agency notes that the placement of investor relations within an organization may relate to company size:

> In large, major corporations, it is not uncommon to have a public relations staff with the many functions divided among different individuals. The investor relations responsibility in such broad-based companies often falls either under the chief financial officer or a subordinate, such as the treasurer. . . . In smaller or medium sized companies, the individual charged with handling investor relations (or overseeing it, if an outside firm or investor relations consultant is used for such services) would typically be responsible for all of the business' public relations activities.[9]

Whether its practitioners report to chief financial officers or public relations managers, investor relations is part of public relations. Investor relations seeks to build relationships with publics that have resources essential to a public company's success. Investor relations professionals who function within a company's financial department should coordinate their relationship-building efforts with other public relations functions within the company, such as media relations and employee relations.

What's in a Name?

You don't need much knowledge of Shakespeare to quote Juliet's famous line: "What's in a name? That which we call a rose by any other name would smell as sweet." However, some public relations educators convincingly challenge the narrow focus of the term *investor relations*. Because of the discipline's relationship-building activities with publics beyond investors—securities analysts, financial news media, and regulators from governments and stock markets—an increasing number of public relations textbooks use the term *financial relations* or *financial public relations*.[10]

Critical Thinking and Investor Relations Careers

Despite the challenges of investor relations—or perhaps because of them—a career in investor relations offers public relations professionals an excellent opportunity to exercise critical thinking skills. Investor relations professionals must analyze complex financial and legal situations, consider both causes and consequences, and develop creative communication tactics that comply with legal and ethical guidelines. Investor relations may be public relations paradise for young professionals with solid critical thinking skills. So how do you prepare for that career? Here's some advice:

- Don't avoid that accounting class—and don't stop with accounting. Enroll in additional business courses. Consider getting an MBA.
- Interview area investor relations professionals. Be sure to ask what college courses they found valuable, or what college courses they wish they had taken.
- Seek internships with investor relations professionals.
- Read company annual reports, including the fine print.
- Read business periodicals, such as the *Wall Street Journal,* the *Financial Times,* and *Investor Relations Business.*
- Familiarize yourself with the Web site of the Securities and Exchange Commission.

And don't forget to study the ethics codes of organizations such as the National Institute of Investor Relations.

At the beginning of the 21st century, investor relations finds itself bathed in the harsh glare of media and government spotlights. Challenges certainly exist—but so does an eagerness to confront them with renewed commitment to the values of honesty and openness. "We must create an environment for the highest ethical conduct in Corporate America," said Louis Thompson of the National Investor Relations Institute. "We have to move forward and make ours, without a doubt, the strongest, most credible financial market in the world."[11]

Discussion Questions ● ● ● ● ● ● ● ● ● ● ● ● ● ● ● ● ●

1. Given your current knowledge of today's financial headlines, what is your impression of investor relations?

2. How do the needs of the different publics in investor relations differ?

3. What, in addition to the coverage in this chapter, can you learn about Regulation Fair Disclosure and the Sarbanes–Oxley Act?

4. Why is critical thinking important to the practice of investor relations?

5. Is investor relations part of public relations? Or has it become an independent discipline? Please explain your answer.

Key Terms ● ● ● ● ● ● ● ● ● ● ● ● ● ● ● ● ● ●

annual meeting, p. 89
annual report, p. 89
disclosure law, p. 88
insider trading, p. 90
institutional investor, p. 87

investor relations, p. 85
mutual fund manager, p. 87
public company, p. 85
securities analyst, p. 87
security, p. 87

shareholder, p. 85
stockholder, p. 85
Webcast, p. 89

Endnotes ● ● ● ● ● ● ● ● ● ● ● ● ● ● ● ● ● ●

1. Canadian Investor Relations Institute Web site, www.ciri.org. All cited CIRI information comes from this site.

2. National Investor Relations Institute Web site, www.niri.org.

3. Securities and Exchange Commission Web site, www.sec.gov.

4. "NIRI CEO Urges 'Outside the Box' Thinking to Restore Public Confidence," National Investor Relations Institute news release, March 2, 2002. Online: www.niri.org.

5. "NIRI CEO Urges 'Outside the Box' Thinking to Restore Public Confidence."

6. "Investor Relations Function Gets Higher Priority, NIRI-Pittsburgh Survey Says," National Investor Relations Institute news release, September 8, 2003. Online: Lexis-Nexis.

7. James G. Hutton, "The Definition, Dimensions, and Domain of Public Relations," *Public Relations Review* (Summer 1999), 199.

8. Robin Londner, "Enron: An Epiphany for IR," *PR Week,* March 11, 2002. Online: Lexis-Nexis.

9. Andrew Edson & Associates, Inc., "The Non-U.S. Company and Investor Relations in the United States." Online: www.edsonpr.com.

10. See, for example, Dennis L. Wilcox, Glen T. Cameron, Philip H. Ault, and Warren K. McGee, *Public Relations: Strategies and Tactics,* 7th ed. (Boston: Allyn & Bacon, 2003); and Dan Lattimore, Otis Baskin, Suzette T. Heiman, Elizabeth L. Toth, and James K. Van Leuven, *Public Relations: The Profession and the Practice* (Boston: McGraw-Hill, 2004).

11. "NIRI CEO Urges 'Outside the Box' Thinking to Restore Public Confidence."

Short Story

Thwarting Short Sellers Becomes a Tall Order for 4Kids Entertainment and KCSA

Many readers of this book have fond memories of Pokémon, the "gotta catch 'em all" Nintendo game that swept the world at the turn of the century. But 4Kids Entertainment, the company that owns worldwide licensing rights to the Pokémon phenomenon, may have felt as if it owned Pikachu, the beloved Pokémon that sometimes blasts its owner with a painful thundershock. Pokémon brought incredible wealth to 4Kids—and, paradoxically, its amazing success threatened the company's financial future.

In 1998, on the eve of the Pokémon blitz, the price per share of 4Kids stock was about $2. One year later, share price had exploded to $93 as 4Kids sold Pokémon licensing rights for T-shirts, card games, board games, snacks, and much more. And that's when the short sellers moved in.

Short sellers are stock market players who try to complete a complicated but potentially profitable maneuver. They borrow stock, promise to return it by a certain date, and sell it without paying for it yet—all in the hopes that share prices will plummet so they can buy back the stock at a lower price, return it to the owner, and keep the profits. Short sellers look for stocks that seem to be enjoying short-lived success. The stunning surge of 4Kids' stock dazzled the short sellers.

In a 1999 interview with 4Kids CEO Alfred Kahn, Terry Keenan, host of CNN's *In the Money*, twice called the Pokémon boom a "craze." And then Kennan stated the obvious: "Short sellers have targeted your stock." Noting the swarm of short sellers around 4Kids, *Crain's Business New York* magazine called the company "a one-hit wonder" and quoted a well-known short seller who said, "This is a classic fad stock."

The swarm of short sellers succeeded in generating alarm among 4Kids' other stockholders. Regular stockholders began to sell their shares, and the feeding frenzy began. By the end of 1999, share prices had nose-dived from almost $100 to a little more than $8.

"It is just frustrating to see the price," said Kahn. "It makes me crazy. It's not justified."

Kahn believed that the true story of 4Kids wasn't being told. Thanks to Pokémon, 4Kids had huge profits to acquire new properties—among them a new TV show called *Yu-Gi-Oh!* that showed promise. That's when Kahn turned to KCSA of New York to help tell the real story of 4Kids Entertainment.

Surrender Now, or Prepare to Fight

KCSA's research of 4Kids revealed that Kahn was correct: The company did have a good story to tell. As the KCSA team interviewed company executives and studied stock-related documents that 4Kids had filed with the Securities and Exchange Commission, it gleaned these key facts: Pokémon revenues accounted for 85 percent of 4Kids' 1999 revenues. That had attracted the attention of the short sellers. But with the profits, 4Kids was purchasing new licensing rights in several other properties. 4Kids was diversifying, creating a solid foundation for continued growth.

Concurrent research showed that many investors didn't know about 4Kids' long-range plans. To study 4Kids stockholders, KCSA created a special hotline so that 4Kids investors could call the company with questions. It also reviewed past meetings that 4Kids had held with investors, studied the investment habits of 4Kids' most active stockholders, monitored conference calls with investors, and interviewed stockholders and their advisers. From that research, two conclusions surfaced: Of 4Kids' 35,000 stockholders, most were parents or grandparents of kids who loved the Pokémon games; those stockholders didn't know anything about the company beyond Pokémon. And because the company's success had been so rapid, stockholders hadn't had time to hear 4Kids' story about its solid future. That combination of facts led to jittery investors who would overreact to the pressures of the short sellers.

KCSA also studied two other important publics: securities analysts and the news media. Interviews with analysts showed that, like investors, they didn't know much about 4Kids' diversification. Ditto for the journalists: KCSA conducted a media analysis to discover the amount and content of coverage of 4Kids stock. Members of KCSA's investor relations and media relations teams also interviewed journalists who had written negative or inaccurate stories about 4Kids.

From all the research, a clear conclusion emerged: Events had moved so quickly that short sellers, traditional investors, analysts, and the news media didn't understand how 4Kids was using the success of Pokémon to establish a solid, diverse foundation for the future. Like the Pokémon game's Team Rocket, the company had blasted off at the speed of light. And as its communications were lost in the roar, 4Kids had to consider Team Rocket's famous taunt: "Surrender now, or prepare to fight."

With KCSA, 4Kids prepared to fight.

Short-Circuiting the Short Sellers

Victory meant reaching several goals: Stabilize the stock price; create awareness of 4Kids' business strengths and growth strategy; and establish management's credibility. To reach these goals, 4Kids established four objectives:

1. Squeeze out the short sellers by building positive momentum for the stock
2. Increase institutional ownership of the stock
3. Correct misperceptions about 4Kids' growth potential and business value
4. Rebuild management's credibility following the significant decline in stock price

KCSA's communication tactics targeted several publics: securities analysts, the news media, and several different groups of stockholders, including short sellers,

In Pokémon games, Pokéballs restrict the movements of captured creatures. In reality, 4Kids Entertainment used award-winning public relations to restrict the impact of short sellers. (Courtesy of the U.S. Consumer Product Safety Commission)

institutional investors, new individual investors who would appreciate 4Kids' strengths, and stockholders who invested in other KCSA clients.

KCSA tackled the short sellers head-to-head, meeting with them and showing them 4Kids' plans and new acquisitions. The key message? 4Kids was not a one-hit wonder. KCSA also used its own proprietary databases to find, inform, and attract investors who sought undervalued stocks.

To rebuild management's credibility, KCSA helped 4Kids move from the NASDAQ stock exchange to the more established New York Stock Exchange. The move generated publicity and questions, allowing 4Kids once again to tell its story. KCSA also helped set up meetings with 4Kids stockholders who had been vocal in their misunderstanding of the company's long-range plans. In addition, KCSA created investor kits that specified how Pokémon had provided a profitable, diverse future for 4Kids.

For investors, possible investors, and analysts, KCSA helped 4Kids sponsor a series of road shows, in which 4Kids executives met face to face with the investment community to answer questions and tell the true story of 4Kids.

At one such show in Pennsylvania, Alfred Kahn spoke with characteristic bluntness. "We have to get people to understand that it ain't just Pokémon," said the CEO. "The highs and lows do not accurately reflect the stock."

KCSA also identified major institutional investors that would appreciate 4Kids' vision of the future. It then helped schedule individual meetings between 4Kids executives and representatives of those institutions.

Media relations included three sustained tactics. KCSA used news releases to announce breaking news, such as continued record profits. It also used news releases and other contacts with reporters to continue to push stories on 4Kids' diversification and long-range strategies. Finally, KCSA helped introduce 4Kids' new investors—investors who believed in the company's future—to journalists who remained noncommittal about 4Kids' future. If reporters were skeptical about statements from 4Kids' management, they might believe the testimony—third-party endorsements—of investors who backed 4Kids with their money.

KCSA worked with a budget of $60,000 per year for research and $120,000 per year for the execution of the communication tactics.

To Be a Master

In the Pokémon game, a player's greatest honor is to become a Pokémon Master. In the stock market game, KCSA and 4Kids proved to be Public Relations Masters. Short sellers fled from 4Kids, surrendering approximately 3 million shares of the company's stock. Institutional investors increased from less than 20 percent to 33 percent of the company's total. By the end of 2001, share price had more than doubled, from $8 to $20—and this increase occurred in a declining stock market. In both 2000 and 2001, *Fortune* magazine ranked 4Kids Entertainment No. 1 in its list of America's Fastest Growing Companies. And 2002 revenues beat 2001 earnings by 28 percent, topping $53 million.

As for respect in the news media, late in year 2000—when KCSA and 4Kids were hoping to see the results of the campaign—*Animation World* magazine declared, "The future for 4Kids looks bright. . . . Efforts to diversify away from Pokémon dependency are increasing."

For its extraordinary success in helping 4Kids Entertainment set the record straight, KCSA won a national 2002 Silver Anvil Award, the highest honor from the Public Relations Society of America.

But an even sweeter award may have come from *Crain's Business New York,* the prestigious magazine that had labeled 4Kids a "one-hit wonder." In an article one year after that blow to the company, *Crain's* ran a story titled "4Kids Entertainment Sheds One-Hit Wonder Tag." In that story, the reporter wrote, "4Kids Entertainment Inc. is shaking its one-hit-wonder image with a new red-hot character called Yu-Gi-Oh. . . . [4Kids'] stock price has been one of the few bright spots on Wall Street."

Sources

Rosland Briggs-Gammon, "Pokemon Licensing Royalties Pay Off for New York-Based Firm," *Philadelphia Inquirer,* February 3, 2000. Online: Lexis-Nexis.

CNN: In the Money, November 12, 1999. Online: Lexis-Nexis.

Lisa Fickensher, "Stock Watch: 4Kids Entertainment Sheds One-Hit Wonder Tag," *Crain's New York Business,* October 7, 2002. Online: Lexis-Nexis.

"Fortune Ranks America's Fastest Growing Companies; 4Kids Entertainment Tops List for Second Year in a Row," BusinessWire news release, August 13, 2001. Online: Lexis-Nexis.

"4Kids Entertainment Announces Fourth Quarter and Year-End Results," 4Kids Entertainment news release, March 28, 2003. Online: Lexis-Nexis.

"Give Us Your Money: 4Kids Entertainment Attains Poké-Momentum," *Animation World,* October 2000. Online: www.awn.com/mag/issue5.07.

KCSA Web site, www.kcsa.com/case.

Charles Keenan, "Life after Pokemon," *Crain's New York Business,* October 9, 2000. Online: Lexis-Nexis.

Public Relations Society of America Web site, www.prsa.org.

Enron De-energizes

Faulty Investor Relations Contributes to a $60 Billion Failure

"Nobody bothered to look," said journalist Bethany McLean. "Everybody counted on somebody else. The Wall Street analysts thought, *Well, the credit rating agencies say it's okay, so it's got to be okay.* The portfolio managers thought, *Well, the Wall Street analysts say it's okay.* The journalists thought, *Well, the Wall Street analysts and the portfolio managers say it's great.*"

It, in this case, was Enron, the worldwide energy company—and it was far from great. In 2002, Enron became one of the largest corporate bankruptcies in U.S. history.

In happier days, Enron included this self-description in company news releases:

Enron is one of the world's leading electricity, natural gas, and communications companies. The company, with revenues of $101 billion in 2000, markets electricity and natural gas, delivers physical commodities and financial and risk management services to customers around the world, and has developed an intelligent network platform to facilitate online business.

Enron was large, diverse, and innovative, and its complexity defied easy investigation. Securities analysts joked about being unable to understand Enron's complicated financing—but recommended the company anyway, charged London's *Financial Times.*

Allan Sloan, business columnist for *Newsweek,* pointed the finger at Enron's accounting firm. "Don't blame the usual suspects: stock analysts," he wrote. "Rather, blame Arthur Andersen, Enron's outside auditors, who didn't blow the whistle until too late."

Plenty of blame to pass around. But where were Enron's investor relations practitioners? Where were the public relations professionals who should have explained the company's financial status to the investment community?

Special Purpose Vehicles

The beginning of the end for Enron was its creation of so-called Special Purpose Vehicles—partnerships that Enron wasn't required to publicize as long as it owned 97 percent or less of the company. Enron created several SPVs and used them to absorb losses and pump money into Enron. Essentially, much of Enron's impressive balance sheet rested on little-known SPVs. If they stumbled, so would the company.

In 2001, the SPVs stumbled. In October, Enron announced an unexpected charge against earnings of more than $1 billion. The questions began, the role of the SPVs emerged, and Enron stock prices swooned from $83 to 26 cents per share.

"We need better disclosure about these matters," said Robert Herdman, chief accountant of the Securities and Exchange Commission.

What was Enron's investor relations goal? If the company had followed the advice of the National Investor Relations Institute, its investor relations team would have created a program to ensure "effective two-way communication between a company, the financial community, and other constituencies, which ultimately contributes to a company's securities achieving fair valuation."

Instead, Enron's goal seemed to be to cast a veil of mystery over company finances. "Wall Street never knew the extent of these deals until they went sour and Enron was forced to publicly write them off," concluded *U.S. News & World Report.*

"A Monstrous Fraud"

One word that characterized Enron's investor relations efforts was *opaque*—hard to see through. "We all hate to see the kinds of things that happened with Enron through opaque reporting," said Kurt Kuehn, vice president of investor relations for UPS. The *Financial Times* headlined an Enron story "A Victim of Its Opacity," and, in the story, declared, "Its accounts are impenetrable. . . . The company posted answers to 'most frequently asked questions' about its financial dealings on its Web site, but they were too ambiguous to ease investors' anxieties."

As for Enron's claim that it revealed its SPVs in a federal 10-K form, the *Houston Chronicle* noted that the references consumed only a few lines on page 78 of the document. The newspaper quoted an energy industry consultant as saying, "There's no way you could have reconstructed any of the facts about them from just this one filing. . . . To say this was an accurate picture of the company's finances obviously is preposterous."

A second Enron investor relations tactic, intended or otherwise, was silence. "It's taken a silent posture and is hiding at precisely the wrong time," said one securities analyst. Said another, "I am increasingly puzzled by management's reluctance to address Enron's financial situation publicly . . . and lay to rest rumors, innuendos and general market hysteria."

During the weeks after Enron's announcement of the billion-dollar charge against earnings, CEO Ken Lay held only one conference call with securities analysts to explain the move. "You really need to give us a lot more information," one analyst told Lay during the phone call.

"When you don't disclose a lot of data, investor sentiment can turn against you quite quickly," said an analyst.

In an article titled "Is Enron's IR Hobbled by Its Lawyers?" *Investor Relations Business* magazine speculated that fear of legal liabilities had silenced Enron's communications with investment publics.

U.S. Securities and Exchange Commission

SEC Charges Kenneth L. Lay, Enron's Former Chairman and Chief Executive Officer, with Fraud and Insider Trading

FOR IMMEDIATE RELEASE
2004-94

Complaint Alleges Participation in Scheme to Defraud With Skilling, Causey and Others; Seeks Civil Penalty and Recovery of Over $90 Million in Unlawful Proceeds from Stock Sales

Washington, D.C., July 8, 2004 - The Securities and Exchange Commission today initiated civil charges against Kenneth L. Lay, former Chairman and Chief Executive Officer of Enron Corp., for his role in a wide-ranging scheme to defraud by falsifying Enron's publicly reported financial results and making false and misleading public representations about Enron's business performance and financial condition.

The Commission also alleges Lay profited from the scheme to defraud by selling large amounts of Enron stock at prices that did not reflect its true value. The sales also occurred while Lay was in possession of material non-public information concerning Enron and generated unlawful proceeds in excess of $90 million during 2001. Specifically, Lay sold over $70 million in Enron stock back to the company to repay cash advances on an unsecured Enron line of credit. In addition, while in possession of material non-public information, Lay amended two program trading plans to enable him to sell an additional $20 million in Enron stock in the open market. Lay's proceeds from the sales constitute illegal gains resulting from his scheme to defraud.

In this action, the Commission is seeking disgorgement of all ill-gotten gains, civil money penalties, a permanent bar from acting as a director or officer of a publicly held company, and an injunction against future violations of the federal securities laws.

"From the very beginning, our mandate has been to hold accountable those who contributed to the false portrayal of Enron as a viable, thriving entity. As Enron's Chairman and Chief Executive Officer, Mr. Lay was an engaged participant in the on-going fraud, and must therefore be called to account for his actions," said SEC Enforcement Division Director Stephen M. Cutler.

Added Deputy Director Linda Chatman Thomsen, "Today, the Commission and the Department of Justice have once again demonstrated our collective commitment to use every tool available under law to pursue those who violated the law in connection with Enron's collapse. It is our sincere hope that others who might someday be tempted to dissemble to the investing public and improperly place their personal interests ahead of those of their shareholders will be deterred by the specter of a determined and multi-

On July 8, 2004, the Securities and Exchange Commission issued a news release announcing fraud and insider trading charges against Enron's former CEO, Ken Lay. (Courtesy of the U.S. Securities and Exchange Commission)

A harsher view of Enron's investor relations tactics characterizes those actions as deceptive. *Governing Magazine* asked, "The question at hand is how such a monstrous fraud could be perpetrated on the company's stockholders."

"Ken Lay got up and lied to our faces," said a securities analyst, recalling Lay's description of the sudden retirement of former Enron CEO Jeffrey Skilling. "That was representative of the trust that has declined."

In the news release announcing Skilling's retirement, Lay said, "Our business is extremely strong, and our growth prospects have never been better." Within three months, Enron had taken its billion-dollar charge, its chief financial officer had been replaced, the company had restated its earnings for the past four years, and the SEC had announced an investigation of the company's finances.

A national survey conducted five months after the billion-dollar charge found that 88 percent of U.S. investors believed that Enron had intentionally misled them.

"This was not an IR issue," said securities analyst Jeffrey Zack of Morgan-Walke Associates. "It was an issue of fraud."

If deception occurred, one of its cruelest forms affected Enron's own employees. As senior managers were selling their own stock in the company, some were assuring Enron employees who owned company stock for their retirement funds that all was well with their employer. (Lay and Skilling combined sold more than $30 million in Enron stock during seven months in 2001.) According to *Newsweek:*

> In September [2001], Lay told employees: "Talk up the stock, and talk positively about Enron to your family and friends." The company's upcoming financial report was "looking great." . . . Employees who saw their [savings] wiped out were furious, especially at executives like Lay who had been systematically unloading stock for years.

Mysterious Motivations

Why would investor relations professionals at Enron allow such mysteries and misrepresentations of reality? The investment community has offered answers that include ignorance, helplessness, and willful unethical behavior.

Perhaps some top Enron officials didn't understand Enron's complex financial maneuverings. "The company was growing so fast and conquering so many new and unsupervised areas that even Enron had a hard time explaining all it did," reported the *Financial Times.*

Some investment relations professionals, however, believe that ignorance should not be an excuse. Point 6 of the NIRI Ethics Code states, "As a regular member of the National Investor Relations Institute, I will discharge my responsibilities completely and competently by keeping myself abreast of the affairs of my company or client as well as the laws and regulations affecting the practice of investor relations."

"Being blindsided by ignorance is not acceptable," said Donni Case, president of the Financial Relations Board, an investor relations agency. "IR specialists definitely need more knowledge of finance and accounting in order to provide meaningful guidance to management."

A second explanation for Enron's investor relations practices might be helplessness. "They've been overwhelmed with events, and they're punch-drunk" was one analyst's explanation for Enron's lack of coherent financial explanations.

"The IR department would not comment to *PR Week*," wrote Robin Londner in that magazine's account of the investor relations debacle at Enron. "However, a PR representative from the company explains that a deluge of media requests is mostly going unanswered by what she says is a two-person IR department struggling to complete normal tasks related to bankruptcy—with no time left over to speak to the press."

A third explanation might be that officials at Enron simply decided to behave unethically. In its assessment of Enron's insurance liability, *Claims Magazine* wrote, "The *Wall Street Journal* reported that Enron's directors waived the company's ethics code to allow finance chief Andrew Fastow to set up a private partnership that would do business with Enron. The directors waived the code again to allow Fastow to set up an even larger venture."

Said one securities analyst: "It was their hyperaggressive rogue financing, which did such damage to them that they lost all financial credibility then lost all moral credibility."

Enron: The Aftermath

The Enron scandal dramatically changed investment policies and practices in the United States. In the months following the scandal, 43 percent of investors said they had less confidence in the stock market. Seventy-three percent were "very angry" at Enron. Seventy-four percent of companies said they would pay more attention to investor relations practices.

A former Enron vice chairman committed suicide, shooting himself in his car.

The Sarbanes–Oxley Act of 2002 requires company leaders to take direct accountability for financial statements.

"From an IR perspective, [Enron] didn't do a good job of telling investors what it was all about," concluded *Investor Relations Business* magazine. "So when something bad happened, there was a significant backlash."

"Enron's blow to investor faith is the Watergate of business," said Alan Towers, president of the TowersGroup public relations agency. "Trust will no longer be assumed. Companies will have to earn it with behavior, communications, and leaders that inspire confidence."

Sources

"The Burning Issue," *FT Expat,* May 1, 2002. Online: Lexis-Nexis.

Steve Caulk, "Fund Analysts Report Distrust," *Rocky Mountain News* (Denver), May 16, 2002. Online: Lexis-Nexis.

"Enron Announces Skilling Resignation," Enron news release, August 14, 2001. Online: Lexis-Nexis.

The *Houston Chronicle* Web site, www.houstonchronicle.com.

"Investor Relations Function Gets Higher Priority," National Investor Relations Institute news release, September 8, 2003. Online: Lexis-Nexis.

"Is Enron's IR Hobbled by Its Lawyers," *Investor Relations Business,* November 21, 2001. Online: Lexis-Nexis.

Marianne Lavelle and Matthew Benjamin, "The Biggest Bust," *U.S. News & World Report,* December 10, 2001. Online: Lexis-Nexis.

Robin Londner, "IR—Enron: An Epiphany for IR," *PR Week,* March 11, 2002. Online: Lexis-Nexis.

Rich Long, "Enron: Countering Corporate Arrogance," *The Public Relations Strategist* (Spring 2002).

Susan Massmann, "Enron Spotlights Directors and Officers Liability Issues," *Claims Magazine,* April 2002. Online: Lexis-Nexis.

Sheila McNulty, "A Victim of Its Opacity: Enron," *Financial Times,* November 12, 2001. Online: Lexis-Nexis.

Jim Morrison, "Delusions of Grandeur," *American Way* (October 15, 2003).

National Investor Relations Institute Web site, www.niri.org.

Pamela Paul, "Fear and Loathing," *American Demographics,* October 2002. Online: Lexis-Nexis.

"A Question of Trust," *Distribution Management Briefing,* March 29, 2002. Online: Lexis-Nexis.

"SEC Hastens Disclosure Overhaul," *Investor Relations Business,* January 28, 2002. Online: Lexis-Nexis.

Allan Sloan, "Lights Out for Enron," *Newsweek,* December 10, 2001. Online: Lexis-Nexis.

Evan Thomas and Andrew Murr, "The Gambler Who Blew It All," *Newsweek,* February 4, 2002. Online: Lexis-Nexis.

Jonathan Walters, "The Snoozing Watchdogs," *Governing Magazine,* March 2002. Online: Lexis-Nexis.

case **5.3**

The No-Hype IPO

Buffalo Wild Wings Shuns Stock Market Flights of Fancy

"Speak softly," said President Teddy Roosevelt, "and carry a big chicken wing."

OK, that's not quite how he put it. But that's how Buffalo Wild Wings, a restaurant chain, may have heard it.

When BWW decided to go public—to sell shares of ownership—in 2003, it produced one of the quietest investor relations campaigns in the recent history of initial public offerings. An IPO is a company's first offering of stock to the investment community. During the gold rush of Internet dot.com companies in the 1990s, IPOs became glittering, splashy affairs that dazzled investors—until the dot.com bust at century's end. When BWW designed its IPO, it shunned hyperbole, spoke in almost a whisper, and hoped that its impressive business record would do the talking.

Better Be Ready

BWW's decision to soft-pedal its IPO publicity reflected the company's core values: While the investment community is important, it isn't the company's primary public. BWW's Mission Statement emphasizes results for stockholders, but it first pledges loyalty to customers, employees, and communities. Devoting its attention to those publics, BWW maintains, will help produce returns for stockholders. Its Mission Statement begins with these words: "Our mission is to WOW people every day!"

Founded on the Ohio State University campus in 1982, BWW made its reputation selling spicy chicken wings named after the city of their origin, Buffalo, New York. BWW features 12 sauces for its wings, including Better-Be-Ready Blazin', Spicy Garlic, Smoky Southwestern, and Teriyaki. Most BWW restaurants have at least 20 beers on tap, including local brews. Average checks total $8. At the time of its IPO, BWW had 227 restaurants in 28 states. The company is based in Minneapolis, Minnesota.

Under the leadership of CEO Sally Smith, a no-nonsense certified public accountant, BWW had turned a $1.8 million loss in 1995 into annual average profit increases of 29 percent—just the kinds of numbers that attract investors willing to do research.

However, initial public offerings can be unpredictable. BWW had planned an IPO in 1998 but had backed away at the last moment when the stock markets sparked and fizzled like damp fireworks.

"We looked at it . . . ," Smith said, "and felt that the market was not steady enough."

Of the 25 companies that had planned an IPO at the same time as the 1998 BWW venture, 23 canceled. For the next five years, BWW remained a private company, watching as IPO campaigns slowed to a trickle.

In 1999, almost 600 companies had launched IPOs. In the first six months of 2003, the year of BWW's IPO, 10 companies announced initial public offerings.

"A sluggish economy, depressed stock market, and post-Enron regulations affecting publicly traded companies have hit the IPO market hard in the past couple of years," declared the *Minneapolis Star Tribune.*

"IPOs were hot in the 1990s when the stock market was hot," reported the *Alameda* (Calif.) *Times-Star,* "but as the market slumped though 2000, 2001, and 2002, they virtually disappeared."

Six other companies were set to join BWW in launching IPOs in late November 2003. Most balked at the last moment. "Buffalo Wild Wings alone braved the markets Friday," wrote *The Deal,* an investors publication.

BWW's confidence impressed securities analysts: In recent years, successful restaurant IPOs had been as common as real wings on real buffalos. BWW offered the first restaurant IPO of 2003. Only two restaurant IPOs had been offered in 2002, and neither had fared well. "Buffalo Wild Wings is . . . something of a novelty since Wall Street hasn't seen many restaurant IPOs," one securities analyst said.

Wanted: Informed Investors

IPOs generally attract large, institutional investors that closely follow the markets. The mass failure of dot.com IPOs drove many individual investors toward established, better-known stocks. That trend suited BWW's plans for a low-key launch: The company primarily sought knowledgeable investors that would buy and hold the stock, preventing dizzying ups and downs that might damage BWW's hard-won reputation for stability.

The goals of BWW's IPO investor relations campaign were to attract stable investors and raise $43 million to $45 million. With that money, BWW proposed to eliminate a $10 million debt and increase its number of restaurants. To raise that lofty sum, BWW and its investment advisers decided to sell 2.7 million shares at approximately $16 apiece.

Many of BWW's investor relations tactics were mandated by law. On Sept. 11, 2003, it submitted a formal request to the Securities and Exchange Commission, seeking approval for the IPO. In a news release announcing the filing, BWW introduced the straightforward, matter-of-fact tone that characterized its entire IPO campaign: "Buffalo Wild Wings Inc. today announced that it has filed a registration statement with the Securities and Exchange Commission for an initial public offering of common stock."

Having shunned in-your-face publicity, BWW caught some investors by surprise with its IPO. "Wall Streeters are used to a fast food lunch . . . ," wrote New York's *Newsday,* "but few of them had ever heard of a company called Buffalo Wild Wings until it came to the market."

Prudent investors studied BWW's SEC filing—a form called an S-1—and liked what they saw. "The company's S-1 filing is interesting stuff, including a discussion of corporate history and strategy," wrote Dave Marino-Nachison on The Motley Fool business Web site. "Investors now have access to information about a quality chain that's growing fast and has plenty of room in which to do it."

The SEC approved the company's IPO plans, and BWW issued another "just the facts, ma'am" news release Nov. 21, the day of the launch. Once again, the release's first sentence showed scrupulous regard for company values and the new legislative climate of investor relations. Hyperbole and hoopla were nonexistent: "Buffalo Wild Wings Inc. (Nasdaq: BWLD), which owns and operates or franchises 227 Buffalo Wild Wings™ restaurants in 28 states, today announced its public offering of 3,000,000 shares of Common Stock at a price of $17.00 per share."

As filed with the Securities and Exchange Commission on September 11, 2003

Registration No. 333-

SECURITIES AND EXCHANGE COMMISSION
Washington, D.C. 20549

FORM S-1
REGISTRATION STATEMENT
Under
THE SECURITIES ACT OF 1933

Buffalo Wild Wings, Inc.
(Exact name of registrant as specified in its charter)

Minnesota	5812	31-1455915
(State or other jurisdiction of incorporation or organization)	(Primary standard industrial classification code number)	(I.R.S. employer identification number)

1600 Utica Avenue South
Suite 700
Minneapolis, MN 55416
(952) 593-9943

(Address, including zip code, and telephone number, including area code, of registrant's principal executive offices)

Sally J. Smith
Chief Executive Officer and President
Buffalo Wild Wings, Inc.
1600 Utica Avenue South
Suite 700
Minneapolis, MN 55416
(952) 593-9943

(Name, address, including zip code, and telephone number, including area code, of agent for service)

Copies To:

Melodie R. Rose, Esq.	Jonathan B. Abram, Esq.
Fredrikson & Byron, P.A.	Dorsey & Whitney LLP
4000 Pillsbury Center	50 South Sixth Street
200 South Sixth Street	Suite 1500
Minneapolis, Minnesota 55402	Minneapolis, Minnesota 55402
(612) 492-7000	(612) 340-2600

Approximate date of proposed sale to the public: As soon as practicable after the effective date of this Registration Statement.

If any of the securities being registered on this form are to be offered on a delayed or continuous basis pursuant to Rule 415 under the Securities Act of 1933, as amended (the "Securities Act") check the following box. □

If this form is filed to register additional securities for an offering pursuant to Rule 462(b) under the Securities Act, check the following box and list the Securities Act registration statement number of the earlier effective registration statement for the same offering. □

If this form is a post-effective amendment filed pursuant to Rule 462(c) under the Securities Act, check the following box and list the Securities Act registration statement number of the earlier effective registration statement for the same offering. □

Before launching its IPO, Buffalo Wild Wings filed a Form S-1 with the U.S. Securities and Exchange Commission. The SEC's EDGAR database provides access to corporate securities filings. (Courtesy of the U.S. Securities and Exchange Commission)

BWW issued its news releases through the Business Wire distribution service and posted them on its Web site in a new Investor Relations section.

As the date of the launch had neared, BWW's evaluative research had indicated a very positive response among established investors. The company therefore bumped the IPO's number of shares and share price above the original numbers of 2.7 million shares at approximately $16 apiece. To attract the attention of institutional investors, BWW had set up informational sessions during a two-week period before the Nov. 21 launch.

BWW posted financial information in the Investor Relations area of its Web site, including current stock prices, a graph charting the stock's movements, a corporate profile, news releases, SEC filings, and answers to frequently asked questions. Interactive features included e-mail alerts upon request: "Alerts are e-mailed to you whenever certain new company information is posted to this site."

On launch day, BWW declined offers to speak with the news media. Even the hometown *Minneapolis Star Tribune* noted that BWW's executive team "declined to comment on the offering." The company did find a nonverbal way to communicate with the sales team at RBC Capital Markets, the bank that sold the first shares to investors: BWW brought the RBC sales team 24 buckets of chicken wings.

Winged Victory

Buffalo Wild Wings' IPO exceeded expectations, generating $51 million. Its opening price of $17 per share jumped 35 percent to $22.95 by the close of first-day trading. Within a month, share price had risen to $26. Analysts praised BWW's plain-facts investor relations campaign.

"This is a company with a solid operating history and, most significantly, profits, which is not always the case in the restaurant business," reported one financial adviser.

Six weeks later, when BWW announced that quarterly profits had risen 37 percent from the previous year, low-profile investor relations became a challenge. "Buffalo Wild Wings Inc. did well in its first quarter as a public company," concluded the *Minneapolis/St. Paul Business Journal*. To accommodate market interest, the company increased its investor relations communications.

In January 2004, BWW discussed earnings through a conference telephone call and a simultaneous Webcast. Company officials also agreed to present at two investor conferences, provided that those proceedings also were streamed live to the Web.

True to form, however, BWW complied with federal law and advised investors that its financial plans were projections, not guarantees. Near the end of the news release announcing the impressive quarterly profits, BWW included these plain-spoken passages:

> Certain statements in this release . . . are forward-looking statements that involve risks and uncertainties. . . . Investors should take such risks into account when

making investment decisions. Shareholders and other readers are cautioned not to place undue reliance on these forward-looking statements.

BWW's factual, low-key investor relations campaign reflected company values and complied with the investment world's new legislative realities. But to quote another president (accurately, this time), "facts are stubborn things." John Quincy Adams no doubt would have supported BWW's decision to let the facts tell the company's story. And it was quite a story.

"No matter how you serve it up," said one financial journalist of BWW's IPO, "$50 million isn't chicken feed."

Sources

Jeff Benjamin, "IPO Market Begins to Awaken from Its Very Deep Slumber," *Investment News,* December 1, 2003. Online: Lexis-Nexis.

Warren Berry, "The Buck Starts Here," *Newsday,* January 11, 2004. Online: Lexis-Nexis.

"Buffalo Wild Wings Files Registration Statement for Initial Public Offering," Buffalo Wild Wings news release, September 11, 2003. Online: Lexis-Nexis.

"Buffalo Wild Wings Inc. Announces Preliminary 2003 Fourth Quarter Results," Buffalo Wild Wings news release, January 13, 2004. Online: Lexis-Nexis.

"Buffalo Wild Wings Inc. Announces Pricing of Public Offering," Buffalo Wild Wings news release, November 21, 2003. Online: Lexis-Nexis.

"Buffalo Wild Wings Inc. Announces Sale of Over-Allotment Shares," Buffalo Wild Wings news release, November 26, 2003. Online: Lexis-Nexis.

"Buffalo Wild Wings IPO Brings in $51 Million," *The Business Journal* (Minneapolis/St. Paul), November 21, 2003. Online: www.bizjournals.com/twincities/stories.

"Buffalo Wild Wings Preliminary Numbers Up," *The Business Journal* (Minneapolis/St. Paul), January 13, 2004. Online: www.bizjournals.com/twincities/stories.

"Buffalo Wild Wings Set for IPO," *Nation's Restaurant News,* September 22, 2003. Online: www.findarticles.com.

"Buffalo Wild Wings Stock Moving Up," *The Business Journal* (Minneapolis/St. Paul), December 30, 2003. Online: www.bizjournals.com/twincities/stories.

Buffalo Wild Wings Web site, www.buffalowildwings.com.

Tara Croft, "Buffalo Wild Wings IPO Takes Flight," *The Deal,* November 24, 2003. Online: Lexis-Nexis.

Susan Feyder, "Would You Like Fries with That IPO?" *Minneapolis Star Tribune,* November 22, 2003. Online: Lexis-Nexis.

Steve Gelsi, "Buffalo Wild Wings Makes Tasty Debut." Online: www.cbsmarketwatch.com.

Benno Groeneveld, "Buffalo Wild Wings Prices IPO at $43M to $45M," *The Business Journal* (Minneapolis/St. Paul), October 23, 2003. Online: www.bizjournals.com/twincities/stories.

Tim J. Johnson, "Buffalo Wild Wings' IPO Is on Back Burner," *The Business Journal* (Minneapolis/St. Paul), August 21, 1998. Online: www.bizjournals.com/twincities/stories.

Dave Marino-Nachison, "Hot Wings, Hot IPO," *The Motley Fool.* Online: www.fool.com.

Dave Price, "Investors Display Appetite for Buffalo Wild Wings Shares," *Finance and Commerce* (Minneapolis/St. Paul), November 22, 2003. Online: www.finance-commerce.com.

"Smart Investors Stay Clear of IPOs," *Alameda* (California) *Times-Star,* December 7, 2003. Online: Lexis-Nexis.

ACT file # 5

Advanced Critical Thinking

Issues Management

Nostradamus has nothing on W. Howard Chase.

Many people in the 21st century believe Nostradamus had an uncanny ability to predict the future. While the 16th century French scholar wrote extensively about his visions of the future, he did nothing to change the course of "future history." Enter W. Howard Chase, a corporate public relations practitioner who designed the first issues management model in 1977.[1] Predicting the future wasn't good enough for Chase. He wanted to do something about it.

Issues management is the process of identifying emerging issues and trends that may affect an organization—and then preparing a proactive response to deal with them. Think of the major issues of our time, such as health care, terrorism, and the environment. None of these appeared overnight: They evolved over a period of time. Organizations that took notice of these issues as they developed are probably better positioned than most others to address the problems and challenges of the future. By engaging in issues management, organizations are able to identify challenges and administer solutions on their own terms, rather than on someone else's.

Terminology is important in issues management. There is a difference between an incident and an issue. An *incident* tends to be a one-time episode isolated from those not directly involved. For example, a random act of violence that is not repeated may be traumatic for those involved but of little meaning to society at large. For something to be an *issue,* it must meet three criteria: It must be evolving, it must influence the actions of multiple stakeholders, and it must have the potential of evolving into some form of policy. If the aforementioned act of violence involved the use of a concealed handgun on school grounds, that, unfortunately, would not be the first time something like that had happened. It would become part of a much wider debate over gun laws involving a variety of stakeholders. Under these conditions, it would be part of an issue.

In many ways, issues management is similar to crisis management (see Chapter 13). Both are forward-thinking exercises that first identify potential risks and then develop contingencies to address them. However, issues management is more strategic than crisis management. Crisis plans tend to be tactical, event-specific. They provide guidance for how organizations should act under certain specific circumstances. Issues management tries to identify social and political trends as they emerge. Using this knowledge, organizations mold responses that help organizations use this knowledge to achieve their strategic goals before they reach a crisis stage.

As you might imagine, issues management starts with identifying issues. This is often referred to as *scanning,* as in scanning the horizon to see what is coming. Organizations can scan in a variety of ways. John Naisbitt won acclaim as a sort of modern-day Nostradamus with the publication of *Megatrends: Ten New Directions Transforming Our Lives* in 1980.[2] However, his vision of the future did not involve magical powers or the use of a crystal ball. Through content analysis of hundreds of newspaper clippings and magazine articles, Naisbitt identified the predominant forces pushing society at the start of the Information Age. That was heady stuffy back then—and very influential. It was also the product of research—something anyone can do.

The problem with adopting Naisbitt's approach to scanning is that most organizations lack the time, resources, and patience for that level of content analysis. Instead, they prefer quicker, less costly alternatives, such as subscriptions to news clipping services, focus groups, meetings with advisory boards, and in-house surveys. Like Naisbitt, they gather scraps of information as if each were a piece of a puzzle that when properly assembled provides a clear picture. A military intelligence officer does the same thing when trying to determine an adversary's intentions. If scanning identifies a relevant issue, organizations study the issue's evolution, a process known as *monitoring*.

Regardless of the scanning methodology used, an organization should address these questions:

- What trends/issues are emerging that could affect our organization's ability to achieve its goals? How can they help us? How can they hurt us?
- What trends/issues are emerging that could affect our stakeholders' ability to achieve their goals? How can those issues help them? How can the issues hurt them?
- For each of these issues/trends, where will our goals and values align with those of our stakeholders? Where will they conflict?
- Do these trends/issues suggest a need to establish new relationships and/or strengthen existing ones?
- What are the risks in taking preemptive actions to address these trends/issues? Are there risks in taking no action?
- Do we have the necessary resources to address these trends/issues?

Once these questions have been answered, the next step is to move to a traditional strategic planning process. As with any such process, the plan should be driven by the organization's values and goals.

Practically all managers say they want to be proactive. Everyone wants to see into the future and "be ahead of the curve." An ongoing program of issues management allows them to do it—and they don't have to be a Nostradamus, either.

Discussion Questions •

1. Using the three-part definition of an issue, identify emerging issues within your community. Defend your answer.

2. How would you go about identifying emerging issues within your community?

3. What are the similarities and differences between issues management and crisis planning?

4. What is the role of values in issues management?

Endnotes

1. Robert L. Heath and Richard Alan Nelson, *Issues Management: Corporate Public Policymaking in an Information Society* (Beverly Hills, CA: Sage, 1986), 7.

2. John Naisbitt, *Megatrends: Ten New Directions Transforming Our Lives* (New York: Warner Books, 1980), 290.

CHAPTER 6

Media Relations

It has become an all-too-familiar image in our media-saturated society: someone in the midst of a personal crisis, trapped on the courthouse steps, bathed in the harsh glare of artificial light and confronted by a phalanx of reporters and television cameras. It is a scene that many find troublesome. While a recent Gallup Poll determined that a little more than half of those surveyed said they have "a great deal" or "a fair amount" of trust in the fullness, accuracy, and fairness of what they see and hear on the news, they do not completely trust the media. Forty-five percent of the respondents in the same survey said they believe the news media in the United States are too liberal, while 14 percent said the news media are too conservative.[1]

It is sometimes easy to forget that journalists play an important role in democratic societies. They are often referred to as the Fourth Estate, an unofficial fourth branch of government. At their best, reporters are the people's representatives. They are eyewitnesses to history. They report on things that matter—or at least *should* matter—to us.

The nation's founders understood the importance of a free press when they gave it constitutional guarantees under the First Amendment. Thomas Jefferson wrote, "Our liberty depends on the freedom of the press, and that cannot be limited without being lost."[2] One of Jefferson's successors in the White House, Harry Truman, had a more pragmatic view of the media. "Whenever the press quits abusing me I know I'm in the wrong pew," Truman said.[3]

Journalism is big business. Advertising expenditures in the United States were expected to top $247 billion in 2003—nearly a quarter of a *trillion* dollars.[4] At the beginning of this decade, there were 1,480 daily newspapers[5] and 7,689 weekly newspapers[6] in the United States. Add to that the more than 13,000 radio stations, 1,700 television stations,[7] 17,815 magazines,[8] and millions of people surfing the Internet.

With this media saturation comes a high-stakes competition for the attention of viewers, readers, and listeners. With increasing frequency, individuals and organizations get caught in the middle of this battle for truth, justice, and higher ratings. At those times, the services of public relations practitioners are most needed.

Students often ask why so much literature on public relations addresses the care and feeding of the news media. The answer is simple: Although reporters are not the only target public important to your organization, they sometimes are the most important. This is a relationship that places great demands on public relations practitioners' critical thinking skills.

A wise old sage once said that you shouldn't get in an argument with someone who buys paper by the ton and ink by the barrel. That is a profound truth in media relations. In a free society with constitutional protections for the media, it is more likely that the media can harm your organization than that you can harm the media. In a sense, the fostering of good media relations is an act of self-preservation.

However, public relations is more than just keeping something bad from happening to your organization. It is also about making something good happen. When executives wish to move an organization from **reactive media relations** to **proactive media relations,** a strong working relationship between the journalist and the practitioner can become a valuable asset.

Media Relations Strategies

As practitioners engage in the critical thinking necessary for developing effective media relations strategies, one thought should come first: In many ways, journalists are no different from any other target public. They can be segmented into many smaller publics, whether by the size of the audience they serve (local, regional, national, or international), the scope of that audience (mass circulation or specialized), or the medium they use (newspaper, radio, television, magazine, or the Internet). Reporters also generally respond to messages that address their self-interests, which are often defined by their segmentation. For example, "hometown" journalists are more likely to write about national news stories if they can identify a local angle, and television reporters are more willing to report on stories with a strong visual element. In short, successful media relations practitioners have to think like journalists.

The Elements of News

The first challenge of thinking like a journalist is to understand what constitutes **news.** Paradoxically, this subjective decision-making process—known as **news judgment**—requires objectivity. Just because you think something is newsworthy doesn't automatically mean that it is. It all depends on whether you can answer "yes" to any of the following questions:

1. **Does the story affect a large portion of the reporter's audience?** While a story about Medicare may generate interest in retirement communities, it may not have the same weight in a college town.
2. **Is it happening now, or is it about to happen?** Timeliness is at the heart of news. People want to know "the latest" or "what's happening next."
3. **Is the story unusual for the reporter's audience?** Is it the first, the biggest, or the only one of its kind? People are interested in the novel and unique.
4. **Is the story relevant to the reporter's audience?** Does it address the audience's self-interests? Does it touch their hearts?
5. **Does it involve someone the reporter's audience knows?** People are attracted to celebrities—even though the definition of a celebrity can vary from one location to another.

You may have noticed a recurring theme in those five questions: News is more about a journalist's readers, viewers, and listeners than it is about his or her personal interests. That is because practitioners usually target the media as an intervening public (see page 24). Reporters and editors are the gatekeepers who stand between you and their audience. Because ratings and circulation determine how much the media can charge advertisers, journalists want to attract the largest audience possible. To do that, reporters have to serve the interests of each medium's audience—the same as any public relations practitioner trying to generate publicity.

During times of crisis, the news media become an essential intervening public. After the terrorist attacks of Sept. 11, 2001, President George W. Bush invited reporters into the Oval Office so he could update the nation about the government's response. (Photo by Paul Morse. Courtesy of the White House)

Turning Knowledge into Strategy

While research about the needs of the reporter's audience is an important aspect of the critical thinking that goes into developing media relations strategies, so is knowledge of the technical and timing challenges facing journalists operating in different media. Each medium has its own deadline requirements, competitive edges, and special needs, as noted in Table 6.1.

table 6.1 *Media Comparisons*

	Deadlines	*Competitive Edge*	*Special Needs*
Daily newspapers	Around midnight for morning papers, late morning for afternoon editions.	Usually better staffed than other media. Often the most important news outlet in the market. Most likely to take an editorial stand.	Require quick access to details for in-depth reporting of breaking news stories, as well as pictures and artwork to illustrate stories.
Magazines	Depending on the publication, once a week or once a month.	Can't compete in the area of daily breaking news coverage, but excel in longer feature and analytical reporting.	In-depth reporting requires thorough research. Higher-quality printing requires added attention to artwork, photography, and design.
Radio	Capable of reporting breaking news anytime. Morning and afternoon commuter drive times are most important.	A portable medium reaching listeners where others can't—in their cars. Minimal logistics for reporters. A quick capsule of the news.	Requires tight writing and short soundbites (actualities). Natural sound effects and music aid in telling stories.
Television	Capable of reporting breaking news anytime. Early and late evening news broadcasts are most important.	The most dramatic because of sight and sound dynamics. Where most people get their news.	Compelling pictures drive story selection. Not well suited for stories with significant detail.
Internet	Twenty-four hours a day, seven days a week.	Brings together the best of all media: pictures, video, sound, and text. Has worldwide reach.	Requires the talents of a reporter, editor, designer, and programmer. With constant deadline pressure, accuracy is critical.

The benefit of understanding a reporter's needs cuts both ways. While it certainly assists the reporter in gathering information, this knowledge can also shape public relations strategies and, in turn, shape the news itself:

• Organizations with bad news to announce often choose to do it on Friday afternoon because they know that the size of media audiences drops on the weekends. They also know that most news organizations operate with smaller, less experienced staffs on weekends, which means less in-depth reporting. By the time Monday comes around, the negative item is often old news.

• Whenever a new medicine is announced, do you wonder how television newscasters are able to get laboratory video of pharmaceutical researchers developing the new miracle drug so quickly? They can because drug companies anticipate television's need for pictures. Drug companies shoot their own video of the laboratory testing of the drug—test tubes, Bunsen burners, and all. On the day of the big announcement, they supply reporters with videotaped footage to assist in the preparation of news stories.

• When a former governor of North Carolina announced a major prison construction program, he waited until 4 p.m. on a weekday afternoon to conduct his news conference. That hour was carefully chosen. It was early enough in the day to dominate early evening television news coverage, but too late for newspaper reporters to gather countering arguments from legislative opponents who had already scattered for the evening. In essence, the governor assured that his side of the story would dominate the first 24-hour news cycle.

• If your university is seeking donations from alumni for a new fine arts center or athletic facility, it probably chose to do so in its alumni magazine. While letters and telephone solicitations can be very effective, nothing stirs the imagination as much as a full-color architect's rendering of the new building printed on the alumni magazine's high-quality glossy paper. The same picture on television or in newsprint doesn't have the same impact. Nor is it as well targeted.

Some stories—usually the bad ones—command reporters' attention no matter what. However, on most days reporters and editors have much to choose from when determining which stories they will cover. The competition is stiff among those who want reporters to cover their issue or event. Amid so many choices, journalists generally choose to cover stories that best suit their professional needs and the interests of their audience.

Media Relations Tactics

There are many ways to reach reporters. The challenge is to know which way of reaching them is best. But the solution is simple: Just ask them. Journalists are no different from any other public. There are certain channels of communication they prefer. Some reporters may prefer e-mail. Others may want their news releases faxed. One of your authors knew a reporter who would not open any letter addressed with a mailing label. He preferred that it be addressed with a more personal touch. The reasons for this eccentricity do not really matter. If you wanted to reach him, you had to do it his way. The moral? Like any other public relations challenge, do your research first.

Sometimes the best way to reach reporters is to speak directly with them either in person or over the telephone. All things being equal, interpersonal communication is the best way to reach a common understanding. When making these contacts, get directly to the point. Journalists are busy people with little time to waste. In their world, there is no time to "schmooze." Journalists are more likely to listen to you if they know that you have a reputation as a professional who values their time and only calls when you have legitimate news.

News releases are the most used—and misused—tool of media relations. These documents, usually one or two pages in length, are written just like news stories. Approximately nine out of 10 news releases wind up in an editor's trash can. Why? Usually because they either do not contain information that appeals to the reporter's audience or their tone is too promotional.[9] Just as in talking with reporters, make every encounter meaningful and professional. When trying to attract reporters to cover an upcoming event, practitioners often distribute **media advisories,** bare-bones explanations of the who, what, where, why, and how of the event. They may also include technical/logistical information, such as the availability of electrical outlets or television lights. Some practitioners use **pitch letters** to encourage reporters to write about stories that lack a hard news edge but may still be of value to the journalist's audience.

Practitioners often use **media kits** to help journalists write complex stories. Although their content can vary, media kits usually include a news release, **backgrounders,** and **fact sheets.** Backgrounders are exactly what their name implies—background information on a certain topic. They are written more like encyclopedia entries than news stories. They provide detailed information about a certain topic, such as executive biographies or company histories. From these, reporters glean bits of information that aid in writing a news story. Fact sheets are similar to media advisories—plain recitations of the most basic facts of a story or event. They are usually limited to one page. Media kits may also include supplemental materials such as photographs, charts, maps, speech texts, and article reprints.

Video news releases can be a valuable tool in generating television news coverage. Just like their print cousins, the most effective VNRs address the interests of the reporter's audience and are not promotional. In addition to a produced news story—usually no longer than 60 to 90 seconds—VNRs often contain unedited footage and interviews for the broadcaster's use. The radio version of a VNR is known as an **actuality feed.** Each contains a produced radio news story, background information, and taped interviews with newsmakers. Because of their growing presence on the Internet, newspapers have discovered that VNRs and actuality feeds on their Web sites complement their print coverage.

Companies often use **news conferences** and **special events** to generate news coverage. When one is struck by the urge to conduct a news conference, however, the best thing to do is to stop and think about it. Just like news releases, news conferences are often misused. Unless a compelling reason exists for conducting one, don't do it. A news conference is an uncontrolled environment in which the news you make may not be the news you want. And if there isn't really any news at all, you can forget about reporters coming the next time. Special events, such as rallies and public meetings, are conducted both for the people who attend and the people who learn of what happened in the news. They can be excellent vehicles for encouraging public discussion of important matters. However, just like news conferences, special events should be used sparingly and with caution. If they won't attract journalists' attention, avoid them.

Key Considerations

There is no such thing as a single recipe or road map to better media relations. The ability to develop good relationships with reporters is both an art and a science and is usually gained from experience. Because of the naturally adversarial relationship between the reporter and the practitioner, the maintenance of good media relations requires constant attention. These are a few tips to help you meet that challenge.

• **Be prepared.** With apologies to the Boy Scouts, this is a pretty good motto for just about everything in life, especially public relations. It means anticipating reporters' questions and needs. To do that, you have to be familiar with both your subject matter and the requirements of the various media.

• **Be cool.** Reporters sometimes say and do things that prompt an emotional response. This is often a deliberate ploy to provoke a reaction that can get bigger play in the media than the substance of the response. Remember for whom you are speaking. Losing your cool reflects as much on your client as it does on you.

• **Never lie.** There are times when a practitioner may have legal, ethical, and security considerations for withholding information. However, there is no excuse for deliberately deceiving people. Whatever short-term gains may be realized by lying, they will evaporate—along with your reputation. Without credibility, a public relations practitioner is of little value. When that happens, it's time to look for a new career.

• **Demand accuracy.** The practitioner shares the journalist's need for accurate information. The failure to provide accurate information to reporters, even if by an honest mistake, can cast serious doubt on your competence and credibility.

Verify your facts first. When you make a mistake, move as quickly as possible to correct the error.

- **The burden of context is on you.** Journalists know that it isn't enough to quote someone accurately, word for word. Words must also be placed in an appropriate context. Rather than assume that reporters understand the context in which you are speaking, spell it out for them. Most reporters are generalists, knowing a little about a lot of things. It is better to be thorough in answering questions and to risk being called long-winded than to give short, snappy answers and be misunderstood.

- **Don't go off the record.** Because most journalists are honorable people, the advice against going off the record with reporters is not a statement about trusting reporters. Most disputes about what was and was not off the record stem from misunderstandings. Confusion won't happen if you avoid the practice. However, if a situation justifies going off the record, make certain everyone understands the ground rules before saying anything.

- **Never speculate.** Reporters love to ask speculative questions. Just because they ask them does not mean that you have to answer them. Speculative answers can create false expectations that come back to haunt an organization. Leave speculation up to gold prospectors and people with tarot cards and a crystal ball.

- **"No comment" is a nonstarter.** Blurting out those two words in response to a question leaves the impression that you have something to hide. If you are not in a position to answer a reporter's question, explain your reasons. When you are candid about your reasons for silence in certain matters, you improve your chances of being asked a follow-up question that you can answer.

- **Be there in good times and bad times.** Take a long-term view of your relationship with reporters. If you want the media to respond to you when times are good, you have to respect their need for information when times are bad. Reporters respect candid practitioners who answer tough questions. That, in turn, reflects well on the organization.

As is true in developing relationships with any other public, organizations must be true to their values when engaged in media relations. Doing the right thing is not always easy, especially when they are forced to take necessary, but unpopular, actions. It can be tempting to allow the conventional wisdom of editorial writers and television commentators to dictate future actions. Like any other public, their views should be thoughtfully considered. However, in the final analysis, public relations practitioners need to be comfortable in who they are, the organizations they represent, and what they believe. While it is important to have a good relationship with journalists, that desire should not compromise a commitment to core values.

Discussion Questions

1. How does a reporter or an editor decide whether a story is newsworthy?

2. How do the news-gathering requirements of a newspaper journalist and a television reporter differ?

3. What are some of the traditional tactics used in media relations?

4. Under what conditions should a public relations practitioner go off the record with a journalist?

5. Is it ever appropriate to lie to a reporter? What is an alternative if the practitioner either doesn't want to answer the question or for legitimate reasons can't answer it?

Key Terms

actuality feed, p. 118
backgrounders, p. 118
fact sheets, p. 118
media advisories, p. 118
media kits, p. 118
news, p. 114

news conferences, p. 119
news judgment, p. 114
news releases, p. 118
pitch letters, p. 118
proactive media relations, p. 114

reactive media relations, p. 114
special events, p. 119
video news releases, p. 118

Endnotes

1. "Are the News Media Too Liberal? Forty-Five Percent of Americans Say Yes," Gallup Poll Organization, October 8, 2003. Online: www.gallup.com.

2. Thomas Jefferson, Letter to James Currie, January 28, 1786. In *The Papers of Thomas Jefferson,* Vol. 9, ed. Julian P. Boyd et al., 1950. As cited online: www.bartleby.com.

3. Harry S. Truman, Speech, February 22, 1958. Reported in *The New York Times,* February 23, 1958, p. 46. As cited online: www.bartleby.com.

4. *Insider's Report: Robert Coen Presentation of Advertising Expenditures,* June 2003, Universal McCann, New York, Online: www.interpublic.com.

5. "Industry Outlets of Different Media," Northwestern University Media Management Center. Online: www.mediainfocenter.org/compare/outlets/.

6. "Total U.S. Non-Daily Newspapers," Newspaper Association of America. Online: www.naa.org/info/facts02/13_facts2002.html.

7. "Broadcast Station Totals as of June 20, 2003," Federal Communications Commission. News release, July 22, 2003.

8. "Number of Magazine Titles," Northwestern University Media Management Center. Online: www.mediainfocenter.org/magazine/size/titles.asp.

9. David W. Guth and Charles Marsh, *Public Relations: A Values-Driven Approach,* 2nd ed. (Boston: Allyn & Bacon, 2003), 274.

Talking Trash

Oklahoma's Antilittering Campaign Helps "Keep Our Land Grand"

When trash pickup crews patrol Oklahoma's roadsides, they are likely to find almost anything—including the kitchen sink. Among items found littering the Sooner State's highways are clothing, cameras, life jackets, bathing suits, towels, mattresses, appliances, furniture, car parts, ballet tutus, wheelchairs, money, drugs, pornography, and beer coolers—beer included. And this doesn't take into account the countless pop cans, fast-food wrappers, rags, tire treads, boxes, and cigarette butts.

Just as staggering as this mountain of trash is the clean-up cost—an estimated $4 million a year. "We could resurface nearly 100 additional miles of roadway with $4 million," said John Fuller, former Oklahoma Department of Transportation maintenance division engineer.

Don't Lay That Trash on Oklahoma

Oklahoma became one of the first states to tackle the problem in 1988, when it launched a $1 million "Don't Lay That Trash on Oklahoma" antilittering campaign. According to ODOT Chief of Public Affairs Terri Angier, the amount of roadside litter collected declined significantly in each of the first three years of the effort. However, as legislators faced mounting budget pressures in the early 1990s, the campaign's war chest diminished. Angier said state officials were forced to convert the program into a public service campaign—meaning that they no longer purchased advertising time and space—and "Don't Lay That Trash on Oklahoma" eventually fizzled.

When Gov. Frank Keating took office in 1995, new life was breathed into the state's antilittering efforts. Keating saw these efforts as part of the state's overall economic development strategy. "We can't expect visitors and potential investors in Oklahoma to go home with a positive impression if we look like a trash dump," said Keating.

However, officials faced the same old problem: lack of money. "We didn't want to do another public service announcement campaign," said Angier. "We knew that you had to be consistent and that you had to get the frequency of the message before it could be effective."

ODOT officials initially received little encouragement when they looked to the federal government for help. Federal Highway Administration officials insisted that antilittering campaigns were not eligible for enhancement funds under the Intermodal Surface Transportation Efficiency Act of 1991. But when Angier scoured through the regulations and found language that suggested antilittering programs were an appropriate use of the funds, the agency reversed its position and provided ODOT with $2 million over three years. Soon thereafter, ODOT contracted Visual Image Advertising of Oklahoma City to help develop a new campaign.

Pick-up Truck Males

Secondary research based on the experience of other states identified rural young males as the group most likely to litter the highways. Many owned open-bed pick-up trucks and allowed trash to blow onto the roadside during routine travel. The same research indicated that 60 percent of littering was deliberate. People younger than 25 were found to generate more than 76 percent of all litter in parks, roadside parks, and recreational areas. Another important finding was the tendency among elementary school children to place upward pressure on family members when it came to responsible social behavior.

"If you can instill those habits and values at a young age, then hopefully they are carried on," said Visual Image President Tim Berney. "If you get young children involved, they often turn out to be ambassadors to the rest of their family."

In a statewide telephone opinion survey, 61 percent of the 321 respondents said they felt litter was a problem in Oklahoma. However, an almost equal number disagreed with the statement that littering was a greater problem in Oklahoma than it was in other states. And most said they did not know anyone who litters. When asked why they felt people litter, two out of three respondents cited laziness or apathy as the reason. The top three reasons cited for people choosing not to litter were concern for appearance, state pride, and concern for the environment.

The "Don't Lay That Trash on Oklahoma" campaign earned mixed reactions. In unaided recall, nearly 70 percent of the respondents said they did not remember it. However, when reminded of the campaign, six out of 10 said the slogan had been effective.

There were also mixed reactions over whether the old slogan should be retained. Nearly 70 percent disagreed with the statement that the slogan should be changed. Much of this lingering support may be attributed to the popularity of the campaign's theme song, which had been set to the music of the 1957 hit "At the Hop." However, when the same question was asked a different way, the exact opposite was true—most favored change. More significant, 71 percent of 16- to 25-year-old respondents—the group identified as most likely to litter—favored a new approach. Those numbers, along with the financial burden associated with paying the $20,000 annual royalty fee for use of "At the Hop," convinced ODOT and Visual Image that a new campaign theme was in order.

Singing a Different Tune

The new theme, "Keep Our Land Grand," came from the lyrics of the state song, the title song of the Broadway classic *Oklahoma!* One phrase in the chorus—"We know we belong to the land. And the land we belong to is grand"—speaks to the pride Sooners hold for their state. By evoking this powerful message, campaign organizers hoped that they could tap into state pride to curb littering. The owner of the music copyright was also willing to let ODOT use "Oklahoma" for a nominal fee of $1 a year.

The awareness phase of the campaign was launched on the steps of the state Capitol in August 1997. With officials from each of Oklahoma's 77 counties standing behind him, Gov. Keating vowed to a gathering of reporters, government workers, and curious bystanders to make litter "a thing of the past." The kickoff event was followed by an integrated advertising and public relations campaign. The advertising—print, broadcast, and billboards—was heaviest during the six-week kick-off phase. Ads were later scheduled around what were considered peak littering times, including summer holidays and hunting season. Berney said that officials succeeded in extending the reach of the campaign by convincing media companies to donate free time and space to augment paid advertising.

One television ad featured the governor and his wife talking about the pride and economic benefits that come with a litter-free state. Another featured the state song, beautiful Oklahoma landscape, and carelessly tossed trash.

A later series of ads targeted young rural males. They featured an edgy, in-your-face guy, the Litter Ranger. Berney described him as a character with David Letterman-like humor that would be "endearing" to the target audience.

Typical of the Litter Ranger television spots was one in which our hero, looking at a discarded cup on a park bench, screamed into the camera, "Is this any way to spend $4 million?" As he sifted through a pile of roadside litter, he added in a voice thick with sarcasm, "I think people litter because there is something missing inside. They are trying to fill a hole. I just wish that hole led to a trash can."

Special events were an important part of the campaign. They targeted two groups, the people who were present at the special events and the audiences of the reporters who covered them. A highlight was an Oklahoma City amusement park appearance by popular television personality Bill Nye, the Science Guy. His appearance coincided with Anti-Litter Day, the spotlight event of Green Days, the educational component of the Keep Our Land Grand campaign. Nye also lent his voice to a series of public service announcements.

There was also the "Anti-Litterbug," a Volkswagen Beetle donated by a Tulsa automobile dealer. The car was decorated with antilittering messages and made stops at high schools, malls, and community events during Anti-Litter Month activities in April 1999. Local radio stations provided music for Anti-Litterbug events, and promotional items such as posters and trash bags were distributed.

One of the most visible—and measurable—components of Keep Our Land Grand was the antilittering hotline. When citizens spotted a motorist littering, they were asked to report the offender on a toll-free number. Polite reprimands—not citations—were then mailed by postcard to each vehicle's registered owner. In its first three years of operation, the hotline netted over 9,000 calls. The public's use of the hotline also generated news stories about the campaign and its antilittering message.

Media relations was an important element of the Keep Our Land Grand campaign. Media kit materials such as these helped generate publicity that, combined with advertising and special events, helped increase public awareness of the state's littering problem. (Courtesy of Oklahoma Department of Transportation, Public Affairs Division)

Antilittering curricula and classroom projects were developed for distribution to teachers across the state. Typical of these was an annual poster contest, with 12 winning entries used in ODOT's annual calendar. A story book for kids, *Billy's Day in the Woods,* was sent to schools and libraries. Educational support materials were also made available to teachers on a Keep Our Land Grand Web site.

Name That Tune?

A February 2000 survey noted that half of the respondents remembered seeing, hearing, or reading advertisements about littering in Oklahoma. More males heard or saw those messages than females. People living in rural areas were more likely to have heard or seen campaign messages than those living in the Oklahoma City or Tulsa metro areas. Two out of three said they thought there was a lot less litter on the state's highways than in the past. However, half of the respondents confused the Keep Our Land Grand theme with the earlier "Don't Lay That Trash on Oklahoma" campaign. Most said they didn't recall seeing or hearing anything about the antilittering hotline. The study concluded that "income, education, years lived in Oklahoma, presence of school age children in the home, age, or gender were not significant predictors of attitudes toward litter."

What had started as a three-year program outlasted the Keating administration and was continued by his successor, Gov. Brad Henry. But even before Henry took office in January 2003, Keep Our Land Grand had evolved into a public service and media relations campaign. "We knew going in that habit-changing campaigns take time to be effective," Angier said. Another factor in the decision to scale back was the need to reapply for the federal funds. Budget considerations also caused abandonment of plans to measure the campaign's success by comparing amounts of roadside trash collected in selected areas.

Sources

Terri Angier, interview, July 10, 2003.

Tim Berney, interview, July 15, 2003.

Frank Keating, "Let's Help Keep Our Land Grand," *Daily Oklahoman,* September 2, 1997. Online: http://archives.oklahoman.com.

Oklahoma Keep Our Land Grand media kit, Oklahoma Department of Transportation.

Penny Owen, "Oklahoma's Trashy Habits Spoil Scenery." *Daily Oklahoman,* July 8, 1998. Online: http://archives.oklahoman.com.

Research Solutions of Oklahoma, "Oklahoma Department of Transportation: 'Oklahoma Keep Our Land Grand' Awareness Study" (Norman, OK: February 9, 2000).

Smith Consulting Group, "Results and Analysis of the Oklahoma Department of Transportation Survey on Anti-Litter Awareness and Opinions" (Oklahoma City: 1997).

Steve Wedel, "Road Litter Costly for State—$4 Million Spent Each Year to Clean Up," *Daily Oklahoman,* June 29, 2000. Online: http://archives.oklahoman.com.

Pink Ribbons and Blue Jeans

case **6.2**

*Lee National Denim Day® Raises Millions
for Breast Cancer Research*

In the time it takes an average person to read this case, another woman will have been diagnosed with breast cancer. That's more than 200,000 mothers and daughters every year. According to health experts, one in every eight women is at risk of developing breast cancer in her lifetime. It is the leading cause of cancer deaths for women aged 40–59.

As compelling as the statistics are, they do not tell the whole story. Breast cancer not only affects those who have it but also casts a shadow over its victims' families, friends, and communities. But as much as it is a story of sorrow and affliction, it is also a story of courage, determination, and the human spirit.

This case is about a clothing manufacturer that had originally set out to solve a business problem but has since been recognized as a leading advocate for breast cancer research and awareness.

Two Strategies, One Goal

According to industry data, approximately 576 million pairs of jeans made of denim, twill, corduroy, or other fabrics were sold in the United States during 2002, representing a retail sales market of $11.7 billion. Despite their popularity, jeans have been long considered a fashion taboo in the professional workplace. Executives at Kansas-based Lee Jeans felt the 1990s trend toward more casual office apparel had presented them with a business opportunity. However, there was a lingering reluctance to accept denim as workplace attire—especially for women, Lee's core consumers. In 1996, Lee hired a Kansas City agency, Barkley Evergreen & Partners Public Relations (BE&P/PR), to help jeans gain workplace acceptance.

About the same time, Lee made another strategic decision. Its leadership decided to focus its corporate philanthropy on a single cause: breast cancer. It was a very personal decision, as the lives of many within the Lee organization had been touched by the disease, either directly or through loved ones and friends. When BE&P/PR learned of Lee's commitment to the battle against breast cancer, the idea of a cause marketing campaign began to form. It was strengthened when secondary research uncovered the *Cone-Roper Cause-Related Marketing Trends Report,* which noted that when price and quality are equal, 76 percent of consumers said they would probably switch to a brand associated with a good cause.

"The concept was very simple," said BE&P/PR President Mike Swenson. "It was to tie Lee's passion for breast cancer with its business challenge to open companies' eyes toward allowing denim in the workplace."

Thus was born Lee National Denim Day®, which has since evolved into the largest single-day fund-raising event for breast cancer research, education, screening, and treatment programs. Participating companies allow employees to wear jeans on the job—any brand—in return for a $5 donation to support breast cancer research. Lee National Denim Day is held every year on a Friday in October, which is National Breast Cancer Awareness Month. The fund raising effort has netted more than $43 million in its first eight years.

A Rewarding Marriage

Most cause-related programs involve strategic partnerships between a company and a nonprofit organization. The nonprofit partner provides an outlet for the money raised in support of a particular cause. Just as important, this relationship allows the nonprofit to share its credibility and specialized expertise with the corporate partner.

Lee Jeans chose to work with the Susan G. Komen Breast Cancer Foundation. The Komen Foundation was founded in 1982 by Nancy Brinker in the name of a sister who died of breast cancer at the age of 36. Over the years, the foundation and its 75,000 volunteers have raised more than $600 million for the fight against breast cancer. The money has been earmarked for cutting-edge medical research, community-based breast health education, and cancer screening and treatment programs.

"In a cause branding program, you are marrying two brands," said Swenson. "We went with the Komen Foundation because of its singular focus on breast cancer."

From the Komen Foundation's perspective, it has been a rewarding marriage. "Funds raised from Lee National Denim Day have helped fund valuable programs that might not have been funded elsewhere," said Susan Braun, foundation president and chief executive officer. "We should not underestimate the power of programs like Lee National Denim Day to help raise much-needed funds and help raise public consciousness that breast cancer has not been cured—yet."

Painting the Golden Gate

Each year's Lee National Denim Day campaign begins in late fall with the selection of the celebrity spokesperson. Since the very first year, when women's basketball star Rebecca Lobo filled that role, celebrities have been at the center of the promotion. Planners look for someone who has personal ties to breast cancer, generates media attention, and connects with the target audiences: women 25–54, men 25–54, corporations, schools, and social or civic organizations. For example, at the time Lobo was the Denim Day spokesperson, she was promoting a book written with her mother in which they candidly discussed her mother's battle with breast cancer.

Denim is powerful stuff.

Because Lee National Denim Day is a grass-roots event, Lee and its agency provided local organizers with a fulfillment kit to help plan and publicize the event. This fill-in-the-blank poster features 2003 spokesperson Christina Applegate. (Courtesy of Lee® Jeans)

Other Denim Day spokespersons have included Yasmine Bleeth, Patricia Arquette, Lucy Liu, and Rob Lowe. The selection of Lowe, whose grandmother had breast cancer, marked the first time a man was selected. Lowe was effective in delivering a different kind of message: Men have a responsibility to ensure the women in their lives get regular breast health check-ups. Lowe's message reach was extended because of his connection at that time to a popular network television show, *The West Wing*. Good fortune—as well as extra media attention—smiled on another Lee National Denim Day spokesperson when actress Christina Applegate won her first Emmy for a guest appearance on the hit series *Friends* just a few weeks before her 2003 campaign. Applegate, who believes an early diagnosis of breast cancer helped save her mother's life, told reporters, "Lee National Denim Day is an easy way to help create awareness about the importance of early detection."

The build-up to Lee National Denim Day quickens during late spring. This is when the celebrity spokesperson is announced and the sign-up of participating organizations begins. A toll-free telephone number, direct mail, and a Web site are also used to encourage participation. Much of this activity is aided by a database of past participants and vigorous networking within the cancer-prevention community. As a result of these efforts, the number of participating organizations has swelled from approximately 3,000 in 1996 to more than 24,000 in 2003.

Participating companies and organizations receive a fulfillment kit—materials for organizing Lee National Denim Day activities at the grass-roots level. The kit includes a book with instructions and ideas for event planning, a poster, sign-up and donation envelopes, a personalized certificate of appreciation, breast cancer fact sheets, and pink ribbon pins for participants to wear and show their support.

During the summer, targeted advertisements are placed in select women's, fashion, and business magazines. In the early fall, BE&P/PR arranges guest appearances for the celebrity spokesperson on prominent national television shows with a largely female audience, such as *Live! with Regis & Kelly* and morning news programs such as *Today*. The celebrity spokesperson also conducts major market radio interviews and a satellite media tour.

"Lee National Denim Day is kind of like painting the Golden Gate Bridge," Swenson said. "Everyone thinks of it as one day in October, but it is a year-round effort."

Sept. 11

The Sept. 11, 2001, terror attacks on New York and Washington, D.C., came less than a month before Lee National Denim Day. The nation was focusing its attention on terrorism and fund raising for victims' families. It was not the nation it had been when that year's campaign was launched. Some hard decisions had to be made quickly.

Lee Jeans President Gordon Harton set the tone just two days after the attacks when he unequivocally said that Lee National Denim Day would not be cancelled. The decision was made to go on with the event because of its importance to breast cancer research. "We decided it doesn't matter if we raise only $1 million, $5 million, or $7 million dollars," said Kathy Collins, vice president of marketing for Lee Jeans. "We decided let's give it everything we've got."

Out of sensitivity, plans for a New York City media tour with Lucy Liu were scrapped. Much of the promotional focus was shifted to the entertainment media in Los Angeles. A radio interview tour and a satellite media tour substituted for the traditional Lee National Denim Day news conference at Lee Jean's corporate headquarters. Even in the shadow of terrorism, the 2001 campaign exceeded expectations, generating 100 million media impressions, a number representing the size of the audience exposed to campaign messages in different media. The 2001 campaign raised $6.3 million.

"It was a great lesson and reminder that in the midst of one of our nation's greatest tragedies, life has to go on," said Swenson.

A Life-Changing Experience

As already noted, Lee National Denim Day has evolved into the largest single-day fund raiser for breast cancer research. Each year's event receives substantial media coverage—an estimated 138,462,391 impressions in 2002. More than one million people participate each year. According to Lee tracking studies, women who are aware of Lee National Denim Day are more likely to have a better perception of Lee as fashionable. Lee's retailers also credit Lee National Denim Day with a rise in sales, especially during the heaviest promotional periods. The Komen Foundation became the first nonprofit to receive the Cause Marketing Forum's Golden Halo Award. The foundation, Lee Jeans, and BE&P/PR also received a silver award for Lee National Denim Day.

The program also has had unexpected side effects. Several of the celebrity spokespersons have continued speaking out about breast cancer and Lee National Denim Day long after their official affiliation with the program has ended. For many companies, it has become part of an internal team-building strategy. Many organizations plan an entire week of activities around Lee National Denim Day. For BE&P/PR, the experience has transformed it into a company now recognized for its cause-branding solutions.

"It has totally changed our company," Swenson said. "It was a turning point and a catalyst for the direction we are going today."

Sources

"Breast Cancer Awareness Heightens Despite National Crisis," *PR News,* vol. 57, no. 39. October 15, 2001. Online: Lexis-Nexis.

"Christina Applegate Proves Denim Is Powerful Stuff; Applegate Teams up with Lee Jeans for Lee National Denim Day, the World's Largest Single-Day Fundraiser for Breast

Cancer," Lee Jeans news release, July 30, 2003. Distributed online by Business Wire: www.businesswire.com.

Halo Awards, Cause Marketing Forum. Campaign background summary for Lee National Denim Day (Barkley Evergreen & Partners Public Relations, undated).

John Frank, "Lee Proceeds with Denim Day in Style," *PR Week* (November 26, 2001), 34.

"Lee National Denim Day Challenges America to Make Breast Health a Priority," Lee Jeans news release, September 15, 2003. Distributed online by Business Wire: www.businesswire.com.

Susan G. Komen Breast Cancer Foundation Web site, www.komen.org.

Mike Swenson, interview, October 7, 2003.

V F Corporation 10-K filing, January 14, 2003, U.S. Securities and Exchange Commission. Online: www.sec.gov.

case **6.3**

Masters of Disaster

The Augusta National Golf Club Becomes the Focus of Women's Rights Protests

It may surprise a lot of people to learn that Martha Burk considers herself a golf enthusiast. She grew up around country clubs in her native Texas. Burk enjoys the game and is a big fan of Tiger Woods.

That's why a newspaper item about Woods winning the 2002 Masters golf tournament caught her eye. It noted that the Augusta National Golf Club, the site of each year's Masters, does not consider women for membership. As chair of the National Council of Women's Organizations, a Washington-based coalition of 170 women's advocacy groups, she couldn't help but notice that provocative tidbit of information.

However, it wasn't until the next NCWO board meeting that she remembered the story. "By the way," Burk told the board members, "I learned about this golf club that doesn't allow women members. Why don't we write them a letter?

"It was such a small deal, we didn't even vote on it," she said.

Ironically, this "small deal" quickly escalated into a major political confrontation involving women's rights groups, the golf world, the media, some of the world's largest corporations—and two very stubborn people.

"We Do Not Intend to Become a Trophy"

Burk wrote a four-paragraph letter to Augusta National Chairman Hootie Johnson on June 12, 2002. "We know that Augusta National and the sponsors of the Masters do not want to be viewed as entities that tolerate discrimination against any group, including women," Burk's letter said. "We urge you to review your policies and practices." She would later say that she expected "a polite response from Johnson that would say something like 'Thank you for your interest, we are working on it.'"

For those who know him best, Hootie Johnson is one of the last people they would have expected to be accused of discrimination. Born William Woodward Johnson in 1931, he became a leading banker in South Carolina and a liberal leader in state politics. In both words and deeds, Johnson took courageous stands against racial injustice. In 1968, he persuaded the state legislature to fund an undergraduate business program at predominantly black South Carolina State University. As state Democratic Party chairman, Johnson helped elect three black state legislators—the first in South Carolina since 1902. As late as 2000, he was credited with orchestrating the compromise to remove the Confederate battle flag from atop the state Capitol in Columbia.

However, Johnson's friends also knew that he could be headstrong when threatened. Johnson rejected Burk's suggestions in a three-paragraph letter on July 8. He wrote that he found her letter to be "offensive and coercive" and that "any further communication between us would not be productive." This was followed the next day by a three-page, 932-word statement to the media. "We do not intend to become a trophy in their case," Johnson wrote. "There may well come a day when a woman will be invited to join our membership, but that timetable will be ours and not at the point of a bayonet."

The battle had been joined.

Guilt by Association

Having been rebuffed, Burk wrote the CEOs of Coca-Cola, IBM, and Citigroup on July 30 and asked them to suspend their television sponsorship of the Masters. IBM responded in an August 15 letter by saying that it did not see a Masters sponsorship as contradictory to its commitment to diversity. Citigroup's answer came a week later, with the company indicating that it would privately communicate its views on the issue to Augusta National.

Johnson provided cover for Augusta National's corporate partners by announcing on August 20 that he had dropped them from the telecast and that the 2003 Masters would be televised by CBS commercial-free. This was a bold move, considering *Advertising Age*'s estimate that each company paid Augusta National $5 million to $7 million for its sponsorship.

"Augusta National is NCWO's true target," Johnson said. "It is therefore unfair to put the Masters' media sponsors in the position of having to deal with the pressure."

Some later questioned whether Burk's targeting of the corporate executives was fair. For example, an *Atlanta Journal-Constitution* investigation of 26 publicly traded companies led by Augusta National members showed that representation of women in high-profile executive positions was on par with all *Fortune* 500 companies. One example cited was telecommunications giant SBC Communications, where six of the company's 21 directors and 23 of its 83 corporate officers were women.

"This company is probably one of the more diverse that you can come across," said SBC spokesman Sam Bingol. "If people want to know where the company's heart lies, they should look at the numbers."

Although contacting corporate sponsors did not achieve the desired effect, the NCWO's pressure caused other high-profile members to seek cover—especially after a previously secret Augusta National membership list was leaked to *USA Today*. In the months that followed, several members, such as U.S. Olympic Committee Executive Director Lloyd Ward, promised to lobby aggressively for female memberships from the inside. Several others resigned, including John Snow, who had been nominated as Treasury Secretary by President George W. Bush, and former CBS executive Thomas Wyman, who called Johnson's position "pigheaded."

Eye of the Tiger

At the same time that Burk targeted Augusta National's corporate sponsors, she also asked Professional Golfers' Association Tour Commissioner Tim Finchem to withdraw recognition of the Masters as an official tournament. "After having considered this matter, we have decided that we must continue to recognize the Masters tournament as one of professional golf's major championships," Finchem answered.

Burk won a symbolic victory when Ladies Professional Golf Association Commissioner Ty Votaw said it was time to open Augusta National to women. "It is Augusta's right as a private organization to not admit women," Votaw said. "But it is not the right thing to do."

Tiger Woods, the two-time defending Masters champion, became an unwilling focal point of the controversy. The *New York Times* called on Woods to boycott the tournament in a Nov. 18 editorial. "A tournament without Mr. Woods would send a powerful message that discrimination isn't good for the golfing business," the *Times* opined. Woods called the editorial "frustrating because I'm the only player they are asking." The Rev. Jesse Jackson, whose Rainbow/PUSH Coalition was planning to support NCWO, said the *Times* editorial was "unfair and inconsistent" in singling out Woods.

At that time, an Associated Press poll reported that Americans were evenly divided on whether Augusta National should have women members. However, by a three-to-one margin, the poll also said Americans felt that Woods should play in the Masters. Woods decided that he would play in the tournament and said that the club should admit women "because it is the right thing to do." Hootie Johnson's response was "I won't tell Tiger how to play golf if he doesn't tell us how to run our private club."

Heated Words

In the months leading up to the 2003 Masters, the rhetoric on both sides became more intense—sometimes generating more heat than light. NCWO launched a

Web site—www.augustadiscriminates.org—on Dec. 17. In it, the organization displayed what it called its "Hall of Hypocrisy," featuring the corporate logos of companies it said sanctioned sex discrimination at Augusta National. "Augusta is considered a model tournament for its beauty, decorum and tradition," the Web site said. "But it has a rotten underbelly."

Burk was sharply criticized in March 2003 when she tried to link her Augusta crusade to the outbreak of war in Iraq. "It's appalling that the women who are willing to lay down their lives for democratic ideals should be shut out of this club," Burk told a New York audience.

Augusta's supporters, in and outside the news media, blasted her for trying to link the golf crusade with Operation Iraqi Freedom. Jim McCarthy, the club's Washington-based crisis management consultant, said, "To use the war as an opportunity to inject yourself into the news is just disgraceful."

These words came from the same man who just a few months earlier had told Scotland's national newspaper that Burk was "a bomb-thrower" and that "even a blind drive-by shotgunner is going to hit a target once in a while." After receiving two letters of complaint from Burk's attorneys, McCarthy toned down the violent imagery of his rhetoric.

Burk's organization sought permission to picket outside the club's front gates during the Masters. When local authorities denied the permit, the protest was moved one-half mile from the club—well out of the range of CBS television microphones and cameras.

And as if the Augusta National Golf Club needed any more controversy, the ultraracist Ku Klux Klan asked for a permit to protest in support of the club. Augusta National spokesman Glen Greenspan said, "Anyone who knows anything about Augusta National Golf Club or its members knows this is not something the club would welcome or encourage."

When the National Council of Women's Organizations was denied permission to protest at the gates of the Augusta National Golf Club, it staged a rally one-half mile away. NCWO's controversial tactics focused national attention on women's rights. (Courtesy of Ralph Estes)

Both Sides Claim Victory

The 2003 Masters came and went without any disruptions. NCWO's protest rally attracted 25 people—or 200—depending on who was counting. However, an even more impressive number was 34.5 million—the number of people who watched CBS Sports' final-round coverage, the third-highest for a Sunday at the Masters. The lost revenues from the commercial-free coverage did not affect Augusta National's charities. The club gave $3.3 million to various organizations, the same amount as the year before. Johnson announced his intention to have another commercial-free Masters in 2004.

Johnson has told reporters that although he had made a mistake by reacting so angrily to Burk's first letter, he did not think the club was damaged by the controversy. "The time may come when we have women in our club," he said. "But for the time being, we hold dear our traditions and our constitutional right to choose and associate."

"We've won," Burk said, "because we've raised the national consciousness about this issue." She said the club will have to change its rules or be "marginalized" and lose membership. "I'm not going to back off."

Sources

Tommy Braswell, "Golfers Try to Avoid Augusta Controversy," *The Post and Courier* (Charleston, SC). January 26, 2003, 9A. Online: Lexis-Nexis.

Mark Craig, "2003 Masters Preview: Hootie Johnson," *Star Tribune* (Minneapolis, MN), April 6, 2003, 6C. Online: Lexis-Nexis.

Karen Crouse, "Martha Burk," *Palm Beach* (FL) *Post*, April 6, 2003, 1B. Online: Lexis-Nexis.

"KKK Wants to Protest at Augusta National," Associated Press, February 28, 2003. Online: Lexis-Nexis.

Richard Justice, "Spar for the Course; Female Furor at Augusta National Rages On," *The Houston Chronicle*, December 15, 2002, 1 (Sports). Online: Lexis-Nexis.

Michael O'Keeffe, "Crashing the Gates, Burk Presses on," Knight Ridder/Tribune News Service, *New York Daily News*, April 8, 2003. Online: Lexis-Nexis.

"National Council of Women's Organizations Hall of Hypocrisy." Online: www.augusta discriminates.org.

"Signs of Bias by Augusta's Corporate Titans Lacking," *Atlanta Journal-Constitution*, March 17, 2003. Online: Lexis-Nexis.

Alan Thays and Craig Dolch, "LPGA Chief Gives Augusta National a Bogey," *Palm Beach* (FL) *Post*, November 21, 2002, 1A. Online: Lexis-Nexis.

Rich Thomaselli, "Masters May Face Sponsor-Less Future," *Advertising Age*, March 10, 2003, 39. Online: Lexis-Nexis.

"Timeline of the Augusta National Controversy," Associated Press, April 9, 2003. Online: Lexis-Nexis.

Jay Weiner, "2003 Masters Preview: Martha Burke," *Minneapolis Star Tribune*, April 6, 2003, 6C. Online: Lexis-Nexis.

"Without Commercial Interruption: Augusta National Says Masters Will Again Have No Sponsors," Associated Press, June 3, 2003. Online: *Sports Illustrated*.

ACT file # 6 · · · · · · · · · · · · · · · ·

Advertising Value Equivalency

Public relations practitioners face constant pressure to show that the fruits of their labors are of measurable value to the organization's bottom line. This is especially true when times are hard and budgets are lean. Practitioners need to be able to answer that toughest of all questions: "Am I getting my money's worth?" And while a recitation of the importance of relationships and the role that resource dependency theory (page 22) plays may be *theoretically* sound, it's not the kind of answer that always wins over the bean counters in the boardroom. They want numbers.

Advertising value equivalency (AVE), therefore, appears to be an answer to practitioner prayers. The concept is simple: Determine a monetary value based on the advertising rates for the amount of media coverage received from publicity. Calculating the AVE of publicity is a relatively easy proposition. Determining whether it is a valid measure of public relations value is another matter.

First, let's look at the process of calculating AVE. Although a wide variety of AVE formulas exist, all of them use two common factors: the amount of space or time the publicity received within a particular medium, and that medium's advertising rate. For example, suppose a public relations agency distributed a news release that generated a story that took up 10 column-inches of space in the local newspaper. To calculate the AVE of the publicity received as a result of that news release, research the newspaper's advertising rates. If advertising in the newspaper is $100 a column-inch, the math would be simple:

10 col. in. publicity × $100/col. in. ad rate = $1,000 AVE

Some take the process a step farther. They note that because of third-party endorsement, publicity is more credible than advertising. For that reason, they argue that there should be a credibility multiplier (CM) included in the AVE formula to account for publicity's added value. For example, the Texas Commission on the Arts advises its stakeholders that "a good rule of thumb is to mark up the advertising value by a factor of three for a general story." If the story includes photographs, logos, or other graphics, it says practitioners should add another multiple to the CM.[1] Following this model and assuming that the newspaper story did not have any pictures or graphics accompanying it, the formula would look like this:

10 col. in. publicity × $100/col. in. ad rate × 3 CM = $3,000 AVE

If you are asking what the basis is for using a multiplier of three—as opposed to two, 10, or even 100—then you have gotten to the heart of the controversy over AVEs. "The weightings for 'third-party' endorsement are totally made up," wrote

Professor James Grunig.[2] The Institute for Public Relations Research has gone so far as to suggest that these "arbitrary weighting schemes" are "unethical, dishonest, and not supported by the research literature."[3]

AVE opponents ask other questions. Is a story in the local newspaper as important as one in the *Wall Street Journal*? Just because you reached a large audience in a certain medium, did it have the demographic and psychographic composition you desired? How do you quantify the value of a story that depicts your organization in a positive, negative, or neutral light? Did the readers, viewers, or listeners take a desired action as a result of the story? When you compare advertising to public relations, aren't you comparing apples to oranges? As a practitioner, can you ethically tell a journalist that your news release contains news—but then evaluate it using advertising rates?

In fairness, AVE has its champions. Gary Getto, vice president of Surveillance Data, said that the public relations industry "may have thrown the baby out with the bath water" by rejecting AVE. Citing research conducted by his and two other firms, Getto said, "We think this study helps to put to rest the claim that AVE is not as valid a tool as audience impressions and article counts."[4]

In light of the controversy over AVE, the Public Relations Society of America warns practitioners against comparing publicity efforts with advertising, saying they might find themselves "in a situation that is indefensible." PRSA says the alternative to AVE is reaching agreement with the client on benchmarks, strategic objectives, and goals at the beginning of every public relations campaign.[5]

Discussion Questions

1. What are the arguments for and against the use of AVE in measuring public relations outcomes?

2. What are some of the alternatives to using AVE to measure public relations outcomes?

3. How does someone compute AVE?

4. On what basis do practitioners believe that a credibility multiplier should be used when figuring AVE?

Endnotes

1. "The Power of Public Relations: A Basic Guide to Getting Noticed—Measurement/Evaluation/ Wrap-up," Texas Commission on the Arts, 1999. Online: www.arts.state.tx.us/news/prpower/measure. htm.

2. James Grunig, "Evaluation," International Public Relations Association e-group, August 4, 2000.

3. "Guidelines and Standards for Measuring and Evaluating PR Effectiveness," Institute for Pub-

lic Relations, University of Florida, 2000. Online: www.instituteforpr.com.

4. "Ad Value Equivalency Comes out of the Shadows, but Is It Still Considered 'PR Witchcraft'?" *Ragan Media Relations Report*, October 1, 2001.

5. "Tips & Techniques: Advertising Equivalency," Public Relations Society of America. Online: www.prsa.org.

7

Community Relations

Ask anyone what comes to mind when you say the word *community.* It will conjure different images for different people. Some think of **geographic communities,** the places where people live, work, and play. Others think of **demographic communities,** in which folks share common nonattitudinal attributes, such as people with the same ethnic heritage or annual income. Others are part of what are known as **psychographic communities,** in which people share similar philosophies or lifestyle attitudes. A fairly recent creation is **virtual communities,** in which people build relationships and share their common interests via Internet list serves and chat rooms. Because the concept of community is as much a state of mind as it is a state of being, a person can be a member of several communities at the same time.

Identifying, building, and maintaining strategic relationships with this vast array of communities are among the greatest critical thinking challenges facing public relations practitioners in the 21st century. Successful community relations often hinges on a willingness to step outside your comfort zone to explore new cultures and ideas.

A Tale of Two Cities

To get a sense of these challenges, one need only to compare two great U.S. cities, San Francisco and Omaha. At first glance, the fact that both are located on the North American continent seems to be one of the few things they have in common. According to the U.S. Census Bureau, San Francisco has twice the population of Omaha. (If you compare the two metropolitan areas, the population of the

San Francisco is one of the most ethnically diverse cities in the United States. Although their city is indeed unique, San Franciscans have much in common with residents of other communities. Public relations practitioners often face the challenge of bridging such differences and identifying common interests. (Courtesy of David Guth)

San Francisco Bay Area is 10 times that of Omaha.) Almost half of the California city is nonwhite, compared with the almost 79 percent white residents in Omaha. More than 92 percent of the Nebraska city residents are native-born U.S. citizens. That compares with just 63 percent in San Francisco. Black residents constitute the largest minority group in Omaha at 13.4 percent. In San Francisco, persons of Asian descent make up nearly one-third of the city's population.

Other significant differences separate the two cities. The median age of San Franciscans is almost three years older than the median age of Omaha residents. Almost half of the people living in San Francisco have a college degree, compared to 29 percent of those living in Omaha. San Francisco has a higher percentage of its workforce in management positions than Omaha, which, in turn, has a higher percentage of people employed in the service and sales/office sectors. The Northern Californians tend to vote for Democrats. The Nebraskans tend to vote for Republicans. For San Francisco residents, the good news is that their median household income is substantially higher than that of their Omaha counterparts, $59,192 to $38,719. However, the people of Omaha have reason to smile as well: The median cost (based on value) of owner-occupied housing in Omaha is only $96,827, compared with $441,080 in San Francisco.[1]

By now you probably think that the residents of these two cities couldn't possibly have *anything* in common. However, if you brought San Francisco and Omaha residents together, you might find that they are not as different from one another as you first thought. Listening in on their conversations, you might find that they have a common love for their country and their families. They might talk about their kids, express concern for their health and safety, and wonder about the quality of their education. It wouldn't be long before you learn that both San Francisco and Omaha are good baseball towns—and do they love their football! Not everybody in San Francisco votes for Democrats, and not everyone in Omaha votes for Republicans. Some may work in the same kind of jobs or have similar hobbies. Who knows? By the time this great social experiment is complete, you may have created a whole new community unto itself!

This takes us back to the process of identifying, building, and maintaining strategic relationships with disparate communities. The critical thinking challenge rests in the practitioner's ability to identify common interests and values—even with stakeholders with whom there is no prior relationship. This is true whether dealing with a single community or, more likely, several communities at the same time.

Why Community Relations Matters

The need to successfully engage different stakeholders within a community should be obvious. As noted in the discussion of resource dependency theory in Chapter 2, no individual or organization is entirely self-sufficient. Each party relies on the goodwill and/or resources of others. For example, when a company decides to move its operations into a new community, it does so to satisfy a variety of needs. These may include the need for a stable, well-trained workforce, easy access to transportation, a stable market, and favorable tax policies. At the same time, the community may actively recruit the company to fulfill its own needs. These may include desires to attract better-paying jobs, increase the community's tax base, and establish philanthropic partnerships to help fund civic and social programs.

It is important to remember that we are not necessarily discussing a one-to-one relationship. The essence of community relations is that many players sit at the table at any given time. While company executives may be negotiating for favorable tax breaks with local government, public officials must answer to voters/taxpayers representing a wide range of constituencies. At the same time, the company needs to establish favorable relations within the neighborhood in which it plans to locate, as well as with potential employees, vendors, and customers. There can even be forces outside of the immediate geographic area, such as labor unions, human rights groups, and environmental organizations, that can wield influence over these relationships.

Analyzing this dynamic mix of interests is known as **coorientation.** Public opinion is shaped not only by one party's take on a situation but also by what it believes are other stakeholders' perceptions.[2] While coorientation is a factor that is present throughout the practice of public relations, it is especially important in the area of community relations. To illustrate this point, let's say a company wants to expand its manufacturing operations. That requires government support in terms of zoning changes, building permits, and infrastructure improvements. Through coorientation, the company determines the appropriateness of its actions in its relations with others. In this case, the company's decision to pursue or delay its expansion may be determined by its perception of whether it has or lacks necessary public support.

The give-and-take between organizations and community stakeholders is an application of **social exchange theory.** Its premise is that people seek to minimize costs and maximize rewards within their relationships. There is an expectation of reciprocity: You scratch my back, and I'll scratch yours. And if that expectation is not met, the danger exists that one party may end the relationship in favor of another seen as more satisfying. Social exchange theory, which was first identified in the early 1950s, is consistent with the more recent research on the components of relationships by Hon and Grunig (Chapter 2).[3]

The practical implication of social exchange theory is a need for organizations and their stakeholders to commit the time, energy, and resources necessary to build and maintain relationships. There has to be a certain level of trust so that all parties involved can rely on one another. This, in turn, requires dependability and forthrightness. There also has to be a level of comfort with what are known as **relational dialectics,** the numerous forces that can pull a relationship in opposite directions. An example would be a community's desire for openness and a company's desire to protect private, proprietary information.[4]

Community Relations Publics

As is the case with other areas of public relations, one of the first challenges in developing a community relations program is to define the stakeholders. Some of these publics are easy to identify. Others are not.

Traditional community stakeholders include public officials, educators, religious leaders, professionals (such as doctors and lawyers), bankers, labor leaders, ethnic leaders, and neighborhood leaders. Also included in this mix are media, both mass circulation media (such as newspapers, radio, and television) and specialized media (such as trade association newsletters and entertainment magazines). It is also common to target community relations efforts toward **special publics,** organized stakeholder groups formed out of a common interest. Some of these are considered **inward special publics** because their mission is focused more on the needs of their members. Examples of inward special publics include members of a local country club, a neighborhood association, or a recreational league. **Outward special publics** are organizations whose mission extends beyond their membership, such as civil rights organizations, social service charities, and service clubs. When several publics sharing common interests combine resources to increase their numbers and political clout, they become **coalitions.** (See Case 4.1.)

Many of the aforementioned traditional stakeholders fall within relatively easy to identify geographic or demographic publics. As a general rule, psychographic publics, whose members share common attitudes and/or lifestyles, are more difficult to identify and are often considered nontraditional publics. These groups often form around a single issue, such as abortion, gun control, smoking, or school bonds. A psychographic special public could even involve a controversy that may seem trivial to most, but that to an energized group is not.

The late Carl Vinson served the people of Georgia in the U.S. House of Representatives for more than a half-century. Vinson was chairman of the House Naval Affairs and Armed Services Committee for a record 29 years during a turbulent period of history. In that position, he earned recognition as the father of the United States' two-ocean navy and played a major role in his nation's victory in World War II. Despite his critical role in national security, Vinson told one reporter that the largest outpouring of public opinion he ever dealt with concerned a highway construction crew's plan to cut down an old tree in Milledgeville, Ga. "I heard more about that damn tree than I ever did about spending billions and billions of dollars on the Navy," he said.[5]

While some nontraditional publics are temporary in nature and disappear once an issue is resolved—such as when Congressman Vinson's tree was spared—others evolve into more permanent and traditional publics. As recently as a generation ago, the gay and lesbian community was considered a nontraditional public. In recent years, it has become a major political force in many communities. Major retailers, resorts, and public officials seek this community's financial and political support. This reminds us of an important lesson, not just for community relations but for life itself: It is best to take a long-term view when dealing with people. You never know how important today's new relationship may become in the future.

Cultural Diversity

Any discussion of community relations has to take into account the evolving composition of the community itself. This is especially true in the United States, where the myth of the melting pot has been replaced with the realization that the nation's racial and ethnic composition is more like a mosaic. According to U.S. Census Bureau projections, the United States is a nation that will become even more diverse in coming decades. (See Table 7.1.)

The 2000 U.S. Census also revealed that Hispanics represent 35.7 percent of the U.S. population below the age of 18, compared with 23.5 percent for whites of the same age. Birth rates of foreign-born Latino immigrants are fueling population growth faster than new immigration.[6]

"The economic importance of the Spanish language population has grown disproportionately to their size," said David C. Schmittlein, a marketing professor at the Wharton School of the University of Pennsylvania.[7] The Selig Center for Economic Growth at the University of Georgia estimates that Hispanic spending power will pass the $1 trillion mark in the next few years.[8]

One word of caution: Don't assume that everyone counted as being of Hispanic origin by the U.S. Census Bureau considers himself or herself to be "Hispanic." This t a b l e **7.1** *Projections of U.S. Population by Race and Hispanic Origin*

	All	White	Hispanic	Black	American Indian, Eskimo, and Aleut	Asian and Pacific Islander
July 1, 2004	285,266,000 (100%)	232,673,000 (69.7%)	37,059,000 (13.0%)	35,050,000 (12.3%)	2,146,000 (0.8%)	12,117,000 (4.2%)
July 1, 2050	403,687,000 (100%)	212,991,000 (52.7%)	98,229,000 (24.3%)	53,466,000 (13.2%)	3,241,000 (0.8%)	35,780,000 (8.9%)

Note: Persons of Hispanic origin may be of any race. For purposes of comparison, the numbers for the non-Hispanic categories reflect persons not of Hispanic origin, by race.

Source: "Projections of the Population by Age, Sex, Race, and Hispanic Origin for the United States: 1999 to 2100 (Middle Series)," U.S. Census Bureau. Online: www.census.gov.

is a broad population classification that serves as an umbrella for people from a wide range of cultures. Persons of Mexican, Cuban, and Argentinean heritage may be considered Hispanic for counting purposes but are of distinct cultures with their own values and motivations. Some bristle at the Hispanic label, preferring Latino. The difference is in bloodlines: Hispanics derive from the Iberian Peninsula, which comprises Spain and Portugal, while Latinos descend from the indigenous populations of Central and South America.[9] Even people from different regions of the same country may be dissimilar. Remember our comparisons of the residents of San Francisco and Omaha?

What this means for organizations seeking to communicate with a diverse array of stakeholders from distinctly different cultures can be summed up in one word: research.

Key Considerations

Strategic and tactical decisions in community relations can be as complex as defining the stakeholders they target. When trying to navigate through the potential minefield of organization–public relationships, practitioners need to address a number of key considerations:

• **Conduct stakeholder research.** This is good advice for any form of public relations. However, because of the complexity and diversity of community relations, this is an especially critical step. Practitioners must understand the different communities they serve and recognize that one size does not fit all. Different stakeholders have different cultures and values. The challenge is to find common ground.

- **Define organization priorities.** In an ideal world, organizations would give all stakeholders the same level of attention. However, time and resources are limited. Therefore, an organization's efforts are best spent addressing the publics and issues that most affect its ability to achieve its goals. This includes planning for philanthropic activities, which should be based on organization strategic needs.

- **Think long term.** While a group of stakeholders may not be a high priority for an organization today, it may well become important in the future. For that reason, no group should be ignored. Even at a lower level of activity, a fledgling relationship is better than having none at all.

- **Pick your partners carefully.** When it comes to special events and strategic campaigns, partnerships with other stakeholders are often beneficial. However, the first two questions you should ask are do we need partners and, if so, who? The key consideration is the credibility and resources of the potential partners. If their presence improves the organization's ability to deliver strategic messages to the targeted publics, bring them on board. However, if the reputations of potential partners add nothing or even detract from message effectiveness, it is best to go it alone.

- **Mirror the community.** Organizations have a much greater chance of establishing strong relationships with community stakeholders if the organization reflects the ethnic, racial, and cultural makeup of the community it serves. This is especially important among the ranks of management. When an organization mirrors the community its serves, it sends a powerful message of inclusion.

- **Remember employee ambassadors.** An important part of community relations is employee relations. Employees serve as unofficial ambassadors to the community. How they feel about their employer and how their employer feels about the community will be communicated with or without the organization's blessing. Many companies encourage their employees to take an active role in the community through volunteerism and membership in civic groups.

When making the critical choices that go into developing an effective community relations program, organizations have to be true to themselves. An organization's values, as articulated in its mission and/or values statement, should govern its actions. Often this isn't as easy as it sounds, and it can be controversial. For example, several major corporations have risked the threat of consumer boycott because of antidiscrimination policies that provided employee benefits to gay and lesbian couples that were normally reserved for more traditional married couples. Actions speak louder than words. Doing the right thing—even when it isn't the easiest thing to do—is always good community relations.

Discussion Questions • • • • • • • • • • • • • • • • •

1. What are some of the different ways people define a community?

2. What is coorientation, and why is it important to public relations practitioners?

3. What is a special public? Why are some defined as inward while others are defined as outward?

4. In terms of its diversity, how is the demographic composition of the United States changing? What are some of the implications of this change?

5. What are the demographic and psychographic characteristics of the community in which you were born?

Key Terms • • • • • • • • • • • • • • • • •

coalitions, p. 142
community, p. 139
coorientation, p. 141
demographic community, p. 139
geographic community, p. 139

inward special publics, p. 142
outward special publics, p. 142
psychographic community, p. 139

relational dialectics, p. 142
social exchange theory, p. 142
special publics, p. 142
virtual communities, p. 139

Endnotes • • • • • • • • • • • • • • • • •

1. 2000–2001 American Community Survey Change Profile (San Francisco County and Omaha City). U.S. Census Bureau, Demographics Surveys Division. Online: www.census.gov.

2. Scott M. Cutlip, Allen H. Center, and Glen M. Broom, *Effective Public Relations,* 8th ed. (Upper Saddle River, NJ: Prentice Hall, 2000), 271–274.

3. J. W. Thibault and H. H. Kelley, *The Social Psychology of Groups* (New York: Wiley, 1952).

4. John A. Ledingham, Stephen D. Bruning, and Laurie J. Wilson, "Time as an Indicator of the Perceptions and Behavior of Members of a Key Public: Monitoring and Predicting Organization-Public Relationships," *Journal of Public Relations Research* (1999), vol. 11, no. 2, 167–183.

5. Former Congressman Carl Vinson relayed that story to author David Guth in November 1976 while Guth served as news director of a Milledgeville, Georgia, radio station.

6. "Habla Espanol? Your Company Will Soon Have to Do That," Knowledge @Wharton, The Wharton School, University of Pennsylvania. Online: http://knowledge.wharton.upenn.edu.

7. "Habla Espanol?"

8. "Habla Espanol?"

9. Darryl Fears. "Latinos or Hispanics? A Debate about Identity," *The Washington Post,* August 25, 2003, A01. Online: www.washingtonpost.com.

Letting Go

*Strategic Partnerships Help Celebrate
Colorado's Year of Trails*

For the folks who manage Colorado's state parks system, "A Little Help from My Friends" is more than just an old Beatles song your parents used to hum. It is a public relations philosophy.

One of the first lessons new practitioners learn is that there is almost never enough time, money, or staff to run public relations campaigns the way they would like. However, when you believe in your mission and can identify others who share that vision, a lot can be accomplished. Working together, like-minded individuals can create synergy, in which the results are much greater than if all of the parties had acted independently.

By building a broad coalition of public and private organizations during 2002, the Colorado Department of Natural Resources did more than celebrate the natural wonders of the Centennial State. The Colorado Year of Trails campaign also generated support for an important public policy initiative, created goodwill among groups that had not always agreed with one another, and boosted the political agenda of the agency and the state's governor.

Quality of Life

Nearly 11 million people visit Colorado's 40 state parks every year. And that doesn't take into account the millions of others who visit federal, local, and private parks and recreational facilities. CDNR's mission is "to develop, protect and enhance Colorado natural resources for the use and enjoyment of the state's present and future residents, as well as visitors to the state." This includes stewardship over the state's more than 11,000 miles of hiking trails.

According to a Great Outdoors Colorado study, 90 percent of Coloradans surveyed used the trails, and the typical household used the trails 78 times a year. While these numbers may seem high, State Parks Director Lyle Laverty said these figures include trails not maintained by the state, such as community trails that wind through local neighborhoods. "Almost anywhere you look, someone is walking the trails," he said.

Research has also shown that Colorado residents value their quality of life. Laverty believes the state's extensive trail system contributes to it by improving cardiovascular health, reducing health care costs, and increasing workplace productivity. "We want to make people aware of the unique system of parks and trails we have in Colorado and that it does, in fact, affect the quality of life," said Laverty.

More than 80 percent of Colorado's 4.3 million residents live along the Front Range, the area of the state east of the Rockies. However, a majority of the state's parks and trails lie in the mountains and to the west. For that reason, Gov. Bill Owens supported creation of the Colorado Front Range Trail, a hiking trail easily accessible to most of the state's population. It would stretch from Fort Collins near the Wyoming border in the north to Trinidad, Colo., near the New Mexico line in the south. In addition to including 250 miles of new trails, the Front Range Trail would incorporate 450 miles of existing community trail systems, linked at an estimated cost of $14–16 million.

Colorado, along with other states, had just completed a successful year-long celebration of state parks. Eager to demonstrate leadership in an issue important to the state's voters, the Owens administration was looking for a vehicle to launch the Front Range Trail initiative. In January 2002, just three months before its projected kickoff, the idea for a Colorado Year of Trails (CYOT) was born.

"All of these pieces came together," said Laverty. "The focus on the trails became an almost no-brainer."

The Value of Partnerships

With an abbreviated planning period and small staff comprised mostly of college interns, State Parks Public Affairs and Marketing Director Steven Hall knew he would have his hands full. And with a budget of only $75,000, Hall, who has since moved on to a position with the U.S. Bureau of Land Management, also knew that he would need the support of other public and private agencies.

"Unless you have limitless staff and resources, you have to learn to bring in partners," Hall said.

While many organizations share a love of Colorado's trails, they do not necessarily share the same values. For example, off-road vehicle enthusiasts are often at odds with those who want to restrict their access to the wilderness. Then there are the dozens of local, state, and federal agencies that approach their individual missions from unique perspectives. And, of course, there are commercial interests that directly and indirectly rely on state's natural resources for profits.

In the end, a coalition of 25 organizations came together as partners for CYOT. Additionally, a number of counties, municipalities, and civic groups participated in the campaign by sending letters of support, planning events, and distributing promotional materials. This coalition was achieved through the creation of objectives on which all the partners could agree. One was "to raise awareness of the role trails play in Colorado's quality of life while encouraging a sense of discovery and fun." Another was "to encourage and support the mission of our partners and the trails community." The campaign was also designed to promote the Front Range Trail, as well as volunteerism, stewardship, and trail etiquette.

"Learn to let go of some of the control of the campaign," Hall said. "If you have good partners and stakeholders, let them run with it. They will come up with much more creative ideas than you could have alone."

Publicity and Promotions

Standing in front of a climbing wall at an outdoor specialty supplies store in Denver, Gov. Owens kicked off CYOT on March 7. It would be the first of more than 200 CYOT events.

"Trails are vital to our healthy Colorado lifestyle, and they provide the perfect outdoor classroom for Coloradans to learn more about our incredible landscape," Gov. Owens said. "Enjoying a trail this year will provide the perfect opportunity to help our state and local economy while rediscovering Colorado."

Owens also announced plans for the Front Range Trail, calling it "an incredible resource for all Coloradans to enjoy." Hall said that linking the CYOT kickoff to the Front Range Trail helped generate more than 2 million impressions during the first two days of the campaign. "While the goals that we had for Year of the Trails were laudable, the fact that we were also kicking off this big effort to build a very important trail helped to generate a lot of media coverage," he said.

CDNR launched a CYOT Web site a few days before the kickoff. It included an event calendar and planning guide, fact sheets, Front Range Trail plan information, and links to partner organizations. It also identified the location of more than 100 trails at state parks. While the Web site generated approximately 15,000 hits during the campaign, Hall said it was an even more valuable tool for sharing information with the partner organizations.

Perhaps the most innovative aspect of the campaign was the distribution of 100,000 CYOT Trails Journals. According to Hall, the idea for the journal came from past experience at state parks, where a Year of the Parks passport had been very popular with families. Hikers were encouraged to record their trail experiences. The journals promoted trail etiquette and volunteerism. They also included contact information for partner organizations.

Twenty CYOT news releases and a number of media kits were distributed during the campaign, with a special push during National Trails Month in June. Two public service announcements sent to 55 Colorado radio stations generated 585 minutes of free airtime. More than a quarter-million promotional items featuring the CYOT logo—such as hats, hiking sticks, key chains, and T-shirts—were distributed at state parks, CYOT partners, and special events.

As might be expected in a huge effort such as this, not everything went as planned. For example, the kickoff event was delayed and eventually forced indoors by Colorado's notoriously rugged winter weather. But that was a minor inconvenience compared with the problems created by the state's worst-ever drought and

One of the popular aspects of the Colorado Year of Trails observance was the Trails Journal, which allowed visitors to state parks to record their experiences while hiking. (Courtesy of Colorado Department of Natural Resources)

forest fire season. At the very peak of the hiking and camping seasons, operations at approximately one of every three state parks were curtailed due to low water levels or nearby wildfires.

"By mid-July, everyone had much bigger things on their minds than trails," Hall said. "I had to focus on my day job."

By the Numbers

Organizers estimate that the CYOT campaign generated more than 50 million impressions during its six-month run. They also say that publicity and public service announcements generated $232,287 of advertising equivalency (see page 137). The campaign also came in under budget, spending only $66,214. However, these numbers do not begin to address the value of attracting and keeping volunteers.

"Budgets are so tight right now," Laverty said. "When you really begin to put a value on what those volunteers contribute and the significance they have on just the resources we have here in Colorado, it is truly phenomenal."

And lest we forget, there is benefit in being seen doing a job well. For state officials and agencies operating in a political environment, this is an important message to both taxpayers and state legislators. Hall said, "If you are going to do this stuff, you have to demonstrate to decision makers that what you are doing matters and that your constituencies matter."

Sources

Colorado Year of Trails media kits, postevent evaluations. Colorado Department of Natural Resources.
Colorado Department of Natural Resources Web site, http://parks.state.co.
Steven Hall, interview, August 6, 2003.
Lyle Laverty, interview, July 25, 2003.
U.S. Bureau of the Census Web site, www.census.gov.

case **7.2**

Teacher on the Trail

Wells Fargo Integrates Its Values with Alaska's Heritage

When Gunner Kaassen drove his dog sled team down an almost deserted First Avenue in Nome, Alaska, in 1925, he was in a race against death. Kaassen was the last of 20 sled dog team drivers to relay desperately needed diphtheria antitoxin serum the 674 miles along the Iditarod Trail from Nenana to Nome. Countless lives were saved because these "mushers" and their more than 150 dogs braved 80 mile-an-hour gales and wind chills of 100 degrees below zero to complete the trek in 127 hours and 30 minutes.

This act of heroism is celebrated every winter with the running of the Iditarod, a 1,049-mile dog sled race that draws participants from around the world. As one Nome newspaper writer noted at the start of the 2003 race, "Today's Iditarod is not just a race, but a celebration and commemoration of the bravery of the men and dogs that made the first run to save lives."

The cultural significance of the Iditarod was not lost on management of Wells Fargo Bank–Alaska, which saw it as an opportunity to introduce its services to a new territory and to connect with several strategically significant community publics.

Continuing a Tradition

San Francisco-based Wells Fargo is a diversified financial services company with more than $370 billion in assets and 136,000 employees. Wells Fargo has more than 3,000 banks—what it refers to as banking stores—in approximately two dozen states, including 51 stores in Alaska. The nation's largest retail home mortgage lender, Wells Fargo serves 4.4 million customers nationwide. According to company literature, Wells Fargo's combined retail and wholesale lending operations provide funding for approximately one of every eight homes financed annually within the United States.

In a statement of corporate values published by the company, Chairman and CEO Richard M. Kovacevich committed Wells Fargo to being "an active community leader in economic development, services that promote economic self-sufficiency, education, social services, and the arts. Wherever you go across Wells Fargo territory you'll see our team members rolling up their sleeves—on community fund raising campaigns, nonprofit boards, and community events."

That territory grew to include Alaska in June 2000, when Wells Fargo purchased the state's oldest and largest financial institution, National Bank of Alaska. NBA had been one of the major sponsors of the Iditarod for 15 years. Wells Fargo not only continued its support but also increased its sponsorship and committed to a five-year contract.

"The Iditarod sponsorship was something that was near and dear to our hearts," said Wells Fargo Bank–Alaska Assistant Vice President Debbie Grahek. "We felt that it showed strong support for a piece of Alaskan heritage and culture. The Iditarod represents the spirit that Alaskans have—that they will persevere, they will survive."

Teacher on the Trail

The first Iditarod Trail sled dog race was held in 1973. Since then, there has been steadily growing interest in the event, especially among educators. This attention helped spawn the Teacher on the Trail program in 1999. Each year, a teacher selected from a pool of applicants travels to Alaska for the race. As part of the program, the Teacher on the Trail develops a curriculum for use by elementary and secondary school students, and flies to various checkpoints along the course to file daily Internet reports on the progress of the race.

Cassandra Wilson, a fourth-grade teacher from Applegate Elementary School in Portland, Ore., was one of the teachers selected. She developed several Iditarod-based lesson plans covering subjects as varied as math, science, and the arts. One included the creation of a student play adapted from *Where's the Boss,* a book for beginning readers that focuses on the teamwork required for mushing. Wilson also carried a laptop computer, a modem, and a digital camera to record her experiences. An estimated 50,000 students—both in and outside Alaska—followed her daily accounts of the race online.

Wells Fargo took over the sponsorship of Teacher on the Trail with its acquisition of NBA. "One of the reasons we decided to sponsor it was because it fit with our interests in education," Grahek said. "We found that it had a world of potential."

One of the benefits of the sponsorship was the use of the Wells Fargo logo on the Iditarod Web site, on official publications, and at various race venues. One story in the *Anchorage Daily News,* the state's largest newspaper, included two color photos that prominently displayed the logo.

Classroom Kits

In an effort to promote Wells Fargo's race sponsorship, as well as the Teacher on the Trail program, 2,500 Iditarod Classroom Kits were produced for the first time in 2002 for distribution to every elementary school teacher along the trail. Additional kits were sent on request to teachers around the world. Materials in each kit included an overview flyer introducing the Teacher on the Trail, a full-color poster featuring the race's route map, an Iditarod trivia game, a coloring poster, and a catalog of educational materials available for purchase from race organizers. Another popular item was a Wells Fargo headband. The kits were promoted through school visits by the Teacher on the Trail, as well as through the posting of supporting materials on the race's official Web site. A self-mailing survey asking teachers to evaluate the materials and curriculum was included in the packet. Wells Fargo established a budget of $18,400 for the promotion.

To kick off the promotion, the Wells Fargo Bank–Alaska marketing staff made a presentation to 100 Anchorage School District principals and administrators. The educators were challenged to a game of Iditarod trivia, with Wells Fargo promotional items used as prizes. After obtaining permission to distribute the kits in school districts along the trail, the materials were mailed to elementary schools three weeks before the start of the race.

"The Iditarod is so popular among teachers as a teaching tool," said Michelle Nelson, Wells Fargo Bank–Alaska assistant vice president. "They are able to use it to

To help build relationships with Alaskan consumers, Wells Fargo lent its financial support to the state's most recognized event, the Iditarod. By sponsoring the Teacher on the Trail program and providing classroom materials, Wells Fargo also demonstrated its commitment to education. (The 2003 Iditarod Classroom Kit and related promotional materials are used with permission from Wells Fargo & Company.)

teach math, English, everything." The kits became so popular that teachers from outside Alaska requested them. "I really cannot believe the amount of enthusiasm that comes from people and especially from teachers outside of Alaska," Nelson said.

By the time of the 2003 race, Wells Fargo officials saw an opportunity to cross-promote their Banking on Our Future program. The cornerstone of the program is an interactive Web site, which encourages students to learn to manage their money, and includes lessons about banking basics, savings and checking accounts, budgeting, credit, and investing. Wells Fargo developed different modules for different age levels. In addition to the English language site, there is a parallel site for Spanish-speaking students.

The 2003 Iditarod Classroom Kits included information about Banking on Our Future, a CD-ROM (both Windows and Macintosh compatible) containing recommended curricula, and a Wells Fargo hand-held calculator.

"The objective of Wells Fargo Bank–Alaska is to support the people of Alaska and education efforts in Alaska," Nelson said. "With the Teacher on the Trail program, the classroom kit was just one more way we could leverage our sponsorship."

A Clash of Values

Although the Iditarod is a popular event among Alaskans, not everyone is enthusiastic. Animal rights groups have raised objections to the race, saying it unnecessarily places the dogs at risk. The clash of values was especially acute in 2003, when unseasonably warm weather and safety concerns prompted race organizers to add 70 miles to the course to avoid thin ice and melting snow.

"The move is simply to ensure that the race goes on, not that animals are not injured or killed," said Amy Rhodes, a spokesperson for People for the Ethical Treatment of Animals. Race opponents had counted at least 118 dog deaths during the 30-race history of the event. And while the rate has fallen in recent years, opponents say that even one sled dog death along the trail is too many.

Iditarod officials say they are committed to dog safety, pointing to the 35 volunteer veterinarians who monitor the dogs during the race. They also note other precautions, such as random drug testing and mandatory rest stops. Veteran musher Aaron Burmeister told the *Nome Nugget* that his dogs "are like family" and challenged PETA to come out and see "how healthy, happy, and excited" his dogs are.

Aware of the controversy, Wells Fargo officials have remained unwavering in their support of the race. "The bank wholeheartedly supports Iditarod," Nelson said. "We think they do a good job of dog safety.

"I think it is more an education issue—educating the public about it," she said.

Evaluation

Wells Fargo officials say the Iditarod Classroom Kits are a big success. After their initial distribution in 2002, bank officials say they received several calls from teachers expressing gratitude and requesting more materials. The Teacher on the Trail program received statewide media coverage, as well as some in the hometown media of each year's teacher participant. The program also received coverage in *NEA Today,* the magazine of the National Education Association. The Iditarod Web site received 120 million hits during the 10-day race. Race organizers reported receiving e-mails from teachers in schools worldwide. All of this was accomplished under budget—except for unexpected costs incurred when a photographer was weathered-in for two days in Bethel.

Sources

Brian Albright, "High Hopes for Mushers as XXXI Iditarod Begins," *Nome Nuggett,* March 6, 2003. Online: www.nomenuggett.com.

Don Bowers, "The Iditarod Sled Dog Race," Iditarod Trail Sled Dog Race Web site. Online: www.iditarod.com.

Debbie Grahek, interview, August 12, 2003.

Abby Haight, "A Teacher's Dogged Determination," *The Oregonian,* February 16, 2003. Online: www.oregonian.com.

Richard M. Lovacevich, "The Vision & Values of Wells Fargo." Wells Fargo Web site. Online: www.wellsfargo.com.

Michelle Nelson, interview, August 12, 2003.

Rachel D'Oro, "Activists Howl at Longer Race," Associated Press, *Anchorage Daily News,* March 1, 2003. Online: www.adn.com.

"The 1925 Serum Run to Nome," Iditarod Trail Sled Dog Race Web site. Online: www.iditarod.com.

"Wells Fargo Today: Company Fact Sheet, 1st quarter 2003," Wells Fargo Web site. Online: www.wellsfargo.com.

case 7.3

Fear the Turtle

The University of Maryland Rallies to Save the Diamondback Terrapin

To people other than fans of the Maryland Terrapins, the idea that anyone should "fear the turtle" might seem a ludicrous notion. The small, inoffensive reptile from which the University of Maryland's intercollegiate athletic teams derived their nickname doesn't appear to be a likely candidate to generate strong emotion. In fact, it used to be that *fear* and *turtle* seldom appeared in the same sentence. Even Maryland's athletics department recognized the image problem in the 1990s when it changed its Terps logo from a scrawny, smiling, and friendly tortoise to a buff and defiant ninja turtle—prompting *Time* magazine to proclaim that the era of "No More Mister Nice Mascot" had arrived.

But Testudo the Terrapin is not all that has changed.

What was once a grass-roots rallying cry for Maryland sports fans has taken on a new meaning. "Fear the Turtle" has become an integral part of the branding of one of the nation's leading universities as well as a means for creative community outreach.

An Endangered Species

To set the record straight, if any creature has something to fear, it is the diamondback terrapin (*Malaclemys terrapin*). Native to the shores of Chesapeake Bay, it is distinguished by the diamond-shaped, concentric rings on the scutes of its upper shell. Marguerite Whilden, a conservation specialist with the Maryland Department of Natural Resources, describes it as "a magnificent creature that charms even the most seasoned waterman with its penetrating gaze and seemingly perpetual smile."

The terrapin has been under almost constant assault since the first English settlements in Maryland in 1632. Colonists roasted the abundant and easy-to-catch turtles over hot coals. Before the Civil War, landowners frequently fed the diamondbacks to their slaves and indentured servants. Later in the 19th century, turtles came into vogue as a delicacy, especially in stew laced with cream and sherry. According to state archivists, terrapin harvests in Maryland topped 89,000 pounds in 1891. The diamondback terrapin was hunted almost into extinction before laws were enacted to protect it.

Despite these restrictions, the assault continued. Human development along the heavily populated Chesapeake watershed has severely limited the terrapin's natural habitat. Natural predators such as ducks, crows, and herons also threaten its eggs and hatchlings. Scientists have estimated that of the approximately 2,000 eggs a female terrapin lays in her 40- to 50-year lifetime, only one reaches the age of reproduction.

The University of Maryland's association with the diamondback terrapin dates back to football coach H. Curley Byrd and the class of 1933. Feeling that the university needed an official mascot, Byrd nominated the diamondback terrapin. Graduating seniors donated a bronze terrapin statute they christened Testudo. Today it stands watch over the campus' large central mall from its pedestal in front of the main library. Students often stop by Testudo on their way to exams and touch his nose for good luck.

Through the years, sports writers have shortened the team's moniker from Terrapins to Terps. As the university's athletic programs have gained prominence by winning national championships in football, basketball, and lacrosse, so has the school's unusual mascot. In what would later prove to be a fortunate move, the Maryland General Assembly, at the request of university officials, made the diamondback terrapin the official state reptile and the official mascot of the University of Maryland College Park in 1994.

A Shell Game

The history behind the "Fear the Turtle" rallying cry is less clear. Many have laid claim to its creation. The *Baltimore Sun* credits Drew Elburn, a Baltimore computer consultant, with dreaming up the slogan. Elburn said he first used the slogan on a hand-made sign during a nationally televised basketball game. "People started hooting and hollering," he told the newspaper. "Then my cell phone starts ringing and people are telling me [broadcaster] Dick Vitale saw me and now he's screaming 'Fear the Turtle, baby!' "

As the slogan caught fire, so did the battle to claim its ownership. Elburn had registered "Fear the Turtle" with the U.S. Patent and Trademark Office, and the university wanted it as its own. "I thought it would be a neat thing to broaden the university's interests beyond sports," said Brian Darmody, the university's assistant vice president for research and economic development. "I wanted to make it a rallying cry for other things at the university and to highlight some of our research and conservation programs."

Elburn quickly ceded the rights to the slogan to the university for a relatively small fee and acknowledgment that he, in fact, was the creator. However, the saga didn't end there. A second company that specializes in abandoned trademark claims filed a competing application. However, officials in the patent office took judicial notice that the diamondback terrapin's status as official state reptile and university mascot had been enshrined in state law. "Many people thought it was trivial legislation at the time it was passed," Darmody said. "As it turned out, it had practical value that helped us in our trademark litigation."

Fear the Turtle

With trademark questions resolved and Fear the Turtle merchandise flowing off store shelves, Darmody approached the state DNR with a novel idea: Why not dedicate a portion of the licensing revenues from these sales toward preservation of turtle habitat? Normally, retailers pay schools 8 percent of each item's wholesale price for the use of a team name or logo. To raise additional funds for turtle habitat, UM tacked another 2 percent on Fear the Turtle merchandise licensing fees. While some of the additional funds were earmarked to cover trademark litigation costs, 75 percent of it went toward research and field programs administered by the DNR.

The campaign kicked off in June 2002, just two months after the school had won its first national championship in men's basketball. UM Vice President and Provost William Destler said, "We believe establishing a partnership with DNR and leveraging interest in the university coming from a national championship season for an important conservation program is consistent with the university's statewide role in research and service."

The initial project included support for a senior UM biological sciences student to carry out fieldwork at three terrapin monitoring stations. The student was also slated to assist in mentoring Maryland elementary schoolchildren in the raising of terrapins. Darmody estimates that the campaign raised approximately $70,000 to support these programs during its first year.

"The diamondback terrapin is more than just a beloved state symbol; it is also a critical part of our environment, and they must be protected," said then Maryland Gov. Parris N. Glendening. "We not only want people to fear the turtle, but, working together, we want terrapins to not fear that Marylanders are going to destroy their homes."

The Turtle Roars

As the Fear the Turtle campaign evolved, so did the use of creative and, at times, unusual media. A car featuring the terrapin logo on the hood was entered in NASCAR's Busch Series and driven by Donnie Neuenberger. Darmody said that sponsorship generated another $20,000 through the sale of miniature car replicas at car shows and other personal appearances. In an even less traditional medium, a Southern Maryland farmer carved a 15-acre cornfield into a maze the shape of the Maryland Terrapin. Unfortunately, Mother Nature did not show proper fear for the turtle, as storms damaged the crop art beyond repair. In what would be another unusual but highly visible medium, Darmody said officials are exploring the possibility of a Fear the Turtle state automobile license tag.

"This thing has certainly taken a lot of twists and turns," Darmody said.

By fall 2003, use of the popular slogan had taken a new turn. Fear the Turtle became the centerpiece of a campaign highlighting the recognition of UM as one of the nation's 20 best public universities according to *U.S News & World Report*. Including graduate programs, the magazine ranked 67 of the university's academic programs among the top 25 in their fields.

This new campaign featured the slogan in both online and printed materials, as well as in a series of television public service announcements. "Fear the Turtle has typically been associated with our athletic teams," the UM Web site proclaimed. "But as the university continues to thrive in virtually every area—the quality of our students, our nationally ranked programs, our renowned faculty—we find that competitors Fear the Turtle not just on the playing field, but in labs and classrooms too."

Symbolic of this confident attitude was a public service announcement in which, through the magic of special effects, a diamondback turtle roars like a lion. The spot aired as part of Maryland football and basketball telecasts.

Although the Fear the Turtle campaign may have been born of happenstance, its impact has been significant. More than money, it raised public awareness about

Fear the Turtle.

Maryland is on a path to meet its destiny. We're already among the **Top 20 national public universities.** More National Merit, National Achievement and Distinguished Scholars in the state choose University of Maryland over all other public and private institutions combined. In just five years, our incoming freshman class average **GPA soared from 3.5 to 3.9.** Our top-notch faculty includes six Pulitzer Prize winners, a Nobel Prize winner and scores of Fulbright scholars. But, if you think that's all we're destined to accomplish, then you don't know your Terrapins. **ROAR!**

UNIVERSITY OF
MARYLAND
www.maryland.edu

What started as a handmade sign at a basketball game became a rallying cry for the University of Maryland, the centerpiece of a branding campaign, and an opportunity to save the diamondback terrapin—the official state reptile. (Courtesy of University of Maryland College Park)

the need to preserve terrapin habitats. It also linked the state's leading public university to one of Maryland's most enduring symbols.

The level of public awareness generated by the campaign became evident following the August 2003 layoff of conservation specialist Marguerite Whilden as part of a $4.5 million cut in the DNR budget. Newspaper readers had come to know Whilden as "the turtle lady." When she lost her job, it was big news. Marylanders were quick to let their public officials know that they felt survival of the turtles was important. Defensive DNR officials found themselves scrambling for new funding sources and reassuring citizens that the state's commitment to turtle conservation would continue.

"I think the animal was a good vehicle to engage the public in our work," Whilden said.

What had started as a simple handmade sign at a basketball game just a few years earlier had become a force in Maryland politics. Perhaps it is just one more reason to fear the turtle.

Sources

Carol Casey, "Success Yields Help for Terrapins," *College Park,* University of Maryland magazine (Fall 2002), 8.

Kevin Cowherd, "Terrapin Shell Game Is Over," *The Baltimore Sun,* March 29, 2001. Online: www.sunspot.net.

Brian Darmody, interview, September 16, 2003.

"Fear the Turtle! Save a Terrapin," University of Maryland news release, June 26, 2002.

Darragh Johnson, "Tide Turns for Terrapins; State Budget Cuts Don't Thwart Symbol's Protection," *The Washington Post,* August 21, 2003, T02. Online: www.washingtonpost.com.

"Maryland at a Glance—State Symbols," Maryland State Archives Web site. Online: www.mdarchives.state.md.us.

ACT file # 7   • • • • • • • • • • • • • • • • • • •

Coorientation

Whether you call the world's most popular sport soccer or—like most people in the world—call it football, everyone can agree that one of the game's most exciting moments comes during a penalty kick. That's when the goalkeeper, standing alone on the goal line, goes one-on-one against an opponent intent on scoring. Put yourself in the mind of the goalkeeper in those tension-filled seconds just before the shot is taken. At that critical moment, the goalie is trying to figure out what the kicker is planning to do. Goalies also play a mind game that goes something like "I wonder if the kicker is thinking that I am thinking that the kicker is thinking. . . ."

The goalkeeper may not know it, but that moment of guessing and second-guessing is an example of an important communication theory known as coorientation. It is the belief that people act not only on the basis of their own perceptions, but also on what they believe are the perceptions of others. It is an idea first articulated by researchers Jack M. McLeod and Steven H. Chaffee in 1973, and it has important implications for the practice of public relations.[1]

There have been many examples—too numerous to count—where organizations and individuals have misinterpreted the intentions of key stakeholders. These missteps can have a wide spectrum of consequences, ranging from inconvenience and waste to conflict and failure. Avoiding these kinds of problems requires an understanding of coorientation, the publics we are trying to influence, and ourselves.

For example, think of the problems that a social service agency might have in trying to establish a drug rehabilitation center in a residential neighborhood. The success or failure of the venture will depend on the perceptions of the key players in the drama: the agency and the neighborhood's residents. If the agency underestimates the neighborhood's concerns about the center or fails to identify any misperceptions residents may have, the result could be a political controversy that kills the project. However, if the agency overestimates the neighbors' concerns and perceptions, it could engage in costly, time-consuming, and potentially antagonistic strategies that are counterproductive.

Understanding an organization's coorientation with its stakeholders on a particular issue involves asking four questions:

1. What is our organization's view of this issue?
2. What is the stakeholder's view of this issue?
3. What does our organization *think* is the stakeholder's view, and does this agree with reality?
4. What does the stakeholder *think* our organization's view is, and does this agree with reality?

Advanced Critical Thinking

When asking these questions, it is important to remember that the various parties may define the issues differently. Turning to our scenario for an example, the social services agency may see the need for a neighborhood drug rehabilitation center as a public health issue. However, some residents, concerned about introducing substance abusers into their neighborhood, may define the issue as a matter of public safety. Both may be valid points for discussion. However, if the parties involved don't know each other's frame of reference, they could end up talking past each other.

This is why McLeod and Chaffee wrote that accuracy, which they defined as the extent to which an organization's estimate of the stakeholder's views actually matches those views, should be a major focus of any communication program. All parties must know precisely what the other is thinking. A common understanding of areas of agreement and disagreement is a crucial first step in building mutually beneficial relationships.

In our neighborhood drug rehabilitation center scenario, the social service agency's first step should be to ask itself the four questions listed above. If it doesn't know the answers, it should conduct research. Even if the agency *thinks* it knows all the answers, coorientation research remains the best option. After all, how will it *know* that it knows without first testing all assumptions?

Like the goalkeeper at the beginning of this discussion, coorientation gives practitioners a fighting chance to succeed. Conducting a public relations campaign without coorientation is a lot like the goalie taking the field wearing a blindfold.

Discussion Questions

1. What are some research methods one can use to conduct coorientation research?

2. Is coorientation an issue with internal publics such as employees or members? Explain your reasons.

3. How do changes in a community's demographic and/or psychographic composition influence coorientation?

4. Cite an example from the case studies in this chapter in which coorientation research did or could have made a difference.

Endnote

1. Jack M. McLeod and Steven H. Chaffee, "Interpersonal Approaches to Communications Research," (March–April 1973), in *Interpersonal Perception and Communication,* a special edition of *American Behavioral Scientist,* vol. 16, no. 4, 483–488.

CHAPTER 8

Consumer Relations

A nnual business expenditures in the United States total about $1.5 trillion. That's a lot of money.

Government expenditures account for about $2.5 trillion a year. That's even more money.

But consumer expenditures—that's all of us paying for music downloads, buying jeans, and shelling out for a tank of gas—total about $8 trillion annually. That's a huge amount of money—more than two-thirds of the U.S. economy.[1]

The average household in the United States earns about $50,000 before taxes—and almost $41,000 goes right back out the door in consumer expenditures.[2] (See Table 8.1.) "Nothing props up the economy more than consumers," reports the *New York Times*.[3]

table 8.1 *Average U.S. Household Income and Expenditures, 2002*

Total household income	$49,430
Food	$5,375
Housing	$13,283
Apparel and services	$1,749
Transportation	$7,759
Health care	$2,350
Entertainment	$2,079
Insurance and pensions	$3,899

Source: Data from U.S. Bureau of Labor Statistics Web site, www.bls.gov.

As much as the authors of this book respect critical thinking, we'd be the first to concede that you don't need a Ph.D. in economics to reach an important conclusion: Most organizations must build relationships with this financial juggernaut, the U.S. **consumer.**

Consumer Publics

The availability of medical care for babies still in the womb helps illustrate the difficulty of defining consumer publics: Most of us were consumers—of medical services, in this case—even before we were born. And we remain consumers for the rest of our lives. Of the almost 300 million citizens of the United States, the consumer public comprises—you guessed it, almost 300 million people. We can segment that huge public with variables such as income, geography, race, gender, and age—and with customer data such as frequency of purchases—but the fact remains that everyone you meet is a consumer.

Despite the size and diversity of the overall consumer public, we do know a great deal about its values and habits. For example, the No. 1 New Year's resolution for U.S. adults in 2004 was to get out of debt. For the first time, that financial pledge squeaked past losing weight in an annual survey.[4]

We also know that Americans prefer to shop on weekends (excluding online shopping), and that prime-time spending hours are 2–4 p.m. On those weekend sprees, shoppers spend $78 on average—compared with $67 per trip on weekdays.[5]

All that shopping, however, doesn't automatically translate into loyalty: Fifty-five percent of consumers feel only a lukewarm commitment to stores they frequent, citing lack of customer service as a top problem.[6] Research shows that one dissatisfied customer will, on average, tell eight to 10 other people about poor service.[7]

In his book *The Loyalty Effect,* consumer researcher Frederick Reichheld reports that most businesses could increase profits anywhere from 25 to 100 percent simply by retaining 5 percent more of their current customers.[8] Attracting new customers costs six times as much as keeping current customers.[9] In fact, 70 percent of customers with complaints will remain loyal if their problems are solved quickly and satisfactorily.[10]

Trends in Consumer Behavior

To celebrate its 25th anniversary in 2003, *American Demographics* magazine identified six trends that had characterized consumer behavior over the past 25 years—and, the publication predicted, would continue to do so for the next 25.[11]

The Growing Power of Women

Women outnumber men by a few percentage points in the U.S. population[12]—but they control a disproportionate amount of wealth when it comes to consumer spending. Martha Barletta, author of *Marketing to Women,* notes that women account for 80 percent of consumer spending in the United States. By 2010, says Barletta, women will control 50 percent of the nation's private wealth.[13]

An Increasingly Diverse Marketplace

The facts speak for themselves. Ethnic minorities in the United States are growing in size and purchasing power. "Companies that are currently working to understand emerging ethnic groups will have a huge advantage over the companies that wait another 10 years," says Mark Seferian of EchoboomX, a Denver-based marketing agency.[14]

Hispanic citizens are the country's largest minority group, totaling almost 13 percent of the national population.[15] By 2007, the annual purchasing power of Hispanic citizens will be an estimated $926 billion.[16]

Black citizens currently are 12 percent of the U.S. population, making them the second largest minority group.[17] By 2007, the annual purchasing power of black citizens will be an estimated $853 billion.[18]

Today, Americans of Asian ancestry are 4 percent of the nation's population.[19] By 2007, the annual purchasing power of Asian Americans will be an estimated $455 billion.[20]

Native Americans are approximately 1 percent of the U.S. population. By 2007, the annual purchasing power of Native Americans will be an estimated $57 billion.[21]

Census Bureau Director Louis Kincannon tells the League of United Latin American Citizens that new Census Bureau estimates show Hispanics as the largest minority group in the United States. By 2007, the annual purchasing power of Hispanic citizens will be an estimated $926 billion. (Courtesy of the U.S. Census Bureau)

Diversity extends beyond ethnicity, of course. New York-based advertising agency Double Platinum estimates that in the United States, a gay and lesbian population of approximately 20 million citizens spent almost $450 billion in 2003.[22] "Whatever the product or service," says Double Platinum Creative Director Arthur Korant, "as with other multicultural segments, the gay and lesbian segment appreciates being spoken to in its own tone of voice."[23]

The Entrepreneurial Explosion

American Demographics predicted in 1979 that the advent of desktop computers might lead to an increase of entrepreneurs able to work from their homes.[24] Today, almost 24 million Americans use personal computers in home-based businesses that they launched. Another 23 million work for organizations but remain at home, using computers and telephones to communicate with the main office—a concept known as **telecommuting.**[25]

Health Care, Aging, and Alternative Medicine

In 2000, 46 million Americans were aged 60 or older. By 2025, that number will almost double, to an estimated 89 million.[26] Spending on health care products increased more than any other household expenditures category from 2000 to 2001—up almost 8 percent.[27]

Rising Demand for Adult Education

Continuing education for adults is expanding through so-called distance learning— at-home college courses offered via the Internet. In the workplace itself, a desire for continuing education and training characterizes almost a quarter of workers age 35 and younger.[28]

Surging Demand for Luxury Goods

In a 2003 article titled "Why Americans Must Keep Spending," the *New York Times* reported that yesterday's luxuries, such as second cars and expensive child care, had become today's necessities—and that new luxuries, such as cell phones, cable TV, and Internet access, were rapidly becoming indispensable. "These lifestyle and expenditure norms have risen pretty dramatically for the middle class and the upper middle class," said Juliet Schor, author of *The Overspent American.*[29]

Another trend worth considering is the growth of **e-commerce,** the purchasing of goods and services via the Internet. Although more than 90 percent of e-commerce involves business-to-business transactions (see Chapter 9), the remaining portion—consumer spending—still accounted for more than $70 billion in 2001.[30] As online shopping becomes easier and more secure, that number has grown every year. During the 2003 holiday season, online purchases totaled $18.5

billion, a 35 percent jump over 2002 figures. Top holiday product categories included clothing, toys, video games, and consumer electronics.[31] As we note in Chapter 14, however, e-commerce represents only a fraction—approximately 2 percent—of total retail sales in the United States.

Building Relationships with Consumers

When public relations practitioners build relationships with consumers, they participate in the discipline known as **marketing.** Marketing is the process of researching, creating, refining, and promoting a product and distributing it to targeted consumers. When public relations practitioners participate in the promotional phase of marketing, their efforts are known as **marketing public relations.**

In the promotional phase of marketing, advertising professionals often join public relations practitioners. **Advertising,** of course, is the process of creating and sending a persuasive message through controlled media, allowing the sender, for a price, to dictate message, placement, and frequency.

When the strategies of public relations, advertising, marketing, and sales join in a coordinated communications campaign, the process is known as **integrated marketing communications,** or IMC. IMC strives to send one clear message through a variety of media, often to individual consumers. New technology, such as computer databases and interactive media, helps IMC practitioners build relationships with small groups or even single consumers.

An enduring misperception among some communication professionals is the belief that public relations is merely a subset of marketing—that all business communication eventually focuses on selling products to consumers. However, in a landmark study of excellence in public relations, the Research Foundation of the International Association of Business Communicators concluded that public relations and marketing are, and should remain, separate but related disciplines: "The public relations function of excellent organizations exists separately from the marketing function, and excellent public relations departments are not subsumed into the marketing function."[32] A separate panel of public relations and marketing experts, convened in 1991, similarly concluded that the two professions are "separate and equal, but related functions" that should exist in separate departments.[33] In IMC, public relations joins aspects of marketing to build relationships with consumers, but public relations is not part of marketing. As the case studies in this book illustrate, public relations practitioners work with a host of publics besides consumers.

The Legal Environment

Various federal agencies regulate marketing communications, and, like advertisers, public relations practitioners must comply with the law. The Federal Trade Commission prohibits false or misleading product publicity. The Food and Drug Administration regulates the disclosure of information about foods and health-related products and, like the FTC, prohibits misleading product publicity. As noted in Chapter 5, the Securities and Exchange Commission protects consumers when they purchase stock, prohibiting companies from distributing false or misleading information regarding their performance. The SEC also forbids the withholding of essential information regarding company plans and performance.

Tactics of Marketing Public Relations

The varied tactics that create an IMC campaign are known as a **marketing mix.** Public relations practitioners can supply a variety of consumer-oriented tactics to an integrated campaign:

• **Product-oriented news releases and media kits:** Because news coverage can supply a third-party endorsement—an independent judgment that a new product is newsworthy—public relations practitioners strive to place product stories in relevant media.

• **Special events:** Attention-grabbing occurrences, such hiring a radio DJ to broadcast outside a new store, not only can gain the media's notice but also can appeal directly to participating consumers.

• **Open houses and tours:** Like special events, inviting consumers and news media into interesting facilities can gain attention and build relationships.

• **Bill inserts:** Few customers like to open bills, so some companies soften the blow with insert sheets containing special offers about company products.

• **Responses to consumer contacts:** Unlike the actions listed above, this tactic is reactive—yet it may be the most important marketing public relations tactic of all. When a consumer contacts a company, whether via phone, U.S. mail, e-mail, or instant messaging—some companies now sponsor instant messaging dialogues with customers through their Web sites[34]—the company must respond as quickly as possible. Remember the point made earlier in this chapter: Displeased by poor customer service, more than half of consumers feel little loyalty to particular companies.

As consumer publics change, no doubt marketing public relations tactics will change as well. New practitioners should understand traditional consumer relations tactics—but they also must be ready to meet evolution with innovation.

The great challenge for consumer relations during the next 25 years, say the editors of *American Demographics,* will involve deciphering "the consumer kaleidoscope" and "devising marketing campaigns that appeal to many demographic segments."[35] American consumers have indeed become a kaleidoscope, a constantly shifting pattern of colors that come together to form a unity from diversity. Discovering who these consumers are and what they want—and determining how public relations can work with marketing to form effective IMC campaigns—will provide ample critical thinking opportunities for a new generation of public relations practitioners.

Discussion Questions
······························

1. If everyone is a consumer, in what ways can you segment the U.S. consumer public?

2. In your opinion, why do women dominate consumer spending in the United States?

3. In your opinion, what changes in public relations and marketing will the increasing percentage of older Americans prompt?

4. What is your experience with e-commerce? What promotes its growth? What inhibits its growth?

5. How would you respond to an acquaintance who says, "Oh, public relations—that's part of marketing, isn't it?"

Key Terms
······························

advertising, p. 169
consumer, p. 166
e-commerce, p. 168
integrated marketing
   communications, p. 169

marketing, p. 169
marketing mix, p. 170
marketing public relations,
   p. 169
telecommuting, p. 168

Endnotes
······························

1. Louis Uchitelle, "Why Americans Must Keep Spending," *The New York Times,* December 1, 2003. Online: Lexis-Nexis.

2. "Consumer Expenditures in 2002," Bureau of Labor Statistics news release, November 21, 2003. Online: www.bls.gov.

3. Uchitelle.

4. "28% of Americans Say Getting out of Debt Is Their Top New Year's Resolution," Cambridge Consumer Credit Index news release, January 8, 2004. Online: Lexis-Nexis.

5. "Shop around the Clock," *American Demographics* (September 2003), 18.

6. Sandra Yin, "Chronic Shoppers," *American Demographics* (December 2003/January 2004), 13.

7. "Getting Close to Your Customer," *Business Line,* December 19, 2002. Online: Lexis-Nexis.

8. Frederick Reichheld, *The Loyalty Effect* (Boston: Harvard Business School Press, 1996), 33.

9. "Getting Close to Your Customer."

10. "Getting Close to Your Customer."

11. Peter Francese, "Consumers Today," *American Demographics* (April 2003), 28–29.

12. Francese.

13. Trendsight Web site, www.trendsight.com. SalesOverlays Web site, www.salesoverlays.com.

14. Alison Stein Wellner, "The Next 25 Years," *American Demographics* (April 2003), 26.

15. "How to Succeed in Multicultural Marketing: A Special Supplement to *American Demographics,*" *American Demographics* (November 2003), 3.

16. "How to Succeed in Multicultural Marketing," 6.

17. "How to Succeed in Multicultural Marketing," 3.

18. "How to Succeed in Multicultural Marketing," 6.

19. "How to Succeed in Multicultural Marketing," 3.

20. "How to Succeed in Multicultural Marketing," 6.

21. "How to Succeed in Multicultural Marketing," 3.

22. Double Platinum Web site, www.plangeapartners.com.

23. "How to Succeed in Multicultural Marketing," 13.

24. Francese, 28.

25. Sandra Yin, "No Shows," *American Demographics* (November 2003), 11.

26. Wellner, 24.

27. "Consumer Expenditures in 2002."

28. "SHRM/CNNfn Job Satisfaction Survey Says More Employees Satisfied with Benefits at Large Organizations versus Small," Society for Human Resource Management news release, December 4, 2003. Online: www.shrm.org.

29. Uchitelle.

30. "E-Stats," 2003 U.S. Census Bureau report. Online: www.census.gov.

31. "Online Spending up 35 Percent over 2002," Goldman Sachs news release, January 5, 2004. Online: Lexis-Nexis.

32. William P. Ehling, Jon White, and James E. Grunig, "Public Relations and Marketing Practices," in *Excellence in Public Relations and Communication Management,* ed. James E. Grunig (Hillsdale, NJ: Lawrence Erlbaum Associates, 1992), 390.

33. Glen M. Broom, Martha M. Lauzen, and Kerry Tucker, "Public Relations and Marketing: Dividing the Conceptual Domain and Operational Turf," *Public Relations Review* (Fall 1991), 223–224.

34. "Should You IM with Customers?" *Sales & Marketing Management* (May 2003), 21.

35. Wellner, 26.

Purple Passion

Jack Horner Communications Catches up with a Leading Ketchup

Kermit the Frog, from television's long-running *Sesame Street,* warbled his way into the hearts of millions with the song "It's Not Easy Being Green." But in 2001, the public relations team at Jack Horner Communications of Pittsburgh was singing a different song: "It's Not Easy Beating Green."

Why would one of the nation's top agencies sing the blues? It all started with the color purple.

In 2000, JHC and H. J. Heinz Company, best known as the producer of best-selling Heinz Tomato Ketchup, scored one of the market coups of the new millennium by introducing green ketchup. In less than a year, kids' demand for the new product had made competitors—well, green with envy. With its factories working around the clock to keep up with demand, Heinz sold more than 10 million bottles of the new product. And now, the ketchup king wanted Jack Horner Communications to score another hit with the color purple.

Actually, instead of singing the blues, agency president Jack Horner saw the new color as a golden opportunity. "If you're not having fun, you're doing it wrong," Horner said.

The Gross-Out Factor

Fortunately, Heinz wasn't seeking another 10-million-bottle extravaganza. Marketers at the $10 billion-a-year Pittsburgh-based company understood that part of the success from the green gusher grew from kids' realization that ketchup didn't have to be red. That realization couldn't be duplicated. But Heinz still had lofty goals: It wanted to sell 1 million bottles of purple ketchup and increase market share to 60 percent. And it wanted JHC to help develop and execute the master plan.

Heinz conducts its own market research, much of which is confidential. But for JHC, Heinz opened its files on the undeniable target market: Kids, especially, ages 8 through 12, consume almost 5 billion ounces of ketchup annually. Heinz research showed that green ketchup had succeeded because, in addition to the novelty, kids loved decorating their food and grossing out their parents. Now that the shock value of green had receded, Heinz research showed that kids wanted a new color—and they were making their preference known.

"Literally thousands of people called, wrote or e-mailed us demanding a new Heinz EZ Squirt color," said Casey Keller, Heinz's managing director for ketchup, condiments, and sauces. "The vast majority of kids asked for purple. And when kids tell us something, we listen."

Given that preference, JHC and Heinz consulted the Color Marketing Group, a nonprofit association of designers that studies the use of colors in marketing, to ensure that purple would appeal to both genders. "Purple is color with attitude that appeals to kids of all ages and is equally liked by both boys and girls," reported association President Jay de Sibour.

Finally, the research also revealed the obvious: Kids don't buy ketchup on their own. JHC expanded the target audience to parents with kids and began exploring which media—such as NBC's *Today* show—were favored by parents.

Grab Your Buns, and Brace Yourself

Research includes gathering information about a client's values—and JHC knew that Heinz is like an artistic accountant: It demands both creativity and responsibility. Heinz wanted a clever campaign with clear goals.

"We look for people who are highly creative, motivated, very quick in responding to change and good with the media," said Debbie Foster, director of corporate communications at Heinz. "We want great ideas, great service, and great relations with the media."

To achieve that greatness, Heinz gave JHC a budget of $100,600.

JHC responded with specificity and innovation. Under the overall goal of selling 1 million bottles, the agency established these objectives to reach its target audience:

- Accumulate at last 150 million media impressions (exposures to readers, viewers, or listeners) and a minimum of 500 media stories
- Secure at least 100 television stories (including five national TV shows)
- Obtain an advertising equivalency of more than $2 million (see ACT File #6)
- Increase Heinz ketchup's market share to 60 percent

To meet Heinz's demand for creativity, JHC decided to tantalize journalists and families alike. "No self-respecting member of the media likes to be told that he or she cannot have *all* the information," Horner explained.

Playing off that human desire to know, JHC created a two-phase campaign. Phase One would create mystery: Heinz would market a new color of ketchup—but which? Phase Two would blitz the media with the answer.

Phase One launched June 19 with a news release containing a memorable lead: "Grab your buns, and brace yourselves. A new addition to the growing Heinz

Heinz EZ Squirt Funky Purple
B-Roll Storyboard

Communications tactics to promote Heinz Funky Purple ketchup included a video news release with b-roll (unedited footage). A storyboard indicates the VNR's b-roll shots. (Courtesy of H. J. Heinz Company and Jack Horner Communications Inc.)

EZ Squirt color palette is just around the corner." The news release revealed only that the new color would be orange, purple, hot pink, or yellow, and it directed kids to www.EZSquirt.com for more information. The news release closed by teasing readers, promising only to "satisfy their condiment curiosity" within the next few weeks.

Distributed through Business Wire, the news release was accompanied by a photograph of a shadowy EZ Squirt ketchup bottle, flanked by its red and green cousins but bearing no label—only a stark white question mark. After the news release, Heinz and JHC refused to divulge more details.

Forty-two days later, on July 31, JHC launched Phase Two, which solved the mystery. The new color would be Funky Purple.

"From a creative brand like Heinz EZ Squirt, media would expect more than just a press release," said Horner. "So our in-house designers created a customized press kit box to grab the interest of any who saw it and to provide a full-size bottle of the new Heinz EZ Squirt Funky Purple."

Covered with question marks, the box opened to reveal a purple interior, the new product itself, a news release headlined "Heinz Ketchup Gets Funky with New Purple EZ Squirt," and two photos: one of the product itself and another of a young Asian American girl decorating lunches (see page 20), reflecting both the fun of the new product and the commitment of Heinz and JHC to diversity. JHC also distributed the news release and photos through Business Wire.

JHC particularly targeted television, sending blind-taste-test baskets to national television shows. To assure journalists that the new product tasted as great as Heinz's other ketchup products, the baskets contained samples of Funky Purple ketchup as well as Heinz' traditional ketchup. The baskets also contained dip cups, chips, blindfolds, and instructions on how to conduct an "Are Your Taste Buds Color Blind?" taste test. Finally, each basket included a news release and promotional photos.

JHC also targeted television though satellite distribution of video footage. The video contained segments of the product and kids, both a boy and a girl, having fun decorating their food.

"Television is still king in terms of reaching the most eyeballs," reported *PR News.* "When Heinz introduced its new Funky Purple EZ Squirt ketchup, the company knew it wanted to reach media that would attract millions of consumers—which meant going after TV reporters."

To cap that media blitz, JHC personnel telephoned each major media outlet that received a media kit or taste test basket. Staff members ensured that journalists had received the materials, promoted the newsworthiness of the story, and answered questions. And then, collectively, they took a deep breath and waited.

Purple Turns to Silver

JHC had early indications that the plan was working. After Phase One and the launch of the mystery, *PR Week* magazine declared the news release a "Play of the Week." The news release generated 55 stories in newspapers and magazines and 10 television stories.

After Phase Two rolled out on July 31, there was no mystery about instant success. The campaign not only met its goals; it shattered them:

- Instead of accumulating 150 million media impressions and a minimum of 500 media stories, the campaign generated 328 million impressions and almost 2,000 media stories.
- Instead of securing 100 television stories, the campaign generated more than 1,000 TV stories. National coverage was gained on the *Today* show, *Live! with Regis & Kelly, ABC World News Now, CNN Headline News,* and several other national news and entertainment programs.
- Instead of obtaining an advertising equivalency of $2 million, the campaign generated $6.4 million in ad equivalency.
- The campaign helped raise Heinz ketchup's market share to 60 percent.

With those objectives met, the sales goal of 1 million bottles was reached—and exceeded. From August 1 to Nov. 15, 2001, Heinz sold 2.5 million bottles of Funky Purple EZ Squirt.

That kind of success gains notice. For its outstanding work in promoting Heinz's Funky Purple EZ Squirt Ketchup, JHC won a prestigious Silver Anvil Award from the Public Relations Society of America. Perhaps just as gratifying to Jack Horner and his team was Heinz's eagerness to work again with JHC when three new ketchup colors debuted in 2002.

Sources

John Frank, "Corporate Case Study," *PR Week,* April 29, 2002. Online: Lexis-Nexis.
"Heinz EZ Squirt Adds a Little 'Mystery' to Its Colored Condiment," Heinz news release, February 27, 2002. Online: Lexis-Nexis.
"Heinz Ketchup Gets Funky with New Purple EZ Squirt," Heinz news release, July 31, 2001. Online: Lexis-Nexis.
Jack Horner Communications Inc. Web site, www.jackhorner.com.
Public Relations Society of America Web site, www.prsa.org.
Public Relations Society of America, Central Iowa Chapter, Web site, www.prsaciowa.org.
Upstart Vision.com Web site, www.upstartvision.com.

Harry Potter and the Magical Marketing Campaign

Harry Potter and the Order of the Phoenix *Makes Publishing History*

Not even Harry Potter and all the wizards of Hogwarts School of Witchcraft and Wizardry could make 11 million books disappear from bookstores in 12 weeks during the summer of 2003. In setting sales records for *Harry Potter and the Order of the Phoenix,* the fifth book in the series about young wizards, Harry and his author, J. K. Rowling, needed a little help from media relations, special events, advertising, and sports promotions—courtesy of Scholastic, the series' U.S. publisher.

Since the debut of *Harry Potter and the Sorcerer's Stone* in 1998, Scholastic had known it had a magical publishing phenomenon on its hands. The promotional events surrounding the debut of each new novel had grown until eager readers—and journalists—expected the appearance of a new volume in the series to generate almost as much buzz as the Super Bowl. How could Scholastic fulfill such high hopes for hoopla and for sales?

Scholastic even was seeking a little magic for itself. Industrywide, books sales were down in the aftermath of the Sept. 11 terrorist attacks and consequent economic slowdown. Scholastic wasn't hurting—its $58 million in annual profits could buy a lot of Bertie Botts Every Flavor Beans—but the company needed a touch of Harry's wizardry. Scholastic wanted record-setting sales for *Harry Potter and the Order of the Phoenix.*

Harry Potter versus Harry Potter

You may know Scholastic well: The company is the world's largest publisher and distributor of children's books. Its best-known distribution channels are grade-school book clubs and school book fairs. The odds are pretty good that you've bought and read a Scholastic book besides one of the Harry Potter series. But Harry Potter and J. K. Rowling changed everything: As *Harry Potter and the Order of the Phoenix* went to press, 80 million copies of the previous four novels already were in circulation. Each of the four had been a No. 1 bestseller. Topping the record-setting sales of *Harry Potter and the Goblet of Fire* would be about as easy as an undefeated quidditch season.

From its earlier successes with Harry, Scholastic knew the primary target publics: kids, bookstores, and the news media. Complications facing the upcoming campaign included a sluggish sales market and economy in the wake of the Sept. 11 terrorist attacks and the pressure Scholastic felt in competing against the success of the previous *Harry Potter* volumes. When *Harry Potter and the Goblet of Fire* had appeared in July 2000, it crushed existing sales records: Muggles (humans) purchased almost 3 million copies during the first weekend of sales.

"J. K. Rowling and Harry Potter have created publishing history with the extraordinary first printing and subsequent sales of *Harry Potter and the Goblet of Fire*," said Barbara Marcus, president of Scholastic Books, a division of Scholastic. "It is extremely gratifying to publish a book which is being read and loved by so many children and adults."

In other words, the new Harry Potter had to defeat not only a stagnant market. It had to outperform an even more formidable foe: the old Harry Potter.

Are You Ready?

The goal of the marketing plan for *Harry Potter and the Order of the Phoenix* was for the new book to outperform its predecessors and set new sales records.

Scholastic created a two-phase plan to introduce the new book to readers—and, ideally, to the publishing hall of fame. Phase One would include prerelease publicity and would carry the campaign name of "Is Harry Ready? Are You?" Phase Two would launch as sales began at 12:01 a.m.—just past midnight—June 21, 2003, and would be called "Deeper Secrets, Darker Powers, Stronger Magic."

In Phase One, Scholastic whetted readers' appetites with a series of diverse tactics. On March 20, three months before the book's debut, the company released the cover. Designed by Mary GrandPré, illustrator of the previous four covers, it featured 15-year-old Harry, wand in hand, confronting a series of doors. Scholastic distributed the cover illustration with a news release, a tactic it used throughout each phase of the campaign. Each new tactic was announced and, afterward, summarized by a Scholastic news release.

At almost the same time, Scholastic issued a news release noting that the size of the first printing had reached an unprecedented 8.5 million copies.

Perhaps Scholastic's most elaborate prerelease tactic was a contest coupled with a special event. The contest was an essay competition for youth ages 18 and younger. The topic: "If you could have one special power taught at Hogwarts, what would it be—and why?" And the special event truly was special: Ten winners and their chaperones would win a trip to London, complete with an evening at Royal Albert Hall, during which J. K. Rowling would read from the new book and answer questions. The event also would be the subject of a live Webcast.

Announced via news release May 2, the essay contest ran six weeks. When Scholastic announced the winners on June 11—nine days before the book's release—company leaders probably felt as if they had created a little magic of their own. More than 12,000 writers entered the competition—but the wishes of the winners may have created the most unexpected magic. Daniel, from Camarillo, Calif., wished

Three months before the book's debut, Scholastic released the cover of the fifth Harry Potter novel, *Harry Potter and the Order of the Phoenix*. (Courtesy of Scholastic Inc. Harry Potter Publishing Rights © J. K. Rowling)

for a cure for autism so that he could help his sister. Marty, from Marlboro, Vt., wished that he could help his older brother learn to read better. Other winners wished for better health for parents and help for a blind classmate.

David, a winner from Saint Petersburg, Fla., wrote, "Although I am only 14 years old, I have the experience of a broken heart due to the death of my mother, and it still has not healed. For this reason I am determined to learn how to acquire the power of healing broken hearts. . . . I loved my mom, and she is gone. I would like the sadness to start lifting somewhat."

One week before the June 21 release, Scholastic flew the first signed copy of *Harry Potter and the Order of the Phoenix* from Scotland to New York. Company officials carried the book in a lockbox and were met at the airport by an armored van. Whisking the book away to a secret hiding place, they awaited a June 20 delivery to the New York Public Library. In a subdued reference to the terrorist attacks of Sept. 11, 2001, the book was inscribed "To the People of New York with Love and Admiration from J. K. Rowling."

Phase Two of the promotional campaign began at 12:01 on the morning of June 21. Expecting the top sales day of the year, bookstores opened at midnight, prepared by Scholastic with event kits that, earlier, had helped them plan opening-day events and festivities such as costume parties, trivia games, decorations, invitations, and other party ideas. In New York, the bookstore parties began when an electronic billboard in Times Square flashed an on-sale signal. Similar billboards kicked off the frenzy in Atlanta, Chicago, Cincinnati, Dallas, Denver, Los Angeles, Minneapolis, Nashville, Orlando, and Phoenix.

After the early-morning debut, four Major League Baseball teams honored *Harry Potter and the Order of the Phoenix* during games, with players in special outfits, costume contests, raffles, free bookmarks, and other promotional giveaways.

Otherworldly Places

Scholastic's promotional magic met the goal: First-day sales of *Harry Potter and the Order of the Phoenix* reached 5 million copies. By June 24, three days after the book's release, Scholastic announced plans to print an additional 800,000 copies, pushing the total number in print to 9.3 million copies.

"We are thrilled with the phenomenal sales of *Harry Potter and the Order of the Phoenix* and are shipping copies of the book to customers that need additional stock," reported a delighted Marcus, president of Scholastic Books.

On Sept. 23, three months after the June 21 debut, Scholastic announced that sales of *Harry Potter and the Order of the Phoenix* had reached 11 million copies.

The record sales had an immediate impact on Scholastic's bottom line. First-quarter revenue jumped 55 percent compared with first-quarter figures from the previous year.

Each aspect of the promotional campaign became newsworthy. Magazines, television stations, and Web sites eagerly snapped up the advance release of the cover. And the armored-van delivery of the signed copy of *Harry Potter and the Order of the Phoenix* won media coverage from the Associated Press, CNN Radio, Fox News, CNBC-TV, MSNBC-TV, WABC-TV of New York—and, of course, *Library Journal*.

For its success in achieving record sales, Scholastic's Harry Potter promotional campaign was named one of 2003's Top 12 promotional campaigns by *Promo* magazine. "A major marketing push by publisher Scholastic sent sales of the fifth Harry Potter title, *Harry Potter and the Order of the Phoenix,* soaring off to otherworldly places," declared the magazine.

The hoopla over Harry also created quieter, more private results. Fourteen-year-old David, the essay contest winner from Florida, journeyed with his grandmother to England to see Rowling read from the new book. After the death of David's mother, his grandmother had purchased the Harry Potter books for him.

"They really helped me," he told reporter Lane DeGregory of the *St. Petersburg* (Fla.) *Times.* "I got them at just the right time."

Harry Potter, an orphan, might understand David's reaction to winning.

"I know my mom would be excited," David said. "I just wish I could tell her."

Sources

"Christmas Arrives on First Day of Summer," Scholastic news release, June 22, 2003. Online: www.scholastic.com.

Lane DeGregory, "If I Could Do Magic Like Harry Potter . . . ," *St. Petersburg* (Fla.) *Times,* June 12, 2003. Online: Lexis-Nexis.

Patricia Odell, "Promotion Leads Branding," *Promo* (September 2003), 85.

"Scholastic and *Harry Potter and the Goblet of Fire* Break All Publishing Records in First Weekend on Sale," Scholastic news release, July 11, 2000. Online: www.scholastic.com.

"Scholastic Announces First Quarter Results," Scholastic news release, September 23, 2003. Online: www.scholastic.com.

"Scholastic Announces Fiscal 2003 Results and Fiscal 2004 Outlook," Scholastic news release, July 15, 2003. Online: www.scholastic.com.

"Scholastic Announces Harry Potter Contest for American Kids," Scholastic news release, May 2, 2003. Online: www.scholastic.com.

"Scholastic Announces Multi-Million Dollar Marketing Campaign for *Harry Potter and the Order of the Phoenix,*" Scholastic news release, May 19, 2003. Online: www.scholastic.com.

"Scholastic Delivers U.S. First and Only Signed Copy by J. K. Rowling of *Harry Potter and the Order of the Phoenix* from Scotland," Scholastic news release, June 13, 2003. Online: www.scholastic.com.

"Scholastic Goes Back to Press for a Third Printing of 800,000 Copies of *Harry Potter and the Order of the Phoenix,*" Scholastic news release, June 24, 2003. Online: www.scholastic.com.

"Scholastic Releases Cover of Highly Anticipated *Harry Potter and the Order of the Phoenix,*" Scholastic news release, March 20, 2003. Online: www.scholastic.com.

"Scholastic Sells 11 Million Copies of *Harry Potter and the Order of the Phoenix* in 12 Weeks," Scholastic news release, September 23, 2003. Online: www.scholastic.com.

"Ten Children Announced as Winners of Scholastic's *Harry Potter and the Order of the Phoenix* Contest," Scholastic news release, June 11, 2003. Online: www.scholastic.com.

No Ordinary Joe

Grocery Store Chain Trader Joe's Prefers Customer Relations to Advertising

If you're puzzled by the theory of relativity or why the quadratic formula works and who would ever need it, don't even ask about Italian wine laws—you just don't want to know.

To make an impossibly complex story short, to keep prices high, only a certain number of the very best grapes become premium wines. Surplus grapes go to more prosaic, less intoxicating uses—unless you find a loophole in the law and mix different premium grapes together, forming an impure but fascinating mongrel elixir. And if you do so, you have to hope that buyers from Trader Joe's, a quirky grocery store chain in the United States, will find your wine, call it something like Nerello del Bastardo, and sell it for $6.99 a bottle. With Trader Joe's fanatically loyal customers, you'll make a fortune.

Trader Joe's buys and stocks exotic merchandise from around the world. It bought the mixed wine and called it Nerello del Bastardo, which roughly translates as "bastard grapes" because of the illegitimate pairing. It charged only $6.99. And because the store chain passionately follows its primary value of customer service, it does indeed have fanatically loyal customers.

Based in Monrovia, Calif., Trader Joe's had—as of 2004—approximately 220 smallish stores in 17 states. Founded by Joe Coulombe in 1967, the store now features exclusive, private-label foodstuffs, often with outlandish names. For example, its Mexican line is Trader José's. Chinese is Trader Ming's. Italian, Trader Giotto's. Health foods are Trader Darwin's—for survival of the fittest. Prices for the exotic fare average about 20 percent less than prices for similar items at regular supermarkets. For example, at Trader Joe's, you might snag a 9-ounce tin of Dutch Stroopwafels for $2.99. Or a 1-pound bag of peanut-butter-filled pretzels for $2.69. Or a 1-pound package of garlic and herb pizza dough for 99 cents.

Trader Joe's mission statement focuses squarely on pleasing customers. The first sentence reads: "At Trader Joe's, our mission is to bring all our customers the best food and beverage values to be found anywhere, and the information to make informed buying decisions." To serve its customers, Trader Joe's has created a relationship-building program as effective, off-the-wall, and low-cost as the artichoke tortellini, French opera cake, and other rarities that line the shelves of its stores.

"The Educated Consumer"

Trader Joe's conducts both formal and informal research into who its customers are and what they want.

"Our people are price-conscious but are interested in food," says Pat St. John, Trader Joe's vice president of marketing. "They want to go beyond what they can find in the mainstream."

In describing his original target public, founder Joe Coulombe used only three words: "the educated consumer."

To attract educated consumers, Trader Joe's carefully researches store location. St. John says that the store chain prefers to place its stores among well educated residents. Sure enough, when a reporter from the Copley News Service corralled a Trader Joe's customer to interview for a rave review of the store chain, the shopper turned out to be a high school teacher. "There are a lot of things here that just aren't available anywhere else," said Tom Deets, the teacher. "We come here about once every two weeks to store up."

Trader Joe's also formally surveys its customers just, in the words of its Web site, "to see how we're doing."

Integrity and Terrible Puns

Part of Trader Joe's mission is to provide unrivaled customer service. To do so, the store chain strives to achieve these customer-focused objectives:

- To instill within each employee Trader Joe's customer service values
- To make each store visit exciting and fun
- To communicate with customers outside the store, informing them about Trader Joe's products

Trader Joe's instills customer service values in its employees by asking them to know their customers. As reporter Janet Adamy of the Portland *Oregonian* discovered, "Employees know customers by name." Trader Joe's Web site proclaims, "We like to be part of our neighborhoods and get to know our customers. . . . Trader Joe's Crew Members are friendly, knowledgeable, and happy to see their customers. They taste our items too, so they can discuss them with their customers."

The Web site philosophy seems to exist in the real world of Trader Joe's crowded stores. "The company's employees, decked out in Hawaiian shirts, are a friendly and knowledgeable presence for customers navigating the aisles stocked with unique products," wrote columnist Chris Penttila of *Entrepreneur* magazine.

"Our first value is integrity, which is pervasive in all we do," says CEO Dan Bane. "We infuse integrity into what we buy, the way we operate the stores, and the way we deal with people. Integrity for us is really golden-rulish—to treat others like you want to be treated, in all facets of the business. But the other way we like to define it is to act as if your customer is looking over your shoulder all the time."

If customers really are peering over shoulders, they may find free samples or recipes waved in their faces. Besides wearing Hawaiian shirts, Trader Joe's employees dispense unusual freebies to ensure that each store visit becomes a fun adventure. "A walk through one of the grocery chain's stores is likely to turn up a taste of a good-looking pasta salad, made with fresh ingredients from the

Panettone (p.21) Brie en Croute (p.16) North Atlantic Scallops (p.6) Tiramisù (p.6) Apple Cider (p.15) Cranberry Chutney (p3) Olives (p.16) Five Layer Fiesta Dip (p.10) French Green Beans (p.7)

TRADER JOE'S

Serving customers with a smile since 1958

A Grocery Store of Great Values

Holiday Guide, 2003

Nerello Del Bastardo
Red Wine with a Pedigree

This premium red wine is the "bastard" child of two famed varietals. Only a certain amount of wine annually, regardless of how much is produced, can legally be called the highly selective Barolo or Barbaresco (which can sell for $30 per bottle and up). Clearly, this leaves some very nice wine on the vine. That value opportunity has a nice nose... seems vaguely Cyrano de Bergerac-esque, no?

These are leftover pedigree grapes that when blended, yield a full bodied, intriguing red wine. This wine complements red meat, pasta and rich cheeses. It also stands well alone.

Our tasting panel tried this wine and loved it. It's a Trader Joe's exclusive. We're selling each 750 ml bottle of **Nerello Del Bastardo**, imported from Italy, for **$6.99**. This is simply a terrific price for wine of this quality.

Adam's Reserve Extra Sharp
Cheddar • $3.99 per pound

Adam's Reserve Extra Sharp Cheddar, produced in New York, is a traditionally aged Cheddar that's been cured for over eighteen months. It's treated with special care and handling during the aging process, resulting in an appealing sharpness that stimulates the taste buds. It also slices well and melts nicely for a great sandwich fixin'.

This award winning cheese recently won "Best of Class Gold," in the United Stated Championship Cheese Contest, hosted by the Wisconsin Cheese Makers Association. The cheese was evaluated on a number of attributes, including taste, body and texture. We're selling **Adam's Reserve Extra Sharp Cheddar** for $3.99 per pound. This is a great price for Cheddar of this quality.
MW

Wow! $8.79 per pound!
Colossal Shrimp
Our lowest price ever!

Shrimp prices are falling! Shrimp prices are falling! We buy huge quantities of shrimp, so we keep a close eye on that market. We were shocked and pleased when pricing dropped to the lowest level in decades. Trying to keep our composure, we sprang to action and purchased record quantities of shrimp so we could offer shrimp at simply an amazing deal.

These are cultivated **Tail-On Cooked Colossals** (21-30 shrimp per pound) that make for a beautiful presentation. They're cooked, peeled, deveined and individually quick frozen (IQF). They're a great choice for the ever-popular shrimp cocktail (perchance with our **Seafood Cocktail Sauce**, pg. 20). So convenient: just thaw and serve.

We're selling **Trader Joe's Tail-On Colossal Cooked Shrimp** for just **$8.79** per pound. At these low prices, there's no need to skimp on the shrimp.

Truffles for a trifle...
French Cocoa Truffles
A Mere $2.99 for 8.8 ounces

Here's a sophisticated sweet with youthful exuberance. Sure, this decadent truffle is made of strictly top drawer ingredients. But even the most refined amongst us may be compelled to lick one's fingers to ensure this sweet is appropriately devoured *in toto*.

Simply an exquisite delicate confection rolled in cocoa, these truffles have the traditional truffle coating. Unlike some others, they don't have a hard outer shell – rather a smooth, rich texture throughout.

We're selling each 8.8 ounce box of **Trader Joe's Original French Truffles** for **$2.99**. This is an excellent price for imported French truffles.

Trader Joe's *Fearless Flyer* customer newsletter seems to be produced by the weird offspring of a college honors student and a Comedy Channel writer. (Courtesy of Trader Joe's East Inc. Prices and availability may vary.)

store's shelves," declared *Promo* magazine. "A 'crew member' hands out recipes so shoppers can purchase the fixings for themselves. An abundance of samples draws crowds of shoppers."

Despite the effectiveness of its free samples and knowledgeable employees, Trader Joe's greatest customer relations tactic may be its *Fearless Flyer,* one of the most uncorporate newsletters in corporate America. Why "fearless"? Because the publication will stoop, with no trepidation, to any outrageous pun. For example, "Absence makes the heart grow fondue" and "Orange you ready for some citrus fruit trivia?" The newsletter introduces products that could be named only by the weird offspring of a college honors student and a Comedy Channel writer:

- Mini quiche hors d'oeuvres are called Prelude to a Quiche (from the play and movie *Prelude to a Kiss*).
- A sweet popcorn–nut snack mix is called Rosencrunch and Guildenpop (from the false friends Rosencrantz and Guildenstern in Shakespeare's *Hamlet*). Just in case you missed the pun, the newsletter article adds, "Share the sweet sensation with the people in your hamlet. Get it? Hamlet?"
- A premium guacamole mix is named "Avocado's Number Guacamole" (from the figure known as Avogadro's Number). If the dust lies thick on your chemistry notes, the article even supplies Avogadro's pride and joy: $6.02221367 \times 10^{23}$.

"The *Flyer* . . . is not your everyday supermarket mailer," concludes the *Los Angeles Times* in a dramatic understatement. The newsletter, 24 pages and decorated with weirdly captioned 19th century engravings, began as an informal handout to employees to educate them about the store's European wines. But when customers saw the photocopied flyer, they asked, received, and enjoyed. "Our *Fearless Flyer* is a somewhat irreverent description of a timely selection of our products," reports Trader Joe's Web site. "It's sometimes been called a cross between *Consumer Reports* and *Mad Magazine.*"

The *Fearless Flyer* has become so effective that Trader Joe's channels most of its marketing efforts into public relations rather than traditional advertising. "Consider the fact that the company does little advertising and relies mainly on its newsletter, the *Fearless Flyer,* to promote its products, new and old," says *Entrepreneur* magazine.

A focus on customer relations rather than advertising has become a key strategy at Trader Joe's. "No amount of advertising can create what we want to create with our customers," says St. John, the marketing vice president. "It can't create an experience. It's the personal relationship with these people that builds loyalty."

"We violate all the rules," said John Shields, a former Trader Joe's CEO. "We do little advertising and no television. Our customers are our advertisements."

Running down the Center Aisle: The Triumph of Customer Relations

Trader Joe's emphasis on customer relations has earned both profits and plaudits. Analysts estimate that the privately held company's annual revenues approach $3 billion. *Consumer Reports* ranks Trader Joe's tops in service in the national specialty groceries category. *Promo* magazine named Trader Joe's one of the 12 "most exciting and innovative brands" of 2003.

Both the *San Francisco Examiner* and *U.S. News & World Report* have used the term "cultlike" to describe the devotion of Trader Joe's customers. *Strategy and Leadership* magazine writes that the company has "a fervently enthusiastic fan club of customers."

"I probably get about 10 letters a day, talking about the great things that happened to our customers in our stores," says CEO Dan Bane. "And the best ones get published in our bulletin. And they are really emotional letters, people talking about it being *their* Trader Joe's and how it really provides a sense of community."

When the Trader Joe's in Cambridge, Mass., opened its doors for the first time, *U.S. News & World Report* was there to witness the hoopla. Writer Kerry Hannon dutifully reported prices, selection, and history. But Hannon also saw the results of an effective customer relations program:

> In Cambridge, Mass., a long line of shoppers formed outside Trader Joe's an hour before the door slid open on its first day of business not long ago. As the locks clicked free, a perfectly sane looking woman, in all likelihood a onetime Los Angeles area resident [where Trader Joe's began], broke ranks, grabbed a cart, and began running down the store's center aisle, shouting, "Yahoo!"

Sources

Stan Abraham, "Dan Bane, CEO of Trader Joe's," *Strategy and Leadership* 2002, vol. 30, no. 6. Online: ABI-INFORM.

Janet Adamy, "Chain Is Not Your Average Joe's," *The Oregonian* (Portland), July 2, 1999. Online: Lexis-Nexis.

"Another Joe: Discount Grocer Trader Joe's Extends Its Reach in the City," *San Francisco Examiner,* November 21, 1997. Online: Lexis-Nexis.

Adam Eventov, "A Changing Market," *Press Enterprise* (Riverside, CA), December 1, 2002. Online: Lexis-Nexis.

Frank Green, "On the Cheap," Copley News Service, September 29, 2003. Online: Lexis-Nexis.

Kerry Hannon, "Let Them Eat Ahi Jerky," *U.S. News & World Report,* July 7, 1997. Online: Lexis-Nexis.

Brad Haugaard, "Trader Joe's Marketing Savvy," *Los Angeles Times,* April 11, 1990. Online: Lexis-Nexis.

Patricia Odell, "Promotion Leads Branding," *Promo* (September 2003), 88.

Chris Penttila, "Brand Awareness," *Entrepreneur* (September 2001). Online: Lexis-Nexis.

Brad Smith and Sarah Rottenberg, "Innovating in the Food Industry," *Prepared Foods,* June 2002. Online: Lexis-Nexis.

"Store Makes Good on Pledge; Trader Joe's to Open Monday," *Los Angeles Daily News,* November 18, 2003. Online: Lexis-Nexis.

Trader Joe's Web site, www.traderjoes.com.

ACT file # 8 ....

The Strategic Message Planner

In an integrated marketing communications campaign, members of the communications team—whether public relations practitioners, advertisers, or marketing specialists—strive to deliver one clear, strategic message across several media. To develop a highly focused, well-researched message, marketers use a critical thinking tool called a strategic message planner.[1] Other terms for *SMP* include *creative work plan, creative platform,* and *copy platform.*

Consumers do not see the strategic message planner. Instead, this concise document stays within the team that creates the marketing campaign.

An SMP helps you summarize and analyze your research in order to develop an idea that will motivate the target market. For example, before marketers begin to think of an ad's visuals or the headline of a product-related news release, they first conduct research and complete an SMP to ensure that they have a well-researched, on-target, persuasive message. An SMP clarifies information in 10 distinct areas: client and product, target market, product benefits, current brand image, desired brand image, direct competitors and brand images, indirect competitors and brand images, advertising goal, strategic message, and supporting benefits.

In this description of an SMP, we use the term *product* generically. A product can be a tangible object, a service, a person, or an idea.

1. Client and Product. Completing this section involves more than just writing the names of your product and the organization that produces or offers it. Include specific details of both the company and the product. Marketers call product details "features," and they compile them in extensive lists. In ACT File #14 (Creative Thinking), we describe how knowing these details can help you generate ideas.

2. Target Market. Your client or boss often will specify the target market. However, you still must dedicate yourself to understanding the people in that group. To define and understand a target market, include both demographic information (such as age, gender, race, income, education level, and purchasing patterns) and psychographic information (such as values, religious beliefs, political persuasions, and social attitudes).

3. Product Benefits. A benefit is a product feature that appeals to the campaign's target market. Which features from your information in Section 1 will address the self-interests of the consumers listed in Section 2? If you list more than one benefit, which benefit would your target market see as most important? Probably, you will present some or all of those benefits in your campaign.

4. Current Brand Image. Brand image is your target market's impression of your product. Describe your product's brand image as your target market really would; don't indulge in wishful thinking. Your client needs—and deserves—an honest evaluation. Your entry in this section should be just a sentence or two. Most consumers don't offer detailed analyses of brand image. Instead, they simply base their impressions on how they feel about the brand.

5. Desired Brand Image. Desired brand image is the impression that you *wish* the target market had of your product. Your client may be able to specify desired brand image for you. That hoped-for image often is the result of extensive research, which may be available for you. If your integrated marketing communications campaign succeeds, the desired brand image would be your target market's new impression of the product.

Like the previous section, your entry for this section should be only a sentence or two.

6. Direct Competitors and Brand Images. List products that compete directly with your product, and specify the brand image of each. For example, if your product is a new diet drink, list competing products as well as your target audience's brand image of each competitor. Understanding competing brand images is important: One goal of the SMP is to help you create a brand image that will beneficially distinguish your product from direct competitors.

7. Indirect Competitors and Brand Images. List products that compete *indirectly* with your product, and specify the brand image of each. Indirect competitors are in a different product category from your product. However, they could prevent your target market from buying your product. For example, an indirect competitor for your diet drink could be an exercise center.

8. Advertising Goal. What, according to your client, is the goal of the IMC campaign—besides selling the product? For example, the advertising goal for your new diet drink might be "To prove to the target market that this drink tastes better and costs less than its leading competitor." Or the goal might be to establish a new, more beneficial relationship with the target market.

Your entry for this section should be one sentence—or even a sentence fragment. The entry may be similar to your entry for the desired brand image section.

9. Strategic Message. Specify the one, clear message of the campaign. In the book *Creating the Advertising Message,* Professor Jim Albright says that a good way to concisely state the strategic message is to finish this sentence: "Target market, you should buy this product because _____."[2] Whatever words follow *because* are your campaign's strategic message.

Use the previous eight sections to develop your strategic message. For example, the strategic message will, ideally, move the target market from the current brand image to the desired brand image. A good strategic message gives your product a unique and positive position in the target market's mind. A good strategic message makes a beneficial promise that no other competing product can make.

The strategic message should be brief—ideally, one sentence that coordinates well with the eight sections that precede it.

10. Supporting Benefits. Supporting benefits are the selling points you could include in the ads, news releases, and other tactics that support the promise of your strategic message.

A good strategic message (from the previous section) is brief, so it usually doesn't include evidence. The supporting benefits supply the evidence. Given your answer to the first seven sections of the SMP, you know which product features your target market will view as benefits.

A successful SMP builds to Sections 9 and 10. Those sections provide the key message and the supporting evidence for an IMC campaign.

Discussion Questions • • • • • • • • • • • • • • • • • • •

1. Can you explain how each of the first eight sections of an SMP influences the strategic message developed in Section 9?

2. Why is it important for marketers to understand the difference between a product feature and a product benefit?

3. In each of the cases in this chapter, do you think the communications professionals used some form of an SMP? Does each campaign have a clear, well-focused message?

4. How might public relations professionals modify the SMP to use it for nonmarketing message development?

Endnotes • • • • • • • • • • • • • • • • • • •

1. Charles Marsh, David W. Guth, and Bonnie Poovey Short, *Strategic Writing* (Boston: Allyn & Bacon, 2005).

2. Jim Albright, *Creating the Advertising Message* (Mountain View, CA: Mayfield, 1992).

CHAPTER 9

Business-to-Business Relations

Welcome to the Twilight Zone of public relations: business-to-business relations, B2B for short.

Public relations practitioner Jeanne Russo speaks for many of her colleagues in describing her first encounter with B2B:

> When I joined a business-to-business (B2B) public relations agency, I soon discovered that much of what I had learned . . . didn't exactly fit the B2B landscape. . . . Few colleges and universities teach even one course in B2B PR. No graduate or practitioner has been formally trained in it. And I've yet to find a single book devoted to it.[1]

B2B's lost-child status in public relations is puzzling. Estimates place U.S. spending on B2B communications and promotions in 2004 at $82 billion.[2] Recent British studies found that 45 percent of all public relations work in England is B2B and that seven of England's 10 most profitable public relations agencies earn more than half their revenues from B2B efforts.[3]

Business-to-business relations is the management of relationships with businesses that have resources that *your* business needs to achieve its goals. B2B publics can include customer businesses, suppliers or vendors, distributors, and even competitors who wish to work together in governmental lobbying efforts. In the few existing studies of B2B relations, however, one public dominates the spotlight: customer businesses.

B2B's Customer Focus

The prominence of customers in B2B relations is logical: Business spending in the United States totals more than $1.5 trillion annually.[4] Recent figures from the U.S. Census Bureau show that business e-commerce dwarfs ordinary consumer e-commerce, totaling more than 90 percent of online expenditures.[5]

Definitions of B2B relations often focus on the customer public. "To the best of my knowledge, there is no textbook definition of B2B PR," says Frank Shediac, founder of Shediac Communications in Hong Kong. "We at Shediac Communications define it as the promotional activities required to get customers to give you their money for your products and services."[6] A 2004 survey of B2B communicators found that their top goal was "driving sales," followed by "customer acquisition."[7]

Despite the prevalence of B2B marketing tactics such as advertising and direct mail (or e-mail), public relations plays a significant role in building relationships with business customers. Unlike most individual purchase decisions, business purchase decisions often require teamwork. Accountants, engineers, buyers, and even CEOs can weigh in, each with different needs and different sources of information. Russo explains:

> B2B buyers go through a long, complex sales cycle that requires agreement among numerous decision makers, each with his/her own buying motivations, objectives, and concerns. . . . PR is the only marketing communication channel capable of cost-effectively handling the complex task of delivering multiple messages to multiple audiences reading multiple publications.[8]

When public relations practitioners coordinate their media messages with marketing tactics such as direct mail, personal selling, and advertising, the effect can be powerful. "Together," says Russo, "they comprise the multilevel communication approach that B2B's different target audiences demand."[9]

B2B communicators also recognize the value of crisis communications, an important component of public relations (see Chapter 13). Describing Boeing's B2B crisis communications following possible marketing irregularities, *BtoB* magazine concluded, "Boeing, of course, isn't the only b-to-b organization to find itself in the bull's-eye of a scandal in the past year. Companies beset by ethics flaps and hounded by the media are using an increasingly necessary marketing discipline: crisis communications."[10]

Like business-to-consumer communication, B2B relations operates in a regulated environment. B2B practitioners must understand the regulations imposed by these federal agencies:

- Regulations of the Federal Trade Commission prohibit false or misleading product publicity.
- Regulations of the Securities and Exchange Commission prohibit false or misleading information regarding the performance of companies that sell

stock. The SEC also prohibits the withholding of essential information regarding company plans and performance.

- Regulations of the Food and Drug Administration promote the disclosure of information about foods and health-related products, and they prohibit misleading publicity in regard to such products.
- Regulations of the Department of Justice promote antitrust policies, which prohibit anticompetitive actions such as price fixing among competing companies.

Partner Relationship Management

Partner relationship management, a new direction within B2B communication, may expand the discipline beyond a tunnel-vision focus on business customers. PRM is an offshoot of **customer relationship management,** a marketing process that uses individual consumer information, stored in databases, to identify, select, and retain customers.

CRM Today Web site defines PRM as "a business strategy for developing and improving relations between companies and their suppliers/channel partners."[11] **Channel partners** are separate businesses, such as warehouses, that help move a company's products through the distribution channel to customers. Although this definition of PRM still focuses on selling, it incorporates more publics than customers alone.

A key part of critical thinking, of course, is definition—and the definition of PRM remains uncertain within public relations. In a recent survey of what the word *partnering* means to public relations practitioners, "approximately half of the respondents were not familiar with the term."[12] One survey respondent, however, defined *partnering* as "a relationship between two or more companies which mutually benefit from the relationship."[13] That comprehensive view of PRM can include a wide scope of companies—for example, a company that supplies security for a power plant. Such a supplier falls outside a traditional sales or product distribution relationship.

"PRM companies seem to agree that PRM is about aligning the goals of disparate companies and making this so financially attractive to partners in the form of [sales] leads and other incentives that they never want to leave your company's sphere of influence," says Josh Krist of SalesLobby.com, a networking site for B2B marketers.[14]

Stephen McNally of Centra Software says he believes that PRM can deepen relationships among businesses that need one another. "By sharing more with them, it encourages them to share more with us," he says. "It builds trust."[15]

Like customer relationship management, PRM incorporates software programs to help companies manage their various partnerships. Though analysts expect annual sales of PRM software to hit almost $600 million by 2006,[16] partnership relationship management means more than data input and computer projections. "The most important word in PRM is the middle one—*relationship*," says Bob

Thompson, editor of *ePartner Insights* newsletter. "Good relationships are valuable to both parties. Effective PRM means delivering value to partners to help them be successful. . . . Of course, helping partners makes good business sense because successful partners are more likely to be loyal."[17]

Tactics of B2B and PRM

Tactics in business-to-business relations and partner relationship management help companies build productive relationships with other companies.

"Help partners to build their businesses," says John Addison, author of *Revenue Rocket: New Strategies for Selling with Partners*. "You can create dialogue through one-on-one discussions, partner advisory councils, surveys, and collaboration. The idea is to understand their issues and help partners grow."[18]

In addition to Addison's suggestions, practitioners can create newsletters and seminars, and they can work with other professionals to create training programs, awards programs, and continuing education materials. But the most powerful medium in modern B2B is the Web site. (See Table 9.1.)

B2B Web Sites

A sweeping survey of B2B marketers showed that their top marketing tool in 2004 was the Web site.[19] In its annual evaluation of hundreds of B2B Web sites, *BtoB* magazine had a tough time naming a winner in 2003. "Choosing the best sites is a task that has grown increasingly difficult as companies devote larger portions of their staffs and budgets to building and maintaining a strong Web presence," the magazine reported. Hewlett-Packard won the competition, earning this evaluation: "Fantastic site with lots of useful computing tools and tips. First-class e-commerce function; customer service options abound, including online chat. Beautiful, modern design."[20]

table 9.1 *B2B Digital Marketing Fact Sheet*

- 62 percent of B2B marketers increased their online budgets in 2004.
- The top three goals of B2B digital marketing in 2003 were finding new customers, driving traffic to company Web sites, and educating current customers.
- Web site development was B2B companies' second most-important strategy for reducing marketing costs in 2003, following bringing more marketing duties in-house.
- 63 percent of B2B companies had online relationships with suppliers in 2003.
- 99 percent of supplier businesses did not participate in online B2B relationships in 2003.

Sources: Data from *BtoB* magazine, Reponsys, and Forrester Research.

Like the Hewlett-Packard site, effective B2B Web sites feature a variety of communication tactics, the magazine noted: "The Web sites we judged are offering users more resources, such as white papers, e-mail newsletters, and in-depth customer case studies. More sites are enabling users to browse in different languages. And many more are making pronounced efforts to determine what customers want by surveying them."[21]

A **white paper** is an objective, fact-laden business report. "What's so great about a wordy piece explaining the technical aspects of products and services?" asks *Sales & Marketing Management* magazine. "It lends credibility that other marketing avenues lack, especially when written with an objective third party."[22]

Despite the surge in online relationship building, B2B communicators give themselves low marks for success in the broader field of **digital marketing.** Besides Web sites, digital marketing tactics include e-mail campaigns, advertising on other Web sites, and electronic newsletters. Responsys, an e-mail marketing company, surveyed online marketers in 2003 and concluded, "Nearly 40 percent graded their use of online marketing at a C, D, or F, admitting there is plenty of room for improvement utilizing digital marketing more effectively."[23]

Public relations practitioners often use a critical thinking tool known as a communication audit to assess the effectiveness of tactics, particularly from a target public's viewpoint (see ACT File #3). Kathy Gogan, vice president of marketing for Responsys, believes her agency's audits have identified one explanation for the mediocre performance of some B2B digital marketing efforts. "Although business-to-business companies are dramatically increasing their spending for digital marketing," she says, "they seem to be focusing on one-way information transfer. The business-to-business consumer market has recognized digital marketing as an effective vehicle for personalized, two-way dialogues, which are critical for maximum results.[24]

"Digital marketing isn't . . . mature yet," Gogan concludes. "It's going to take some patience and some more learning."[25]

Innovation and Tradition

High-tech B2B tactics can extend beyond Web sites. Ohio-based AK Steel earned widespread media attention in 2002 for a bold public relations tactic that targeted the construction and home-appliance industries: It built a so-called concept home, using its new germ-killing coating on steel surfaces, and invited the news media to a housewarming party. "It became a magnet of attention for the media," reported *BtoB* magazine, "and the home was featured on NBC's *Today* show and CNBC as well as in the *New York Times, Popular Science,* and *Popular Mechanics.*" AK Steel and HSR Business to Business, a B2B marketing agency, estimated that the home generated 130 print articles, totaling almost $800,000 in advertising equivalency (see ACT File #6).[26]

Perhaps most important, the high-tech house showed the importance of public relations in the emerging world of B2B communications. "The most effective part

Not all business-to-business communication tactics are conventional.
To demonstrate the effectiveness of its germ-killing coating on steel
surfaces, AK Steel built an entire demonstration home. (Courtesy
of AK Steel)

of the campaign," *BtoB* concluded, "may have been a very unusual public and media
relations strategy . . . the concept house."[27]

B2B relations may well be one of the most important elements in the future
of public relations. Much of its terrain is new and unfamiliar—different publics,
unique self-interests, and innovative approaches such as PRM. However, as long
as B2B practitioners seek shared values and mutually beneficial relationships, they
will feel at home—even in high-tech concept houses.

Discussion Questions

1. Have you studied B2B public relations in other
   courses? If so, what do you recall about that
   area of public relations? If not, why do you
   think B2B relations has such a low profile?

2. Why, in your opinion, does customer relations dominate B2B communication?

3. How does partner relationship management
   compare with traditional B2B communication?

4. In your opinion, why are Web sites the dom-
   inant tactic in B2B communication?

5. If you currently work in a part-time or full-
   time job, with what other companies does your
   employer have relationships?

Key Terms

business-to-business
  relations, p. 191
channel partners, p. 193

customer relationship
  management, p. 193
digital marketing, p. 195

partner relationship
  management, p. 193
white paper, p. 195

Endnotes

1. Jeanne Russo, "Building a New Public Relations Model for the Special Needs of B2B Marketers." Online: www.schubert.com/pressroom.

2. Rebecca Gardyn, "Moving Targets," *American Demographics,* October 2000. Online: Lexis-Nexis.

3. "PR League Tables: Top 50 Business-to-Business," *Marketing,* May 21, 1998. Online: Lexis-Nexis. "PR League Tables: Why Trade PRs Are Hooked on the Net," *Marketing,* May 25, 2000. Online: Lexis-Nexis.

4. Louis Uchitelle, "Why Americans Must Keep Spending," *The New York Times,* December 1, 2003. Online: Lexis-Nexis.

5. "E-Stats," U.S. Census Bureau report, 2003. Online: www.census.gov.

6. "Interviews," *PRPoint Newsletter,* March 2002. Online: www.prpoint.com/INTERVIEWS.

7. Sean Callahan, "Marketers Opt for Short-Term Results," *BtoB: The Magazine for Marketing Strategists,* January 19, 2004. Online: www.netb2b.com.

8. Russo.

9. Russo.

10. Sean Callahan, "Boeing, Others Crank up Crisis Communications," *BtoB: The Magazine for Marketing Strategists,* December 8, 2003. Online: www.netb2b.com.

11. "What Is PRM?" CRM Today Web site. Online: www.crm2day.com.

12. Gayle M. Pohl and Dee Vandeventer, "The Workplace, Undergraduate Education, and Career Preparation," in *Handbook of Public Relations,* ed. Robert Heath (Thousand Oaks, CA: Sage, 2001), 365.

13. Pohl and Vandeventer, 365.

14. Josh Krist, "Partner Relationship Management: The Next Business Revolution?" Online: www.SalesLobby.com.

15. David Joachim, "Online Tools Drive New Sales through Old Channels," *BtoB: The Magazine for Marketing Strategists,* September 15, 2003. Online: www.netb2b.com.

16. Joachim.

17. Bob Thompson, "Partner Relationship Management: A Critical eBusiness Strategy for a Multichannel World," *ePartner Insights,* August 2000. Online: www.frontlinehq.com.

18. John Addison, "10 Mistakes to Avoid with Partners," *VARBusiness,* July 7, 2003. Online: Lexis-Nexis.

19. "New Study Finds Marketers Investing More This Year in Digital Marketing to Stay Competitive," Responsys news release, January 19, 2004. Online: www.responsys.com.

20. Mary E. Morrison, "The 2003 NetMarketing 100: Best B-to-B Web Sites," *BtoB: The Magazine for Marketing Strategists,* August 11, 2003. Online: www.netb2b.com.

21. Morrison.

22. Jennifer Gilbert, "White It Down," *Sales & Marketing Management* (February 2003), 50.

23. "New Study Finds Marketers Investing More This Year in Digital Marketing to Stay Competitive."

24. "New Study Finds Marketers Investing More This Year in Digital Marketing to Stay Competitive."

25. Larry Dobrow, "Marketers: Broader Acceptance, Bigger Budgeting Plans for Interactive," *MediaPost,* January 19, 2004. Online: www.mediapost.com.

26. Roger Slavens, "AK Steel Campaign Brings Home the Point about New Coatings," *BtoB: The Magazine for Marketing Strategists,* June 9, 2003. Online: www.netb2b.com.

27. Slavens.

Through the Mummy's Eyes

Silicon Graphics Inc. and Portfolio Communications Return to the Past for a Futuristic Campaign

The scientists waited until the last of the patients in the CAT scan room at London's National Hospital for Neurology had departed into the evening. Then they quietly wheeled in their "patient," immobile and swathed in ancient wrappings.

Shooting 1,500 detailed images took hours, but the patient didn't complain. After all, he had been dead for almost 3,000 years.

"I know—sounds like a bad science fiction movie," CNN correspondent James Hattori confessed in trying to explain the story to his viewers.

Hattori might have started by discussing the philosophy of Portfolio Communications, a London-based public relations agency. On its Web site, the agency emphasizes a key value: "Portfolio believes strongly in creativity, but only to meet communication goals rather than for its own sake."

The patient in the London hospital was the mummy of an Egyptian priest named Nesperennub. And he was there at the suggestion of Portfolio, all to help launch a business-to-business public relations campaign for a company every bit as creative as Portfolio itself: Silicon Graphics Inc.—also known as SGI—of California.

The Museum Connection

SGI is a high-tech powerhouse, best known for its computer visualization innovations. Engineers, entrepreneurs, and others have used SGI imaging technology to design safer cars, forecast weather, and create visuals for such movies as *Jurassic Park* and *Toy Story*. In 2002, SGI's hottest new development was its three-dimensional visualization technology, built into facilities that SGI called Reality Centers. To help boost its business in England, SGI sought a unique way to present the new technology to British business managers, scientists, and engineers.

For insight into how to reach those target publics in a memorable way, Portfolio turned to its sister agency, the Metrica research group. Metrica's research showed that almost half the members of SGI's target publics in England had visited a museum within the past year. In England, any list of museums begins with the imposing complex near Russell Square: the venerable British Museum.

Nesperennub wasn't the automatic first choice for a visualization subject. Instead, Portfolio approached John Taylor, an Egyptologist at the museum, for permission and advice on a suitable subject. Together, Taylor, Portfolio, and SGI selected the 3,000-year-old mummy as an ideal candidate for the campaign. SGI's 3D visualization technology, combined with CAT scan images, would allow scientists to construct manipulable internal and external images of Nesperennub. Scientists knew that Nesperennub's cartonnage, or papyrus outer casing, contained more than his remains: Mysterious objects lay beneath the coverings—but removing the coverings would destroy the mummy.

Chief among the mysteries was a hatlike object on the skeleton's skull. Egyptologists had known that something crowned Nesperennub's head, since the mummy had been X-rayed in the 1960s. Some scientists speculated that it might be Nesperennub's placenta, saved since his birth, and buried with his mummy as a religious rite. If SGI's visualization technology could solve an enduring museum mystery, it might win the notice and respect of the campaign's British target publics.

Nesperennub was a crowd favorite, a resident of the museum since 1899. Museum research showed that he had been a priest in Thebes. He died in approximately 800 BC and was buried on the west bank of the Nile River. But now, millennia later, his mummy was a silent partner in a creative public relations plan. The goal? To show the benefits of SGI 3D visualization technology to British business managers, scientists, and engineers.

"We Can See inside the Skull"

To introduce SGI's new technology to the target publics, Portfolio developed several objectives:

- To raise the company's profile and position it as a leader in 3D visualization technology
- To demonstrate the power of the new technology in solving complex, data-intensive problems in science or business
- To win popular acclaim for the effectiveness of the technology
- To highlight SGI's integral role and strong reputation among the world's scientists

Tactics devised to achieve the objectives came in two phases: creating the mummy's internal–external 3D images and then promoting that success.

The gadgets SGI used to create the 3D images were a techie's dream. In a news release celebrating the success of the process, SGI officials declared, "Using the SGI Reality Center facility, investigators have been able to create a virtual image of Nesperennub while keeping the casing intact. SGI used data from a recently conducted computed axial tomography (CAT) scan . . . to reproduce the mummy, using an SGI Onyx 3000 series InfiniteReality3™ visualization system running OpenGL Volumizer™ graphics software." (College students and professors may want to remember that they were not the target audience for such a complex description.)

But as he played with the images, one SGI employee became so excited that he spoke in a language a little more like common English: "You can rotate it and

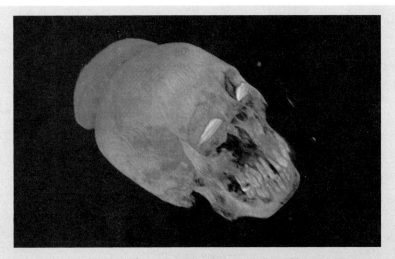

SGI technology allowed scientists at the British Museum to peer inside
the wrappings of Nesperennub, a 3,000-year-old mummy. (Courtesy of
Silicon Graphics Inc.)

really explore it interactively. For instance, I could cut away the back of the skull so
that we can see inside the skull—I mean, more than that, get inside and look out
through Nesperennub's eye sockets!"

"The initial results have absolutely exceeded our expectations," said the British
Museum's John Taylor. "They have solved some of the unanswered questions about
Nesperennub and have opened up exciting new avenues of investigation."

Among the questions answered was the status of the mysterious hatlike object on Nesperennub's skull. SGI's 3D visualization revealed the object to be not a
placenta but, rather, an unfired ceramic bowl. The image of the bowl was so precise
that Taylor and other investigators could see bumps and scratches on its surface.

"This is quite a puzzle because we've never seen anything like this in a
mummy before," Taylor confessed.

SGI's technology also revealed an unexplained hole near Nesperennub's left
temple.

"It really was exciting to be able to see such detail so vividly, and it will help
enormously to advance our knowledge," Taylor said.

With images completed, old mysteries solved, new mysteries created, and scientists almost dancing with excitement, Portfolio knew SGI had a story to tell. Metrica's research had shown that the demographics of the campaign's target publics
strongly matched the readership demographics of London's *Financial Times,* a newspaper with worldwide readership. So Portfolio offered exclusive coverage of the entire process to *Financial Times* science reporter Fiona Harvey, who earlier had written
favorably about SGI technology. Harvey not only wrote an SGI–Nesperennub piece
for the *Financial Times,* she also wrote a similar feature for *New Scientist* magazine.

The articles appeared March 9, 2002. A few days later, SGI and the British Museum presented the images at SGI's Visualization Summit at the Glasgow Science Center. Portfolio organized a special viewing for leading technology and science journalists and ensured that they received media kits—both paper and CD—with a news release, a backgrounder on Nesperennub, and, of course, spectacular images of the computer-visualized mummy.

At the same time, SGI and Portfolio launched a worldwide news release, using companies such as PR Newswire to announce the dramatic success of the 3D visualization technology.

Who's Your Mummy? Nesperennub Rules

With the articles in *Financial Times* and *New Scientist,* SGI and Portfolio scored a direct hit on its target publics. Additional media coverage in England exceeded the campaign team's expectations. Metrica counted more than 40 stories, 45 percent of which were "strongly favorable" and 55 percent of which were "slightly favorable"—for a total of 100 percent favorable coverage. The prestigious *Times* of London reported that SGI had given scientists "an unprecedented opportunity to study the interior of a mummy." Metrica calculated that SGI's media coverage shot far beyond the target public, reaching 48 percent of adults in English with repeated exposures to the story.

The *Times* story—certainly not aimed precisely at SGI's target public—even detailed the precision with which the 3D visualization technology identified interior objects besides the bowl: "The scans have revealed several linen-wrapped amulets on Nesperennub's chest, to ward off the perils of the afterlife. One is a winged figure, while another is egg-shaped and may be a heart scarab—a beetle-shaped charm to protect the dead man's heart."

Internationally, newspapers as far away as Australia picked up the story. Germany sent a television crew to record the mummy and the new images, as did CNN. In the CNN report, John Taylor told the world, "This technology is ideal for investigations of this kind because it doesn't touch the mummy at all. It's completely nondestructive."

The Nesperennub campaign also earned praise from public relations organizations and their competitions. SGI, Portfolio, and Metrica won first-place honors from both the Public Relations Consultants Association and England's Institute of Public Relations.

Said David Hughes, manager of collaborative visualization at SGI, "The project has resulted in exactly the kind of media coverage that SGI wanted and helped us to achieve our aim of spreading the word about visualization and what it can be used to achieve."

Even Nesperennub gained additional star status. Most media reports noted his history, and the *Times* story even explored his fascinating family tree. His father, Ankhefenkhonsu, was also a Theban priest, and the mummy of Nesperennub's wife, Neskhonspakhered, now resides in the Lowie Museum of Anthropology in

Berkeley, Calif. Regrettably, there seems to be no news of Nesperennub's—well, of his mummy.

Sources

CNN Daybreak, April 3, 2002. Online: Lexis-Nexis.

Mary Cowlett, "SGI Exhibits Its Tech with Egyptology," *PR Week,* September 27, 2002. Online: Lexis-Nexis.

Fiona Harvey, "Tomb Raiders," *New Scientist,* March 9, 2002. Online: Lexis-Nexis.

Mark Henderson, "Wraps Come off Ancient Egypt with Virtual Perfection," *The* (London) *Times,* March 13, 2002. Online: Lexis-Nexis.

Next@CNN, March 31, 2002. Online: Lexis-Nexis.

"Planning Counts." Online: www.metrica.net.

"The 3D Mummy." Online: www.portfoliocomms.com.

"3D Technology Unlocks Secrets of 3,000-Year-Old Egyptian Mummy," SGI news release, March 11, 2002. Online: Lexis-Nexis.

Bad Scents and Good Sense

case 9.2

An American City Turns Its Offensive "Tacoma Aroma" into the Sweet Smell of Success

If a city can have an inferiority complex, Tacoma, Wash., did. Since the 1960s, crime had increased, businesses had fled, and the stench of despair permeated the city's air—literally. "For those in the region," *American Demographics* magazine explained, "the city's image was one of gangs, high crime rates, and the distinctive 'Tacoma aroma' of its nearby pulp mills." When Toyota named a pick-up truck after the city—thinking the name might connote rugged Northwestern individualism—knowledgeable auto critics howled and asked if the vehicle spewed noxious fumes and moved only in reverse. Even Tacoma's Economic Development Department conceded, "Positive coverage of Tacoma was virtually nonexistent."

Change for the better began quietly. Faced with economic disaster, the City Council cracked down on crime, cleaned up the air, and, in its most audacious move, sank $100 million into what it called the Click! Network, a lightning-fast fiber-optic telecommunications system that linked the city's business district with the world's telecom networks. Hoping to transform the city's image, the council then hired Development Counsellors International, a company that specializes in helping cities and regions market themselves. DCI had helped reinvigorate cities such as Richmond, Va., and Charleston, S.C. Could it do the same for Tacoma?

A Unique Selling Proposition

Even DCI's president seemed daunted by the challenge of presenting Tacoma as an emerging paradise. "Tacoma's image was that of a blue-collar town dominated by pulp and paper mills," recalled Andrew Levine. "Residents joked about the 'Tacoma Aroma.'"

DCI and the Economic Development Department set to work, beginning with an analysis of national news coverage of Tacoma and interviews with national site-selection consultants who helped organizations select locations for business headquarters or expansions. The conclusions were grim. In the words of the Economic Development Department, "Tacoma had an entrenched, negative image in the Pacific Northwest, and nationally the city was virtually unknown."

The research team also interviewed local business and city leaders—and found a glimmer of hope. The Click! Network far exceeded expectations, energizing Tacoma businesses and winning praise even from skeptics. The research team learned that Click! was the nation's largest city-owned telecom network and that new businesses could tap into the system in a matter of days rather than the months such access might require elsewhere. The glimmer of hope evolved into an idea—a unique advantage that Tacoma could offer to high-tech businesses.

"Every town, city or state should have a unique selling proposition that encapsulates what that area is about," said Levine.

Tacoma's "#1 Wired City" campaign included Web cartoons featuring skeptical executives won over by Tacoma's business advantages. (Courtesy of Tacoma Economic Development Department; City of Tacoma; and Augustus Barnett Advertising, Fox Island, Wash.)

DCI and the Economic Development Department created more than two dozen campaign themes and tested them with a community focus group. From that process came a slogan that city leaders hoped would help transform Tacoma's business image: "Tacoma: America's #1 Wired City."

Business leaders dominated the target publics as the communications team planned its upcoming campaign. With DCI's assistance, Tacoma would send its message to site-selection consultants, CEOs of high-tech companies, local business leaders, and the news media. Among these publics, DCI labeled local business leaders as the "most critical audience" because of their potential role as independent, knowledgeable ambassadors for Tacoma's Click! Network and the city's commitment to high-tech expansion.

Third-Party Credibility

The goal of Tacoma's public relations plan reflected its business-to-business orientation: to position Tacoma as a home for high-tech businesses. To reach these publics with its unique selling proposition, the planning team created four objectives:

1. To change local negative perceptions of Tacoma by generating at least 20 positive articles in local news media
2. To change regional negative perceptions of Tacoma by generating at least 10 positive articles in Seattle media
3. To win national and international attention by generating at least five articles in leading national or international news media outlets
4. To create at least five new business leads generated through media coverage for Tacoma

Generating positive media coverage meant developing knowledgeable, enthusiastic sources for the news media, so the planning team first created tactics to win over Tacoma's current business leaders. The team met with those leaders and developed educational business-to-business materials to familiarize them with the scope of Tacoma's commitment to becoming a high-tech haven. Armed with such knowledge, the business leaders could act both as credible media sources and as Tacoma ambassadors in their meetings with other business leaders. To enhance those outreach efforts, Tacoma added the #1 Wired City logo to city business cards and changed the city e-mail and Web addresses to wiredcityusa.com.

At the same time, the team took its high-tech message to the local news media, holding a news conference to announce the campaign and the "Tacoma: America's #1 Wired City" slogan to Tacoma journalists.

To reach regional and national media, DCI and Tacoma held a media day in nearby Seattle, briefing business journalists on the campaign and the scope of the city's Click! Network. The team also pitched individual story ideas to the Seattle bureaus of national and international news media.

"We want to position Tacoma in national media because business leaders read the national media," said Julie Curtin, vice president of DCI's western region office.

Just in case national and international site-selection consultants missed the national media coverage, DCI and Tacoma officials secured reprint permissions for such articles and sent them to members of that key target public.

Local journalists understood and appreciated the decision to employ media relations rather than advertising. "Media coverage carries third-party credibility, and it doesn't cost much," Tacoma *News Tribune* columnist Dan Voelpel explained to his readers.

DCI's Curtin was equally blunt. "This will not be an advertising campaign," she said. "It will be a public relations campaign."

In the early days of the campaign, however, some Tacoma residents expressed skepticism. "Not everyone was impressed. Many rolled their eyes," wrote *News Tribune* columnist Art Popham. "A year ago, when DCI announced its 'America's #1 Wired City' slogan as one element of its effort to create a new image for Tacoma, even more locals, including me and others here at the *News Tribune,* wondered if the city was wasting taxpayer money."

Clearing the Air

The first clue that Tacoma city leaders hadn't wasted taxpayer money came when more than 20 national and regional journalists descended on the city after the Seattle media briefings.

In all, the DCI/Tacoma plan generated more than 200 stories in local, regional, national, and international news media. Favorable stories appeared in the Tacoma *News Tribune,* the *Los Angeles Times,* the *Dallas Morning News,* the *Boston Globe,* the *Wall Street Journal,* the *New York Times,* and other newspapers. Influential professional magazines such as *Business Week, Area Development, Site Selection,* and *Global Business* carried the news of the new Tacoma. Web sources such as Business 2.0 and Site Selection Online praised the city's business climate. Internationally, stories on America's #1 Wired City appeared in Asia and Europe. Tacoma's resurgence was a cover story in *Inc.* magazine, and a headline in the *Seattle Times* proclaimed, "Tacoma Emerges as a Tech Center."

"A well-crafted marketing/PR campaign has succeeded in giving Tacoma an entirely new image—America's #1 Wired City," wrote the Tacoma *News Tribune.* "This is the kind of publicity that money can't buy."

"These kinds of efforts . . . are of immeasurable value for communities," national site-selection consultant Dennis Donovan told the *News Tribune.* "It legitimizes the communities in the eyes of the corporate executives."

In the wake of the #1 Wired City campaign, more than 100 high-tech companies have located or expanded in Tacoma, including Amazon.com. *Entrepreneur* magazine named Tacoma the nation's best mid-sized city for businesses, and *Industry Standard* magazine designated the city one of the "Top Five Tech Towns" in the United States.

Tacoma's #1 Wired City campaign dazzled public relations professionals around the world. The campaign won a prestigious annual Business Issue Award from the International Association of Business Communicators. In that competition, IABC selects the single best business-issues campaign from among its international Gold Quill winners. Tacoma's campaign also won a Silver Anvil Award from the Public Relations Society of America for the year's best institutional program. And the *Bulldog Reporter,* a media relations newsletter for public relations professionals, gave the campaign its annual Bulldog Reporter Award for Not-for-Profit/Association/Government campaigns. Tacoma's #1 Wired City promotion had become one of the most honored campaigns in public relations history.

As high-tech businesses continued to establish themselves in Tacoma, city leaders announced the renewal of their contract with DCI—and the targeting of a new public: tourists.

And what of Art Popham, the *News Tribune* columnist who wondered if DCI and city leaders were wasting taxpayer money?

"Well, the numbers are in, and I was wrong," Popham wrote. "And glad of it." Popham went on to say that his favorite media coverage of Tacoma's new high-tech image had come from the German newspaper *Die Welt,* which had included this assessment of America's #1 Wired City: "Tacoma . . . is an oasis of peace, space, and good air."

Good air.

Those two little words may have meant more to DCI and Tacoma than all their campaign awards combined.

Sources

"Case History: Tacoma Economic Development Department," Development Counsellors International. Online: www.dc-intl.com.

Marcelene Edwards, "The Selling of Tacoma," (Tacoma) *News Tribune,* August 21, 2000. Online: www.tribnet.com.

Cliff Enico, "Finding That Perfect City," *Entrepreneur,* August 5, 2002. Online: www.Entrepreneur.com.

Andrew Gordon, "Tacoma Sets Its Sites on Tourists in Latest Initiative," *PR Week,* August 5, 2002. Online: Lexis-Nexis.

Robin Londner, "Image Enhancement," *PR Week,* January 7, 2002. Online: Lexis-Nexis.

Seema Nayar, "Brand Fever," *American Demographics,* January 2002. Online: Lexis-Nexis.

Art Popham, column, (Tacoma) *News Tribune,* January 4, 2001. Online: Lexis-Nexis.

Public Relations Society of America Web site, www.prsa.org.

Jim Syzmanski, "Public Relations Firm Hired to Bolster Tacoma, Wash.'s Image," (Tacoma) *News Tribune,* November 4, 1999. Online: Lexis-Nexis.

Dan Voelpel, column, (Tacoma) *News Tribune,* July 16, 2003. Online: Lexis-Nexis.

Shootout in the E-Frontier

case 9.3

St. Paul Travelers Wants Businesses to Fight Back against Hackers, Viruses, and Bugs

With apologies to poet Elizabeth Barrett Browning, how do they hack us? Let us count the ways.

- A hacker stole 300,000 credit card numbers from CD Universe and posted them online.
- Another hacker posted almost 60,000 credit card numbers that he or she had stolen from Creditcards.com.
- Yet another hacker penetrated Microsoft's defenses twice in five days and left system operators a message recommending improvements in the company's online security measures.
- Still another hacker gained access to the computer files of a Florida bank, stealing the names and addresses of almost 3,600 customers.
- Other hackers have penetrated the online defenses of NASA, the CIA, and other government agencies.

And that's just hacking. Additional dangers loom in what international insurer St. Paul Travelers calls "the E-Frontier." Online perils that confront modern businesses include computer viruses, loss of service, misuse of intellectual property, failure to protect private files, and much more. In 2002, the FBI and the Computer Security Institute set the price tag for business losses due to recent online crime at $455 million.

St. Paul Travelers of Saint Paul, Minn., one of the world's largest property-liability insurers, specializes in diagnosing, preventing, and insuring against online threats. In 2004, The St. Paul Companies merged with Travelers Property and Casualty Corp. In 1961, St. Paul became the first company to issue insurance covering electronic data processing. In 1984, it launched a new unit dedicated to providing specialized insurance for electronics manufacturers, computer services, and software companies. In 2001, the company asked Imre Communications of Baltimore, Andrew Edson & Associates of New York, and research agency Schulman, Ronca & Bucuvalas Inc. of New York to help it assess and communicate the dangers in the E-Frontier to the world's business community.

Ignorance Isn't Bliss

The St. Paul corporate communications team initiated the campaign's research phase by discussing risk assessment and risk management with top executives at the company's technology unit, which oversees insuring and assisting businesses operating in the E-Frontier. The researchers used that information to create a series of focus groups for three distinct publics: risk managers for companies with annual revenues of $500 million-plus, risk managers for high-tech companies, and the independent insurance agents and brokers who sell St. Paul insurance.

A summary report of focus group findings indicated three possible trends, which survey research might confirm:

- Risks involving computers, networks, and the Internet "kept insurance buyers awake at night."
- Companies doing business in the E-Frontier were not well informed about current and emerging risks and relevant insurance coverage.
- Insurance agents and brokers who sold St. Paul policies also lacked extensive information about E-Frontier risks and the effectiveness of in-place insurance policies.

With the assistance of Schulman, Ronca & Bucuvalas Inc., St. Paul also used the focus groups to develop and refine questions for a comprehensive multinational survey of corporate risk managers and brokers who sold St. Paul policies. The company hoped the survey findings would identify the extent of the recipients' knowledge of existing E-Frontier risks and the consequent insurance options. SRBI conducted more than 1,300 telephone interviews with risk managers at hundreds of companies in the United States, Belgium, Denmark, France, Germany, Ireland, Italy, the Netherlands, Norway, Portugal, Spain, Sweden, Switzerland, and the United Kingdom. SRBI also interviewed more than 150 insurance agents and brokers in the United States.

The survey results were sobering:

- Computer and Internet risks were the No. 1 concern of European risk managers and the No. 2 concern of U.S. managers (just behind employment liability issues).
- Only one-quarter of U.S. companies and slightly less than one-third of European companies managed technology risks with formal structures and policies.
- Programs to educate employees about E-Frontier risks existed in only 60 percent of U.S. companies and 56 percent of European companies.
- Significantly, even with those alarming numbers, U.S. insurance agents and brokers believed that their clients underestimated cyber risks and overestimated their preparedness.

"Compared to more traditional property-casualty risks, companies are poorly prepared for the risks posed by technology and e-commerce," said Kae Lovaas, St. Paul vice president of technology in 2001. "Not only are companies unsure of the risks presented by their business operations, they also have substantial difficulty understanding what types and levels of insurance coverage they need."

With such information in hand, the St. Paul communications team knew it could strengthen the company's position as an international cyber-risk expert and problem solver. To solidify that reputation, the team targeted three publics for a business-to-business public relations campaign: current and potential St. Paul customers; independent agents and brokers who sell St. Paul policies; and St. Paul employees, who needed to understand their company's emerging leadership role. St. Paul's focus on its own employees may have been sparked by a significant finding of the survey: "Employees—the people who employ technology daily in their jobs—are described as the least knowledgeable about technology risk and its potential impact on their companies."

News Conferences, Road Shows, and Intranets

To reach its goal of positioning itself as an international expert in E-Frontier insurance issues, St. Paul's corporate communications department and its agency partners devised four objectives:

- To increase relevant E-Frontier business by 25 percent in 2001
- To generate noteworthy media coverage of the survey results, with at least one major feature in the *Wall Street Journal,* the *New York Times,* or the *Financial Times*
- To feature survey results in a "road show" to reach at least 400 of St. Paul's top agents and brokers
- To position The St. Paul Companies as a leading E-Frontier source for journalists and organizations seeking speakers.

The centerpiece of the campaign's tactics was the survey itself. The communications team packaged the findings in an extensive report titled "The E-Frontier: New Challenges to Corporate Risk Management" and created an elaborate plan for its distribution.

The team selected Jan. 31, 2001, for the kickoff of publicity. On that day, St. Paul presented its report in simultaneous news conferences in New York and London. Linked by satellite, the conferences allowed reporters at one site to ask questions of presenters at the other site. Journalists not able to attend could participate through online video and could e-mail questions to participants. (For better or worse, hackers, bugs, and viruses didn't thwart the high-tech news conference.)

To ensure same-day coverage of the report, St. Paul negotiated an exclusive advance look at the survey findings for journalists at the *Financial Times.*

On Jan. 30, the evening before the transatlantic news conferences, St. Paul previewed its findings for key insurance industry executives and analysts in invitation-only banquets in New York and London.

On Jan. 31, the day of the conferences and the *Financial Times* exclusive, St. Paul also issued a comprehensive seven-page news release, detailing the survey's findings. Titled "Survey: U.S., European Businesses Are 'Overconfident, Underprepared' for

High-Tech Risks," the release contained a lead paragraph that didn't sugarcoat the situation:

> NEW YORK—Businesses do not adequately understand the risks posed by technology, have difficulty identifying potential risks and lack the tools to manage them effectively, according to a major survey of executives at 1,500 companies in the United States and Europe released today by The St. Paul Companies, the Saint Paul, Minn.-based global insurer.

The news release also joined other documents in a comprehensive media kit that St. Paul translated into French, Spanish, German, and Dutch and distributed to selected journalists throughout the world. It also posted the report, translated into those languages, on its Web site.

Mindful of uninformed employees among its clients, St. Paul delivered the transatlantic news conferences to its own employees via the company intranet, and, as the campaign progressed, the company issued internal updates on media coverage and business results.

To reach key agents and brokers, St. Paul prepared a road show of presentations, handouts and PowerPoint slides and took it to 10 cities: Atlanta, Boston, Chicago, Dallas, Denver, Los Angeles, Philadelphia, Saint Paul, Seattle, and Washington, D.C.

Celebration and Concern

The turmoil in the E-Frontier captured the attention of the world's business media. St. Paul's media relations efforts generated more than 60 stories in almost 100 media outlets in the first year of coverage. In addition to the *Financial Times* kickoff story, media coverage included a front-page story in *Business Insurance* magazine, an industry leader. Stories appeared in the United States, Europe, Asia, and Latin America.

More than 500 agents and brokers attended St. Paul's E-Frontier road shows, and reporter inquiries and speaker requests increased at corporate headquarters. Within a year, St. Paul reported a 30 percent increase in technology-related business.

For the success of its E-Frontier campaign, the St. Paul corporate communications team and its agency partners won a 2002 first-place Silver Anvil Award from the Public Relations Society of America.

And there the story might stop. But it doesn't.

As St. Paul Companies celebrated the success of its E-Frontier campaign, the terrorist attacks of Sept. 11 occurred. Even before the attacks, company officials had wondered if the 2001 report would change corporate attitudes and behaviors. After Sept. 11, concerns about cyber terrorist attacks increased. And so The St. Paul Companies and SRBI launched a 2002 cyber-risk survey, this time focusing on 460 companies in the United States.

Executive Overview

Technology is re-shaping the way business is done in the new millennium. More and more companies rely on the Internet as an essential part of their day-to-day activity. Few, however, understand the range of potential liabilities involved in e-commerce, including:

- Intellectual property risks, including infringements of copyrights, trademarks, and patents.

- Privacy risk, for example, via the disclosure of others' confidential information.

- Network security risk, including external hacking intrusions, computer viruses, web site attacks, denial of service attacks and reputation loss.

How serious are the potential liabilities involved in e-commerce? The Computer Emergency Response Team (CERT) at Carnegie Mellon University in Pittsburgh, Pa., found that the number of *reported* computer security incidents more than doubled between 2000 and 2001. In a separate study, the Computer Security Institute of San Francisco reported that of respondents who acknowledged a loss due to computer breaches, 44% quantified their cumulative losses at nearly $500 million.

For complete survey results go to www.stpaul.com/cyberrisk-survey. For more information, call Kim O'Connell, The St. Paul Companies; 651.310.2883 or via e-mail: kim.o'connell@stpaul.com.

In 2001, The St. Paul Companies released the results of *The E-Frontier: New Challenges to Corporate Risk Management*, a survey of 1,500 corporate risk managers in the United States and Europe. It showed that businesses did not adequately understand the risks posed by technology, had difficulty identifying potential risks, and lacked the tools to manage them effectively. The survey also found a lack of communication and cooperation between risk managers and I.T. managers when dealing with cyber-risks.

In January 2002, The St. Paul commissioned a follow-up study to explore the lack of communication and cooperation between risk managers and I.T. managers, and to gauge U.S. companies' perception of and preparedness for cyber-risk, particularly in light of the September 2001 terrorist attacks.

The following pages outline the key findings of *The E-frontier 2002: Continuing Threats to Corporate Risk Management*.

1

The Executive Overview of St. Paul Companies' 2002 cyber-risk survey contains an eye-opening statistic: Corporate computer security incidents more than doubled between 2000 and 2001. (Courtesy of St. Paul Travelers. Copyright St. Paul Companies Inc.)

Once again, the results were cause for concern: Though recognition of cyber risks had increased a bit, risk managers believed such risks would increase, felt they didn't communicate well with information-technology employees, and thought they were unprepared to deal with emerging cyber threats.

Fewer than one-quarter of corporate risk managers said that their senior management had become more involved in assessing and managing possible cyber terrorist attacks since Sept. 11.

"While [the Sept. 11] attacks didn't involve high tech risks, the heightened attention to security that resulted needs to extend to cyber risks," says Bill Rohde, president of St. Paul's Global Technology unit. "As companies conduct business via the Internet, they are opening themselves up to a new set of risks and dangers, and those risks must be better understood, quantified and managed."

The St. Paul E-Frontier reports are online at www.stpaul.com.

Sources

Imre Communications Web site, www.imrecommunications.com.

"Survey: U.S., European Businesses Are 'Overconfident, Underprepared' for High-Tech Risks," St. Paul Companies news release, January 31, 2001. Online: www.stpaul.com.

"The E-Frontier: New Challenges to Corporate Risk Management," St. Paul Companies. Online: www.stpaul.com.

"The E-Frontier 2002: Continuing Threats to Corporate Risk Management," St. Paul Companies. Online: www.stpaul.com.

Public Relations Society of America Web site, www.prsa.org.

The St. Paul Companies Web site, www.stpaul.com.

"U.S. Businesses 'Continue to Underestimate' the Risks Involved in E-Commerce, According to New St. Paul Companies Survey," St. Paul Companies news release, June 12, 2002. Online: www.stpaul.com.

ACT file #9

SWOT Analysis

If your game is poker, pinochle, hearts, crazy eights, gin rummy, canasta, or even go fish, you know the routine. Once the cards are dealt, the first thing you do is pick them up and start arranging your hand to figure out what kind of combinations you have. To put it another way, you are trying to make sense of a batch of raw data and figure out your possibilities.

That, in essence, is what a SWOT analysis does. It serves as a bridge between research and planning. It allows practitioners to bring order to a flood of information gathered during the research phase of the public relations process. In helping to organize this information, a SWOT analysis can also suggest directions for public relations planning.

SWOT stands for strengths, weaknesses, opportunities, and threats. Those terms have specific meanings best explained with the help of the diagram in Figure 9.1, known as a SWOT analysis grid.

Two factors influence definition of each term. The first is whether an issue or condition influencing an organization reflects positively or negatively on its ability to achieve its goals. On the SWOT analysis grid, the vertical axis represents this factor. The second factor is whether the impact of an issue, fact, or condition on the organization's ability to achieve its goals is in the present or is something that will appear in the future. On the SWOT analysis grid, the horizontal axis represents

Advanced Critical Thinking

	The Present	The Future
Positive Factors	Strength	Opportunities
Negative Factors	Weaknesses	Threats

figure 9.1

SWOT Analysis Grid

this time element. With this as background, the four elements of a SWOT are defined as follows:

1. **Strengths**—What do we see as positive current issues or conditions influencing our organization's ability to achieve its goals? Having a strong membership base is an organizational strength.
2. **Weaknesses**—What do we see as negative current issues or conditions influencing our organization's ability to achieve its goals? An example of a weakness is an existing shortage in the skilled labor pool.
3. **Opportunities**—What do we expect to see in the future as positive issues or conditions that will influence our organization's ability to achieve its goals? Increased productivity brought about by future technological improvements is an example of an opportunity.
4. **Threats**—What do we expect to see in the future as negative issues or conditions that will influence our organization's ability to achieve its goals? An example of a threat is the prospect of increasing foreign competition.

When conducting a SWOT analysis, you must do more than look at your own organization. Practitioners also need to look hard at the competition. In this context, a competitor is not necessarily defined as a rival company, product, service, or point of view. It can be anything that competes for the attention of targeted publics. For example, many charitable organizations had fund-raising problems following Sept. 11, 2001. These charities may not have competed directly with the many relief funds established for the victims of the terror attacks, but their messages were drowned out by public attention on the War on Terror.

Practitioners must also be objective and define issues and conditions as they are and not as practitioners *hope* they are. Organizations need professionals who can put aside their feelings and see the world as it really is—even if that image is unflattering. However, seeing a less-than-perfect picture is one thing, telling management is another. This can involve courage—especially regarding an unpopular issue or condition. When practitioners must be messengers of bad news, they should remember that they were hired as public relations counselors, not as cheerleaders.

As any card player knows, luck comes from the cards that are dealt. However, skill comes from analyzing the situation before making the next play. For public relations practitioners, a SWOT analysis is that important step toward a winning hand.

Discussion Questions

1. What is the value of a SWOT analysis?
2. When conducting a SWOT analysis, how does one define the competition?
3. Why is it important for a practitioner to be objective when conducting a SWOT analysis? What, if any, challenges are associated with being objective?
4. How might you apply a SWOT analysis to any of the companies/organizations profiled in this chapter?

CHAPTER 10

Cross-Cultural and International Relations

Pop music may be the key to improving relations between the United States and Iran. When Iranian citizens overthrew the U.S.-supported Shah of Iran in 1979 and captured the U.S. Embassy, as well as 54 hostages, the two nations severed diplomatic relations and began years of mutual hostility and distrust. In 2003, when a violent earthquake destroyed the Iranian city of Bam, Iranian officials accepted U.S. aid but turned away a U.S. delegation that had hoped to begin an improved relationship with the Islamic nation.

Enter Radio Farda, a new tactic for building relationships with Iranian citizens. Sponsored by the Broadcasting Board of Governors, a U.S. agency that oversees the government's international public relations radio efforts, Radio Farda targets Iranians under age 30, a group comprising 70 percent of that nation's population. Beamed into the country from beyond Iranian borders, Radio Farda—translating as Radio Today—plays a mixture of American and Iranian pop music, with 12-minute newscasts on the hour. When the station launched in 2003, Britney Spears and Enrique Iglesias dominated airtime. Within its first month, the station had received more than 1,000 e-mails from listeners. In nearby Jordan, a similar U.S.-government station is the most-trusted radio news source among 39 percent of its young target audience.[1]

Not all **cross-cultural communication** efforts are as large or successful. When a representative of the state of Washington recently toured China to build markets for agricultural products, he wondered why men grimaced as they accepted the green baseball caps he presented as gifts. Wearing a green cap in China, he finally learned, signifies that a man's wife has rejected him and taken a lover—perhaps the person who gave him the cap. Kind of gives a new meaning to the term *international affairs*.[2]

table 10.1 *International Terms for Public Relations Tactics*

English	Public relations
German	Öffentlichkeitsarbeit
French	Relations publique
Italian	Relazione pubbliche
Spanish	Relaciones públicas

Source: Adapted from *Harrap's Five Language Business Dictionary* (London: Harrap, 1991).

Cross-cultural communication lapses also can have tragic consequences. A misunderstanding of a Japanese communiqué may have helped persuade U.S. President Harry Truman to order the use of atomic bombs in World War II.[3]

Communicating across cultures can be like tiptoeing through a minefield. "Culture is often at the root of communication challenges," write Marcelle DuPraw, of the National Institute for Dispute Resolution, and Marya Axner, a consultant in diversity awareness. "Our culture influences how we approach problems and how we participate in groups and in communities."[4]

Defining Culture

Because critical thinking generally begins with definition, we should establish what we mean by *culture*. And that might be hard.

"Even in the field of anthropology, in which the central focus involves studying culture, there is no universally accepted definition of the term," say public relations scholars Krishnamurthy Sriramesh and Dejan Vercic.[5] As early as 1952, in fact, anthropologists had identified more than 150 definitions of *culture*.[6]

DuPraw and Axner offer this definition: "*Culture* refers to a group or community with which we share common experiences that shape the way we understand the world. It includes groups that we are born into, such as gender, race, or national origin. It also includes groups we join or become part of."

A culture's relationship with communication can be cyclical. "Communication influences and is influenced by culture," Sriramesh and Vercic explain.

Cultures at Home and Abroad

We need not cross national borders to encounter new cultures. In helping Pacific Gas & Electric draft a plan to reach out to low-income customers in California, the Hill

This McDonald's restaurant in Beijing is tangible proof of globalization. Doing business internationally requires an understanding of each country's culture. (Courtesy of Robert R. Basow)

& Knowlton public relations agency quickly learned that it needed to communicate in five different languages (Case 10.2). The agency responded by expanding its staff, becoming more representative of California's multicultural environment. Research from the Population Studies Center at the University of Michigan shows that throughout the United States, minority groups tend to cluster into communities, preserving and promoting cultures that lie outside the mainstream.[7] "To operate successfully on a global scale requires acute sensitivity to cultural diversity that may exist even in countries which on the surface appear broadly similar in terms of economic development, consumption patterns, or political systems," write public relations professors Danny Moss and Barbara DeSanto.[8]

Moving across national borders, however, can take us into new and unfamiliar cultures. For example, a recent study by the International Public Relations Association revealed that, in some nations, public relations practitioners routinely pay journalists to either run or suppress news stories. According to the study, China, Saudi Arabia, Vietnam, Bangladesh, and Pakistan head the list of nations in which media relations can be cash-based. Countries in which the practice would violate powerful cultural norms include Finland, New Zealand, and the United States.[9]

The likelihood of such cross-cultural surprises increases as **globalization**— the growing economic interdependence of the world's people—affects more and more organizations. The International Monetary Fund has identified four trends that increasingly fuel globalization:

- Trade—import and export transactions among nations
- Movement of capital—the flow of investment money between countries, including foreign aid and private stock purchases
- Movement of people—the mobility of workers who cross national borders in search of better jobs or in fulfillment of employment obligations
- Spread of knowledge and technology—the exchange of information and equipment among nations

"The **global village** predicted 30 years ago by communications scholar and philosopher Marshall McLuhan is here," says Michael Morley, deputy chairman of Edelman Public Relations Worldwide.[10]

Fortunately, globalization may also be strengthening tolerance as interactions between cultures increase. Did you inadvertently show the sole of your shoe to colleagues from a Middle Eastern nation—a serious insult? They may forgive you. "Happily, such cross-cultural faux pas are no longer deal killers,'' reports the *New York Times*. "Globalization has narrowed the cultural divide."[11]

Analyzing Cultures

The cultural divide may be narrower, but it still exists, presenting a treacherous chasm for the unwary. Several critical thinking tools for studying different cultures exist, among them Hofstede's Cultural Dimensions (ACT File #10). DuPraw and Axner offer five characteristics that help distinguish different cultures.[12]

Different Communication Styles

"The way people communicate varies widely between, and even within, cultures," DuPraw and Axner write.[13] In many Latin American nations, for example, interrupting a speaker indicates interest and good manners. In Asian nations, however, many of which value silence, interruptions are rude.[14]

Different Attitudes toward Conflict

"Recognition that parties to a conflict can hold vastly different basic assumptions about the purposes, benefits, and procedures for engaging in conflict is essential to effective conflict communication," says public relations Professor Stephen Banks. Attitudes about violence also differ. Professor Michael Kunczik notes, "Certain forms of terrorism, namely, those designed to reach the public through media coverage, are specially staged for the mass media"—and he terms such efforts "terrorism as international public relations."[15]

Different Approaches to Completing Tasks

Some cultures are more deadline- and clock-oriented than others. In a survey of national attitudes regarding punctuality, *American Demographics* magazine reported that, of more than 30 nations studied, Switzerland ranked first in desire to comply with schedules and timetables. The United States ranked in the middle, and Mexico ranked last.[16]

Different Decision-Making Styles

"The roles individuals play in decision-making vary widely from culture to culture," say DuPraw and Axner. "For example, in the U.S., decisions are frequently delegated. . . . In many Southern European countries, there is a strong value placed on holding decision-making responsibilities oneself."[17]

Different Attitudes toward Disclosure

Different attitudes about candor can surface even within the same culture. Public relations practitioner Alejandra Brandolini of Buenos Aires, Argentina, recalls:

> One of our clients wanted to create a culture of open communication within the organization. During the change-development process, however, we discovered that the practice of hiding information with the intention of using it to blackmail others or for personal advancement was so deeply rooted that a change in corporate values would be very difficult. For the culture change to be successful, all members of the organization had to share and buy into the new values. This meant that the leaders of the old culture had to be identified and separated from the organization.[18]

Different Approaches to Knowing

Psychologist Geert Hofstede, creator of the cultural dimensions reviewed in ACT File #10, has found that the ability to deal with uncertainties is a primary distinguishing characteristic among national cultures. Citizens of the United States, for example, tolerate uncertainty fairly well. Costa Ricans and Germans are less tolerant, and Swedes and Malaysians are more tolerant.[19]

To this list of cultural indicators, we might add gestures, levels of formality, religion, and other demographic or psychographic traits that help distinguish one culture from another. Though fascinating, the study of different cultures is a never-ending process.

Successful Cross-Cultural Public Relations . . . .

As noted in Chapter 1, successful public relations is not an accident. Public relations triumphs are planned, using research of the situation, the client, and the stakeholders. In addition to the four-step process of public relations—research, planning, communication, and evaluation—we recommend a nine-step process for successful cross-cultural public relations.

Awareness

You don't need to wait until you're on the job to increase your awareness of other nations and cultures. In a recent survey, 95 percent of college students who studied abroad said their international experience continued to influence their perceptions of the world (and 96 percent reported that the experience increased their self-confidence).[20] At your own college or university, you might consider joining an international students association.

Commitment

With the increasing influence of globalization, as well as the growing diversity of the United States, organizations must have a constant commitment to cultural sensitivity. For example, Worldcom Public Relations Group, with offices in 35 countries on six continents, has incorporated commitment to cross-cultural awareness into its mission statement: "Worldcom was formed primarily to serve national, international, and multinational clients needing in-depth marketing and communications support and expertise from professionals who understand the language, culture, and customs of the domestic and foreign arenas in which they operate."[21]

Research

"There is very little empirical evidence on the nature of public relations in many regions of the world," write Sriramesh and Vercic.[22] If you can't find existing research on particular aspects of cultures or cross-cultural communication, you may need to generate your own findings—perhaps through public relations practitioners within the relevant culture. "Knowing the values, assumptions, and identity issues of diverse populations is necessary for sensitive communication of any sort," writes Banks.[23]

Local Partnership

A key to successful cross-cultural public relations, according to *PR News* magazine, is "finding the right playmates and learning to share the sandbox nicely."[24] That usually involves finding a public relations professional who understands the local sandbox. Like the Worldcom Group, the Pinnacle Group has offices throughout the world staffed by members of local cultures. "What this means to you," the agency declares on its Web site, "is that Pinnacle partners have long-standing relationships with key media, government, and other important audiences in every region."[25]

Diversity

Cultural awareness begins at home. As you approach graduation and seek employment, study possible employers. Are their staffs diverse? That doesn't guarantee successful cross-cultural communication, but it's a step in the right direction.

What do the values statements and mission statements of those employers say about diversity? Do their actions reflect their values?

Testing

Test messages on representatives of target publics before you distribute them to entire publics. A test might help you avoid the faux pas of the airline that, trying to impress Asian passengers, handed each a white carnation before a flight. In many Asian nations, the color white symbolizes death. "Nobody wanted to get on the plane," recalls one observer.[26]

Evaluation

We can't learn from our successes and failures until we conduct evaluation. World-com Group assures its clients that "we have a quality control task force which actively monitors assignments being undertaken across transnational borders to help ensure the very best effort is being expended on the client's behalf."[27]

Advocacy

Organizations face dozens of competing demands for their attention. Enduring commitment to cross-cultural sensitivity requires a steadfast advocate. Someone must remind the organization that cultural sensitivity is more than political correctness; it's an organizational value. In your workplace, that person might be you.

Continuing Education

As noted earlier, the study of different cultures is a fascinating, never-ending process. The Pinnacle Group has established Pinnacle University, which sponsors mandatory seminars, teleconferences, and forums for its international members. "By attending regional and international meetings, we cultivate our knowledge through continuous learning and sharing," the agency declares on its Web site.[28]

In the 21st century, the forces of globalization are a little like your college courses: Deal with them, because they're not going away. If you gain a career in public relations, you will encounter cross-cultural communication—ready or not, eager or not. The profession of public relations has discovered the global village that Marshall McLuhan predicted—and found it to be a very diverse place. Who knows? In your cross-cultural public relations campaigns, one of your colleagues may be a young Iranian now listening to Radio Farda.

Discussion Questions

1. In your own words, what is a culture? How would you describe the culture in which you live?

2. How are the concepts of cross-cultural communication and international communication similar? How are they different?

3. How would you respond to a boss who said, "You're always after us to do that cross-cultural stuff. You need to face it: We're all basically the same."

4. What blunders in cross-cultural communication have you heard of—or experienced yourself? What were the consequences?

5. What opportunities to increase your knowledge of different cultures exist at your college or university?

Key Terms

cross-cultural communication, p. 215

culture, p. 216
global village, p. 218

globalization, p. 217

Endnotes

1. Dan Gilgoff, "Wolfman in Farsi?" *U.S. News & World Report,* January 20, 2003, 28.
2. Craig S. Smith, "Beware of Green Hats in China and Other Cross-Cultural Faux-Pas," *The New York Times,* April 30, 2002. Online: Lexis-Nexis.
3. David W. Guth and Charles Marsh, *Public Relations: A Values-Driven Approach,* 2nd ed. (Boston: Allyn & Bacon, 2003), 140.
4. Marcelle DuPraw and Marya Axner, "Working on Common Cross-Cultural Communication Challenges," *Webster's World of Cultural Democracy.* Online: www.wwcd.org/action.
5. Krishnamurthy Sriramesh and Dejan Vercic, "A Theoretical Framework for Global Public Relations Research and Practice," in *The Global Public Relations Handbook,* eds. Krishnamurthy Sriramesh and Dejan Vercic (Mahwah, NJ: Lawrence Erlbaum Associates, 2003), 8.
6. Stephen P. Banks, *Multicultural Public Relations,* 2nd ed. (Ames, IA: Iowa State University Press, 2000), 9.
7. William H. Frey, "The Diversity Myth," *American Demographics* (June 1998), 39, 41.
8. Danny Moss and Barbara DeSanto, *Public Relations Cases: International Perspectives* (London: Routledge, 2002), 1.
9. "Researchers Release First-Ever Global Index Revealing Where Media Bribery Most Likely," International Public Relations Association news release, September 8, 2003. Online: www.ipra.net.
10. Michael Morley, *How to Manage Your Global Reputation* (New York: New York University Press, 1998), 1.
11. Smith.
12. DuPraw and Axner.
13. DuPraw and Axner

14. Dana Ambrosini, "Connecticut Consultant Lectures Business Reps on Cross-Cultural Communication," *Connecticut Post,* July 9, 2002. Online: Lexis-Nexis.
15. Michael Kunczik, "Transnational Public Relations by Foreign Governments," in *The Global Public Relations Handbook*, eds. Krishnamurthy Sriramesh and Dejan Vercic (Mahwah, NJ: Lawrence Erlbaum Associates, 2003), 419.
16. Robert Levine, "The Pace of Life in 31 Countries," *American Demographics* (November 1997), 20.
17. DuPraw and Axner.
18. "What Is Your Greatest Obstacle as a PR or Communication Practitioner?" *Communication World* (April–May 2003), 8.
19. Geert Hofstede, *Cultures and Organizations: Software of the Mind* (New York: McGraw-Hill, 1991). Geert Hoftstede, *Culture's Consequences: Comparing Values, Behaviors, Institutions and Organizations across Nations* (Thousand Oaks, CA: Sage, 2001).
20. Matt Sutorius, "Survey Says Study Abroad an Eye-Opener for Many Students," *The Maneater* (University Wire), October 1, 2003. Online: Lexis-Nexis.
21. Worldcom Public Relations Group Web site, www.worldcomgroup.com.
22. Sriramesh and Vercic, 1.
23. Banks, 51.
24. Sherri Deatherage Gree, "Affiliate Agencies: Pooling Resources Requires a Firm Understanding," *PR News,* July 21, 2003. Online: Lexis-Nexis.
25. Pinnacle Group Web site, www.pinnacleww.com.
26. Ambrosini.
27. Worldcom Public Relations Group.
28. Pinnacle Group.

Gross (Multi) National Product

The United Kingdom's Science Museum Hopes That a Controversial U.S. Exhibition Will Make a Big Stink

Queen Victoria of 19th century England was famous for frosty glances and a bone-chilling phrase of condemnation: "We are not amused." As one of the founders of the London-based Science Museum in 1857, the queen hardly would have found amusement in an exhibition the museum imported from the United States in 2002. Its title? Grossology: The (Impolite) Science of the Human Body. The museum's public relations staff may not have helped much with the headline of its first Grossology-related news release: "Burp, Fart, and Sniff Your Way to Understanding the Science of the Human Body."

The world-traveling Grossology exhibition, created by Advanced Exhibits, a division of Advanced Animations LLC, stems from the best-selling *Grossology* books by U.S. author Sylvia Branzei. "This is science in disguise," Branzei explains. "If we teach students in their own words, they'll understand better and actually learn something."

Still, what would the British—famed throughout the world for culture, civility, and a completely unpredictable sense of humor—make of an exhibition that even the Science Museum described as "dealing with farts, snot, poo, and other 'nasties' not discussed in polite society"?

As if the Science Museum needed more flirtation with disaster (it even sponsored a Grossology Web site that listed euphemisms for passing gas, including "bottom burp" and "trouser cough"), the exhibition came from the United States and used U.S. animatronic technologies in its exhibits—hardly a formula for winning the hearts of skeptical British citizens.

And yet the Science Museum believed in the science and the possible success of Grossology. To help promote the exhibition to the British public, the museum enlisted the services of its own communications staff as well as a public relations agency called mission 21.

Aiming High or Dumbing Down?

Initial research didn't improve the outlook for Grossology's success. Not only was the exhibition controversial, born in the U.S.A., and disgusting, it wasn't free: The museum would charge for admission, a policy it had moved away from in recent months. That meant that an exhibition targeting children would compete with movies, video arcades, and every other youth-oriented fee-based attraction in London. Even worse, early discussions of Grossology kept returning to a common misperception: The museum was "dumbing down" science by accepting such an exhibition.

Research into Grossology's U.S. roots, however, showed that even the crustiest critics didn't think Grossology was dumbed-down science. Rather, the books and exhibition used an "edutainment" philosophy to teach children some fundamentals of science. Could the same philosophy work in the United Kingdom?

Further research showed that a primary target public for the Grossology campaign was the Science Museum's own staff. Staff members had to be ready to counter any charges of dumbing down. They needed to present Grossology as a distinguished . . . well, as a reputable . . . well, at least as an interesting and effective way to present science to kids. A related target public was science opinion leaders in the United Kingdom—that is, individuals who influenced public opinion about science issues.

Other primary target publics were, logically, kids themselves; their parents, grandparents, and teachers; and the news media.

Seen in *The Beano:* The Plan

Based on its research, the communications team developed both a campaign goal and an overriding strategy. The strategy was simple: Stay on message! Grossology did not dumb down science; rather, the exhibition presented science to children in a fascinating, effective new way.

The campaign goal supported the museum's broader mission of maintaining the highest standards of science education while avoiding the snootiness and boredom that some associate with science. The goal for the Grossology campaign plan was to help create a financially successful exhibition that expanded the image of the Science Museum as being modern, relevant, and accessible to many.

Under that goal, the communications team created three objectives:

- To further the Science Museum's mission of reaching and engaging new audiences
- To surprise, amuse, and intrigue audiences and help change outdated perceptions of the museum
- To generate 995 paying visitors a day during May and 1,076 a day in June and July, with even higher attendance during school holidays

To achieve the objectives, the Science Museum's communications staff and mission 21 created three phases of public relations tactics: prelaunch tactics (before the exhibition opened); launch tactics (during the opening); and duration tactics (during the life of the exhibit, from May 11 through Sept. 6).

Prelaunch tactics began with formal and informal contacts with science opinion leaders, particular members of the Royal Institute of Science, to secure their endorsements of Grossology. Such endorsements would help combat charges of dumbing down.

The communications team announced the exhibition to the news media with a news release that began "On Saturday 11 May 2002 Grossology: The (Impolite) Science of the Human Body splats, oozes, and bursts into life at the Science Mu-

'Snot your everyday science fair. Nigel Nose-It-All and the Grossology
exhibition wowed kids (and others) at the Science Museum in London.
(Courtesy of Advanced Animations LLC)

seum." Perhaps more important, the media relations effort included persuading *The Beano,* the United Kingdom's wildly popular but irreverent comic book—somewhat similar to the United States's *Mad Magazine*—to feature a favorable (though disgusting) strip on Grossology.

In keeping with the gross-but-relevant strategy, Science Museum President Jon Tucker said, via news release, "This exhibition is an absolute must-see. It hits the pimple on the head. Children love making bodily sounds and asking graphic questions at the most embarrassing moments. This exhibition uses that curiosity to excite them about science and helps to explain it."

Other prelaunch tactics included hosting a video preview for the news media and reviewing question-and-answer sheets with staff members so that they could refute charges of dumbing down and excessive U.S. influence.

Tactics during the launch itself focused primarily on the news media. The day before Grossology opened to the public, the museum treated reporters and editors to a private preview of the exhibition. The communications team ensured that the visiting journalists received copies of favorable media accounts that already had appeared—including the strip from *The Beano.*

Old Underwear and Viral "Fart Organs": More Tactics

The Science Museum's most imaginative tactics occurred during the exhibition itself. Chief among them were a so-called viral fart organ and a notorious online survey of gross behavior. The fart organ—viral because it was a game sent via e-mail in hopes that recipients would spread it like a virus—allowed players to create tunes by programming a series of musical trouser coughs.

The online survey lasted almost the duration of the exhibition. When the museum announced the results, Grossology became front-page news throughout the United Kingdom. Residents of the British Isles learned that 34 percent of their fellow citizens pick their noses and "eat what they excavate." Other findings? Northern Irish audibly burp and pass gas in public more than the rest of their fellow citizens, while the Welsh are most likely to blame their own embarrassing noises on innocent bystanders. Only 3 percent of the men of Kent change their underwear daily. And as for the women of Dorset—well, you probably don't want to know.

"Overall, we're pretty gross," said a Science Museum representative. "But it was a fun survey, and I don't think anyone should take it too seriously."

An irreverent lack of seriousness coupled with good science also characterized Grossology's Web site. The site included such pages as "Gross Facts" (amazing stuff about urine) and "Gross Experiments" (including a "Fake Snot Recipe" and a do-it-yourself belching balloon belly).

Even conventional tactics embraced grossness. Media kits to regional newspapers contained "Foul Facts" sheets. Special events included a loudest burp competition, broadcast live, and live gross experiments at the Covent Garden shopping area. As Sept. 6 and the end of Grossology neared, the exhibition's final news release sent one last invitation to enter the "stinky, slimy, scaly world of Grossology." Primary targets for the news releases and media kits included London tourism and entertainment guides and children's news media.

Evaluation: Nothing to "Bon-Goo" At

Grossology's edutainment blend of true science and true yechiness did win the approval of the prestigious Royal Institute of Science. The exhibition also earned the praise of the country's National Museum Directors Conference. Charges of dumbing down were few, if any.

Media coverage of the exhibition, beginning with the all-important *Beano,* was extensive. Sixty major media outlets attended Grossology's prelaunch preview, and regional distribution of media kits generated more than 120 stories. Even the prestigious *Times* of London declared, "The Science Museum is to be congratulated on boldly going where no sane biology master has gone before"—and the newspaper's science editors proudly joined the fun, offering readers the Korean word for a bottom burp: *bon-goo.* Media coverage for Grossology set a record for the most publicity ever for a Science Museum exhibition.

Attendance in the opening days was double the amount specified in the objectives. Early sessions sold out, and, in all, more than 100,000 grossologists attended the exhibition. More than two-thirds of those surveyed credited news media stories for alerting them to Grossology. And the most-cited medium among kids? *The Beano,* of course.

Awards for Grossology and its promotional campaign were numerous. London's *Time Out* entertainment weekly named Grossology a "Critic's Choice." Both the London Tourist Board and the English Tourism Council named the Science Museum the year's top tourist attraction.

In praising the efforts of Grossology's communications team, the London edition of *PR Week* magazine concluded, "The campaign enhanced the reputation of the 150-year-old institution and was lauded by the media." And in 2003, the Science Museum's Grossology public relations campaign won first place, consumer relationships division, in the United Kingdom's Institute of Public Relations Excellence Awards.

"We took big risks with the PR program for this exhibition," said Stephen Bromberg, Science Museum communications manager. "We could easily have been accused of dumbing down, but instead bold PR earned us great visitor numbers and affection and turned this into a memorable campaign. Most people would not think that edgy, risky, and radical PR would come out of the Science Museum—but it does. Ourselves and mission 21 worked hard to reach new audiences, people the museum wouldn't ordinarily communicate with, earning thousands of new fans."

The Science Museum's final salute to Grossology was typical. In a news release announcing its Institute of Public Relations award, the public relations team stayed on message one last time: "The Science Museum won a prestigious PR award for promoting an exhibition about farts, poo, and snot."

Sources

Will Barker, "1 in 3 Are as Gross as Homer," *The Sun,* August 27, 2002. Online: Lexis-Nexis.

"Burp, Fart, and Sniff Your Way to Understanding the Science of the Human Body," Science Museum news release, March 31, 2002 Online: www.sciencemuseum.org.uk.

"Children: Listings—Critics Choice," *Time Out,* May 8, 2002. Online: Lexis-Nexis.

Gidon Freeman, "Grossology Captures the Imagination," *PR Week* (UK), September 6, 2002. Online: Lexis-Nexis.

Alison Goddard, "For the Farterland," *Times Higher Education Supplement,* August 30, 2002. Online: Lexis-Nexis.

Advanced Exhibits Web site, www.grossologytour.com.

"Homegrown Habits Are Worst of a Bad Bunch," *Irish News,* August 28, 2002. Online: Lexis-Nexis.

Institute of Public Relations Web site, www.ipr.org.uk.

"Last Chance to See the Science Museum's Must-See Exhibition: Grossology," Science Museum news release, August 21, 2002. Online: www.sciencemuseum.org.uk.

"Science Museum Feted for Farting," Science Museum news release, August 7, 2003. Online: www.sciencemuseum.org.uk.

"Science Museum, Grossology, Mission 21," *PR Week* (UK), November 1, 2002. Online: Lexis-Nexis.

"Science Museum Grossology Survey Reveals Who Makes the UK YUCK!" Science Museum news release, August 27, 2002. Online: www.sciencemuseum.org.uk.

Science Museum Web site, www.sciencemuseum.org.uk.

"Science Museum Wins PR Award," National Museum Directors' Conference Web site, www.nationalmuseums.or.uk/news.

Power to the People

*To Communicate with Californians,
a Public Relations Agency Learns
to Speak in Five Languages*

Is the United States a melting pot in which different cultures merge and blend? Or is it a mosaic in which diverse cultures remain unique and form a new whole from distinct segments? Increasingly, sociologists tend to see a mosaic. If the concept is accurate, California is the country's greatest work of art.

In the Golden State, white residents of Anglo-Saxon ancestry constitute less than half the state's population. Residents of Hispanic origin constitute 32 percent; of Asian origin, 11 percent; and of African origin, 7 percent. Foreign-born residents constitute more than a quarter of the population, and households in which the primary language is not English constitute 40 percent, compared with a U.S. average of 18 percent.

Pacific Gas and Electric, a huge power company, confronted that diversity in 2001 when the California Public Utilities Commission ordered it to significantly increase enrollment in a payment-assistance program for low-income customers. PG&E knew that it could communicate in English through traditional channels—but that approach would ignore California's growing multicultural environment. To communicate effectively with a variety of cultures, PG&E hired Hill & Knowlton, one of the world's largest public relations agencies.

Based in New York, Hill & Knowlton provides communication services to national and international clients. It has offices in 36 countries and affiliations with other agencies in additional nations. PG&E requested Hill & Knowlton's help in promoting a statewide program called CARE (California Alternate Rates for Energy), which provided a 15 percent reduction in utility payments. For more than a decade, enrollment in CARE had lagged at less than 40 percent of all eligible customers. In 2001, California's utilities commission ordered PG&E to boost that percentage by the end of the year.

English Channels

Hill & Knowlton began its research process by examining existing information about the different demographic and psychographic communities within California. Using findings from that secondary research, the agency conducted face-to-face and phone interviews with leaders in different ethnic groups to learn why enrollment numbers in CARE remained low among eligible members of their communities. From its research, Hill & Knowlton drew several conclusions that became the basis for a multicultural communications plan:

- More than 90 percent of all eligible customers spoke one of five languages at home: English, Spanish, Cantonese, Mandarin, or Vietnamese.
- Diversity among eligible customers within each ethnic community existed, governed by such things as age and rural–urban status.
- Although the utilities bill generally was sent to the male head-of-household, the top decision maker on family matters often was the female head-of-household.
- Many eligible customers were unaware of CARE because of lack of distribution of promotional materials.

A final research conclusion underscored the need for Hill & Knowlton to craft a respectful, multicultural campaign: Even when eligible customers did find CARE promotional materials, the English-only approach often discouraged them.

180 Days

One unusual aspect of Hill & Knowlton's campaign for CARE was the goal that PG&E stipulated. A goal often describes a general aim. But PG&E's goal for increased participation in CARE was nothing if not specific: Increase enrollment in CARE from 40 percent of eligible customers to 50 percent—a 20 percent increase—in 180 days.

Hill & Knowlton's primary objective in pursuit of that goal was to inform eligible customers in an appropriate language and with appropriate respect for unique cultural norms—in person, when possible. That ambition led to two more objectives: to identify appropriate community organizations and train their members to recruit CARE candidates; and deliver messages about CARE through trusted third parties, particularly community leaders.

Hill & Knowlton's first tactic emphasized cultural awareness and respect. The agency wholly revamped PG&E's CARE-related toll-free call center. The new service—available 24 hours a day, seven days a week—featured recorded messages in five different languages.

To help ensure culturally sensitive, face-to-face recruiting, PG&E attracted community organizations—labeled CARE Community Outreach Coordinators—by offering such groups $1 million in payments for program applications. PG&E thus built additional goodwill by helping fund community services.

"This partnership between our organizations ensures that the information regarding the CARE benefits reaches those individuals and families in most need of assistance," said John Gamboa, executive director of the Greenlining Institute, a minorities advocacy group and an early PG&E partner.

CARE：能源優惠計劃

加州能源折扣收費（**CARE**）是一項對不同類型的能源用戶提供的低收費計劃。

- **獨立家庭用戶的 CARE 計劃**
  此計劃適用于獨立家庭中有自己帳戶的用戶。**CARE** 提供每月煤氣費和電費八折優惠。此外，**CARE** 用戶還可免除近期的電費加價。在簽署之後，每兩年必需續期一次。

- **享用分表設施的住宅用戶的 CARE 計劃**
  這個計劃是給那些享用分表設施的租戶八折優惠。這類租戶電量和帳單均由業主提供（例如，停放的流動房屋，享用分表的公寓和小船塢）。這種優惠是通過業主取得的。每一年必需續期一次。申請表可向業主或經理索取，或聯絡你的能源公司（請看第 2 頁）。

- **符合非牟利社團機構的居住設備的 CARE 計劃**
  從 1992 年開始，原計劃已經擴展到非牟利社團機構的居住單位，無家可歸者庇護所，救濟院和婦女庇護所提供 **CARE** 折價優惠。所有的住客都一定符合 **CARE** 的計劃所定明的收入界限和這些機構必須是聯邦免稅者，例如，"**501(c).**"。這些機構可以符合住宅或商業收費，但是一定要每一個分表中 **70%** 的能源是作住宅用途。

- **農業僱員住宅的 CARE 計劃**
  1996 年立法更進一步擴至加州政府臨時工人服務處（**OMS**）擁有並且管理的臨時農業工人房屋，私人擁有並持有執照的僱員房屋 ，及非牟利的流動的房屋。與非牟利社團機構住所的 **CARE** 計劃一樣，每類住所需有符合自己的資格，執照、免稅和能源用途。

- **收入標準於 2003 年 6 月 1 日生效**
  家庭的所有成員全年收入的總和不可超過以下表格所列之收入。因為通貨膨脹的問題，收入線需要每年調整一次。

家庭人數	全年總收入界限
1-2	$ 23,000
3	$ 27,000
4	$ 32,500
每增加一人請增加	$ 5,500

In its efforts to reach out to all publics in the state, the California Public Utilities Commission posted CARE instructions in Mandarin on its Web site. (Courtesy of the California Public Utilities Commission)

A steady stream of news releases highlighted the above tactics and also sent out a call for the assistance of community leaders. "We are partnering with community groups from Bakersfield to the Oregon border to make sure customers who qualify, regardless of where they live, are aware of the CARE program and are encouraged to enroll as soon as possible," said Guillermo Rodriguez Jr., PG&E's director of external relations. "But to be successful, we also need assistance from leaders across our community to get the word out to every eligible family."

With its finding that females in virtually all the targeted ethnic groups were the primary caregivers for their families, Hill & Knowlton helped PG&E place its message in family-service areas. The agency helped place multilingual CARE brochures in neighborhood laundries, churches, community centers, and schools. It helped design enrollment events at Sears and K-Mart stores and even at a Kwanzaa celebration at a community center. At a K-Mart store in San Jose, for example, the name of every new CARE applicant was entered into a raffle for an energy-efficient refrigerator.

PG&E and Hill & Knowlton also promoted the CARE program through inserts in customer bills, inserts in Hispanic newspapers, and information on the PG&E Web site. Using services and information from the Web site, eligible customers could download an application and fax it to PG&E headquarters through home technology or facilities at community centers.

PG&E also placed advertisements, using research to select print ads for Asian communities, radio for Hispanic communities, and outdoor (billboard) ads for English-speaking customers.

"We are absolutely committed to making sure that every eligible customer is enrolled in CARE," Rodriguez said.

Rolling with the Changes

Operating in a business environment regulated by the California Public Utilities Commission, PG&E had to be responsive to policy changes that affected CARE. Throughout the recruitment campaign, in fact, the company had to announce changes in program details. In April, the utilities commission allowed a rate increase for electrical services but exempted CARE enrollees from the hike. The commission also expanded the pool of residents who qualified for CARE. PG&E adapted its program and announced the changes in a news release.

In June, the utilities commission increased the CARE discount from 15 percent to 20 percent—and, again, PG&E announced the modified CARE program with a news release. In the same news release, PG&E provided a forum for a community-organization partner to call for more enrollments and for more involvement from community leaders. "We encourage families who need help in paying their electricity bill to call PG&E and inquire about the payment assistance programs," said Luis Arteaga, assistant director of California's Latino Issues Forum. "Also, it is important that community leaders become active in educating our community."

Hill & Knowlton made changes of its own to provide complete services in a multicultural environment. To communicate successfully with PG&E's target publics, the agency hired new employees familiar with the specific languages and cultures.

Awards and Expansion

Hill & Knowlton succeeded in helping PG&E meet its ambitious goal for CARE. The new toll-free call center received 51,000 calls in all five languages in its first few months of existence. More than 75 community organizations enlisted as CARE Community Outreach Coordinators. Within 180 days, more than 20 elected officials had endorsed CARE and PG&E's efforts to increase enrollment. Four California communities sponsored a CARE Day. "The energy crisis has been tough on all of us, and I applaud PG&E for its diligence in making sure every eligible family is enrolled in CARE," said Nora Campos, a member of the San Jose City Council.

By the end of 180 days, Hill & Knowlton had exceeded PG&E's goal of 50 percent enrollment. More than 200,000 residents enrolled in CARE during the campaign, increasing the total to 52 percent of eligible Californians. For its success in creating an effective grass-roots multicultural campaign, Hill & Knowlton won PRSA's prestigious Silver Anvil Award for Multicultural Public Relations.

Hill & Knowlton also received an award from PG&E in the form of additional business. PG&E asked the agency to extend its campaign, and in 2002, Hill & Knowlton helped increase enrollment in CARE to 61 percent of eligible customers. For its new efforts, Hill & Knowlton won a Gold SABRE Award for Multicultural Marketing Campaigns from the *Holmes Report,* a public relations newsletter.

Hill & Knowlton's success with CARE has helped the agency solidify its presence in multicultural public relations. In 2003, Hill & Knowlton helped create DIVERSAlliance, a multicultural communications partnership, with Hispanic-owned HeadQuarters Advertising, one of its partners in the CARE campaign. Additional partners in the new venture are SAESHE Advertising, which specializes in marketing to Asian Americans, and the Walker Marchant Group, a minority/female-owned agency.

"We are excited to expand our excellent working relationship with Hill & Knowlton," said Horacio Gomes, HeadQuarters president. "Through DIVERS Alliance, we can offer clients anywhere in the U.S. the full range of public relations, public affairs, and advertising services in a new and different way."

Sources

"CARE Education and Outreach," Pacific Gas and Electric Company Web site, www.pge.com.

"Case Studies 2003: Bring You Energy with CARE," Hill & Knowlton Web site, www.hillandknowlton.com.

"Hill and Knowlton USA Wins Five Gold & Silver SABRE Awards," Hill & Knowlton news release, May 20, 2003. Online: www.hillandknowlton.com.

"Major Multicultural Alliance Announced by Agencies Headquarters Advertising, Hill & Knowlton, SAESHE Advertising and the Walker Merchant Group," Hill & Knowlton news release, February 5, 2003. Online: Lexis-Nexis.

"More Customers of Pacific Gas and Electric Company Now Eligible for Lower Electric Bills," PG&E news release, June 2, 2003. Online: www.pge.com.

"Pacific Gas and Electric Company Announces Changes in the CARE Program," PG&E news release, April 5, 2001. Online: www.pge.com.

"Pacific Gas and Electric Company Reaches out to 600,000 Customers Eligible for CARE Discounts," PG&E news release, September 27, 2001. Online: www.pge.com.

"Pacific Gas and Electric Company to Award Contracts to Community Groups That Help Low-Income Consumers," PG&E news release, August 6, 2001. Online: www.pge.com.

"PG&E Announces Higher Discount for Low Income Assistance Programs," PG&E news release, June 13, 2001. Online: www.pge.com.

"PG&E Joins with Community Groups to Increase Outreach to Low-Income Households," PG&E news release, February 8, 2001. Online: www.pge.com.

"PG&E, Self-Help for Elderly and Other Local Groups Partnering to Reach More than 35,000 San Franciscans," PG&E news release, September 4, 2002. Online: www.pge.com.

"PG&E to Enroll South Bay Customers during October 20 CARE Day in San Jose," PG&E news release, October 16, 2001. Online: www.pge.com.

Public Relations Society of America Web site, www.prsa.org.

Civil Disobedience in Nigeria

case 10.3

An Unusual Campaign Tactic Improves Relationships in a Developing Nation

Roli Ododoh wasn't supposed to be there. The property belonged to others, and the mother of two children had broken the law to set foot upon it. But the danger of her position couldn't compete with the grandeur of what she saw.

"The Bible describes paradise as a beautiful place where there is everything," Ododoh later told a *New York Times* reporter. "When we got in there, it really was like paradise."

Paradise for Ododoh was the ChevronTexaco terminal in Escravos, Nigeria—a compound in the country's southern delta region consisting of holding tanks, docks for ships, an airstrip, offices, and homes for workers. Ododoh lived across the river from the compound in an impoverished fishing village.

"This is a people who are living very close to where they see oil being drilled from the areas in which they live," said Chris Fomunyoh of the National Democratic Institute for International Affairs in Washington, D.C. "And yet they live in abject poverty."

For 10 days in July 2002, Ododoh and hundreds of other women in Nigeria's delta region invaded the Escravos compound, staging a protest that won international attention for peacefulness and success. Much of the world's interest, however, focused on the women's tactics—and one in particular.

Good Neighbors

The Escravos compound is jointly owned by Chevron Nigeria Limited, a subsidiary of international oil company ChevronTexaco, and the Nigerian National Petroleum Company. Nigeria is one of the world's most prolific oil producers, generating approximately $250 billion in revenues since oil was discovered there in the early 1960s.

Despite the poverty of the Escravos region, ChevronTexaco prided itself on being a good neighbor—and with good reason. In Nigeria, ChevronTexaco now generates more than 2,000 jobs, 90 percent of which are held by Nigerians. Almost 75 percent of the Nigerian subsidiary's managers are Nigerian citizens. Since the early 1990s, ChevronTexaco has invested more than $90 million in community development in the country. The company operates the Riverboat Ambulance Services in the Escravos delta area, hosts AIDS-education seminars, and offers scholarships to area schools.

"One of the keys to our success in Africa—and elsewhere—is our commitment to partnership," said ChevronTexaco Chairman and CEO David O'Reilly in accepting a 2002 Sullivan Leadership Award. The Sullivan awards are named for the late Rev. Leon H. Sullivan, a leader in international civil rights. "To us, partnership is not a legal or business term. It is a value. We understand that success among partners must be mutual and sustained. Partnership transcends business—it governs our relationships with our employees, our communities, with governments and with customers."

ChevronTexaco was a good partner and neighbor. But the nearby fishing village of Ugborodo had no gas station—it imported gas for sale at approximately three times the normal price. The people of Ugborodo wanted jobs—and they wanted electricity, water, and schools. They wanted some of the paradise that they saw so nearby.

"How long these two worlds can coexist in such proximity without inflaming violence is a question that increasingly preoccupies the top management of ChevronTexaco," wrote *New York Times* reporter Norimitsu Onishi.

Violence had erupted in the region before. *Platt's Oilgram News,* an industry news service, reported that "previous attacks on the Escravos terminal, which is situated in coastal swampland, have been carried out by armed gangs of local youths." The *London Daily Telegraph* reported that nine tribal leaders had been executed in the mid-1990s for protests that had disrupted the development plans of a rival company.

But the violence hadn't produced changes for Ugborodo. And so a different group of activists—village women—developed a plan to change the village's relationship with ChevronTexaco. Their goal was to win the desired jobs, electricity, water, and schools. And they believed they had a tactic that would work.

The Tactic

On July 8, 2002, the women of Ugborodo gathered in the predawn darkness. In small groups they huddled near a supply boat sent from the terminal to pick up daily workers. Numbering in the hundreds, they suddenly surged toward the boat, forcing the workers off and demanding that the captain take them to the terminal. Taken by surprise, the captain complied, and before the terminal security force realized what was happening, the women were inside the ChevronTexaco compound.

The invasion had not been the attackers' first choice or first tactic. Earlier, the women had written a letter detailing their concerns to company managers, but amid the hundreds of letters ChevronTexaco receives each day, the letter had not gained company attention.

"What's unique this time around is that it's being led by . . . unarmed women, some with kids on their backs," Fomunyoh told CNN Anchor Fredricka Whitfield.

CNN reported that the women had trapped approximately 700 workers inside the compound. They occupied the docks and the airstrip, preventing movements into and out of the oil terminal. *Platt's Oilgram News* reported that operations at the facility were "severely disrupted."

Nigerian military forces and ChevronTexaco's own security personnel were at the Escravos terminal, but Chevron Nigeria Limited's leader gave orders to maintain the peace. African observers doubted, however, that the armed forces would have moved forward even under orders.

Why the reluctance? The women threatened to deploy a tactic of great power in some African cultures. They pledged to remove their clothing—to strip—in front of any attackers.

"The threat that women could disrobe in the presence of men—it's very disarming, even for the military that would traditionally have gone in to try to break up the protest," Fomunyoh said.

"Our ultimate weapon is our nakedness," Helen Odeworitse, one of the women, told a reporter for the *London Daily Telegraph*.

Other African experts agreed. "By the time the women bare their chests and go around, people are really in trouble," Bolanle Awe explained to a *Christian Science Monitor* reporter. Awe, a founder of the Women's Research and Documentation Center in Nigeria, added, "It's a curse on whoever the ruler is."

"Most Nigerian tribes consider unwanted displays of nudity to be an extremely damning protest measure designed to evoke a collective sense of shame among those at whom the action is directed," noted *Platt's Oilgram News*.

CNN reported that the women's nudity would cause "ultimate shame" for any attackers. Onishi, in the *New York Times,* wrote, "Showing nudity, especially by older women, is a weapon of last resort, considered an act of deep shame here and a great curse directed at men."

Cultural Diversity

The nudity tactic surprised some observers in the Western, industrialized world. "The flurry of female radicalism is far removed from the coordinated, Internet-assisted campaigns against multinationals in industrialized countries," concluded the *Christian Science Monitor.* "The villages around the Escravos terminal have no access to telephones or computers."

The threat of disrobing, reported Minnesota Public Radio's *Marketplace,* "takes creative nonviolence to a new level."

Some Western observers noted that other cultures might react differently to the threat of nudity. Columnist Sally Kalson of the *Pittsburgh Post-Gazette* wrote:

> Hard to imagine this kind of naked ploy succeeding in America. . . . Sure, the country would still take note of 600 women threatening to disrobe en masse—but mostly with wisecracks about their age and presumed physical imperfections. . . . Still, it's inspiring to know that somewhere in the world, nonviolent protest is alive and well.

Crossing the Water

True to their word to be good neighbors and good partners, managers of the ChevronTexaco compound crossed the water to the village of Ugborodo to see

U.S. Ambassador to Nigeria Roger Meece, right, toasts Chevron Nigeria Managing Director Jay Pryor for winning a U.S. State Department award honoring commitment to the people of Nigeria. (Courtesy of the United States Diplomatic Mission to Nigeria)

conditions firsthand and speak with other leaders of the protest. They met peaceful protest with peaceful negotiation.

Nine days after the women had occupied the Escravos terminal, their leaders and ChevronTexaco managers signed a memo of understanding that pledged village improvements, including assistance in providing schools, electricity, and water. For their part, the villagers pledged to maintain peace and open dialogue in their relationship with ChevronTexaco.

"We are delighted that this crisis has been resolved peacefully through dialogue," said the chairman of Chevron Nigeria Limited, a U.S. citizen. "The agreement reached today between us and the community demonstrates our unwavering commitment to being a good partner focused on building productive, collaborative, trusting, and beneficial relationships with our communities and other stakeholders."

News media and other observers around the world praised the peaceful resolution of the conflict.

"To the credit of ChevronTexaco, they made commitments to meet some of the demands of the women," Fomunyoh said.

CNN reported that the protest ended peacefully. *Platt's Oilgram News* concluded, "The . . . protest by the unarmed women, whose biggest threat was to remove their clothes, appears to have been more successful for having been nonviolent."

One of the most hopeful reactions came from Mama Ayo, a leader of the Escravos protest. "If Chevron's M.D. [managing director] from America comes here and sees the way we are living, he will do good," she told the *New York Times.* "I am sure of that. We are still friends forever."

Sources

Tim Butcher, "Strip Threat by Women Halts Oil Terminal," *London Daily Telegraph,* July 15, 2992. Online: Lexis-Nexis.

CNN Sunday Morning, July 21, 2002. Online: Lexis-Nexis.

Sally Kalson, "Shame Fuels Nigerian Protest," *Pittsburgh Post-Gazette,* July 17, 2002. Online: www.post-gazette.com.

Marketplace, July 25, 2002. Online: Lexis-Nexis.

Jacinta Moran, "ChevronTexaco near Deal to End Protest," *Platt's Oilgram News,* July 17, 2002. Online: Lexis-Nexis.

"Nigeria Fact Sheet." Online: www.chevrontexaco.com.

"Occupation of Escravos Ends as Chevron and Ugborodo Community Sign Agreement," Chevron news release, July 17, 2002. Online: www.chevrontexaco.com/news/press.

Norimitsu Onishi, "As Oil Riches Flow, Poor Village Cries Out," *The New York Times,* December 22, 2002. Online: Lexis-Nexis.

Michael Peel, "Women Blocked the Entrances of Two Oil Company Facilities, the Latest in a Month of Protests," *The Christian Science Monitor,* December 8, 2002. Online: www.csmonitor.com.

"Remarks by David O'Reilly, Chairman and CEO, ChevronTexaco, Leon H. Sullivan Awards Dinner," June 20, 2002. Online: www.chevrontexaco.com.

ACT file #10 ·

Hofstede's Cultural Dimensions

Flash back to the 1970s. (OK, that may be a little difficult for most readers, but use your imaginations.) You're an IBM executive in charge of a worldwide corporate empire—and you're fascinated by mysterious national and cultural differences that prevent the design of one, uniform employee communications program. So you approach company psychologist Geert Hofstede to study national/cultural differences among your employees.

Hofstede studied the IBM workforce in 64 countries, and his findings launched additional studies that covered other groups, including students and airline pilots, in still other nations. Hofstede concluded that national cultures tend to differ in five basic areas, which he labeled "dimensions." Today, a generation later, students of cultural differences still rely on Hofstede's Cultural Dimensions to analyze unique national cultures. Those five dimensions are power distance, individualism, masculinity/femininity, uncertainty avoidance, and long-term/short-term orientation.

1. *Power distance* measures how tolerant a society is about unequally distributed decision-making power. Countries with a high acceptance of power distance include Mexico and France. Countries with a low acceptance include Austria and the United States.

2. *Individualism,* as contrasted with collectivism, pits loyalty to one's self against loyalty to a larger group. Countries in Asia and Latin America gravitate toward collectivism, while the United States, Canada, and most European countries gravitate toward individualism.

3. *Masculinity/femininity* contrasts competitiveness (traditionally masculine) against compassion and nurturing (traditionally feminine). Masculine nations include the United States, Germany, and Japan. Feminine nations include Sweden and Spain.

4. *Uncertainty avoidance* measures how well a society tolerates ambiguity. Nations that have difficulty functioning in uncertainty include Germany. Nations that tolerate ambiguity include Great Britain and the United States.

5. *Long-term/short-term orientation* measures a society's willingness to consider the traditions of the past and carry them into the future. China and other East Asian nations tend to have long-term orientations. The United States has a short-term orientation.

Advanced Critical Thinking

As long as public relations practitioners avoid simplistic stereotyping, Hofstede's Cultural Dimensions provide a standard system for analyzing national cultures. His analyses of how specific nations embody the five cultural dimensions appear in his books, *Cultures and Organizations: Software of the Mind* and *Culture's Consequences: Comparing Values, Behaviors, Institutions and Organizations across Nations.*[1]

Discussion Questions

1. What countries besides those listed above might have a high tolerance for power distance? Why?

2. Do you agree that U.S. citizens tolerate ambiguity fairly well? Why or why not?

3. Consider recent international news stories. Can Hofstede's cultural dimensions help explain reported differences from your own culture?

4. Discuss Hofstede's cultural dimensions with classmates who have studied abroad. Can they—or you—apply the dimensions to the cultures in which they lived?

Endnote

1. Hofstede, Geert. *Cultures and Organizations: Software of the Mind.* New York: McGraw-Hill, 1991. Hofstede, Geert. *Culture's Consequences: Comparing Values, Behaviors, Institutions and Organizations across Nations.* Thousand Oaks, CA: Sage, 2001.

CHAPTER 11

Ethics and Social Responsibility

S tudents of ethics can serve themselves well by contemplating Jean Buridan's ass. Clearly, this needs a little explanation. Jean Buridan was a 14th century French philosopher, and his ass—a donkey—was a mythical animal that, standing between two equal piles of hay, starved to death because it couldn't decide which pile represented the better choice—the greater good. In philosophy, "Buridan's ass" has become a synonym for befuddled indecision. When we struggle with ethical problems—sometimes with choosing between clashing values—we run the risk of becoming Buridan's ass. Successful public relations practitioners must arm themselves with knowledge and critical thinking skills to avoid becoming, in ethical issues, the professional equivalent of a dead donkey.

To borrow a cliché, ethics is one of those things that says easy but does hard. We can define ethics without much difficulty, but *doing* ethics—and action is the heart of ethics—can be tough. **Ethics** are the values that guide the ways we think and act. That definition possesses two parts, each indispensable. Without values, we have no ethics. But unless we bring forth those qualities in our thoughts and actions, we still have no ethics. Ethics are active, not passive.

Ethics are about integrity. In its fullest sense, *integrity* means an integration of ideals and actions. Integrity means that our values come to life in our daily routines, not just at times of crisis.

Another way to define ethics, say Professors Gene Laczniak and Patrick Murphy, is to substitute the concept of trust: If people are ethical, they are trustworthy.[1] We may not always agree with the decisions they make, but we do trust that they strove, to the best of their abilities, to act on honorable values. And chances are that, even in our disagreement, we respect them.

In a 2003 position statement titled "Restoring Trust in Business: Models for Action," the PR Coalition, a group of leading U.S. and worldwide public relations organizations, compared ethics to "a moral compass" that guides our actions. And in the same document, the coalition linked ethics to trust: "Lack of trust in a business is seen as crucially debilitating. . . . Rebuilding trust is a long-term undertaking. It requires injecting a philosophy of social responsibility and ethical behavior into the company's culture."[2]

Good ethics and social responsibility lead to trustworthiness and respect, two valuable assets in public relations and in life.

Challenges to Ethical Behavior

So who wouldn't act ethically? Who wants to be an indecisive donkey—or, worse, a scoundrel? But as we noted earlier, behaving ethically isn't always easy. Ethics scholar Laura Nash believes that ethics problems can be divided into two categories: *denial* and *dilemma*.[3] Nash's system, however, begins with the belief that we want to be ethical; her system offers little insight to someone determined to be a donkey or a scoundrel.

Problems of **denial,** says Nash, involve powerful temptation. Different courses of action lie before us, and we know which course seems consistent with our values. However, we choose a different course because doing the right thing—honoring the most important values at stake—just seems too hard. Doing the right thing might involve public humiliation, or losing our job, or losing a friend. In problems of denial, we deny the commands of our strongest beliefs. We separate actions from values, and we behave unethically.

As gut wrenching as problems of denial sound, dilemmas may be even worse. We often use the word **dilemma** as a synonym for *problem*—but dilemmas are worse than that. A dilemma is a problem that has no good solution. An ethics dilemma involves a clash of values, and no solution that honors all the involved values seems possible. Harvard Professor of Ethics Joseph Badaracco calls ethics dilemmas "defining moments" because they tell us who we really are and what we really value.[4] For example, a public relations practitioner may be torn between financial obligations to his family and working for a client whose views he opposes. Badaracco offers the depressing but realistic notion that in dilemmas we often get our hands dirty. At best, we get to pick—through a critical analysis of the dilemma—which dirt stains us.

To Nash's two categories of denial and dilemma, your authors would add a third: **ignorance** (we wish it started with the letter *d*). Problems of ignorance come from a lack of awareness that something is challenging our values. Ignorance may stem from inexperience: Young practitioners in particular need to be wary of ethical ignorance—though age is no defense against a lack of critical thinking. One reason for critically analyzing the case studies in this book is to become familiar with the challenges of your chosen profession. In public relations, problems of ethical ignorance tend to cluster into five areas: overwork, legal/ethical confusion, cross-cultural ethics, short-term thinking, and virtual organizations.

1. **Overwork.** Overwork involves taking on so many tasks that we lack time to consider the motivations and consequences of our actions. As a young professional, you know that you'll impress your bosses by arriving early, staying late, and, basically, working like a perpetual-motion machine. However, work in public relations also involves measuring all your actions against your values and those of your client, your organization, your profession, and your society. Don't get so busy with implementing tactics that you can't see a looming ethics problem.

2. **Legal/ethical confusion.** Here's a definite—and unproductive—shortcut in critical thinking: deciding that if it's legal, it's ethical, case closed. But legal actions aren't always ethical. To a lesser degree, ethical actions may not always be legal. For example, it's probably legal to refuse to help an endangered public that has served your organization well for years. Is it ethical?

3. **Cross-cultural ethics.** As the forces of globalization expand the world of public relations (see Chapter 10), practitioners increasingly encounter unfamiliar cultural norms. For example, let's say you possess the value of honoring the religious beliefs of your co-workers and clients. On business in Turkey, you walk onto the grounds of a mosque—with your shoes on. You've just desecrated holy ground and offended your colleagues. Intentionally? Of course not. But ignorance separated your actions from your values.

4. **Short-term thinking.** Short-term thinking is poor critical thinking. It involves refusing to consider the long-term consequences of your actions. Short-term thinking can lead to momentary pleasure at the cost of long-term pain. If we deliberately refuse to consider long-term ramifications, short-term thinking may be more a problem of denial than ignorance.

5. **Virtual organizations.** Made possible by rapid advances in technology, virtual organizations are groups whose members unite, temporarily, to complete a specific job. An independent engineering consultant in New York may team up with an independent public relations practitioner in San Francisco and an independent advertising expert in Dallas to help a new engineering agency develop brand recognition. Do the new, temporary partners know one another's values? Can they trust one another to act ethically on behalf of the team? Will they learn of any incompatible values before damage occurs?

So how do you avoid problems of denial and ignorance? How can you resolve dilemmas? As a public relations practitioner, you can start by understanding the ethics codes that influence your professional environment.

Ethics Codes

Ethics codes specify core values, and they detail acceptable and unacceptable actions within that framework. At the very least, ethics codes, written and unwritten, exist at five levels: personal, organizational, professional, societal, and international.

Personal Codes

Increasingly, professors in public relations ethics courses are asking their students to write personal ethics codes—not just for the profession but for life. Do you have such a code? Is it written? What values and beliefs matter most to you? What thoughts and actions are consistent—and inconsistent—with that ethical foundation? Traditional sources of personal values include parents, education, religion, and culture.

Organizational Codes

You may not be very many months away from a job search. As you consider corporations, agencies, nonprofit organizations, and other entities that employ public relations practitioners, see if you can find their ethics codes. Their Web sites can be a good place to start looking. A good organizational ethics code clearly specifies the values that unite the organization, that guide its ideas and actions. An organizational ethics code can help you determine if an employer would be a good fit for you.

Professional Codes

Like organizations, professions can have written ethics codes. In the United States, the two best-known public relations professional ethics codes are those of the Public Relations Society of America and the International Association of Business Communicators. PRSA's code specifies six core values: advocacy, honesty, expertise, independence, loyalty, and fairness. IABC's code (see Chapter 4) reflects that organization's international standing: The code urges members to "engage in communication that is not only legal but also ethical and sensitive to cultural values and beliefs."

Societal Codes

Societal codes, which generally reflect the values of nations and cultures, may not be as specific as organizational and professional codes—we generally can't point to one document and say, "There it is"—but they are no less binding. Studies of U.S. business culture, for example, show that most participants value honorable, straightforward competition. Where is that societal code written? Don't bother looking—but don't violate the code without understanding the consequences.

Some societal codes *are* written, however. For example, both the Bill of Rights, in the U.S. Constitution, and the Ten Commandments embody social values.

International Codes

As we increasingly build the global village that communication philosopher Marshall McLuhan forecast, we create a world in which actions in Kenya have consequences in Kalamazoo. Is it possible to create an international ethics code that

PRSA Member Statement of Professional Values

This statement presents the core values of PRSA members and, more broadly, of the public relations profession. These values provide the foundation for the Member Code of Ethics and set the industry standard for the professional practice of public relations. These values are the fundamental beliefs that guide our behaviors and decision-making process. We believe our professional values are vital to the integrity of the profession as a whole.

ADVOCACY

We serve the public interest by acting as responsible advocates for those we represent. We provide a voice in the marketplace of ideas, facts, and viewpoints to aid informed public debate.

HONESTY

We adhere to the highest standards of accuracy and truth in advancing the interests of those we represent and in communicating with the public.

EXPERTISE

We acquire and responsibly use specialized knowledge and experience. We advance the profession through continued professional development, research, and education. We build mutual understanding, credibility, and relationships among a wide array of institutions and audiences.

INDEPENDENCE

We provide objective counsel to those we represent. We are accountable for our actions.

LOYALTY

We are faithful to those we represent, while honoring our obligation to serve the public interest.

FAIRNESS

We deal fairly with clients, employers, competitors, peers, vendors, the media, and the general public. We respect all opinions and support the right of free expression.

-more-

The ethics code of the Public Relations Society of America begins with a statement of six core values. The full PRSA code appears in the Appendix. (Copyright PRSA. Reprinted with permission, The Public Relations Society of America, www.prsa.org)

respects cultural differences yet makes Kenya responsible for Kalamazoo—and vice versa? One early effort is known as the Caux Principles, named for the city in Switzerland where business leaders periodically gather to ponder cultural integrity and mutual respect. Available online at www.cauxroundtable.org, the principles begin by acknowledging the difficulty of the task: "We seek to begin a process that identifies shared values, reconciles differing values, and thereby develops a shared perspective on business behavior."

Social Responsibility

In societal and international ethics codes, the concept of **social responsibility** clearly enters the profession of public relations. Social responsibility rests on the notion of a social contract, an idea you may have encountered through the philosophers John Locke and Jean-Jacques Rousseau in your Western Civilization or Great Readings courses. Social contract theory essentially says that we're all in this together, so if you treat me well, I'll treat you well. If we fail to do so, we reduce our society to chaos.

For public relations, social responsibility might best be described by the cliché "a good corporate citizen." Certainly not all organizations that use public relations are corporations; some organizations, in fact, exist solely to address social welfare needs. As we note in Chapter 1, no organization is an island. In public relations, ethics codes insist that we recognize that our actions have social consequences. Ethics codes ask that our organizations and clients function with social responsibility. (For more on corporate social responsibility, see Chapter 14.)

Friends in Need: The KARMA Mnemonic

Despite their usefulness, no ethics code can anticipate and solve every ethics problem, particularly dilemmas. To avoid becoming Buridan's ass, immobilized by the challenge of clashing values, you can turn to various ethics philosophies that have stood the test of time. College ethics courses often focus on five key philosophers or philosophies, and, conveniently, those five form the memorable acronym—a mnemonic device—of KARMA: Kant (Immanuel), Aristotle, Rawls (John), Mill (John Stuart), and agape. (See Table 11.1.) Each of the five offers different, often conflicting, advice. At the risk of sounding flippant on a serious subject, we suggest that during ethics dilemmas, you mentally invite each of the five, one at a time, into a conference room, and say, for example, "OK, Aristotle, what's your advice? How would you approach this?"

This approach can help you critically analyze an ethics dilemma and may even lead you to a solution. If you're called on to defend your decision, you may gain credibility by revealing that you've enlisted the aid of some of the greatest minds of ethical philosophy.

The following summaries can start you on your journey toward KARMA.

table 11.1 *The KARMA Mnemonic*

Philosopher	Philosophy
Kant, Immanuel (1724–1804)	Imagine living in a world in which your decision/action became the universal law. The end cannot justify the means.
Aristotle (384–322 BC)	Avoid extremes, which are unethical. Virtue exists at a point between excess and deficiency.
Rawls, John (1921–2002)	Distribute pain and pleasure fairly. Imagine living as each stakeholder for the rest of your life.
Mill, John Stuart (1806–1873)	Select the greatest good for the greatest number of people.
Agape	Be the earthly agent of a loving god. Love your neighbor and yourself; both have value to God.

Immanuel Kant (1724–1804)

Can the ends justify the means? Can we do a bad thing in order to produce a good thing? Immanuel Kant would say no. Kant termed his most memorable contribution to ethics theory the **categorical imperative.** In plain English, he meant that you should imagine a world in which the basic principle derived from your action would become an unbreakable rule. For example, if you decide to tell a lie, even in pursuit of a greater good, then lying becomes the universal rule. Would you—could you—live in such a world?

Aristotle (384–322 BC)

Unlike Kant, the Greek philosopher Aristotle wasn't fond of behavioral absolutes. In fact, Aristotle believed that extremes were unethical. Virtue, he believed, existed somewhere between a quality's excess and its deficiency. Never lie? Aristotle would say, "Never say never—that's an extreme." Aristotle might allow a lie when the good it generated exceeded the essential evil of the lie itself. He did caution, however, that true virtues, such as justice and courage, already were points between extremes and should not be subjected to a too much/too little philosophy.

John Rawls (1921–2002)

American philosopher John Rawls believed in respect, empathy, and fairness for all stakeholders in an ethics dilemma. In fact, Rawls believed that you, as the decision maker, should figuratively wear a **veil of ignorance** that strips you of your identity so that you can imagine your decision from the vantage point of each stakeholder. Rawls asks you to envision a scenario in which your worst enemy could transform you into any one of the stakeholders. Rawls believed that such an approach would lead decision makers to seek fairness by distributing both pain and pleasure, rather than giving some stakeholders unfair advantages or disadvantages.

John Stuart Mill (1806–1873)

Coming chronologically between Kant and Rawls, John Stuart Mill developed a philosophy that disagrees with both. Mill believed that the end could justify the means and that pain to some stakeholders could be justified by a greater good being delivered to a greater number of stakeholders. Mill helped develop the philosophy of **utilitarianism,** which holds that actions have usefulness only if they produce happiness or reduce pain. The famous maxim of utilitarianism is "the greatest good for the greatest number."

Agape

Agape (pronounced both *AH-guh-pay*) is a Greek word for love. **Agape** symbolizes human love that strives to imitate divine love. This philosophy asks us to act as the earthly agents of a loving god. Jesus, whether recognized as the son of God by Christianity or as prophet by Judaism and Islam, summarized an agape recognized by many religions when he said, "You should love your neighbor as yourself." Agape asks us to ponder how a loving god might resolve a particular ethics dilemma.

Capable of Honor

Professor Tom Bivins offers another way for public relations professionals to ensure that their behavior matches their values. Bivins encourages practitioners to pause at every stage of the public relations process—research, planning, communication, and evaluation—to examine whether their actions reflect their values.[5] Similarly, in its report "Restoring Trust in Business: Models for Action," the PR Coalition urges business leaders to create workplace cultures in which a commitment to ethical behavior permeates every meeting, report, and action.

As you read the case studies in this chapter and throughout this book, you'll find examples of organizations that succeeded in honoring their values—and organizations that failed. Of course, you'll also find some in-between examples. It's no secret that public relations, like any business, has ethical lapses. But the lapses in public relations often are more visible than those of other professions.

The challenges of behaving ethically should not deter you from trying. The occasional ethical failures of others in the public relations profession shouldn't discourage you. In Allen Drury's Pulitzer Prize-winning novel *Advise and Consent,* the daughter of a prominent politician asks her father how he can stay in politics despite the ethical failings of some of his colleagues. His answer provides guidance for many who carry high standards into the challenges of the real world. He believes in his profession, he says, because "it is capable of honor."

Discussion Questions

1. What is the definition of ethics?

2. What might be examples, real or hypothetical, of denial in public relations ethics? Of dilemmas?

3. In your examples of dilemmas, what specific advice might the KARMA mnemonic provide?

4. Do you have a personal code of ethics? What core values motivate your actions?

5. Can you find online examples of organizational ethics codes? What similarities and differences do you find among them?

Key Terms

agape, p. 248
categorical imperative, p. 247
denial, p. 242

dilemma, p. 242
ethics, p. 241
ignorance, p. 242

social responsibility, p. 246
utilitarianism, p. 248
veil of ignorance, p. 247

Endnotes

1. Gene Laczniak and Patrick Murphy, *Marketing Ethics: Guidelines for Managers* (Lexington, MA: Lexington Books, 1985).

2. PR Coalition, "Restoring Trust in Business: Models for Action" (New York: Arthur W. Page Society, 2003).

3. Laura Nash, "American and European Corporate Ethics Practices: A 1999 Survey," in *Business Ethics in a New Europe,* eds. Jack Mahoney and Elizabeth Vallance (Norwell, MA: Kluwer, 1992). Cited in

Bodo Schlegelmilch, *Marketing Ethics: An International Perspective* (London: International Thomson Business Press, 1998), 38.

4. Joseph Badaracco, *Defining Moments: When Managers Must Choose between Right and Right* (Boston: Harvard Business School Press, 1997).

5. Thomas Bivins, "A Systems Model for Ethical Decision Making in Public Relations, *Public Relations Review* (Winter 1992), pp. 365–384.

Death Wish

Last Acts Seeks to Change a Bitter End to a Better End

Public relations practitioners sometimes believe their campaigns are matters of life and death. And sometimes they're right.

"While opinion polls reveal that most Americans would prefer to die at home, free from pain and with their loved ones, the reality is vastly different," concluded a report titled *Means to a Better End: A Report on Dying in America Today.* "Americans often die alone in hospitals or nursing homes, in pain and attached to life support machines they may not want."

Prepared by an organization called Last Acts, *Means to a Better End* graded each state, plus the District of Columbia, on the quality of medical and social services offered to people in their last months of life. The report was a tactic in an unusual public relations campaign, and it attracted national attention.

Last Acts is a coalition of more than 1,000 organizations that represent consumers, health care professionals, religious leaders, educators, and other stakeholders concerned about the quality of health care in the United States and the world. The first sentence in the organization's values statement establishes its focus on improving heath care for the dying: "Last Acts envisions a world in which dying people and their loved ones receive excellent care and are honored and supported by their community."

Founded in 1996 by the Robert Wood Johnson Foundation, Last Acts escalated its efforts in 2002 after evaluating new research that showed most Americans approaching the end of life lacked social and medical services that eased the pain and trauma of dying. Studies showed that up to 75 percent of cancer patients in intensive care units, for example, suffered moderate to severe pain, anxiety, lack of sleep, hunger, or thirst.

The Best Places to Die

Faced with discouraging data that indicated little progress in compassionate care for the dying, the management team at Last Acts brought together leading end-of-life experts to discuss ways of forcing the issue into the public consciousness. Discussion soon focused on the value—and the related publicity—of an unusual tactic: issuing end-of-life report cards to each state and the District of Columbia.

"Magazines have 'The Best Hospitals' and 'The Best Places to Live,'" said Victoria Weisfeld, senior communications officer for Last Acts. "Why not 'The Best Places to Die'?"

Introduction

During the past century, we in the United States have seen significant changes in the way we experience illness and death. A hundred years ago, people usually died from an injury or sudden illness. Farm work, factory work—even childbirth—were risky. Today, with medical and other advances, people live longer and can expect to live several years with an illness that may eventually kill them. Ultimately, many will reach a point where medical technology may be able to keep them alive but can neither restore their health nor even improve their condition. In truth, more treatment may be merely prolonging dying. At that point, patients and families face difficult choices about the kind of care they want.

While opinion polls reveal that most Americans would prefer to die at home, free from pain and with their loved ones, the reality is vastly different. Americans often die alone in hospitals or nursing homes, in pain and attached to life support machines they may not want. And this happens despite modern medicine's ability to ease most pain, the existence of good models of delivering supportive care, and the increasing availability of excellent end-of-life care through hospice and palliative care programs. All these services, however, are underused—in large part because in our death-denying culture, many Americans don't want to discuss death and dying, or because many Americans don't know about these options for good end-of-life care and thus don't ask for them.

> *Many Americans don't know about these options for good end-of-life care and thus don't ask for them.*

The last decade saw an evolution in the way Americans think about death and dying. The debate over physician-assisted suicide, coupled with pioneering studies about patterns of end-of-life care, launched a national dialogue about how we die. In November 1995, the *Journal of the American Medical Association* published initial results from SUPPORT (Study to Understand Prognoses and Preferences for Outcomes and Risks of Treatments), the largest,

Means to a Better End, a report by Last Acts, documents the differences between how we want to die and how we actually die. (Courtesy of Last Acts Partnership)

In gathering state-by-state data, Last Acts also conducted research on the wishes of the dying. Key findings included these facts:

- Although more than 70 percent of Americans would prefer to die in their own beds with loved ones nearby, only 25 percent die at home.
- Approximately 50 percent of all deaths occur in hospitals, but fewer than 60 percent of hospitals offer specialized end-of-life services.

As the staff at Last Acts continued to evaluate incoming research, its members clearly saw the disconnect between what dying Americans wanted and what they received. And with the state-by-state report cards, staff members knew they were armed with research that could generate national as well as local interest. The question now was how to communicate that research.

The Wake-up Call

Last Acts created a public relations plan with two goals: to educate policymakers and citizens about the lack of good end-of-life care; and to use research and media attention to spur policymakers, health care leaders, and citizens to work for reforms. Given those goals, the target publics seemed clear. Last Acts decided to focus its communications efforts on national and local newspapers and broadcast stations, coalition partners in Last Acts and similar organizations throughout the nation, and policy makers at all levels of government.

"We hope that researchers and policy makers will see the need we're identifying and take it on as a challenge," said Judith Peres, deputy director for Last Acts.

To reach the two goals and their related target publics, Last Acts specified four objectives:

1. Generate news coverage that included stories in 25 daily newspapers in the top 50 markets and generate television exposure in at least 50 markets
2. Increase visits to the Last Acts Web site by 50 percent
3. Increase participation from coalition members to 10 percent of the groups (up from the usual 3–5 percent) and gain the participation of at least two large, previously unaffiliated consumer organizations
4. Stimulate policy changes and prompt future collection of related data

"We want to create a wake-up call," Peres said. "We want to let policymakers and people in this country know that we need better care for people at the end of their lives."

Sparking Public Discussion

The key tactic in the Last Acts campaign was *Means to a Better End:* a 94-page report that graded the states on eight different measures, including the location of deaths—for example, hospital or home—and state pain-management policies.

"We hope this report will stimulate efforts to improve the availability and quality of data needed to understand end-of-life care in this country," wrote Peres and Last Acts Director Karen Orloff Kaplan, authors of the report. "But meanwhile we hope to spark a public discussion that cannot wait until more refined data are developed."

Last Acts presented the report in a news conference held in Washington, D.C. Announced by a media advisory, the conference featured a panel of experts that included Jim Towey, director of the White House Faith-Based and Community Initiatives. In the media advisory, the Last Acts team also provided numbers for open phone lines for distant reporters who wanted to hear the proceedings and ask questions. The advisory also gave the Web address for a live Webcast of the event.

Following the news conference, Last Acts sent individualized news releases to each state describing the end-of-life care grades that the state earned. The organization prepared similarly specific video news releases for each state.

To increase media interest in the report, Last Acts enlisted the help of its partner organizations. Members of those organizations received "Seize the Opportunity" action kits that included state-by-state media contacts and a list of key talking points to ensure that all members of the Last Acts coalition delivered the same message. In the months before the debut of *Means to a Better End,* Last Acts blitzed its member organizations, as well as other interested groups, with newsletters, weekly conference calls, fax reports, face-to-face meetings, and frequent mentions of the Last Acts Web site.

Last Acts spent $380,000 on tactics for the *Means to a Better End* campaign.

Reaction to Report Cards: Grounded!

Judith Peres and the Last Acts Team knew the media blitz had succeeded when Peres, Towey, and other leaders appeared on PBS's nightly *News Hour with Jim Lehrer.* Towey, as a representative of President George W. Bush's administration, bluntly declared, "If my children came home with a report card like this, they would be grounded. I think we all have to ask ourselves some tough questions—that in a country that has the finest medical technology on Earth, we haven't made more progress on how we care for our people at the end of life."

Towey's comparison to a child's report card echoed throughout the country. "If our children brought home such grades," one resident of Arkansas wrote to the *Arkansas Democrat-Gazette,* "we would immediately realize the need to be more attentive to their education."

In all, *Means to a Better End* won coverage in 30 of the nation's 50 highest-circulation newspapers. Within weeks, the report had generated more than 120 stories, including at least one in each state. The video news releases were even more successful, sparking 204 stories in 78 media markets and reaching an estimated 5.8 million viewers.

Last Acts also succeeded in using *Means to a Better End* to increase participation among current partners and to attract new partners. More than 20 percent of Last Acts' member organizations participated in the publicity efforts, and traffic on the Last Acts Web site from partners and others jumped more than 130 percent.

Organizations that had not actively worked with Last Acts before, including the American Cancer Society and the Alzheimer's Association, joined the *Means to a Better End* campaign for reforms in end-of-life care.

Perhaps most important, policy makers heard the voices of the Last Acts partners and the media reports. The National Association of Attorneys General distributed *Means to a Better End* to its members in order to lay the foundation for state-by-state changes. Reports of local policy reviews from North Carolina to Montana soon reached Last Acts.

For its impressive efforts to bring an awkward, painful subject to public consciousness, Last Acts won a national Silver Anvil Award from the Public Relations Society of America.

Ethics have been defined as values in action. As Steven Schroeder, director of the Robert Wood Johnson Foundation, surveyed the early successes of *Means to a Better End,* he found strong evidence that Last Acts was acting on its values. "Last Acts is much more than platitudes about a good death," he said. "It has challenged patients, families, health care professionals, medical educators, the clergy, and other stakeholders to undertake new and creative efforts to improve care at a critical time in people's lives. It has pushed for specific reforms across the board, reforms that are involving millions of Americans. Last Acts' successes are tangible proof that care for people near the end of life can be vastly improved."

Sources

Michael V. Aureli, "Letters," *Arkansas Democrat-Gazette,* December 12, 2002. Online: Lexis-Nexis.

"First State-by-State 'Report Card' on Care for the Dying Finds Mediocre Care Nationwide," Last Acts news release, November 18, 2002. Online: www.lastacts.org.

Means to a Better End: A Report on Dying in America Today. Online: www.lastacts.org.

"Media Advisory: Last Acts to Release First-Ever State-by-State 'Report Card' on End-of-Life Care," Last Acts news release, November 6, 2002. Online: Lexis-Nexis.

News Hour with Jim Lehrer, November 19, 2002. Online: Lexis-Nexis.

Public Relations Society of America Web site, www.prsa.org.

Robert Wood Johnson Foundation. Online: www.rwjf.org.

case 11.2

iLoo Meets Its Waterloo

*Microsoft's "Miscommunication"
Inadvertently Misleads Journalists*

"What a long, strange trip," concluded *Marketing News,* quoting those distinguished '60s rock philosophers, the Grateful Dead.

The bizarre journey began when the Microsoft's United Kingdom division announced, via news release, the iLoo, an Internet-wired, computer equipped portable toilet for festivals and rock concerts ("loo" is British slang for bathroom).

"Sit and surf" was the headline in a consequent CNET News.com story.

But that wasn't the strange part.

The trip took an unexpected detour when Microsoft headquarters in the United States confessed that the iLoo was an April Fools' joke—even though the British branch had announced the product almost a month after that notorious holiday.

Using a little bathroom language of his own, a writer for the news service Europemedia—speaking for journalists who felt deceived—declared, "Boy, did we ever feel crappy about leading our esteemed readers down the garden path to the outhouse of untrustworthy news releases."

Still, that wasn't the strange part.

The strange part occurred soon afterward, when Microsoft headquarters retracted its own retraction, declaring that the iLoo had, after all, been real. The hoax wasn't a hoax at all, Microsoft announced, but the company was canceling plans for the iLoo. Angry journalists began to publish their second corrections of Microsoft's version of the story.

"Suffice it to say the software company's credibility has clearly gone down the toilet," wrote Rob Wright, in *VARBusiness,* a magazine for high-tech suppliers.

"Where Do You Want to Go Today?"

In addition to what you'd expect to find in a portable toilet, plans for the iLoo featured wireless networking, a flat plasma screen, and a waterproof keyboard that an occupant could place on his or her lap. Toilet paper would feature popular Web site addresses. Because such amenities might induce a user to stay a little longer than usual, the unit also would feature computers on the external walls as well. (Bemused journalists forgot their anger long enough to craft some predictable jokes. Richard Adams of England's *Guardian* newspaper wrote, "This project gave new meaning to Microsoft's slogan, 'Where do you want to go today?'")

The British Microsoft division announced the iLoo in the spring of 2003. Its public relations agency, Red Consultancy, confirmed the story for incredulous journalists.

"It's a bit of fun, and it allows younger age groups access to our key services, like Hotmail and MSN Messenger in a fun and interactive way," a British Microsoft representative told journalists. He even added that iLoo would include an additional unique feature: a guard. "If we didn't post a guard," he explained, "somebody would probably would just lift the whole thing up and walk away with it."

But the whiplash of retractions began cracking when the company's U.S. headquarters announced, days later, that the iLoo was a hoax.

"This iLoo release came out of the UK office and was not a Microsoft sanctioned communication, and we apologize for any confusion or offense it may have caused," said a Microsoft representative.

"I can confirm it was an April Fools' joke," said another Microsoft spokesperson.

Responded the *Guardian:* "This may not placate furious journalists . . . who were assured by MS-UK's PR at Red Consultancy that the story was legit."

Within 24 hours, Microsoft reversed course again, declaring that the iLoo had been real but that negative publicity had caused the company to change its plans.

"What's true with the iLoo?" queried the Associated Press. "Microsoft Corp. and its public relations firm changed their story—again—yesterday."

So skeptical of Microsoft's latest story was the *Seattle Post-Intelligencer* that it noted that company representatives "did not provide proof of the cancellation, as requested."

Mac Observer, a publication for Macintosh owners (some of whom have little reason to love Microsoft), couldn't resist a comparison to Microsoft's occasional software problems: "Microsoft backpedaled so fast it didn't bother to get the facts straight and released a very buggy statement to the press in the process. As usual, version 3 from the company got it right."

"We jumped the gun basically in confirming that it was a hoax, and, in fact, it was not," said a Microsoft group product manager. "Definitely, we're going to be taking a good look at our communication processes internally."

A Lapse of Values

Compounding Microsoft's embarrassment was its recognition that the misrepresentations to the news media contradicted, albeit inadvertently, the company's value of "integrity." In the midst of the iLoo debacle, the *Seattle Times* reported that, after being admonished by the Federal Trade Commission for deceptive advertisements, Microsoft had added "integrity" to employee evaluation standards. One definition of integrity involves consistency of standards, meaning that a company has integrated its values throughout all its actions. In changing its iLoo story and embarrassing journalists in front of their audiences, Microsoft had not lived up to its new standard of integrating its values into all its actions.

To Microsoft's credit, it publicly analyzed how the initial misunderstanding occurred: After the British announcement of the new iLoo, a British employee had informed the U.S. office that the project had been a hoax—a claim that U.S. officials publicized. When journalists then charged Microsoft with misleading them, further conversations with British employees had revealed the reality of iLoo.

"It looks like there was some miscommunication internally over whether the program was legitimate," a Microsoft representative said.

Specific reactions from journalists to Microsoft's changing story ranged from good humor to charges of deception. "Microsoft Says iLoo a Hoax; Wait, No It's Not!" declared a headline in the Memphis *Commercial Appeal.* "Here's the latest—

we dare not say last—word on iLoo," wrote the *Seattle Post-Intelligencer.* "Leave it to Mr. Gates to put a new twist on bathroom reading."

The *Seattle Times* offered a sterner assessment: "The company has a credibility problem." *VARBusiness* reported that "Microsoft officials falsely called the now-discontinued project a prank." The *National Journal* concluded, "The truth about Microsoft's plans to develop an Internet-ready portable toilet has been hard to determine."

Irate journalists directly associated Microsoft's iLoo mortification with public relations. "The media have now focused on the communications breakdown more than the iLoo itself, calling it everything from a PR embarrassment to a credibility problem to a PR debacle," summarized *PR Week.* "Microsoft has lost its grip on its famously managed public relations," wrote *Marketing News.* Even the *South China Morning Post* of Hong Kong called the episode "a public relations embarrassment," as did the Associated Press.

In their anger, journalists still couldn't resist the obvious puns. "Someone in Microsoft's PR department is in deep do-do," concluded Europemedia. *VARBusiness* scorned Microsoft's "best efforts to flush this news," and *IT Week* charged the company with "a bizarre case of verbal incontinence." The *Seattle Times* wrote that iLoo "became the butt of jokes" and lamented the fate of "Microsoft's new Pee-C."

But the reality of Microsoft's damaged credibility was ultimately sobering. "If something as trivial as this can trip up the whole PR process, that's sad," concluded the Motley Fool, an investment analysis company.

Microsoft itself acknowledged its public relations failure. "It's definitely not how we like to do PR at Microsoft," said a company representative.

Confession and Redemption

Microsoft's U.S.-based officials might have done well to follow the lead of Celia Chong Wu, a regional general manager in the company's Asian division. When a reporter from the *South China News* asked Wu what was true about the iLoo, she offered a response that public relations practitioners occasionally find difficult: She confessed that she didn't know.

As the extent of Microsoft's unintentional deception became clear, company officials did openly accept responsibility for the fiasco. In a series of comments to the news media, a Microsoft representative offered these observations:

- "We jumped the gun basically in confirming that it was a hoax and, in fact, it was not. Definitely, we're going to be taking a good look at our communication processes internally."
- "There definitely was some miscommunication internally."
- "Our objective now is to make sure the facts get out, and make sure the press knows that there was some miscommunication on our part—even if we end up with a bit of egg on our face."

- "We're going to meet with all the parties involved and set forth some processes to ensure that we're absolutely confirmed on different marketing plans before they're communicated externally."
- "We apologize for our mistake and are working on making sure it doesn't happen again."

Microsoft's candor in accepting responsibility for its iLoo April Fools' farce laid the story to rest—until December, when journalists began to reprise their favorite stories of the year. *Marketing News* crafted this headline for a brief, humorous recap of the story: "Yes. No. Yes . . . But."

In its year-end issue, *Plastics News* wrote, "Microsoft in April won the attention of grateful comedians around the world when it proposed the iLoo." Unable to resist a little comedy itself, the magazine gave Microsoft a "Bill Gates Is Full of It Award" and offered a final word in the saga of Microsoft's dizzying potty pronouncements: "The iLoo project went down the toilet."

And that's the bottom line—for now.

Sources

Richard Adams, "City Diary," *The Guardian* (London), May 14, 2003. Online: Lexis-Nexis.

CBS Marketwatch, May 14, 2003. Online: Lexis-Nexis.

Bryan Chaffin, "ILoo Version 3.0: Microsoft Claims Internet Toilet a Hoax, Recants—Real After All," *Mac Observer,* May 14, 2003. Online: www.macobserver.com.

Brier Dudley, "Microsoft Comes Clean on iLoo," *Seattle Times,* May 14, 2003. Online: Lexis-Nexis.

Andrew Gordon, "Microsoft and Wag Ed Tell Conflicting Stories about iLoo," *PR Week,* May 19, 2003. Online: Lexis-Nexis.

Helen Jung, "Microsoft Says iLoo a Hoax; Wait, No, It's Not!" *Commercial Appeal* (Memphis), May 14, 2003. Online: Lexis-Nexis.

L.M.K., "2003 in Review: Strange but True," *Marketing News TM,* December 8, 2003. Online: Lexis-Nexis.

LouAnn Lofton, "Microsoft's PR Needs Flushing," *The Motley Fool Take,* May 14, 2003. Online: Lexis-Nexis.

Carolyn Ong, "iLoo Fiasco Leaves MSN Advocate Temporarily Tongue-Tied," *South China Morning Post,* May 27, 2003. Online: Lexis-Nexis.

Dan Richman, "On-Again, Off-Again iLoo Is Off for Good," *Seattle Post-Intelligencer,* May 14, 2003. Online: Lexis-Nexis.

"Strained Relations," *IT Week,* May 19, 2003. Online: Lexis-Nexis.

"The Truth about Microsoft's Wired Potty," *National Journal's Technology Daily.* Online: Lexis-Nexis.

"2003 Winners Claim Dubious Distinction," *Plastics News,* December 15, 2003. Online: Lexis-Nexis.

"Wi-Fi While You Wee-Wee," *Europemedia,* May 14, 2003. Online: Lexis-Nexis.

Joe Wilcox, "Sit and Surf: MSN UK Tests Portable Potty," CNET News.com, May 2, 2003. Online: www.news.com.

Rob Wright, "Unbelievable but True—Microsoft's Internet Outhouse," *VARBusiness,* June 9, 2003. Online: Lexis-Nexis.

Interns and Ethics

Young Public Relations Professionals Help Navigate a Course among Competing Values

Roger Lang of the New York Landmarks Conservancy stood before the Mayor's Task Force on the Future of Governors Island and spoke from his heart.

"This is a rare opportunity," he said. "The chance to regain 180 acres of Manhattan that was ceded from our control two centuries ago is unprecedented. We believe it calls for bold thinking and risk taking on the part of both public officials and private citizens."

Governors Island lies in New York Harbor at the mouth of the East River. In 1800, the city gave the island to the federal government to help defend against attacks from foreign powers. But in the early 21st century, the U.S. government no longer needed Governors Island, leaving its future uncertain. Would the island with its historic fort and castle be returned to the people of New York or sold for development?

"Ladies and gentleman of the Mayor's Task Force, please do not retreat from the evidence before you," Lang pleaded. "It's your job. Please do the right thing."

But one brief question remained. What was the right thing?

Do the Right Thing?

If an ethics dilemma involves a clash of important values, the fate of Governors Island presented a classic dilemma. Lang and his conservancy formed part of a larger coalition, the Governors Island Group, that championed the value of preserving the historic island for the people of New York. The federal government, bound by the Balanced Budget Act of 1997, had to consider the value of selling the island in the interests of the national budget; the property carried a price of almost $500 million. Before negotiating with the federal government for the return of the island, New York state and city officials had to consider the value of preserving their own budgets. Could they afford the upkeep and maintenance of the island? Federal law even allowed the island to be considered for a homeless shelter, a worthy value in the eyes of social workers. Doing the right thing, as Lang requested, meant different things to different stakeholders.

At the epicenter of the debate was a small island—actually 172 acres—that the National Trust for Historic Preservation had, in 1998, termed one of the nation's "Eleven Most Endangered Historic Places." Said John Nau, president of the national Advisory Council on Historic Preservation:

Governors Island has had many significant roles in the history of our nation. This special but little-known place has welcomed immigrants to America, furnished timber for the Dutch colony, witnessed George Washington's key strategic retreat from Manhattan during the Revolutionary War, and held Confederate prisoners. It was home base for First Army headquarters, including before and after it relocated to England in 1943 to plan and conduct the American landings in Normandy. It was also home to the world's largest Coast Guard station.

Nau might have added that the island was the launching site for Wilbur Wright's historic 1909 airplane flight around the Statue of Liberty and was home to a National Monument area that included Fort Jay and Castle Williams. Purchased in 1637 from the Manahatas Indians for axes, nails, and beads, the island had been the property of early governors of the New York colony. But the Coast Guard left Governors Island in 1996, and in 1997 the federal government announced that it no longer wished to own the property. And so the dilemma began.

Unsuccessful in its attempts to win attention from political leaders and the news media, the Governors Island Group turned to public relations agency Ruder Finn in 2002. Time was running out: The federal government wanted a decision on the island's fate by June. And the timetable wasn't the only problem: The Governors Island Group had a budget of $40,000, not enough to hire an agency and pay for tactics.

Once again, values stood front and center in the saga of the small island. Ruder Finn promptly agreed to waive its fees, accepting the Governors Island Group as a *pro bono* client. In January 2002, the agency and the coalition of concerned organizations went to work.

"Varying Political Goals and Objectives"

Constrained by the small budget, Ruder Finn conducted extensive but inexpensive research by interviewing New Yorkers chosen at random on the streets. The agency also conducted interviews with civic leaders in the city and state. Research results indicated both bad and good news: New Yorkers knew very little, if anything, about Governors Island—but when they learned about the property and its uncertain future, they became advocates for its return to New York.

A second research finding underscored that, despite its tiny size, Governors Island had become the focus of a host of competing values and concerns. "The audiences for this campaign were extremely diverse, with varying political goals and objectives," explained Ed Harnaga of Ruder Finn.

Ruder Finn and the Governors Island Group did agree on the goal of the campaign: the return of Governors Island to the people of New York. To reach that goal, Ruder Finn developed three objectives:

1. Attract attention to the plight of Governors Island
2. Gain support of elected officials
3. Help build a coalition of groups capable of planning a stable future for Governors Island

Advocates for the return of Governors Island now had less than six months to achieve their goal.

The Place That Launched 1,000 Ships

The legendary Helen of Troy reportedly possessed such beauty that she had, in the words of playwright Christopher Marlowe, a "face that launched a thousand ships"—meaning the Greek forces that sought her return from Troy. Governors Island may not have inspired epic poems and plays, but, like Helen, it did help launch 1,000 ships. In an innovative tactic that later won acclaim from awards committees, Ruder Finn helped gather a flotilla of more than 1,000 boats that surrounded Governors Island, symbolically reclaiming it for New York. The event included the hoisting of a flag on the island, mimicking the actions of colonial explorers who claimed land in the name of their governments.

A flurry of tactics designed to win the participation of small-boat owners preceded the flotilla. Ruder Finn worked with the Governors Island Group to send mailings to area marinas and followed them up with hand-delivered flyers. It sponsored a table at New York's annual Boat Show, and it developed a newsletter to sustain boaters' interest in the event. The agency also announced the flotilla

The first boats leave Manhattan in Ruder Finn's 1,000-craft public relations tactic to surround and reclaim Governors Island for the people of New York. (Courtesy of Ruder Finn)

with a news release, and an observation boat was provided solely for members of the news media.

At the same time the flotilla was symbolically reclaiming Governors Island, a rally in New York City—which featured entertainers, politicians, and portrayals of George Washington, Wilbur Wright, and other historic figures associated with the island—was attracting media attention.

Ruder Finn built up to the twin special events by creating a logo and a slogan—"Governors Island: For the People"—as well as a media kit that explained the island's history and unresolved destiny. Working with Level M, a brand-identity group, the agency designed T-shirts with the slogan and logo and created a Web site that reproduced the materials from the media kit and offered updates and directions for a variety of tactics. It also organized a news conference held on the steps of New York's City Hall.

To gain the support of elected officials, members of the Governors Island Group wrote letters to politicians at all levels of government. To U.S. Secretary of the Interior Gale Norton, for example, they wrote, "Ensuring that Governors Island is returned to the citizens of New York and made into a major public amenity is one of the highest priorities of the civic community of this region."

As elected officials signed on to the campaign, they, too, contacted other political leaders. In a message to a prominent Texan—President George W. Bush—House of Representatives members Carolyn Maloney and Jerrold Nadler said, "Remember the Alamo. We know you would never consider selling a historic treasure like the Alamo from your state of Texas."

To build the Governors Island Group into a coalition clearly capable of helping to sustain a New York-owned Governors Island, Ruder Finn helped organize a conference for community groups interested in bringing the island back to the state.

Winning all-important media support required the help of Ruder Finn's interns. Students at the agency helped build media lists and then phoned journalists, pitching the story of New York's grassroots efforts to reclaim the island.

Interns and members of the Governors Island Group even visited the location of NBC's *Today* show, hoping for free national television coverage. "We got [weatherman] Al Roker to come over and give us some quality airtime," said Ruder Finn's Harnaga.

In using interns for such an important campaign, Ruder Finn again honored its own values. "This provided Ruder Finn interns with real life practical experience in dealing with the media," Harnaga said.

The $1 Compromise

Ruder Finn's innovative campaign with a small budget and a limited timetable succeeded. In April 2002, President Bush announced a compromise of competing values: Governors Island, in keeping with the law, would be sold in January 2003—to the people of New York for $1.

Media coverage of the flotilla had been extensive, and more than 50 community organizations had attended the coalition-building conference. To sustain and direct the new ownership of Governors Island, many of those organizations helped form the Governors Island Preservation and Education Corp., the group charged with directing the island's future.

For success against daunting odds, Ruder Finn and the Governors Island Group won several prestigious awards: a Crystal Obelisk for Social Responsibility from the Foundation of Women Executives in Public Relations, a Silver Anvil for Special Events and Observances from the Public Relations Society of America, and an Award for Federal Partnerships from the National Trust for Historic Preservation.

"This highly successful grass-roots campaign demonstrates that with limited resources and a solid PR strategy, an organization can create a single event capable of sending a message all the way to the White House," Harnaga said.

But, even after such a success, the Governors Island campaign had not concluded. Members of the Governors Island Group implemented one final tactic and honored one final value: They wrote thank-you letters to politicians who helped return Governors Island to the people of New York.

Sources

"Governor's Island: The Next Steps," *Waterwire News,* November 12, 2003. Online: www.waterwire.net.

"Historic 1000-Boat Flotilla to Celebrate Governors Island and Reclaim It for the People," Governors Island Group news release. May 13, 2002. Online: http://reclaimgovernorsisland.org.

"The Many Faces of Governors Island," Lower Manhattan.info, August 27, 2003. Online:www.lowermanhattan.info/news.

National Trust for Historic Preservation Web site, www.nationaltrust.org/news.

New York Landmarks Conservancy Web site, www.nylandmarks.org.

Public Relations Society of America Web site, www.prsa.org.

Gian-Claudia Sciara, "Isle Fly Away," *City Limits* (August/September 1997). Online: www.citylimits.org.

Van Alen Institute Web site, www.vanalen.org.

Women's City Club of New York Web site, www.wccny.org.

Women Executives in Public Relations Web site, www.wepr.org.

ACT file # 11 ....

The Potter Box

Ethics dilemmas—that is, seemingly irresolvable clashes among important values—often create paradoxes: At a time when we need to do our clearest thinking because so much is at stake, our thinking becomes muddled—because so much is at stake.

Created by Harvard Divinity Professor Ralph Potter, the Potter Box helps you analyze ethics dilemmas, breaking them down into four specific areas of potential conflict and uncertainty: definition, values, principles, and loyalties.[1] Potter asks us to envision this analytical process as a square divided into four sections. (See Figure 11.1.) You begin in the upper left with Definition and then move counter-clockwise through Values, Principles, and Loyalties. As you move through the process, you may learn things that prompt you to move back, momentarily, to earlier quadrants.

In the Definition quadrant, describe the situation to the best of your abilities, paying particular attention to what you know for certain, what you don't know and what might be described differently by another stakeholder in the situation. Would additional research or additional conversations with stakeholders help you clarify the definition and resolve the dilemma?

In the Values quadrant, list and consider the values involved in the dilemma. A value is a belief or feeling that you wish to honor, that you would make sacrifices to uphold. Again, the painful irony of an ethics dilemma is that important values seem incompatible. Any action you take to resolve the dilemma will violate at least one important value. A challenging duty in the Values quadrant is to rank values, carefully determining which of the competing values are most important to you.

In the Principles quadrant, list and consider the principles that offer guidelines for what your actions might be. For example, consider the principles of personal, organizational, and professional ethics codes. In addition, consider the principles generated by the philosophies of Aristotle, Kant, Mill, Rawls, and religious traditions. What might be the outcome if you followed each principle exclusively? Determine which principles seem most relevant to the dilemma. Would

Advanced Critical Thinking

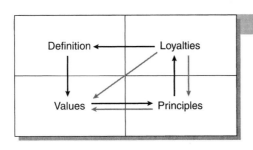

figure 11.1

The Potter Box

Source: David W. Guth and Charles Marsh, *Public Relations: A Values-Driven Approach*, 2nd ed., (Boston, Allyn & Bacon, 2003), 182.

those principles support the most important values you identified in the previous quadrant? If not, how can you resolve that inconsistency?

In the Loyalties quadrant, list all the stakeholders in the dilemma. Just as you did with values, rank the loyalties, determining which stakeholder most deserves your loyalty. Do the top values and principles you identified in the earlier quadrants support your ranking of the stakeholders? If not, how can you resolve that inconsistency?

Unfortunately, the Potter Box won't magically deliver an answer to an ethics dilemma. But by asking you to break the dilemma down into its components, the Potter Box can help you challenge your definition of the situation and rank the competing values, principles, and loyalties. The process helps you identify unities and discrepancies among those competing elements.

When you think you've reached a decision, examine the Definitions quadrant one last time. Does your solution truly address the situation?

The Potter Box can help you justify your eventual decision to others—and, perhaps more important, to yourself.

Discussion Questions • • • • • • • • • • • • • • • • •

1. Why is it important to define the situation before examining values, principles, and loyalties?

2. What is the difference between a value and a principle?

3. In what ways is the Potter Box similar to Platonic dialectic, Act File #1?

4. In the case studies in this chapter, who might have considered using the Potter Box?

Endnote • • • • • • • • • • • • • • • • •

1. Media ethics books often analyze and explain the Potter Box. A good example is Clifford G. Christians, Mark B. Fackler, Kim B. Rotzoll, and Kathy Brittain McKee, *Media Ethics: Cases and Moral Reasoning,* 6th ed. (Boston: Allyn & Bacon, 2001).

CHAPTER 12

Political and Public Policy Communication

The stakes had never been higher. The 2000 U.S. presidential election, for all intents and purposes, ended in a tie. Vice President Al Gore narrowly won the popular vote, but Texas Gov. George W. Bush apparently won a majority of the Electoral College, the only vote that really mattered. However, Florida's 25 electoral votes, enough to change the outcome, were in dispute. The election hinged on how Florida counted ballots—especially faulty punchcards in which the voter's intent was in dispute. It took 36 days and a U.S. Supreme Court decision to settle the issue in Bush's favor.

Although the election was eventually settled in the courts, the seven-week standoff was characterized by intense political debate. Both sides knew they needed public support to maintain the legitimacy of their candidate's victory claim and to raise the money necessary to sustain the legal challenge. Gore's message to the electorate was that all he wanted was a fair and full count. Bush framed the dispute as a case of the opposition trying to overturn the voters' will by changing the rules after the fact.[1] Although there were other options open to him, Gore's decision to concede the election after the Supreme Court decision was based, in part, on the erosion of the political support needed to maintain his challenge.

It is unlikely—although not impossible—that we will see another political drama in which the stakes are as high as they were in November 2000. However, we debate important questions in every community every day. In democratic societies, public policy is achieved through **politics,** a consensus-building process. In this environment, the ability of individuals and organizations to communicate their vision and needs is essential. In democratic societies, those who do not know how to communicate effectively are at a distinct disadvantage.

For this reason, public relations, along with a free press, is critical to the success of democratic institutions. If the system is going to work as intended, then everyone must have access to the marketplace of ideas.

Public Opinion

Because democratic societies govern by consensus, government officials pay close attention to **public opinion.** Public opinion is a public's expressed attitudes on a particular topic at a particular moment in time. It can be very fluid, subject to sudden changes in the environment. Public opinion can also be difficult to measure. Survey results can fluctuate based on who is questioned and how those questions are asked. If you need proof, just ask any of the major television networks that bungled Florida exit-poll projections during their coverage of Election Night 2000.

Not everyone has the same level of knowledge or interest in all issues. Depending on a person's self-interests, some things matter more than others. For that reason, three different levels of public opinion exist:

- **Latent public opinion** occurs when people have an interest in a topic or issue, but are unaware of the interests of others.
- **Aware public opinion** occurs when the people grow aware of an emerging issue.
- **Active public opinion** occurs when the people act—formally and informally, often not in unison—to influence the opinions and actions of others.

Public opinion is a process of constant change. It starts when an **issue** enters the social environment. By definition, an issue must affect a variety of publics and be evolving. Like-minded individuals coalesce into publics who, in turn, engage in debate with other publics holding different opinions about the issue. Over a period of time, a consensus forms—much like the dialectical process described in ACT File #1. It, in turn, translates into a social action, such as a new law, and becomes a social value. And things remain that way until a new issue arises and the process starts again.

Special Interest Groups

As you ponder the role of public opinion in free societies, it is important to remember an essential fact: In Western-style democracies, decision-making authority is diffused throughout the government. The government of the United States was created as a power-sharing arrangement among three branches of government—executive, legislative, and judicial—with equal authority. In doing so, the founders of our nation rejected the notion of concentrated power as embodied by the British monarchy. While these 18th century visionaries may not have predicted the 20th century development of public relations, they clearly understood that governing would depend on the ability to generate and maintain a public consensus—the essence of the practice of modern public relations.

This system of checks and balances operates in a variety of ways. Decision-making authority is shared not only among the branches of government but between the local, state/provincial, and national/federal governments. This means that in certain matters, a city mayor may have more power than the president. Therefore, the first challenge in political and public policy communication is to identify the decision makers. Notice that we use the plural—rarely does the ultimate authority rest in the hands of one individual or group. Also, you should have noticed that what we are describing is essentially stakeholder research. It is not enough to know *what* needs to be decided. You also must know *who* makes that decision.

As discussed in Chapter 2, stakeholders can be divided into two broadly defined groups, primary and intervening publics. *Primary publics* are the decision makers who stand between an organization and the achievement of its goals. In a political and public policy context, these are the elected and appointed public officials entrusted with the responsibility for acting in the public's interests. *Intervening publics* are those with whom one communicates in an effort to reach and influence primary publics. In democratic societies, everyone can be an intervening public because everyone is a **constituent,** or voter. Like-minded constituents—those with common values, interests, and needs—are known as **special interest groups.** It is possible—and likely—that an individual is a member of several special interest groups at once. For example, pretend you own the corner store. For argument's sake, let's say you favor low taxes, desire less government regulation, support law enforcement, and want to restrict competition from out-of-town chain stores. That's four special interest groups you belong to—and we haven't even asked where you stand on such hot-button issues as abortion, gun control, and school prayer. Although there is a tendency to think of others as members of special interest groups, the reality is that we all are.

The Iron Triangle

The degree to which these special interest groups make their voices heard by decision makers influences the outcome of political and public policy debates. While the central tenet of democracy is that all people are created as equals, that is not necessarily true among special interest groups. There are a variety of reasons why some groups have more influence than others. The National Rifle Association and the National Education Association carry considerable sway on Capitol Hill because of their large memberships. That size, especially in terms of the number of votes and campaign contributions it represents, can be the difference in a close election. However, numbers are not always as important in determining influence

President George W. Bush successfully pushed Medicare reform
measures through Congress by winning key support from special
interest groups such as AARP. (Courtesy of the White House)

as who is in charge. For decades, the tobacco industry successfully fought off tighter
regulation by Congress despite growing antismoking sentiment in the country. One
reason for Big Tobacco's legislative success was the disproportionate number of
congressional committees chaired by people representing Tobacco Belt states. The
people in these states opposed tougher regulations, and the committee chairs were
in a position to block legislation.

The process through which special interest groups influence public policy is
known as the **iron triangle.** The first time many people became aware of its existence was in 1961, when President Dwight D. Eisenhower, in his Farewell Address
just days before leaving office, warned of the close relationships between arms
manufacturers, the Pentagon, and sympathetic members of Congress. "This con-
junction of an immense military establishment and a large arms industry is new in
the American experience," Eisenhower said. "In the councils of government, we
must guard against the acquisition of unwarranted influence, whether sought or
unsought, by the military–industrial complex."[2]

Eisenhower was describing a process through which special interest groups
align themselves with like-minded individuals in the executive and legislative
branches of government. This iron triangle is not restricted to just military matters. It has become the way public policy evolves through the legislative process
(see Figure 12.1).

With thousands of pieces of legislation introduced in state legislatures and
Congress every year, it is impossible for elected officials to become experts in the
wide spectrum of subjects those bills reflect. For that reason, Congress and state
legislatures established the committee system. Legislators are appointed to com-

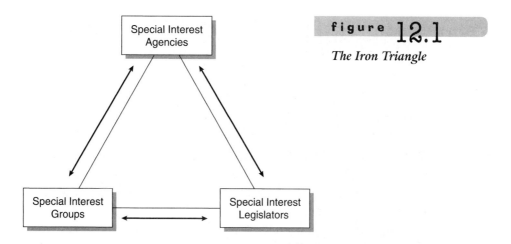

figure **12.1**

The Iron Triangle

mittees that require expertise in a specialized area. Each committee examines proposed legislation and makes recommendations to the entire body. In essence, the members of each of these committees become **special interest legislators.** For example, the Senate Agriculture Committee oversees farm legislation. Senators from states with significant agricultural interests seek appointment to this committee because it is a place where they can exert considerable influence—and be seen by their constituents doing so.

Because of their expertise and influence in a particular area, these legislators develop close relationships with the **special interest agencies** that their committees oversee. In the case of farming issues, the Senate Agriculture Committee has a close relationship with the officials running the Department of Agriculture. These legislators also develop relationships with special interest groups that have a stake in the issues before the committee. An example of this is the National Corn Growers Association—a group that is intensely interested in farm regulations.

In an iron triangle, groups represented at each point of the special interest pyramid communicate with the others as either a primary public or as an intervening public in an effort to influence the third party. For example, let's assume the corn growers want a change in federal farming policy. They may choose to lobby the U.S. Department of Agriculture directly. However, if they don't get satisfaction there, the growers can turn to the special interest legislators who control the agency's budget appropriations. It is important to remember that an iron triangle operates in all directions. The same agency could influence legislators to convince the growers that the current policy is best.

While this may seem an efficient way to do business, the iron triangle has its drawbacks. Members of nontraditional or latent publics with a stake in a particular issue often find themselves on the outside of this process and unable to participate. Because legislators represent a variety of constituencies with varying interests, they can also find themselves in the nexus of competing special interests. That is why lawmakers usually have a difficult time passing comprehensive and complex legislation—there are too many stakeholders with conflicting interests.

Grass-Roots Lobbying

When special interest groups encourage their members to contact government officials, this is known as **grass-roots lobbying.** It is often effective because it conveys an impression of broad public support to vote-hungry politicians. Politicians also like to feel that they are hearing the "real" voice of the people. Some of history's most significant social movements, such as feminism, environmentalism, and civil rights, began at the grass-roots level. Even the American Revolution started as a grass-roots uprising of colonists who challenged British authority at Lexington and Concord.

Because of the success of grass-roots advocacy in shaping public opinion, the creation of this kind of organization has been a favorite public relations tactic since the earliest days of the profession. Public relations pioneer Edward L. Bernays created a grass-roots organization in 1913 to promote *Damaged Goods,* a controversial play about sex education. That was a time when public discussion of anything involving sex was considered socially unacceptable. Because the play's producer was having difficulty securing financial support for the production, Bernays organized the "Medical Review of Reviews Sociological Fund." Money raised from membership dues helped defray the play's costs. It was one of the Bernays' first attempts at influencing public opinion, and it came 10 years before he coined the phrase "public relations counsel."[3]

One of the most successful grass-roots organizations of recent decades has been Mothers Against Drunk Driving. MADD began in 1980 as a loosely organized coalition of mothers sharing a common tragedy, the loss a child at the hands of a drunk driver. Today, it proclaims itself the world's largest crime victims' assistance organization, with more than 3 million members. The organization claims that its grass-roots lobbying has resulted in the passage of thousands of federal, state, and local anti–drunk driving laws, including 1984 legislation that forced states to raise the legal drinking limit to 21 or face the loss of federal highway funds. Its Red Ribbon campaign during the holiday season serves as a vivid reminder against drinking and driving. Perhaps MADD's most noteworthy accomplishment is a 43 percent reduction in annual alcohol-related traffic deaths since 1980.[4]

Because of the popularity of grass-roots advocacy, there are many examples of organizations creating front organizations to give the *impression* of popular support. This controversial tactic is known as **Astroturf lobbying,** a pejorative term that reminds us that the grass roots—and the public support they imply—are fake. For example, the tobacco industry was severely criticized for creating a front organization, the Tobacco Institute Research Committee, to counter scientific research that linked cigarette smoking to cancer.[5]

Another controversial example is Citizens for a Free Kuwait, a supposedly broad-based coalition of Kuwaiti citizens who opposed Iraq's 1990 invasion of their country. The organization lobbied successfully for a U.S.-led liberation. However, widespread suspicion about the true nature of the organization arose when it was later discovered that Citizens for a Free Kuwait had been almost entirely funded by the Kuwaiti royal family and that many of its claims of Iraqi atrocities were unverifiable.[6]

When the Public Relations Society of America Assembly adopted a new code of ethics in October 2000, it included a core principle that "open communication fosters informed decision making in a democratic society." As an example of improper conduct under that provision, the code specifically mentioned front groups that implement "'grass roots' or letter writing campaigns to legislators on behalf of undisclosed interests."[7]

Money and Politics

When individuals of a like mind pool their money to support candidates who share their philosophy, they create what is known as a **political action committee,** or PAC. While PACs may seem like a fairly recent invention, the first one was formed by a labor union in 1944 to raise money for the reelection of President Franklin D. Roosevelt. Because the PAC got its money from individual union members and not the union's treasury, the arrangement skirted existing federal laws prohibiting direct contributions from unions or corporations.[8] As a result of the Watergate scandal, Congress adopted major campaign finance reforms in 1974 that, in effect, encouraged the growth of PACs. (See Figure 12.2.)

According to the Federal Election Commission, 4,594 registered PACs raised $685.3 million and spent $656.5 million during the two-year election cycle ending Dec. 31, 2002. Both reflected a 13 percent increase over the previous election cycle.

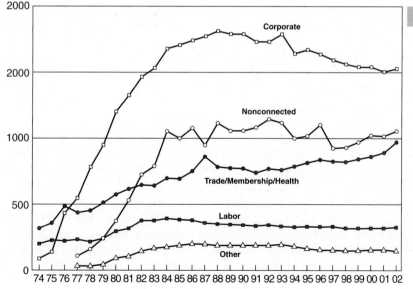

figure 12.2

Number of Political Action Committees, 1974–2002
The chart shows the dramatic growth of PACs since their creation as part of post-Watergate political reforms in 1974. Corporations are the largest segment of PAC contributors.

(Courtesy of the U.S. Federal Election Commission)

Three of every four PAC dollar contributions went to incumbent candidates. Only 10 percent went to challengers, with the rest earmarked for candidates vying for open seats.[9]

As much money as that may seem, it was only the icing on the cake. The FEC estimated that the Republican and Democratic parties raised $1.15 billion during the 2001–2002 election cycle—a 73 percent increase over the 1997–1998 election cycle, the last election cycle without a presidential race on the ballot. The two parties raised $658.8 million in **hard money,** to which limits on contributions and prohibitions on corporate, union, and other sources applied. **Soft money** contributions, money raised that was not covered by federal election laws, totaled $496 million. Soft money was later prohibited from future federal elections under the Bipartisan Campaign Reform Act of 2002.[10]

Under the Federal Election Campaign Act, candidate committees, party committees, and PACs must file periodic reports disclosing the money they raise and spend. The law also limits the amount of money candidates may receive—$2,000 for each election from individuals and PACs and $5,000 from national, state, and local party committees.[11]

Voters and Turnout

While money is important to politicians, their constituents are even more important. After all, constituents have the one thing candidates need the most: votes. However, at a time when democracy is flourishing in places where it had once been only a dream, the percentage of people voting in the more established Western democracies is steadily declining. According to the Stockholm, Sweden-based International Institute for Democracy and Electoral Assistance, the United States ranked 114th in the world, with a 48.3 percent voter turnout between 1945 and 1998. That compares with 96.1 percent in the Seychelles, 92.5 percent in Italy, and 90.5 percent in Cambodia.[12] With so many people choosing to stay home on Election Day, candidates and their supporters spend much of their resources in **GOTV**—get out the vote—efforts.

A study of voter turnout in the 1998 midterm election provides a snapshot of who votes—and who doesn't. In general, the older the citizen, the more likely he or she was to cast a ballot. More than 61 percent of persons age 65+ voted in that election, compared with 56.5 percent of persons between the ages of 45 and 64, 38.7 percent of those 25 to 44, and 18.5 percent of 18- to 24-year-olds. Women voted at a slightly higher rate then men. More than 47 percent of white voters participated in the election, compared with 41.9 percent of black voters, 32.8 percent of Hispanic voters, and 32.3 percent of Asian and Pacific Islander voters.[13]

One statistic that may stand out particularly among typical readers of this book is the low voter turnout among college-age voters. During the 2000 General Election, only 29 percent of eligible voters ages 18–24 cast ballots for president. That compares with 38 percent in 1992, when Bill Clinton defeated the first President Bush.

"Young people don't have an explicitly negative view of government, but they tend to feel it is remote," said William Galston, a University of Maryland specialist on civic engagement. "There has been a huge shift in the past generation toward voluntary sector work, the fact that you can control who receives your services."[14]

As a result of this trend, many candidates have focused their attention toward older, more reliable voters. That is why groups such as Rock the Vote work hard to engage younger voters in the political process.

Government Relations and Public Affairs

Practitioners who help private organizations build or maintain healthy relationships with government agencies work in an area of public relations known as **government relations.** Those who help government agencies build or maintain good relationships with their various constituencies are engaged in what is called **public affairs.** While the two roles are similar, differences exist.

One area in which government relations and public affairs are similar is the boundary-spanning role they play. That means that both kinds of practitioners serve as liaisons between the organizations they represent and their many stakeholders. As the name implies, these practitioners function at the point where the organization and its publics meet and interact.

For government relations specialists, the boundary role involves representing their organization's interests to government officials. This could mean telling government officials about new products and services, informing them of issues that affect the organization, or lobbying on pending legislation. In addition to this outward focus, government relations practitioners must also look inward toward their own organization. These practitioners monitor what the government does and interpret what it means to their organization's leadership. In this capacity, government relations practitioners are often the first to identify potential threats and opportunities.

Public affairs specialists play a similar boundary role. However, when they focus outside their agency, their efforts target constituents and other important stakeholders. In democratic societies, it is important for the government to report to the people on the many issues that may affect them. At the same time, government officials need to gain public support as they try to address those same issues. However, the flow of information goes in both directions. Public affairs specialists are often the channel through which the public exercises its right to petition the government with its grievances. Public affairs practitioners routinely monitor public attitudes on a variety of issues and report their findings to policy makers.

Government relations and public affairs practitioners also use similar tactics. In the world of government and politics, interpersonal communications are the most effective. However, much of this communication is typically done through letters and other forms of written correspondence. Practitioners often prepare white papers, detailed briefings on particular issues facing their organization. Because the media reach a wide range of influential stakeholders both inside and

outside government, political reporters are often seen as an important intervening public. Traditional media relations tactics—such as news releases, media kits,
opinion commentaries, and news conferences—are frequently used. Organizations often conduct public meetings or demonstrations to generate publicity.
Whether the practitioner works on the local, state, or federal level, these efforts
target reporters working in or near the halls of government—whether they be in
city hall, the state capitol, or Washington, D.C. Web sites are also popular tools
for public outreach.

A major difference between government relations and public affairs is the degree of **transparency** under which the practitioners of each must operate. Public
affairs specialists must comply with a variety of open records and meetings laws.
Although government relations practitioners may have to meet various disclosure
requirements—especially if they work in publicly owned companies or tax-exempt
organizations—the degree of scrutiny they face is less than that in public affairs,
where virtually everything is the people's business.

Public affairs practitioners also confront a higher degree of resistance than
their government relations counterparts. This antipathy comes from a variety of
sources: partisan rivalry between different political parties, competition among
the various branches of government, friction that comes from government oversight of private organizations, and resistance among taxpayers to the use of public funds to advocate for programs that will cost them more money. For that
reason, one seldom finds a government practitioner whose title contains the
words *public relations*. Instead, they use titles that include phrases such as *public
affairs, public information,* or *community outreach*. In any event, public affairs practitioners often find themselves limited in what they can do by both restrictive regulations and limited resources.

"A Vital Cog"

Public affairs and government relations practitioners play an important role in democratic societies. This is why there is such rapid growth in public relations education in the world's new and emerging democracies. Public relations allows
organizations and individuals to be heard within the great marketplace of ideas. In
turn, it brings the government and the people much closer together.

Before his death in 2000, noted public relations educator and historian Scott
Cutlip wrote of public relations as being "a vital cog in the nation's public information system." While he believed the profession plays an important role in building social consensus, he was also concerned about its negative effects. "Public
relations has cluttered our already choked channels of communication with the
debris of pseudo-events and phony sound bites that confuse rather than clarify,"
he wrote. "This is especially true of today's damaged political process."[15]

Like any tool found on a workbench, public relations can be used to build,
repair, or disassemble. It all depends on the skill and the intent of the person
using it.

Discussion Questions

1. What is public opinion, and what are its three levels?

2. What is a special interest group, and how does it interact within an iron triangle?

3. What is grass-roots lobbying? How is it different from Astroturf lobbying?

4. What are political action committees? What is the difference between hard money and soft money?

5. How are government relations and public affairs similar? How are they different?

Key Terms

active public opinion, p. 268
Astroturf lobbying, p. 272
aware public opinion, p. 268
constituent, p. 269
GOTV, p. 274
government relations, p. 275
grass-roots lobbying, p. 272
hard money, p. 274

iron triangle, p. 270
issue, p. 268
latent public opinion, p. 268
political action committee, p. 273
politics, p. 267
public affairs, p. 275
public opinion, p. 268

soft money, p. 274
special interest agencies, p. 271
special interest groups, p. 269
special interest legislators, p. 271
transparency, p. 276

Endnotes

1. David W. Guth and Charles Marsh, *Public Relations: A Values-Driven Approach,* 2nd ed. (Boston: Allyn & Bacon, 2003), 144–145.

2. Stephen E. Ambrose, *Eisenhower: Soldier and President. The Renowned One-Volume Life* (New York: Simon & Schuster, 1990), 536–537.

3. Scott M. Cutlip, *The Unseen Power: Public Relations. A History* (Hillsdale, NJ: Lawrence Erlbaum Associates, 1994), 162.

4. Janice Lord, "Really MADD: Looking Back at 20 Years," Mothers Against Drunk Driving, in *Driven* (Spring 2000). Online: www.madd.org.

5. Cutlip, 482–498.

6. Guth and Marsh, 162–163.

7. "Member Code of Ethics 2000," Public Relations Society of America, as published in Guth and Marsh, 556–562.

8. "Important Dates: Federal Campaign Finance Legislation," The Hoover Institution, Stanford University. Online: www.campaignfinancesite.org/history/financing1.html.

9. "PAC Activity Increases for 2002 Elections," News release, Federal Elections Commission, March 27, 2003.

10. "Party Committees Raise More than $1 Billion in 2001–2002," News release, Federal Election Commission, March 20, 2003.

11. "The FEC and the Federal Campaign Finance Law," Federal Election Commission Web site, September 2003. Online: www.fec.gov/pages/borchures/fecfeca.htm.

12. "Turnout in the World—Country by Country Performance," Institute for Democracy and Electoral Assistance Web site, www.idea.int/voter_turnout/voter_turnout_pop2,2.html.

13. "Voting & Registration in the Election of November 1998," *Current Population Reports,* P20-523-RV, U.S. Bureau of Census.

14. "Courting Young Voters Can Yield Meager Results," The Associated Press, November 6, 2003. Online: www.cnn.com./2003/ALLPOLITICS/11/03/elect04.youth.vote.ap/index.html.

15. Cutlip, xiii.

War of Words

The Government Debates the Role of Overseas Information in the War on Terror

Few words in the English language are as emotionally charged or carry as many ethical intonations as *propaganda*. Its use by democratic societies has been controversial for most of the past century. The terrorist attacks of Sept. 11, 2001, brought new life to the debate. They also rekindled interest in U.S. overseas information programs that had lost much of their luster since the end of the Cold War.

Propaganda versus Persuasion

"Propaganda as a label suffered (and suffers) from a certain imprecision," said historian Brett Gray. "It is not unlike Justice Potter Stewart's fabled definition of pornography: 'I don't know how to define it, but I know it when I see it.'" Some see propaganda as an umbrella covering all forms of persuasive communication, including advertising and public relations. Others, such as communication scholars Garth Jowett and Victoria O'Donnell, defined propaganda as "the deliberate, systematic attempt to shape perceptions, manipulate cognitions, and direct behavior to achieve a response." On the other hand, they said persuasion "is interactive and attempts to satisfy the needs of both the persuader and persuadee."

Jowett and O'Donnell identified three forms of propaganda: white, black, and gray. White propaganda comes from a source that the message identified correctly and accurately reported. Black propaganda is "credited to a false source and spreads lies, fabrications, and deceptions." As the name suggests, gray propaganda is a middle ground where the source "may or may not be correctly identified, and the accuracy of the information is uncertain."

Overseas Information

U.S. overseas information programs grew out of two world wars. When the United States was drawn into global conflict in 1917, President Woodrow Wilson saw the creation of the Committee on Public Information as a necessary counterweight against the propaganda of the Central Powers. He took the advice of friend and political ally George Creel, who believed the application of U.S.-style propaganda was preferable to military censorship.

With the outbreak of World War II, President Franklin D. Roosevelt launched a similar effort, the Office of War Information. OWI's services included the Voice of America radio service, modeled after the BBC and beamed into occupied areas. As Allied armies moved across Europe, OWI provided media contacts and established a series of Information Centers, or libraries. The agency engaged in white and gray propaganda. It was left to the Office of Strategic Services to conduct psychological warfare against the enemy, including the use of black propaganda.

These differences led to a philosophical split that influenced U.S. overseas information programs through the end of the century. The opposing views were highlighted in a 1948 Brookings Institute study. One view united those who believed "propaganda should be a part of subversive operations and should consist of any action, true or false, responsible or irresponsible, which would effectively hamper the enemy at any point." The other view included those who thought that overseas information should be "a public, responsible government operation to tell the truth."

President Dwight D. Eisenhower—who held the second view—effectively ended the debate when he created the United States Information Agency in 1953. The new agency's job was to explain government policy objectives to the rest of the world. In addition to Voice of America, USIA also operated a Washington-based news bureau, overseas libraries and cultural bureaus, and citizen-exchange programs. Its annual budget ran to nearly $1.5 billion in the mid-1990s. When the Clinton administration embarked on a cost-cutting program, the agency's days were numbered. USIA was shut down and its functions consolidated within the State Department in 1999.

"We're Losing the Public Relations War"

The Sept. 11, 2001, terrorist attacks on the United States thrust the debate over the role of overseas information back to center stage. Again, the central question was what kind of propaganda, if any, is appropriate?

President George W. Bush met with Karen P. Hughes, counselor to the president, on the morning after the attack. According to official minutes of that meeting, the president told Hughes to develop a "plan, a strategy, even a vision . . . to educate the American people to be prepared for another attack. Americans need to know that combating terrorism would be the main focus of the administration—and the government—from this moment forward."

Secretary of Defense Donald H. Rumsfeld articulated a slightly different philosophy during a Sept. 15 session of the Bush war cabinet at Camp David. The minutes of that meeting indicate that Rumsfeld said, "Need tighter control over public affairs. Treat it like a political campaign with daily talking points."

Hughes spearheaded the creation of the Coalition Information Center next door to the White House in the Eisenhower Executive Office Building in October

Karen Hughes (second, left), shown here in the Presidential Emergency
Operations Center during the Sept. 11 terrorist attacks, was the initial
architect of the White House's communication efforts during the War on
Terror. Also shown are National Security Adviser Condoleezza Rice
(center, seated) and Vice President Dick Cheney (with telephone).
(Courtesy of the White House)

2001. There were also smaller CIC operations in London and Islamabad, Pakistan.
Within the CIC, staffers from the White House, other administrative agencies, and
the British Embassy engaged in what The *New York Times* described as "the most
ambitious wartime communications effort since World War II."

The CIC's stated purpose was to more effectively and quickly communicate
U.S. foreign policy goals to the world—especially a skeptical Muslim world. The
CIC was also established to counter the propaganda efforts of the Taliban regime,
al Qaeda, and Osama bin Laden. The *New York Times* also reported that creation of
the CIC was "an acknowledgment that propaganda is back in fashion after the
Clinton administration and Congress tried to cash in on the end of the Cold War
by cutting back public diplomacy overseas . . . to balance the budget."

The creation of the CIC came at a time when the administration was being
criticized for mistakes during the U.S. bombing campaign in Afghanistan. Twice
during the early weeks of the air campaign, U.S. bombs mistakenly struck Red
Cross facilities. President Bush told the National Security Council on Oct. 29,
2001, "We need to also highlight the fact that the Taliban are killing people and
conducting their own terror operations, so get a little more balance here about
what the situation is." Just two days later, the president repeated his frustration
when he opened a National Security Council meeting by saying, "We're losing
the public relations war."

The first successes of the CIC came within a few days of its creation. Former U.S. Ambassador to Syria Christopher Ross appeared on the influential Arabic news channel Al-Jazeera. It was the first time a U.S. official had addressed the Arab world in its own language since the attacks. On Nov. 17, First Lady Laura Bush presented the White House's weekly radio address as part of a coordinated effort to draw attention to the Taliban regime's brutality against women and children. Just a few days later, the CIC office in Islamabad released a list of 22 atrocities it alleged were committed by al Qaeda and the Taliban.

A Turn to the Dark Side?

The Pentagon established its own information outlet during fall 2001, the Office of Strategic Influence. Its existence remained secret for several months. Defense officials would say later that its objectives were similar to those of the CIC. However, OSI also used gray propaganda tactics as part of military and Central Intelligence Agency operations against the Taliban and al Qaeda. These included dropping leaflets and the use of flying radio stations urging terrorists to surrender.

When media reports surfaced in February 2002 of OSI plans to spread disinformation to foreign journalists, White House aides reportedly "hit the ceiling" and said they were "furious" about the proposal. Hughes, who had been accompanying Bush on an Asian trip at the time the news broke, called a *Washington Post* reporter to assure "that there would be no change in the administration's strict policy of providing reporters with the facts." Rumsfeld shut down OSI the next day and said the Pentagon would not deal in disinformation.

This was not the last flirtation with black propaganda. The *New York Times* reported the existence of a secret effort "to discredit and undercut the influence of mosques and religious schools, as well as planting news stories in newspapers and other periodicals in foreign countries," in December 2002. White House spokesman Ari Fleischer told reporters, "The president has the expectation that any program that is created in his administration will be based on facts, and that's what he would expect to be carried out in any program that is created in any entity of the government." In a Pentagon briefing, Rumsfeld said that the idea might have been discussed "at the 50th level" of the bureaucracy, but that "we don't intend to do things that are in any way inconsistent with the laws, or our Constitution, or the principles and values of our country."

New Approach, New Problems

The White House announced July 30, 2002, that it was establishing a permanent Office of Global Communications to coordinate the administration's foreign policy message and to help shape the country's image abroad. Spokesman Ari

Fleischer said, "Better coordination of international communications will help America to explain what we do and why we do it around the world. It's important to share the truth about America and American values with other nations in the world."

U.S.- and British-led forces ousted dictator Saddam Hussein from power in the controversial Operation Iraqi Freedom during spring 2003. The war was waged over widespread domestic and international opposition that did not see a link between Iraq and the War on Terror. The Bush administration's main argument had been the regime's defiance of United Nations prohibitions against Iraq's development and possession of weapons of mass destruction. In the months following the opening of combat operations, no direct evidence of the existence of those weapons was found. The Bush administration said it acted on what the president felt at the time was accurate intelligence. However, the lack of evidence and continuing violence in Iraq created significant problems for President Bush as he entered his 2004 re-election campaign.

Sources

Mike Allen, "White House Angered at Plan for Pentagon Misinformation," *The Washington Post,* February 25, 2002, A17.

Elizabeth Becker, "A Nation Challenged: Hearts and Minds," *The New York Times,* November 11, 2001, Section 1A, p. 1.

Leo Bogart, *Cool Words, Cold War.* Washington, DC: The American University Press, 1995, xiii.

Donald R. Browne, "United States Information Agency," in *History of the Mass Media in the United States: An Encyclopedia,* ed. Margaret A. Blanchard (Chicago: Fitzroy Dearborn, 1998), 672–673.

Laura Bush, Radio Address to the Nation, Office of Mrs. Bush, The White House, November 17, 2001. Online: www.whitehouse.gov.

Ari Fleischer, Press Briefing Transcript, The White House, July 30, 2002.

Brett Gray, *The Nervous Liberals: Propaganda Anxieties from World War I to the Cold War* (New York: Columbia University Press, 1999), 8.

Fact Sheet: Foreign Affairs Reorganization, The White House, December 30, 1998.

Garth S. Jowett and Victoria O'Donnell, *Propaganda and Persuasion,* 3rd ed. (Thousand Oaks, CA: Sage, 1999), 1–15.

Dana Milbank, "U.S. Takes Offensive in Information War with List of Enemy Crimes," *The Washington Post,* November 22, 2001, A38.

Richard Alan Nelson, *A Chronology and Glossary of Propaganda in the United States* (Westport, CT: Greenwood, 1996), 128, 176, 274.

Donald Rumsfeld, Transcript of U.S. Department of Defense News Briefing (with General Richard B. Meyers, Chairman, Joints Chiefs of Staff), U.S. Department of Defense, December 17, 2002.

Eric Schmitt, "White House Plays down Propaganda by Military," *The New York Times,* December 17, 2002. Online: www.nytimes.com.

Charles A. H. Thomson, *Overseas Information Service of the United States Government* (Washington, DC: The Brookings Institution, 1948), 19 (as cited in Bogart).

Bob Woodward, *Bush at War* (New York: Simon & Schuster, 2002), 41, 88, 272–273, 279.

case 12.2

"Please Help Us"

A Family Campaigns to Keep Dale Earnhardt's Autopsy Records Private

Dale Earnhardt died doing what he loved and knew best—driving hard for the finish line. Earnhardt, 49, was involved in a tight battle for the lead in the final turn of the last lap of the 2001 Daytona 500. In the race to the checkered flag, his black No. 3 Chevy Monte Carlo spun out, hit the outside wall at 180 mph and was then struck by another car.

To the thousands of fans who witnessed the race from the stands and the millions watching on television, the wreck did not appear bad by NASCAR standards. Earlier in the same race, there had been a more spectacular crash in which no one was seriously hurt. That is why the death of arguably the sport's greatest star came as such a shock.

Millions of NASCAR fans mourned the passing of the seven-time Winston Cup champion. The Mooresville, N.C., headquarters of Earnhardt's racing team became the focal point for the grieving. Fans left flowers, posters, and personal notes for the driver they knew as "The Intimidator." NASCAR Chairman Bill France said, "NASCAR has lost its greatest driver ever."

Amid the grieving, however, Earnhardt's death quickly turned into a legal, political, and ethical battle pitting the driver's family and fans against the news media. It also provided a lesson in the power of public opinion and the complexity of the U.S. Constitution.

Official Version Questioned

Five days after the accident, NASCAR President Mike Helton said that a broken safety belt appeared to be a contributing factor in Earnhardt's death. Because of the seat belt failure, Helton said the driver was killed when he struck the steering wheel. This was a controversial finding that would soon be challenged.

Just weeks before the fatal race, the *Orlando Sentinel* had published a series of articles on the potential dangers NASCAR drivers face from head trauma. It noted that four drivers had died within the previous nine months as a result of violent head whip, a potentially preventable injury. Shortly after Helton's statement, the *Sentinel* submitted a public records request to the Volusia County Medical Examiner's Office for the Earnhardt autopsy photographs.

"We are not seeking the photos for some macabre curiosity," said *Sentinel* attorney David Bralow. "We have a very significant news reason to look at these, and we want to do it in a timely manner." He added that the paper had no intention of publishing the photographs.

Concerned that photographs taken during her late husband's autopsy might be published, Earnhardt's widow, Teresa, went to court to seal the records. Her concerns had merit. Shortly after Earnhardt's death, autopsy photographs of NASCAR driver Neil Bonnet, who had died running practice laps at Daytona in 1994, were posted on a Deland, Fla., Web site. It wasn't long before a number of state and national media organizations joined in the legal battle to obtain the autopsy photos.

"Please Help Us"

The Earnhardt family, which had gone to court to block the photos' release, turned to public relations agency Burson-Marsteller for help. While battling the news media over access to public records may seem like a daunting task, the Earnhardts were heartened by private polling that showed that *Sentinel* readers sided with them by a 7-to-1 margin. The family felt it had the public support needed to convince lawmakers to amend Florida's open records law to restrict access to autopsy photos.

They decided to appeal to stock car racing fans through beat reporters covering NASCAR's next event, in Las Vegas. On March 5, a little more than two weeks after the accident, Teresa Earnhardt made her first public comments since her husband's death. The more than 200 reporters at the standing-room-only session were not informed in advance of what she was planning to say.

"The deceased have a right to their dignity," she said in a prepared statement. "Releasing the pictures will serve only to violate the privacy of our family and the integrity of Dale's legacy." Before leaving the room without taking reporters' questions, she asked NASCAR fans to "please help us by speaking out."

The results of Teresa Earnhardt's appearance were an outpouring of public support for amending the open records law and a torrent of criticism toward the *Sentinel*. There were public demonstrations at the county courthouse and in front of the newspaper offices. The *Sentinel* and state officials were inundated with thousands of letters and e-mails supporting the Earnhardts. For example, Gov. Jeb Bush said he had received 20,000 e-mails on the issue. The *Sentinel* also felt a financial backlash in the form of canceled subscriptions and advertising. Within a week, the Florida Family Protection Act, a bill to restrict access to autopsy photos, was introduced in the state legislature.

Still in mourning, Teresa Earnhardt left it to Burson-Marsteller spokespersons and her attorneys to sustain her message. They, in turn, wrote op-ed commentaries for Florida newspapers and participated in a satellite media tour. The public relations agency also enlisted the support of the National Center for Victims of Crime, a group that advocates for the rights and dignity of victims. In an effort to deal with the mounting criticism, the newspaper hired its own public relations agency and sent its managing editor and publisher on a media tour to explain its position.

Both Sides Claim Victory

A Florida judge ordered the two sides into mediation. A settlement was announced March 17. It called for the selection of an independent medical doctor to examine the photographs under court supervision. No copies would be allowed, and the review would be confined to a narrowly defined set of issues. Once the review was completed, the medical examiner would not be allowed to permit anyone else to view or copy the photographs.

"The court is siding with the right of privacy," said family attorney Thom Rumberger. *Sentinel* President and Publisher Kathleen M. Waltz said, "The *Sentinel* is pleased to have amicably reached an accord with Mrs. Earnhardt that allows the newspaper to continue to do its job and at the same time addresses Mrs. Earnhardt's concerns."

After his examination of the autopsy photos, Dr. Barry Myers of Duke University, the court-appointed medical expert, suggested that "restraint failure does not appear to have played a role in Mr. Earnhardt's fatal injury." Because of these and other revelations, NASCAR would later reverse its position and require head and neck restraints for drivers in its three major series.

While the Earnhardt family hoped that the settlement would end the controversy, all it seemed to do was fan the flames. Within days, an independent student-run newspaper at the University of Florida challenged the settlement, saying that it wasn't in the public's best interests. Tom Julin, the lawyer representing the *Independent Florida Alligator*, said he couldn't promise that the pictures would not be published. "Without seeing the photos, it's impossible to know if there's anything to publish," he said.

From Legal to Political Action

While the legal drama played out in Volusia County, a political drama neared its conclusion in Tallahassee. The Florida Family Protection Act, otherwise known as HB1083, moved at unusual speed through the state legislature. The bill's language noted that "photographs or video or audio recordings of an autopsy are highly sensitive" and "could result in trauma, sorrow, humiliation, or emotional injury to the immediate family of the deceased, as well as injury to the memory of the deceased." The bill also noted that "there continue to be other types of available information, such as the autopsy report, which are less intrusive and injurious to the immediate family members of the deceased and which continue to provide for public oversight."

The legislation passed the house 96–12, and the senate 40–0. Gov. Bush signed the measure into law March 29, 2001—only 39 days after the Daytona crash that triggered the controversy. Several news organizations filed a lawsuit challenging the constitutionality of the legislation—specifically citing the First and 14th Amendments to the U.S. Constitution, which deal with freedom of the press and equal protection under the law. In February 2002, the Earnhardt family joined the case as an *amicus curiae*—literally, as a "friend of the court." In that role, attorneys representing the family filed legal briefs and argued in support of the law. The challenge failed in both the state district and supreme courts. On Dec. 1, 2003, the U.S. Supreme Court rejected the student-run newspaper's claims.

Even as the legal issues are decided, the controversy over the Florida Family Protection Act continues. "It guarantees the protection of the fundamental right of privacy without infringing on any other right," said Earnhardt family attorney Parker D. Thomson. "No one need worry about whether investigative reporters, the police, or medical examiners will be able to do their jobs."

Newspaper industry publication *Editor & Publisher* noted in a March 2001 editorial that "autopsy reports and photos have frequently revealed long-buried truth and brought murderers to justice." It went on to say, "Who is not moved by a widow's tears? But compassion must not cloud our clarity—and that, unfortunately, is what is happening in all three branches of Florida's government."

Sources

"Agreement reached on Earnhardt autopsy photos," CNN, March 17, 2001. Online: www.cnn.com/2001/US/03/16/earnhardt.autopsy/index.html.

John M. Daly, "'News' Wrong: Autopsy Laws in Florida Needed Change," *The Stuart News,* January 14, 2002, A8.

"Earnhardt Autopsy Review—A Collision with the Truth," *Salisbury Post,* April 13, 2001. Online: www.salisberypost.com/2001april/041301ed.htm.

"Earnhardt Family Joins New Lawsuit on Family Protection Act; Family of Deceased NASCAR Legend Admitted as Amicus Curae in Broward County Litigation," PR Newswire, February 28, 2002.

"Earnhardt Fans Remember 'Man Like No Other,'" CNN, February 19, 2001. Online: www.cnn.com/2001/US/02/19/earnhardt.fans/index.html.

"Earnhardt's Wife Appeals for Autopsy Photos to be Kept Private," CNN, March 5, 2001. Online: www.cnn.com/2001/US/03/04/earnhardt.autopsy/index.html.

HB 1083, Florida General Assembly Web site, www.leg.state.fl.us.

"Red-Flag Autopsy Bill," *Editor & Publisher, 134*(12), March 19, 2001, 14.

"Student Newspaper Seeks Earnhardt Autopsy Photos," CNN, March 20, 2001. Online: www.cnn.com/2001/LAW/03/20/earnhardt.autopsy/index.html.

case 12.3

Giving an ASSIST

The National Cancer Institute Builds Local Coalitions to Reduce Smoking

After decades of controversy and debate, no one today—not even the tobacco industry—denies that cigarette smoking is a harmful and addictive habit. In an annual report on cancer statistics, the American Cancer Society estimated that there would be more than 1.3 million new cancer cases and 556,000 deaths in 2003. In the United States, cigarette smoking alone causes about 30 percent of cancer deaths and an estimated $157 billion in annual health-related economic losses.

The public relations industry has had a long and controversial association with tobacco. The man most recognized as the "father" of modern public relations, Edward L. Bernays, created a national sensation in 1929 when he had 10 debutantes stroll down New York's Fifth Avenue carrying lighted cigarettes aloft. The so-called "Torches of Freedom" march was a publicity stunt protesting the social taboo against women smoking in public. Years later, Bernays wrote that he regretted his actions.

This historic relationship between public relations and the tobacco industry has resulted in a torrent of criticism from health professionals and social activists. Among the sharpest critics are authors John Stauber and Sheldon Rampton, who lambasted the profession in "How the American Tobacco Industry Employs PR Scum to Continue Its Murderous Assault on Human Lives," a 1995 article in *Tucson Weekly*. "Accusing the PR industry of manipulating the truth is like criticizing sharks for eating meat, or snakes for poisoning their victims," the authors said. "They do what they do because it's in their nature."

For those who believe public relations should be a positive force for social change, a 2003 report in the *Journal of the National Cancer Institute* brought a ray of hope. It credited a federal antismoking campaign with a decline in tobacco use. The program, the American Stop Smoking Intervention Study—or ASSIST—was the largest government-funded demonstration program to help states develop effective strategies to reduce smoking. In the 17 states that participated in ASSIST between 1991 and 1999, smoking dropped by approximately 3 percentage points— more than one-half a point better than in states not engaged in the program. What made the ASSIST program outperform others? The answer, in part, is public relations.

Building Coalitions

The National Cancer Institute focused on four objectives when it launched the program. The first was to launch a public relations effort to counter an estimated $47 billion in tobacco marketing during the same eight-year period. Each of the participating state health departments received $1.14 million a year to implement the program. These public relations efforts were closely linked to the program's remaining objectives: the promotion of a smoke-free environment, limiting minors' access to tobacco products, and the raising of excise taxes to increase the price of tobacco products. With each of these strategies contingent on building consensus, effective public relations became the critical element.

ASSIST enlisted the support of volunteer coalitions in each of the participating states. These coalitions, working in concert with health care professionals, brought pressure to bear on public and private organizations to tighten regulations involving the sale and use of tobacco products. According to *Tobacco Control,* a research publication of the National Cancer Institute, "The underlying assumption is that social change is more likely to succeed when those who will be affected are involved in planning, initiating, and promoting the change." By mid-1996, more than 6,200 community-based organizations were participating in ASSIST coalitions.

Maine's Experience

Maine was one of the 17 states involved in ASSIST. The state Department of Human Services, working with the NCI and the American Cancer Society, administered the program, known locally as the ASSIST Coalition for a Tobacco-Free Maine. The organization, in turn, worked with a network of youth groups and local organizations to develop an antitobacco network that covered the state.

In an effort to reduce illegal sales of tobacco to minors, the department funded five pilot youth access prevention projects in 1993. The money went to a variety of community groups, including schools, town governments, health care advocates, and civic clubs. Campaign organizers conducted compliance checks gauging the level of illegal tobacco sales in 16 communities. These compliance checks found that youth could illegally purchase tobacco products more than 40 percent of the time. This survey served two purposes: to provide a benchmark for program evaluation and to provide ammunition in efforts to lobby the state government for stricter tobacco regulation. On the day the legislature considered the regulations, campaign organizers held a youth rally at Maine's statehouse. Two youths testified before a legislative committee in support of the legislation.

Those lobbying efforts led to enactment of a new state law that created penalties for juvenile possession of tobacco and required special licenses for tobacco retailers. State agencies also were required to work with health care advocates and retailers in implementing the new law. To that end, the state Department of Human Services met with stakeholders in August 1995 to encourage cooperation and collaboration. Four work groups were formed at that meeting: merchant education, public awareness, law enforcement, and smoking cessation.

Along with the compliance checks, the Maine ASSIST coalition launched a program of merchant and community education. One community in the coalition, St. John Valley, enlisted the help of a local television station and developed a public service announcement discouraging illegal tobacco sales. In Portland, the local coalition created an antitobacco video. Other community-developed promotional tools included fact sheets on tobacco use, slide presentations, and a promotional packet sent to retailers when they received their tobacco sales license. The state coalition contracted the American Lung Association of Maine to conduct "The Youth Summit '96: Leadership Training for Smoke-Free Youth." Sixty-one participants, ages 12–18, attended tobacco-prevention workshops to learn leadership and team-building skills.

The ASSIST Coalition for a Tobacco-Free Maine

Comprehensive Tobacco Control Plan

FIFTH ANNUAL ACTION PLAN

October 1, 1997 - September 30, 1998

The ASSIST antismoking campaign involved 17 states, including Maine. It required collaboration at the federal, state, and local levels, as well as from a variety of private, nongovernmental organizations. Researchers estimated that the eight-year campaign resulted in 104,000 fewer smokers. (Courtesy of the Maine Department of Human Services)

Media Advocacy

Maine's ASSIST efforts also focused on training volunteers to generate publicity. According to NCI's *Tobacco Control,* "Using media strategically to advance a social or public policy initiative has come to be defined as 'media advocacy.'" At a media advocacy workshop, 47 participants learned a variety of tactics, including writing letters to the editor, media interview techniques, and lobbying. Coalition members encouraged each participant to conduct two publicity activities per year and to recruit other volunteers into the effort.

These efforts generated a number of success stories. Maine's top youth-oriented radio station started playing daily remembrances of recording artists who had died from tobacco-related diseases. Community-based World No Tobacco Day activities were conducted in 1996 and included a successful 4,000-name petition drive for tougher tobacco control policies at the Naval Air Station at Brunswick. A statewide women's organization adopted a resolution to educate youth and adults about the dangers of smoking and underage tobacco sales. The Greater Portland ASSIST Coalition distributed clean indoor air policy packets to area businesses. The Maine Dental Association embraced tobacco cessation efforts through posters and patient counseling sessions. Even Portland's minor league baseball team got into the act, announcing that its new home stadium would be a smoke-free facility.

One of the Maine coalition's most successful publicity efforts involved Dave Goerlitz, who once had been a successful advertising model for Winston cigarettes. However, his message was much different this time. Goerlitz spoke in 17 central Maine communities during 1993–1994 about both the dangers of tobacco and his criticisms of tobacco advertising. He returned a year later for a more extensive tour of the state, reaching 40 communities and 3,000 people. According to organizers, tour publicity generated 300,000 audience impressions and an advertising equivalency (see ACT File #6) worth almost twice as much as it cost to contract Goerlitz.

Measuring Success

Follow-up compliance checks suggested that the combination of education, enforcement, and advocacy tactics worked. Illegal sales of tobacco products to underage customers dropped in Portland from 43 percent to 24 percent in the first year. In Farmington, the illegal sales dropped from 42 percent to 33 percent during the same period. Between October 1996 and September 1997, more than 1,000 random unannounced inspections of licensed tobacco retailers were conducted.

Successes also occurred on the legislative front. In addition to the previously mentioned tobacco retail sale licensing law, Maine lawmakers doubled the state excise tax on cigarettes. The measure was expected to generate $3.5 million each year for tobacco prevention and control activities. Major legislation aimed at reducing tobacco use among young people passed in 1995 and 1997.

It was left for NCI-funded researchers to assess whether the ASSIST program had produced a measurable reduction in smoking. Their research, published in November 2003, made headlines across the country. Using industry cigarette sales figures and tobacco use surveys for the eight years being studied, researchers determined that the percentage of smokers had dropped from 25.19 percent to 22.17 percent—just over 3 percent—in the 17 states in which the ASSIST program was in place. That compared with a decline from 24.41 percent to 22.30 percent—just over 2 percent—in the rest of the country.

According to researcher Frances A. Stillman of Johns Hopkins University, ASSIST reduced smokers' ranks by 104,000 people. Had the program been in place across the nation, she estimated that the reduction in smokers would have been around 278,000. In the end, the program spent approximately $1,200 for each person who quit smoking.

"Most smoking cessation programs will spend that," said study co-author Elizabeth A. Gilpin of the University of California, San Diego. "When you think about what you save in health care costs, $1,200 is a real bargain."

Not everyone shared Dr. Gilpin's enthusiasm. In a scathing editorial less than a week after the study was released, the *Las Vegas Review-Journal* called the eight-year, $128 million dollar program a "boondoggle." The paper's sharpest criticism focused on the ASSIST program's media advocacy efforts.

"The federal government spent your money coaching people to twist the arms of state lawmakers in Colorado, Missouri, New York, North Carolina, and 13 other states, demanding higher taxes and reduced freedom for business owners to decide whether to allow their customers to smoke," the newspaper said. "And were any of those jacked-up tax receipts then rebated to the federal taxpayers who funded the scheme? Perhaps our checks are still in the mail."

Sources

"ACS Cancer Facts & Figures 2003 Released," News release, American Cancer Society, January 22, 2003. Online: www.cancer.org.

"A Real Bargain," Editorial, *Las Vegas Review-Journal,* November 24, 2003. Online: http://reviewjournal.com.

The ASSIST Coalition for a Tobacco-Free Maine: Fifth Annual Action Plan, Maine Department of Human Services, Bureau of Health, August 1, 1997.

Edward L. Bernays, *Biography of an Idea: Memoirs of Public Relations Counsel Edward L. Bernays* (New York: Simon & Schuster, 1965), 387.

"Smoking Rate Decreases More in States with Cessation Effort," The Associated Press, as reported in the *Houston Chronicle,* November 19, 2003. Online: www.chron.com.

Marc Manley, William Lynn, Roselyn Payne Epps, Donna Grande, Thomas Glynn, and Donald Shopland, "The American Stop Smoking Intervention Study for Cancer Prevention: An Overview," *Tobacco Control, 6,* Suppl. 2 (Winter 1997).

John Stauber and Sheldon Rampton, "How the American Tobacco Industry Employs PR Scum to Continue Its Murderous Assault on Human Lives," *Tucson Weekly,* November 22, 1995. Online: www.tucsonweekly.com/tw/11-22-95/cover.htm.

Frances A. Stillman, Anne M. Hartman, Barry I. Graubard, Elizabeth A. Gilpin, David M. Murray, and James T. Gibson, "Evaluation of the American Stop Smoking Intervention Study (ASSIST): A Report of Outcomes," *Journal of the National Cancer Institute, 95*(22), November 19, 2003, 1681–1691.

"Study Shows Strong Tobacco Control Programs and Policies Can Lower Smoking Rates," News release, National Cancer Institute, November 18, 2003.

ACT file # 12

Force Field Analysis

As a critical thinker, you should challenge the old notion that a picture is worth 1,000 words. But in the case of force field analysis, a diagram can clarify a situation and add drama to client presentations—especially when you want to demonstrate the need to act.

Force field analysis helps public relations practitioners illustrate a situation analysis. In other words, it offers a diagram of the forces that create the environment in which a client operates. To construct such a diagram, you must first conduct research to discover the positive and negative forces that influence your client's current performance. The force field analysis diagram visually represents the results of your research.

Kerry Tucker, president of the Nuffer, Smith, Tucker public relations agency, popularized the use of FFA in public relations.[1] Based on the theories of social scientist Kurt Lewin, FFA helps you generate a diagram that looks something like Figure 12.3. To construct a force field analysis diagram, you use the following conventions.

- Assume that the current state of affairs, the status quo, merits a 5 on a vertical scale of 1 to 10. Indicate the status quo with a line. At the top of the scale, 10 represents the best of all possible worlds in the relevant situation; at the bottom, 1 represents total disaster.
- Identify the most important negative forces that threaten the status quo—forces that try to push the line down to a lower ranking. Indicate each force with a downward arrow. In Figure 12.3, we might label one negative arrow "Voter Apathy" and a second negative arrow "Organized Opposition Group."
- Identify the most important positive forces that strengthen the status quo—forces that try to push the line up to a higher ranking. Indicate each force with

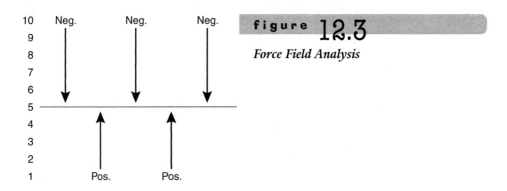

figure 12.3

Force Field Analysis

Advanced Critical Thinking

an upward arrow. In Figure 12.3, we might label one positive arrow "Friendly PAC" and a second positive arrow "New Legislation."

With the major positive and negative forces identified and illustrated, you can discuss plans—based on additional research—to weaken the negative forces, strengthen the positive forces, and add new positive forces. With a presentation program such as Microsoft PowerPoint, you can easily add and subtract arrows during a client presentation. You can show the line—your client's situation—moving upward to a better ranking.

Force field analysis can illustrate the present, the plan, and the future. That just might be worth 1,000 words.

Discussion Questions

1. Could a force field analysis diagram be useful in cases other than those dealing with political and public policy issues?

2. Do you think it's necessary to have an equal number of positive and negative arrows in a force field analysis diagram? Why or why not?

3. Do you think a force field analysis diagram could add drama to a client presentation? Why or why not?

4. Can you construct a force field analysis diagram for each of the cases in this chapter? For other cases in this book?

Endnote

1. Kerry Tucker, Doris Derelian, and Donna Rouner, *Public Relations Writing: An Issue-Driven Behavioral Approach,* 3rd ed. (Upper Saddle River, NJ: Prentice-Hall, 1997).

CHAPTER 13

Crisis Communications

A quick glance at the table of contents of the U.S. government's emergency preparedness guide is enough to scare anyone. First, there are the natural hazards, such as floods, hurricanes, volcanoes, and tsunamis. Then come technological and man-made horrors. Those include hazardous materials incidents, terrorism, biological weapons, and nuclear attacks.[1] And that's just the stuff we know about.

Does anyone doubt the need for crisis communications planning and training? The answer to that question may depend on whom you ask.

Nine out of 10 respondents to a February 2002 American Society of Safety Engineers survey said their company had a written crisis plan. Two-thirds of those firms had conducted mock crisis drills within the previous year.[2] That's the good news. But keep in mind that it was a survey of *safety engineers* and it was published a just few months after Sept. 11, 2001. Now the bad news: According to a 2003 Harris Poll, one-third of the *Fortune* 1000 senior executives surveyed said their companies were no better prepared to protect their digital assets than they were before the terrorist attacks.[3] Through the years, several polls have indicated that only one in three companies have written crisis plans that they have practiced within the past year.[4]

"The unfortunate truth is that many companies have failed to recognize that physical events or nagging perceptions can be their undoing," wrote Richard C. Hyde, director of crisis and issues management for Hill & Knowlton. "As keepers of corporate reputation, we need to step up to one of our most important responsibilities: developing the capabilities for responding to threatening situations."[5]

Regardless of the number of those who are—or are not—prepared, the fact remains that how organizations respond to emergencies often determines whether they survive the storm. History is littered with examples of organizations that faced disaster, responded poorly, and ceased to exist. However, you don't have to look far to find organizations that met these challenges and came out of the experience better and stronger.

Understanding Crises

Crisis is an overused and often abused word. Many use it in a personal way, as if a bad hair day is a crisis. However, even in that context, you can see a working definition of the term begin to emerge. Although **crisis** has been described in many ways, most characterizations contain some or all of these elements:[6]

- **Stressful**—People need to be at their best when things are at their worst.
- **Disruptive**—Crises strain the physical and emotional resources of those they affect.
- **Dangerous**—Crises place an organization or individual's reputation, financial resources, products/services, employees, and survival at risk.
- **Predictable**—Crises don't "just happen." There are usually warning signs of impending trouble. The challenge is to recognize and act on them before real damage occurs.
- **Public**—Crises often happen within full view of important stakeholders, such as the media, regulators, consumers, investors, and employees. The crisis response has a tremendous influence of their perceptions of the organization or individual in crisis.
- **Escalating**—Much like a leaking pipe under a sink, the challenges may start with just a trickle that left unattended or subjected to an inappropriate response could quickly degenerate into a flood.
- **Pivotal**—The resolution of a crisis is in doubt with potential for an outcome either positive or negative—or both.

While the War on Terror may have provided a heightened sense of urgency, crisis communications has been a hot topic in public relations for more than two decades. This interest began with the 1980 accident at the Three Mile Island nuclear power plant in central Pennsylvania. Business executives and public relations practitioners quickly noticed that while no one was injured in the incident, the controversy evolved into a death knell for nuclear power plant construction in the United States. They wondered that if the utility and government had handled crisis communications during the incident more competently, would the outcome have been any different?[7]

Other notable crisis communications failures have occurred. They include the grounding and breakup of the oil tanker *Exxon Valdez* in the pristine waters of Prince William Sound in Alaska in 1989.[8] The resulting spill of 11 million gallons of crude oil contaminated nearly 600 miles of shoreline. Since that time, experts have pointed to the slow and unengaged response of Exxon CEO Lawrence G. Rawl as the prime example of how *not* to manage a crisis. NASA's clumsy actions in the hours after the 1986 explosion of the space shuttle *Challenger* helped fuel a public outcry that led to a major overhaul of the space agency.[9] More recently, the combative actions of Bridgestone/Firestone in the wake of reports of serious defects in tires used on sport utility vehicles made the company the object of public scorn and opened it to expensive lawsuits.[10]

The terrorist attacks on the World Trade Center and the Pentagon forced public and private organizations to use crisis communications to reassure key stakeholders at a time of uncertainty. (Courtesy of the Federal Emergency Management Agency)

However, going back to a point we have made before, the outcomes of crises do not have to be bad. Business analysts say the candid, proactive actions of Chrysler Corp. CEO Lee Iacocca saved the company from bankruptcy in 1981.[11] Both Johnson & Johnson and Pepsi won widespread praise for their forceful responses to product tampering incidents in the 1980s and 1990s.[12] And who can forget the professionalism—and heroism—of the thousands of unnamed individuals in both the public and private sectors who calmed a frightened nation after the Sept. 11, 2001, attacks?

This is the key lesson in managing crises: The outcomes do not have to be bad.

Stopping a Crisis before It Starts

The best crisis is the one avoided. Rarely are crises unanticipated. We may not know exactly when an earthquake, hurricane, or tornado may strike, but we are certainly aware of those risks. And because we have improved our ability to anticipate and plan for such catastrophic events, the number of people killed in those kinds of calamities is at historically low levels. What about the terror attacks of Sept. 11? That wasn't the first act of terrorism against U.S. citizens on U.S. soil. It wasn't the first time terrorists had hijacked planes. It wasn't even the first time they had attacked the World Trade Center. The warning signs were there. We just did not recognize them.

According to Steven Fink, a member of the team that managed Pennsylvania's response to the Three Mile Island accident, crises follow a predictable four-phase pattern:[13]

1. **The Prodromal Crisis Stage**—This is the warning stage, when signs of potential trouble exist—if only we recognize them.
2. **The Acute Crisis Stage**—This is what Fink calls "the point of no return": the moment when we recognize the onset of the crisis. Some damage—physical, financial, and/or in terms of reputation—will occur. How much remains to be seen.
3. **The Chronic Crisis Stage**—Also known as the "clean-up phase," this period features steps taken to resolve the crisis. It is also the period on which stakeholders will judge management's ability to address the crisis. Reputations—and careers—are often made or broken during this phase.
4. **The Crisis Resolution Stage**—This is when things return to "normal." However, there may be a new "normal." This is the time for evaluating why the crisis happened and the decisions that were made. Once that is accomplished, steps should be taken to ensure that history does not repeat itself.

Knowing the cyclical nature of crises, we can see the value of crisis communications planning: the ability to identify signs of trouble quickly and to minimize or eliminate their potential to harm your organization. Let's say you have come to this planet from another world and have never seen clouds before. Under those circumstances, you may not know to carry an umbrella when it is cloudy. However, you only need to be rained on once to learn that dark clouds indicate the possibility of wet weather. From that time on, you keep an umbrella handy.

In the language of crisis communications planning, you have just done a **risk assessment**—a form of research that identifies potential dangers confronting organizations. Risk assessments set the stage for **crisis communications planning**—a contingency plan that outlines an organization's various options for communicating with key stakeholders in the event of a crisis.

Let's say your organization operates a day care center right next to an area where it stores hazardous materials. Obviously, the geography of that situation suggests a potential risk. A good crisis planner would recognize the danger and move one or both of the facilities out of harm's way. However, other, less obvious threats exist. Bad weather could force the early closing or cancellation of day care services. Crisis planners cannot control the weather. However, they can anticipate it and make plans to minimize weather-related disruptions. One example would be the creation of an emergency notification system for reaching parents on short notice.

Crisis Communications Planning

Risk assessment and crisis planning should involve people at all levels of the organization. While managers may be more knowledgeable about an organization's strategic goals, the rank-and-file may better know how things work. With this kind of collaboration, it is less likely that important issues and concerns will fall through the cracks.

Crisis communications plans should contain these key components:

- **Who is the crisis manager?** This is the person who has operational control of the crisis response. While the chief executive officer may choose to fill this role, the CEO sometimes delegates this responsibility to someone he or she trusts.

- **Who is on the crisis management team?** Not everyone in the organization can—or should—be involved in crisis response. The purpose of a crisis management team is to isolate the crisis in order to allow the remainder of the organization to continue to function as normally as possible. CMT members should include financial experts, attorneys, public relations practitioners, technical experts, and support personnel.

- **Where is the emergency operations center?** An emergency operations center is a secure location from which the CMT can manage the crisis without interruption from curious reporters or rubbernecking employees.

- **Where is the media information center?** A media information center is a place the media gather to receive official information about the crisis response. The MIC fosters a mutually beneficial relationship by providing the media a place to work and helping the organization to speak with one voice.

- **How will you communicate with all stakeholders?** Although the media are important, they are not the only stakeholders who will want to know about the crisis response. Employees, shareholders, government officials, and members of the community are among those who will need to know what is happening. Long-term relationships with these groups can depend on the answer to this question.

In addition to these steps, crisis plans should take into account that some crises involve an around-the-clock response. That requires a certain level of redundancy, with several people trained for each CMT position. These backups are especially useful because there is no guarantee that crises will not occur when key people are ill, on vacation, or otherwise unavailable.

It is also a good idea to train all employees about their roles in the crisis plan—even if that role is to let somebody else do it. One of the most important people in any response is the first person to recognize (or fail to recognize) the onset of a crisis. What that person chooses to do or not to do will influence all decisions that follow. Regularly scheduled practice sessions will serve the dual purpose of providing that training and pointing out any holes in the response plan.

The work should not end when the crisis is over. While memories are still fresh, members of the CMT should write an **after-action report** that details the steps they took, what worked well, and potential areas of improvement. This evaluation may help the organization avoid even more severe crises in the future.

Key Considerations

Communicating during a crisis tends to complicate what is already a difficult process. Even in the best of times, people will question one's motives. However, when stress and the stakes increase, everyone's sensibilities are more acute. For that reason, crisis communicators should keep additional things in mind:

- **Make friends before the crisis happens.** The middle of crisis is a difficult time to make new friends. Identify stakeholders as part of the risk assessment process and establish relationships before being forced by events to do so.

- **Candor goes a long way.** Although there may be good reasons you can't tell the public everything you know, there is never a good reason to lie. People respond well to those willing to admit to their mistakes. That is especially true if you volunteer the information, as opposed to having someone force an admission from you.

- **Be prepared.** In anticipation of the variety of crises an organization can face, practitioners should have generic news releases, backgrounders, and fact sheets on file and ready for use at a moment's notice. This will save time—a precious commodity in the middle of a crisis.

- **Address stakeholder needs.** Stakeholders are more interested in their problems than yours. Direct messages to the needs of each public, using the medium or media that each prefers.

- **Speak with one voice.** Designate one person to speak for the organization, preferably from one fixed location, the MIC. Even as spokespersons change during a prolonged crisis, the message should not. This also means coordinating communication efforts with other agencies and organizations involved in the crisis response.

- **Actions speak louder than words.** Saying that you will fix a problem is not enough. Credibility is always important, but especially during crises. Stakeholders will demand that organizations in crisis be true to their word. Failure to do so lessens the likelihood of repairing damaged relationships.

- **Be true to your values.** Never are values more greatly tested than during crises. And never are they more needed to guide you through the storm.

Careers are often defined by crises. Rudolph Giuliani was near the end of an often controversial and sometimes contentious eight-year run as mayor of New York when terrorists destroyed the World Trade Center. Because of his inspired leadership in the hours and days that followed, the man who became affectionately known to millions as Rudy had become an international hero. Conversely, any future political ambitions Secretary of State Alexander Haig may have had in 1981 vanished because of a single, unsettling news conference following an assassination attempt against President Ronald Reagan. Nervous and perspiring profusely, Haig declared, "I am in charge here at the White House." He wasn't—and because of that performance, he never would be.

There is also an ethical dimension to crisis planning. Errors of omission can be as damaging—and deadly—as those of commission. Managers—and we hope that includes public relations practitioners—have a moral responsibility to protect their organizations from potential dangers. That includes protecting the organization's reputation among its key stakeholders. It is never too early to plan for a crisis. History shows the consequences of being late.

Discussion Questions

1. How is a crisis different from an everyday problem?

2. What are Steven Fink's four stages of a crisis?

3. What is risk assessment?

4. What are the key components of a crisis communications plan?

5. Who should be on an organization's crisis management team, and where should it conduct its business?

Key Terms

Acute Crisis Stage, p. 298
after-action report, p. 299
Chronic Crisis Stage, p. 298
crisis, p. 296

crisis communications
  planning, p. 298
Crisis Resolution Stage,
  p. 298

Prodromal Crisis Stage,
  p. 298
risk assessment,
  p. 298

Endnotes

1. *Are You Ready? A Guide to Citizen Preparedness.* Federal Emergency Management Agency (Washington: U.S. Government Printing Office, 2003), v–vi.

2. Steven E. NyBlom, Janine Coy, and William Walker. "Understanding Crisis Management," *Professional Safety* (March 2003), vol. 48, no. 3, 18–25.

3. Leslie Brooks Suzukamo. "Gone in an Instant," *The Kansas City Star* (September 8, 2004), B6.

4. David Guth and Charles Marsh, *Public Relations: A Values-Driven Approach,* 2nd ed. (Boston: Allyn & Bacon, 2003), 390.

5. Richard C. Hyde. "The New Reality: Response to 21st Century Threats," *The Public Relations Strategist,* Fall 2002, vol. 8, no. 4. Online: http://www.prsa.org.

6. The authors acknowledge that two publications were influential in developing this definitional list: Laurence Barton, *Crisis in Organizations: Managing and Communicating in the Heat of Chaos* (Cincinnati: South-Western, 1993); and Steven Fink, *Crisis Management: Planning for the Inevitable* (New York: AMACON, 1986).

7. Fink, 1–14.

8. David Guth and Charles Marsh, *Public Relations: A Values-Driven Approach* (Boston: Allyn & Bacon, 2000), 24–25.

9. Guth and Marsh, 2000, 380–381, 388–390.

10. Guth and Marsh, 2003, 26–27.

11. Barton, 75–76.

12. Guth and Marsh, 2003, 415–417.

13. Fink, 20–28.

Lessons Learned?

NASA *Responds to the* Columbia *Disaster*

For most Americans over the age of 25, the breakup of the space shuttle *Columbia* on Feb. 1, 2003, brought back sad memories of another sunny, cold morning 17 years earlier.

The space shuttle *Challenger* exploded 71 seconds after launch from the Kennedy Space Center, killing its crew of seven on Jan. 28, 1986. NASA's response to the *Challenger* accident left much to be desired. The result was a nearly three-year grounding of the shuttle fleet and a major shake-up of the space agency.

Unlike *Challenger, Columbia* was returning home after a seemingly flawless 15-day mission. But to those old enough to remember, things seemed tragically familiar. And it wasn't long before an important question was confronted: Had NASA crisis communicators learned their lessons?

Triumph and Tragedy

NASA's worst accident before the space shuttle program occurred in January 1967, when three astronauts died in a launchpad fire during a dress rehearsal for *Apollo 1*. Investigators cited faulty wiring and bad quality control practices as causes of the fire. They said that the race to beat the Russians to the moon had created an environment in which safety—often claimed to be NASA's top priority—had taken a back seat. NASA's failure to communicate during the hours after the accident was also severely criticized. Following a reorganization and housecleaning, NASA had a new crisis response plan and a commitment to training people in its use.

The space agency was tested again three years later when an explosion crippled the *Apollo 13* spacecraft en route to the moon. NASA received praise for the open manner in which it dealt with the crisis. Because of NASA's candor and transparency in the face of disaster, the space agency earned a large measure of respect.

That is why NASA's failures at the time of the *Challenger* disaster were surprising. Because of employee turnover and a lack of crisis training, the agency had ignored its crisis plan—one that required a public statement within 15 minutes of an in-flight accident. A five-hour news blackout followed the explosion. NASA officials appeared less than forthcoming at the first news briefing. The lack of communication frustrated agency employees.

An engineering problem—a faulty seal on the shuttle's external rocket booster—was quickly identified as the cause of the accident. However, a presidential review panel, appointed after the public and Congress had lost confidence in NASA's ability to conduct an unbiased investigation, concluded that the agency's culture contributed to the disaster. The Rogers Commission said that NASA had forgotten its core values and had placed its schedule ahead of safety. The panel also cited a flawed decision-making culture in which engineers were afraid to offer constructive criticism.

"We Had a Bad Day." · · · · · · · · · · · · · · · · ·

As subsequent investigations would show, *Columbia* and its crew were doomed from the beginning. Just 81 seconds after launch, a chunk of insulating foam broke off the external fuel tank and struck the orbiter's left wing at high velocity. In doing so, it damaged some of *Columbia*'s external tiles, designed to protect it from the blowtorch heat of re-entry. NASA officials were aware of the foam strike. After an internal debate, flight controllers decided that the incident was insignificant.

The end came with shocking speed. A review of telemetry after the accident showed the first signs of trouble around 8:49 a.m. Eastern U.S. time. At first, a few

The crew members of *Columbia* lost their lives during re-entry into Earth's atmosphere on Feb. 1, 2003. The accident, reminiscent of the *Challenger* disaster 17 years earlier, tested NASA's crisis communications plan. (Courtesy of NASA)

temperature gauges in the left wing failed. Then the problems began to multiply rapidly. On the ground in the southwestern United States, home video cameras recorded the shuttle's fiery descent, which was normal, followed by a sparkling debris field, which was not. NASA lost contact with *Columbia* over Texas at an altitude 207,135 feet and a speed 18 times faster than the speed of sound.

"We lost the data," Chief Flight Director Milt Heflin later said. "That's when we clearly began to know that we had a bad day."

Rapid Response

Many challenges confronted NASA Administrator Sean O'Keefe. The agency had to show that it had learned the lessons of the *Challenger* disaster. A loss in public confidence could pose a significant threat to the space program's budget. Many wondered whether the shuttle had been brought down by an act of terrorism. There was also concern about retrieving wreckage—and possible clues as to what had gone wrong—from a 500-square-mile debris field in two states. Last, but certainly not least, was concern for the astronauts' families and the NASA community.

Within minutes, O'Keefe alerted the White House, which, in turn, mobilized federal, state, and local agencies for shuttle debris recovery. At the same time, NASA's Public Affairs Office announced that a "space shuttle contingency" had been declared.

"Search and rescue teams in the Dallas-Fort Worth area and in portions of East Texas have been alerted," the statement said. "Any debris that is located in the area that may be related to the Space Shuttle contingency should be avoided and may be hazardous as a result of toxic propellants used aboard the shuttle. The location of any possible debris should immediately be reported to local authorities."

NASA posted the statement on its Web site within 30 minutes of the accident. It informed reporters of the satellite coordinates to receive feeds from the space agency's television outlet, NASA-TV. It also announced the times and locations of upcoming press briefings. In the coming months, NASA continued to use the Web as a major point of public access to information generated by the investigation of the accident. The Web site received more than 40 million hits in the first 24 hours, 530 million hits during February 2003, and more than a billion hits in the five months following the accident.

Ironically, NASA had upgraded its Web site just a few hours before the *Columbia* accident. The agency had worked for several months to improve the public's ability to navigate through the system to access general and scientific information. "We later learned that the old Web site we had just taken down would have collapsed under the weight of that traffic," O'Keefe said.

NASA spokespeople conducted live interviews with the major television networks within the first half-hour of the emergency. Although they said they did not have a lot of information, they quickly dispelled concerns that the breakup of the shuttle was the result of an act of terrorism. NASA established telephone numbers and e-mail addresses for reporting debris locations or sharing photographs taken of the shuttle's final moments

President George W. Bush spoke by telephone with members of the astronauts' families less than three hours after the accident. Bush then addressed the nation, saying "These astronauts knew the dangers, and they faced them willingly, knowing they had a high and noble purpose in life." In his own statement to reporters, O'Keefe said, "We diligently dedicate ourselves every single day to assuring these things don't occur. And when they do we have to act responsibly, accountably, and that is exactly what we will do." O'Keefe's remarks were followed a couple of hours later by the first in a series of technical briefings on the accident and its possible causes.

A Question of Independence

Consistent with plans established after the *Challenger* disaster, officials began an internal investigation and moved quickly to secure relevant data and paperwork. Within 90 minutes of the disaster, O'Keefe took the initial steps toward establishing the Columbia Accident Investigation Board, an independent panel chaired by retired U.S. Navy Rear Admiral Harold W. Gehman, Jr. But not everyone was pleased, saying the board was too closely tied to NASA's bureaucracy. To answer congressional critics, O'Keefe expanded CAIB's membership and revised its charter three times. At one point, Gehman wrote O'Keefe, asking that he reassign several shuttle managers involved in the ill-fated mission "in the best interest of these people, NASA, and the progress of the investigation." In a public exchange of letters, O'Keefe complied, even though he complained, "I am convinced this course of action will be viewed as prejudging the facts before the investigation is complete."

Some critics accused NASA of limiting public access to internal documents and e-mail, as well as warning employees not to talk to reporters without prior permission. CAIB was also criticized for reneging on an invitation to reporters to join board members in a Feb. 12 tour of the shuttle facilities at Kennedy Space Center. Instead, reporters were excluded from that tour and Gehman answered only four questions in 10 minutes following his inspection.

"What a Difference"

The *Washington Post* reported that "O'Keefe has won plaudits for accessibility and candor." *USA Today* columnist Peter Johnson wrote, "Reporters covering NASA in the aftermath of Saturday's disaster are buzzing about how this agency bears no resemblance to the secretive, tight-lipped one that treated the media as the enemy after the *Challenger* disaster."

"What a difference 17 years make," said Jim Banke of Space.com, a Web site dedicated to science and space issues. "Information on the *Columbia* tragedy is following as fast as it can."

Public opinion polls taken in the weeks following the accident showed widespread support for the space program. A CNN-*Time* poll said more than seven in 10 Americans felt the space shuttle program was worth its risks. A CBS survey reported that a majority of respondents said the shuttle program contributes a lot to the nation's sense of pride and patriotism.

Not all reviews were positive. Early in the probe, O'Keefe said that he doubted "the smoking gun" would ever be found. However, within a few months, tests concluded that the foam strike was the most likely cause of the accident. Syndicated columnist Rhonda Lokeman wrote, "While on the one hand they publicly sympathized with the memorialized crew, U.S. space agency officials were, on the other hand, incredibly nonchalant about the odds of discovering why the shuttle disintegrated upon re-entry over Texas."

Eight months later, O'Keefe told a gathering of public relations practitioners in New Orleans that he erred when he and others prematurely dismissed a foam strike as the cause of the accident. "Due to our ill-advised speculation," he said, "we took some hits in the press."

CAIB issued its final report August 26, 2003. "The Board recognized early on that the accident was probably not an anomalous, random event, but rather likely rooted to some degree in NASA's history and human space flight program's culture," the report stated. It noted that "cultural traits and organizational practices detrimental to safety were allowed to develop." The report singled out "organizational barriers that prevented effective communication of critical safety information and stifled professional differences of opinion." The report also placed some blame on Congress and the White House for a decade of lean budgeting. In perhaps its sharpest criticism, CAIB criticized the space agency for "ineffective leadership" that "failed to fulfill the implicit contract to do whatever is possible to ensure the safety of the crew."

Even as CAIB was wrapping up its investigation, a Nobel Prize-winning member of the panel expressed doubts about NASA's decision-making culture. "No matter how good the report looks, if we don't do something to change the way NASA makes decisions, I would say that we have been whistling in the wind," said Douglas Osheroff of Stanford University. "At the moment, I'm in a state of depression."

Sources

Scott Banke, "Commentary: NASA's Response to Columbia More Open than Challenger," Space.com, February 06, 2003. Online: www.space.com/missionlaunches/nasa_open_030206.html.

Columbia Accident Investigating Board. Report Volume I, August 2003. Online: www.caib.us.

Nancy Gibbs, "Seven Astronauts, One Fate," *Time* (February 10, 2003), 30–45.

David W. Guth and Charles Marsh, *Public Relations: A Values-Driven Approach* (Boston: Allyn & Bacon, 2000), 380–382, 388–390.

"Investigator Worried NASA Culture Won't Change." CNN, August 1, 2003. Online: www.cnn.com/space.

Sean O'Keefe, Remarks to the Public Relations Society of America World Conference, New Orleans, La., October 28, 2003.

Peter Johnson, "NASA's 'Stunning' Candor Is Praised," *USA Today,* February 3, 2003. Online: http://usatoday.com.

Jeffery Kluger, "What Went Wrong?" *Time* (February 10, 2003) 36–44.

Rhonda Lokeman, "NASA's Management Catastrophe," *Duluth News Tribune,* July 18, 2003. Online: www.duluthsuperior.com/mid/duluthtribune/news/opinion.

News releases and briefing transcripts, National Aeronautics and Space Administration. Online: www.ksc.nasa.gov/columbia.

Eric Pianin and Guy Gugliotta, "O'Keefe: Man with a Past—and a Future?" *The Washington Post* (March 3, 2003), A6.

Working Scenario, Final Version, Columbia Accident Investigating Board and the National Aeronautics and Space Administration, July 8, 2003. Online: www.caib.us.

case **13.2**

A Season of Crises

American Airlines Scrambles to Survive following Sept. 11

Who would have blamed officials at American Airlines if they had paused on the afternoon of Sept. 11, 2001, and thought to themselves that things couldn't get any worse? Two of their aircraft had been hijacked by terrorists and used as weapons of mass destruction. American Flight 11 out of Boston crashed into the north tower of the World Trade Center in New York. A second plane, American Flight 77 out of Washington, was crashed into the Pentagon shortly after takeoff. Those acts of terrorism, combined with the hijacking of two United Airlines flights, resulted in approximately 3,000 deaths and traumatized much of the world in less than two hours.

Despite the horror of that dark day, the terror attacks of Sept. 11 marked just the first in a series of crises that threatened to overwhelm the world's largest airline. American Airlines was on the front lines of the War on Terror. And during fall 2001, its survival was an open question.

Scrapping the Crisis Plan

On the morning of Sept. 11, American Chairman and CEO Donald J. Carty answered the phone at his Dallas home and learned that one of the airline's planes had been hijacked. Before rushing to his office, he paused to see whether news of the hijacking was on television.

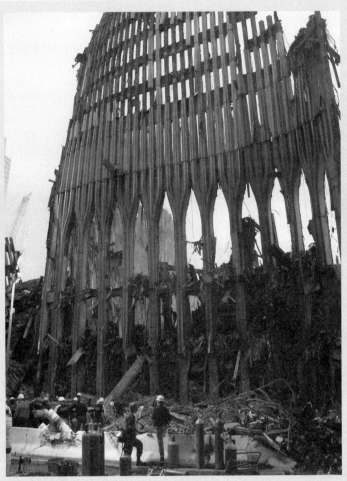

The hijacking of two American Airlines jets and the subsequent attacks on the World Trade Center and Pentagon were just the first in a series of crises that confronted American Airlines during fall 2001. (Courtesy of the Federal Emergency Management Agency)

"I saw them talking about something that struck the World Trade Center," Carty later said. "And just in my gut, I knew it was our airplane."

Immediately, American activated its crisis communications plan, which had been revised only weeks earlier. American opened its crisis command center in Fort Worth. However, it soon became apparent that the new crisis plan had not anticipated a disaster of this magnitude. Who could have known that two American planes would be transformed into suicide bombers, that the airline would have to coordinate with another airline in the same predicament, that the FBI would almost immediately clamp a lid down on airline communications, and that all commercial aircraft operating in the United States would be grounded for days?

Under normal crisis plan procedures, American would have chosen to put its CEO before the public as soon as possible. But this was not a normal crisis. The FBI, in effect, took over the crisis command center and imposed a news blackout. In any event, American officials felt that under the special circumstances of a national emergency the company should defer to the federal government. "It became increasingly obvious to us that the CEO for this crisis wasn't Don Carty," said Timothy Doke, American's vice president of corporate communications. "The CEO in this instance was George W. Bush."

Several hours passed before American released a statement on its Web site. "I know that I speak for every employee at American Airlines when I extend our deepest sympathy to those who lost a loved one, family member, or friend on American

Airlines Flight 11, American Airlines Flight 77, United Airlines Flight 93, United Airlines Flight 175, or at the sites of these tragic accidents," Carty said. American forwarded all media questions to the FBI. The airline also withdrew all of its broadcast advertising and suspended its online ticket-booking site.

The grounding of all air traffic in the United States posed another serious problem: assisting the relatives and friends of the passengers on the doomed flights. Normal procedures would have been to activate the Customer Assistance Relief Effort and send company personnel to both the arrival and departure airports. With air traffic grounded, the airline hatched an alternative plan. Doke called in the services of two public relations agencies, Weber Shandwick Worldwide and Burson-Marsteller. He said their "global reach allows our crisis response team to be based in cities where we simply can't put our own PR people on an everyday basis." These agencies also assisted the airline in filling gaps in headquarters public relations staff created by layoffs and in successfully lobbying Congress for a $15 billion industrywide emergency financial aid package.

Back-Channel Communication

The tragedy of Sept. 11 was more than a national calamity to the employees of American Airlines—it was personal. Not only had they lost their co-workers, but the financial foundation of the company also had been badly shaken. American was forced to lay off 20,000 of its 128,000 employees and to reduce the size of its fleet. Many employees took pay cuts, including Carty. "Perhaps no group is more keenly aware of our problems than our board members, so it is particularly meaningful for them to forgo compensation until the end of the year," he said. The airline established a special Web site for employees to sign up for voluntary pay cuts or to make charitable donations to the families of employees who lost their lives during the attacks.

For these and other reasons, internal communications were a high priority. Staff bulletins and voice-mail recordings provided an important link between management and the rank-and-file. Management employees received an average of seven messages a day in the first few days of the crisis. American established a Web site to communicate with laid-off workers.

The airline took the unusual step of posting many of these messages on its Web site, thus allowing key messages to reach other important publics, such as the media and shareholders. It was with a broader audience in mind that Carty announced the layoffs in a Sept. 28 letter to employees. In what one publication described as a "no-nonsense document," Carty told employees—as well as other stakeholders reading the message on the Internet—that "right now it is survival, not profitability, that is our core challenge."

This tactic was especially useful a few months later, when passengers and crew aboard an American flight from Paris to Miami subdued a would-be terrorist while he attempted to ignite a bomb hidden in his shoe. Once again, the FBI imposed an information blackout. However, the company was allowed to tell employees that the security breach was the fault of French officials and not a result of the airline's actions. American posted the "internal" message on a public Web site, where the news media immediately picked it up.

American officials also used other back-channel communications to protect their interests. Following the terror attacks, the company anticipated media scrutiny over airline passenger screening procedures. After all, how could 19 terrorists board four planes with box cutters? Inhibited by the FBI's gag order, Doke said he spoke to a number of airline security experts to "help carry our message and to put some of the media hysteria into perspective." When Doke related this story to an audience of public relations practitioners more than a year later, he did not identify those experts or how he garnered their support.

More Bad News

Tragedy piled on tragedy Nov. 12, when American Flight 587 crashed into a Queens neighborhood seconds after takeoff from New York's John F. Kennedy International Airport. Fears of another terror attack immediately surfaced but were later dispelled. Unlike Sept. 11, Carty made a brief statement before boarding a plane to the accident site. He held a news conference later that same day at the hotel where the victims' families were housed. The company also posted messages in English and Spanish on its Web site. It sent e-mails to customers. Broadcast advertising, reinstated just 20 days earlier, was once again pulled. Passengers inconvenienced by accident-related airport closings were allowed to rebook their flights at no additional charge.

Two other incidents focused unwelcome attention on American Airlines. The first came less than a month after Sept. 11, when passengers on a Los Angeles-to-Chicago flight subdued a disturbed man who had attempted to break into the cockpit. In December, a few days after the "shoe bomber" incident, an Arab-American Secret Service agent was removed from an American flight at Baltimore-Washington International Airport after the crew accused him of being hostile. The agent accused the airline of racial profiling. In response, an American spokesperson noted that Carty had issued a memo to all employees Sept. 12—the day after the terror attacks—urging them to respect the rights of Middle Eastern passengers and employees.

A Slow Recovery

The fact that American Airlines was still flying and had avoided bankruptcy two years after the terror attacks may be a measure of the company's resiliency, if not success. In part due to a soft economy, the company had been losing money before Sept. 11, 2001. Once the unthinkable had happened, the bottom dropped out. AMR, the airline's parent company, reported total losses of $5.8 billion during 2001 and 2002. An additional 7,000 employees were laid off during 2002. And with the outbreak of war in Iraq in 2003, the nation's economy remained sluggish.

In its 2002 annual report, American said it needed to reduce its annual operating costs by $4 billion "in order to become competitive and sustain its operations." The company identified half of the cuts through a series of cost-reduction measures. In February 2003, it asked labor leaders and other employees for approximately $1.8 billion in permanent annual savings "through a combination of changes in wages, benefits, and work rules." On April 16, 2003, American announced that members of its three major labor unions had ratified the agreements. But the package nearly fell apart when it was learned that Carty had given misleading information regarding the protection of executive bonuses and pension funds, even in the event of bankruptcy. The labor agreements were withdrawn, and modified versions were approved on April 25—one day after Carty submitted his resignation.

By the time of the second anniversary of the attacks, public opinion toward the airline industry, as a whole, was guarded. An August 2003 Gallup Poll said that 37 percent of respondents had a positive view toward the airline industry, while 31 percent said it was negative. According to an April 2003 Harris Poll, 67 percent of respondents said they trusted the airlines to do the right thing if they had a serious safety problem—the third-highest rating among the business categories surveyed. A CBS News Poll taken in January 2002 indicated that 78 percent of respondents felt American Airlines did the right thing when it removed the Secret Service agent from the plane.

American's Timothy Doke was honored as the Public Relations Society of America's 2002 Professional of the Year.

Sources

AMR Corporation Form 10-K for the fiscal year ended December 31, 2002, Securities and Exchange Commission, commission file number 1-8400. Online: www.sec.gov.

AMR Corporation Form 10-Q for the quarterly period ended March 31, 2003, Securities and Exchange Commission, commission file number 1-8400. Online: www.sec.gov.

Chris Barnett, "Crisis Communications Now: Three Views," *Public Relations Tactics* (January 2003), 15–16.

CNN Larry King Live Transcript #111900CN. V22, November 21, 2001. Online: Lexis-Nexis.

"Employees of American Airlines, American Eagle, TWA and the AMR Board of Directors Chip in to Help American through Financial Crisis," American Airlines news release, October 4, 2001, distributed via PR Newswire. Online: www.prnewswire.com.

Sherri Deatherage Green and Claire Murphy, "Client Profile—American Airlines Braces for Most Turbulent Journey," *PR Week*, November 5, 2001, 12. Online: Lexis-Nexis.

"A Message from American Airlines Chief Executive Officer Don Carty," American Airlines Web site, September 11, 2001. Online: www.aa.com.

Jeanne Meserve and Mike Ahlers, "Pilot Acted in 'Best Interest' in Removing Agent, CNN, January 2, 2002. Online: www.cnn.com.

Poll Archives, The Polling Report. Online: www.pollingreport.com.

The Road to Recovery

Toronto Revives Tourism following a Deadly SARS Outbreak

Severe acute respiratory syndrome, SARS, is a pneumonia-like illness first reported in China in February 2003. Over the next few months, the disease spread to more than two dozen countries on four continents. According to the World Health Organization, 8,422 people became sick with SARS and 916 people died before the global outbreak was contained. However, health authorities cautioned that the deadly virus could reemerge at any time in any place.

When an infectious disease such as SARS breaks out, health officials move quickly to keep it from spreading. For example, officials with the Centers for Disease Control in the United States issue *travel alerts* that inform travelers of the potential health dangers and the precautions that should be taken. They also issue *travel advisories* recommending that nonessential travel be deferred. Although these measures are necessary to protect public health, they also can have a lasting effect on the targeted cities and countries. Even after the threat has subsided, the economies of these locales can suffer from decreased tourism and commerce caused by lingering public doubts.

This case study focuses on the efforts of officials in Toronto, Ontario, to restore public confidence in and travel to their city following a SARS scare in March 2003. While the outbreak was not the only cause of the city's economic slump, it ironically served as a catalyst for reviving an economically depressed tourism industry.

The Epidemic Spreads

According to a World Health Organization report, the first cases of SARS emerged in Guangdong Province, China, in November 2002. There, the disease infected 305 people and caused five deaths. At first, health officials were not sure what they were dealing with. SARS is much like pneumonia, with symptoms that include a high fever, headache, and respiratory distress. However, when patients failed to respond to traditional treatments for pneumonia, the alarm—and the disease—spread. Not until Feb. 11, 2003, did WHO officials in Geneva receive their first official report on the unidentified disease from the Chinese Ministry of Health. By then, a doctor in Guangdong had spread it to health care workers in Hong Kong, Vietnam, and Singapore.

"He brought the virus to the ninth floor of a four-star hotel in Hong Kong," a WHO report later said. "Simultaneously, the disease began spreading around the world along international air travel routes as guests at the hotel flew home to Toronto and elsewhere."

Dr. Carlo Urbani first identified the SARS virus in Vietnam on Feb. 28. He died of the disease just one month later. On March 12, the WHO issued a global alert for SARS. Two days later, Canadian health authorities reported four cases of SARS within a single family in Toronto that had resulted in two deaths. By March 26, Ontario health officials ordered thousands of people to quarantine themselves in their homes. On April 23, the WHO issued a SARS travel advisory for Toronto. It lifted the warning a week later, but reinstated it when 26 new cases were discovered in late May. Toronto was finally declared SARS-free on July 2—but only after 252 reported cases and 40 deaths. Ontario had suffered the largest outbreak of the disease outside of Asia.

Toronto Fights Back

"Right now, the real battlefront is on the PR side of things," said Brad Ross, the city of Toronto's chief spokesman, on April 26. "We're trying to get out the message that Toronto is safe and healthy."

Even without SARS, Toronto's tourism sector was reeling from world events. Travel was down everywhere during the first half of 2003 because of the war in Iraq and the sluggish U.S. economy. There were also concerns among some officials that the reduced cross-border traffic was the result of a backlash against the Canadian government's stand against the war. However, others saw the decline in Ontario tourism as a problem that had little to do with war and the economy.

"We had already identified before SARS that tourism was a major issue for Toronto," said David Pecaut, chairman of a public–private partnership created to assist Toronto's ailing tourism industry. He said the city was already losing its share of the tourism market to places such as Chicago and Montreal, which spent much more on tourism marketing than Toronto's annual budget of $9 million. (All monetary references in this case are Canadian dollars.) "Then SARS hit us, and we lost $500 million of tourism activity in a matter of months, with some hotels down to 10 or 20 percent occupancy."

Prime Minister Jean Chretien announced on April 26 that he would move his government's next cabinet meeting to Toronto in a symbolic gesture to show that the city was safe. He also said that the federal government was pitching in $10 million toward a marketing campaign—a fraction of the $100 million it was spending to battle SARS. Three days later, Ontario Premier Ernie Eves announced a two-year, $128 million tourism and investment recovery plan. The effort used advertising and an intensive public relations campaign highlighted by major events designed to raise Toronto's international profile. It also included incentives for meeting and convention planners, marketing grants to local communities, and a five-month moratorium on collecting tourism-related taxes.

"With the summer season around the corner, we want to get the word out that every part of our great province is safe, welcoming, and open for business," said Ontario Tourism and Recreation Minister Brian Coburn.

"Back and Booming"

The first elements of the recovery strategy were quickly executed. On May 5, tourism officials and doctors met with U.S. travel and leisure media in New York. The Canadian Media Marketplace, an annual gathering of travel journalists to learn about Canadian tourism opportunities, had taken on added importance. Federal, provincial, and territorial ministers met five days later in Toronto to map out plans to promote tourism across the country.

On May 9, provincial tourism officials launched a three-week advertising campaign designed to reassure residents and visitors that Toronto and Ontario were safe travel destinations. Thirty-second television spots based on the theme "It's Time for a little T.O." ran in selected markets throughout the province. In addition to the campaign directed largely at the domestic market, tourism officials had planned a similar campaign with different ads for key U.S. border markets starting May 23. However, that was the same day a second outbreak of SARS was announced, and the campaign was pulled. Later radio, print, and television spots targeted the so-called rubber-tire market—U.S. and Canadian markets within driving range of Toronto—as well as key international markets. Those ads featured famous Canadians such as comedian Leslie Nielsen and hockey star Wayne Gretzky.

The first of the special events, "Concert for Toronto," was announced in late May and held June 28 at the SkyDome and Air Canada Centre. It was an all-star, all-Canadian event that included the hometown group Barenaked Ladies and Halifax native Sarah McLachlan. Other special events that summer included Caribana, Gay Pride Week, and the Molson Indy.

The Toront03 Alliance, the public–private partnership chaired by David Pecaut, was announced on June 5. "After several weeks of intensive effort to put together a viable, private sector-led initiative, we're ready to move ahead with solid backing," Pecaut said. Armed with an $11.5 million war chest, the Alliance engaged in a multimedia campaign to promote previously scheduled events such as the annual Toronto Film Festival and newly created events, including a gigantic rock concert featuring the Rolling Stones.

The Stones concert on July 30 attracted nearly a half-million people to Toronto's Downsview Park, twice the crowd initially anticipated. "Toronto is back, and it's booming," proclaimed vocalist Mick Jagger. In fact, it was booming so much that the provincial government had to make a last-minute emergency appropriation of $1 million on top of an earlier $2 million grant to cover the health, safety, and security needs of concert-goers. "This spectacular event is just what we need to put tourism in Toronto and Ontario back on track," Coburn said.

The Rolling Stones concert was followed by a new promotion, the Kids Summer Road Trip. To encourage additional rubber-tire traffic, visiting children 12 and under received free admission to popular attractions such as the CN Tower and the Royal Ontario Museum. The road trip also included a Web site and virtual "postcards" sent to potential visitors via e-mail by sports, media, and political celebrities. The site encouraged Toronto residents to act as ambassadors and send e-mail invi-

In an effort to lure people to Ontario following the 2003 SARS outbreak, Toronto sponsored several special events, including a Rolling Stones concert that attracted nearly a half-million people to Toronto's Downsview Park. (Courtesy of Ontario Ministry of Tourism and Recreation)

tations to friends and family. Such online pass-alongs are known as *viral marketing*—although, for obvious reasons, organizers declined to characterize it by that name.

Running for Coverage

According to government figures, the average hotel occupancy rate dropped from 70.2 percent in June 2002 to 57.8 percent one year later. Experts estimated that Toronto's large chain hotels experienced a $698 million loss in tourism expenditures from March to October 2003—a substantial drop from the same period in 2002. During the seven months following the SARS outbreak, officials estimated that Toronto tourism revenues dipped 27.3 percent from the previous year's levels.

Despite these dismal figures, the Ontario Ministry of Tourism and Recreation was able to report signs of recovery by year's end. A border-crossing survey of U.S. citizens' travel intentions showed SARS-related fears subsiding. While 17 percent of the respondents cited the outbreak as the top reason for not visiting Ontario in June 2003, that percentage had dropped to just 3 percent by August. Research conducted at the end of the year confirmed that a small proportion of potential U.S. visitors still had concerns about SARS. The research also hinted that Toronto and Ontario had bigger "brand confusion" issues that needed to be addressed. Meanwhile, interest in visiting Toronto jumped from 55 percent to 68 percent from June to August.

Ministry officials reported in the newsletter *Tourism Recovery Update* that their advertising had met with "disappointing" results in the Michigan market and would be re-evaluated. However, they also reported that the summer advertising campaign featuring Canadian celebrities had a record 90 percent rate of recall. "The campaign elicited a strong response and generated immediate trip-taking, primarily in the form of short getaways and same-day trips," the newsletter reported. The results of the e-mail virtual postcard campaign were also encouraging, with some postcards getting up to 30 pass-alongs.

"You should not shy away from a crisis," said Pam Johnston, Toront03 Alliance public relations director. "You shouldn't be running for cover. You should be running for coverage."

Sources

Stuart Elliot, "In Advertising: Toronto Polishes Its Image," *The New York Times* Direct, November 25, 2003. Online: www.nytimes.com.

"Eves Government Announces 'Concert for Toronto' Featuring All-Star, All Canadian Cast," Ministry of Tourism and Recreation, Government of Ontario news release, May 28, 2003.

"Eves Government Gives Another $1 Million for Toronto Concert." Ministry of Tourism and Recreation, Government of Ontario news release, July 30, 2003.

"Fact Sheet: Basic Information about SARS," Centers for Disease Control and Prevention, U.S. Department of Health and Human Services, August 19, 2003.

Oakland Ross, "City's Next Battle on Public Relations Front," *Toronto Star* (April 26, 2003), A09.

"Ontario TV Ads Tell Torontonians and Tourists, 'It's Time for a Little T.O,'" Ministry of Tourism and Recreation, Government of Ontario news release, May 9, 2003.

"SARS Case Count Continues Slow Decline," *Guelph Mercury,* (May 6, 2003), A7.

Severe Acute Respiratory Syndrome (SARS): Status of the Outbreak and Lessons for the Immediate Future, World Health Organization, Geneva, Switzerland, May 20, 2003.

"Timeline: SARS Outbreak," CNN, April 24, 2003. Online: www.cnn.com.

"Toronto Back on WHO SARS List," CNN, May 26, 2003. Online: www.cnn.com.

"Toronto Removed from SARS List," CNN, July 2, 2003. Online: www.cnn.com.

"Tourism Ministers Discuss Action Plans to Attract Travelers to Canada," Ministry of Tourism and Recreation, Government of Ontario news release, May 10, 2003.

Tourism Recovery Update, Ministry of Tourism and Recreation, Government of Ontario (August 2003), no. 3, 2.

ACT file # 13 . . . .

Crisis Risk Assessment

The first step in crisis communications planning is risk assessment. By identifying the potential risks an organization may face, public relations practitioners can make plans to effectively deal with crises—or even eliminate the dangers before they happen.

The most effective way to conduct a risk assessment is to create a task force representing a cross section of an organization. This means choosing a combination of people with managerial and technical skills. The committee must understand every aspect of the organization, from front-office operations to how the production line works. The broader the perspectives of this panel, the less likely it is to miss a potential danger.

The first challenge of a crisis-planning task force is to list all the dangers the organization may realistically face. These dangers may be technical, logistical, legal, or cultural in nature and include any natural or human-created situation that could

- Disrupt normal operations
- Cause financial harm to the organization
- Damage the organization's reputation
- Hurt relationships with key stakeholders
- Place employees or stakeholders at risk

The next step is to determine what potential dangers can be eliminated *before* they become a problem. For example, if a company is located next to heavily traveled railroad tracks, it should have a plan of action in the event of a derailment involving dangerous chemicals. Another example is purchasing an electrical generator if the task force identifies the lack of a backup power supply for critical systems, such as computers or pumps.

The third step in risk assessment is to rank crisis planning needs. It is likely that the team has developed a fairly long list of potential crises, but which ones possess the greatest threat and need the most attention? This is where a crisis plotting grid (Figure 13.1) is handy. To use the crisis plotting grid, assign two numbers to each crisis the task force has identified:

- For the first number, estimate on a scale of 1–10 the *probability* that such a crisis could occur. This is what is known as the *crisis probability factor* and is represented by the horizontal axis of the grid. For example, if the company's operations are located in a region that gets plenty of snow each year, the possibility of facing blizzard conditions could be very high. It would be lower for companies operating in warmer climates.

Advanced Critical Thinking

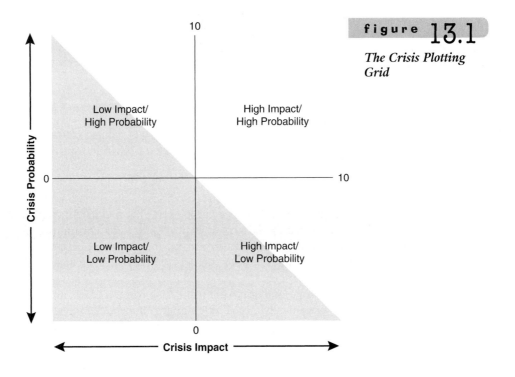

The Crisis Plotting Grid

- For the second number, estimate on a scale of 1–10 the *impact* that such a crisis would have on company operations. This is what is known as the *crisis impact factor* and is represented by the vertical axis of the grid. For example, companies in colder regions may be better prepared to deal with blizzard conditions than those in warmer climates.

  Plot each potential crisis on the grid. Those in the unshaded portion of the grid have greater probability and/or impact and should be your highest planning priorities. Those that fall in the shaded zone have lower impact and/or probability and are lower planning priorities.

Discussion Questions

1. How should organizations conduct a crisis risk assessment?

2. What kinds of risks should be considered when trying to predict potential crises that may affect an organization?

3. What is the value of a crisis plotting grid?

4. What would a crisis plotting grid look like for any of the companies/organizations featured in this chapter?

CHAPTER 14

Cyber-Relations

W hat started as a response to the launch of *Sputnik,* the world's first artificial satellite, has become the fastest-growing and, perhaps, the most powerful mass medium of the 21st century. When military and academic researchers realized in 1957 that they needed to link computers at research centers around the country, they created what would eventually evolve into the **Internet.** And when researchers at CERN, the European Laboratory for Particle Physics, developed a more user- and graphics-friendly Internet service in 1990, they created the **World Wide Web.** The rest, as they say, is history.[1]

As Table 14.1 indicates, the growth of Web sites during the past decade has been nothing short of phenomenal. From just a single site in December 1990, the World Wide Web grew to approximately 45 million sites by the end of 2003.[2] According to the Pew Internet & American Life Project, nearly 59 percent of U.S. adults had Internet access at the end of 2002. That compared with just over 50 percent only two years earlier.[3] The study showed that the New England region had the highest Internet penetration at 66 percent, with the lowest in portions of the South at 48 percent. "The regional variations in Internet use in the United States lies in the traditional factors that drive Internet use: education and income levels," the Pew study said. "Those regions that have more people with substantial household incomes and college degrees tend to have both a higher proportion of Internet users in general and a higher proportion of experienced Internet users."[4]

As of mid-2003, approximately 116 million Americans used the Internet to send e-mail, 110 million used search engines to find information, and another 104 million used the Web to either search for an answer to a specific question or to research a product or service before buying it. Some 43 million U.S. residents do online banking, 27 million participate in online auctions, and 15 million buy their groceries online.[5]

table 14.1   *Web Site Growth*

Year*	Web Sites
1990	1
1991	10
1992	50
1993	693
1994	10,022
1995	100,000
1996	603,000
1997	1,834,710
1998	3,689,227
1999	9,560,866
2000	25,675,581
2001	36,276,252
2002	35,543,105
2003	45,000,000 (estimated)

*Most figures represent the number of Web sites in December of the year indicated. In years in which December figures are not available, figures from January of the next year are used.

Source: Data from Robert H. Zakon. "Hobbes' Internet Timeline." Online: www.zakon.org/robert/internet/timeline.

Is there any doubt that public relations practitioners have found the Internet to be an indispensable tool?

Cyber-Relations Defined

The Internet has created a new front door for organizations that is accessible from almost every point on the globe. The interactivity of the Web can be an effective tool for building and maintaining mutually beneficial relationships—if it is used properly. Organizations can enjoy several positive aspects of this increased interaction. The Internet provides additional opportunities to improve the corporate image. The Internet also provides a means for collecting feedback, as well as collecting and analyzing public opinion. This, in turn, helps make corporations more accountable and responsive to public needs.[6]

Of course, not everyone has the Midas touch when it comes to the Internet. Staffers at eCompanyNow compiled a list of what they called "the 101 dumbest moments in e-Business history." The list included the CEO of an Internet retailer who showed up on a popular cable television business program wearing only boxer shorts—an attempt to demonstrate that consumers could buy anything from their home in their underwear. He resigned seven months later, after the price of the company's stock plummeted. Then there was the CEO who said, "There isn't an Internet company in the world that is going to fail because of mistakes—Internet companies make thousands of mistakes every week." And then there was Mitch Maddox, who legally changed his name to DotComGuy and spent a year living alone in a house filled with Webcams. According to *Public Relations Tactics,* he used "only the Internet to interact with the outside world, an effort that conclusively proves . . . um, nothing."[7]

Because of the value—and challenges—associated with the Internet, organizations must now engage in what we call **cyber-relations,** the use of public relations strategies and tactics to deal with publics via the Internet and with issues related to the Internet. We acknowledge that *cyber-relations* is a term that is not mutually exclusive of other forms of public relations. After all, many different aspects of public relations embrace the Internet, such as media relations, consumer relations, and investor relations. However, the reason we choose to place cyber-relations in its own category is the dynamic nature of the medium. The Internet and its many uses are constantly evolving. This state of flux presents serious challenges for practitioners and the organizations they represent. More people have access to information about an organization, both controlled and uncontrolled, than ever before. Anyone can have a Web site—and essentially the same presence on the Web—as the largest corporation. Because of the many examples in which the Internet has been both problem and solution, we feel the process of conducting public relations on the Internet merits special attention.

Segmentation and the Web

Given its omnipresence, the use of the Internet in segmenting audiences may seem like a contradiction. However, judicious use of the Web can be very effective in reaching specific audiences. As is the case in the selection of any medium, the decision to use the Internet depends on the purpose of the message, the intended audience, and the suitability of the medium.

• **Purpose**—The Internet tends to be regarded as less formal communication than traditional ink-on-paper. That is primarily because of the latter's portability and permanence. However, the Internet is valued as an on-demand repository of information, such as a company Web site that maintains annual reports, a news release archive, and various kinds of corporate background information. Through e-mail or instant messaging, the Internet is ideal for timely, short-form messages. It is also a valuable channel for transmission of data, audio, and video files.

• **Audience**—As has been noted, Internet access is constantly rising. However, it is not universal. The most recent U.S. Census Bureau report on home computers and the Internet suggested that several factors should be considered when targeting online publics. For example, Internet use increases with level of income and education. The Census Bureau reported that 56.2 percent of Asian and Pacific Islander households used the Internet, compared with 46.1 percent among white households, and 23.6 percent among both black and Hispanic households. The heaviest use is among people ages 25–44 who live in urban areas, and among males.[8] These figures tell us that when it comes to the Internet, one size doesn't fit all.

• **Medium**—The suitability of the Internet is best judged on a case-by-case basis. Again, a number of factors relate to the nature of the purpose and the audience. Because the Internet is, in essence, a convergence of all media, very few circumstances exist for which its use is not suitable. However, even in an increasingly wireless world, the Internet is not totally transportable. For that reason, it is most often used to complement more traditional media.

Given these qualities, the Internet has become popular in the execution of employee, media, investor, and consumer relations tactics. For each, the Web promotes two-way communications between organizations and important stakeholders.

Employee Relations

Because the Internet serves as a front door to an organization, it is often the first point of contact a potential employee has during the recruitment process. Many organizations use the Web as a cost-effective substitute for traditional employee newsletters and memos. (However, we should note that an employee's first instinct often is to print a hard copy of electronic communications, thus negating any savings in paper and ink.)

The Web makes employee collaboration easier in corporations with dispersed operations. Its timeliness makes it ideal for transmitting critical information during crises. And because it is interactive, it can help executives keep a finger on the pulse of the organization. To ensure confidentiality, many organizations choose to conduct their internal communications over what is known as an intranet, a controlled-access internal computer network.

Media Relations

Journalists have found that organization Web sites are excellent resources for gathering information. In the deadline-driven news business, the Internet also can serve as an effective way of cutting through the clutter. Organizations often e-mail or Web-post news releases and media kits. E-mail is often used in answering reporters' questions or pitching news stories. However, as in all media selection, it is best to first determine the medium of choice. Some reporters prefer to do business over the Internet, while others don't. That's why audience research is a prerequisite.

Investor Relations

Public companies have discovered that the Web is handy in reaching all their potential stakeholders, from the casual investor to highly critical securities analysts. Companies often post their annual reports, quarterly reports, and other disclosure documents on the Web. (If they don't, the documents are available via the Security and Exchange Commission's online EDGAR database.) Usually, the Internet is not the sole method of disclosure. Instead, companies use the Web to complement other media. Many government agencies and nonprofit organizations under public scrutiny use the Internet in a similar fashion.

Consumer Relations

Because it is more expensive to find new customers than to retain old ones, businesses have found the Internet an important ally in building and retaining consumer relationships. The Web is a handy source of product and service information. In this increasingly technological world, the Web is a place where consumers can go to have their product or service questions answered. Its interactive nature makes the Internet helpful in gaining useful consumer feedback and handling complaints. The Web can also be effective in product recalls, when timely dissemination of accurate and detailed information is critical to averting harm to consumers and the company's reputation.[9]

For more and more people, the Internet is the marketplace of choice. The Census Bureau estimated U.S. retail e-commerce for the third quarter of 2003 at $13.291 billion, or 1.5 percent of all retail sales during that same period.[10] For business-to-business transactions, companies often establish secured **extranets,** controlled access networks open only to authorized buyers and/or vendors.

Other Uses

Internet use is not limited to just these situations. It has strategic and tactical applications in targeting most audiences. Because the Web is a controlled channel, it can deliver important information in a timely manner during crises. For example, during the Sept. 11, 2001, terrorist attacks on New York and Washington, traditional channels of communication were either unavailable or clogged. Many companies kept their employees, investors, and other key stakeholders updated through their Web sites. This, in turn, helped to lessen economic disruption caused by that tragic event.

Usenets, sometimes called *newsgroups, bulletin boards,* or *chat rooms,* provide people an online forum for sharing information and providing feedback. People often engage in threaded discussion, with one person's comments building on another's. Usenet groups can be used for unobtrusive issues research—but also should be taken with a grain of salt. Not everyone knows what he or she is talking about. You should first verify all information gathered from these forums.[11]

Corporate Social Responsibility and Cybersmears

Monitoring the Internet for the latest social trends and industry news has become less optional and more of an imperative. In fact, it has become a forum of choice for debate over **corporate social responsibility.** The Internet has become an arena for the struggle between activists seeking to correct perceived wrongs and corporations feeling unfairly targeted.

W. Timothy Coombs of Illinois State University wrote that the Internet has been an equalizing force in this debate, giving previously powerless advocacy groups a tool that makes their voices heard in corporate board rooms. "The Internet can be a useful tool for changing the activist group's standing in the organization's stakeholder network," Coombs said. "In turn, the power dynamic shifts making the activists and their concerns more salient to an organization."[12]

INTELLIGENCE NOTE
6/30/2003

Prepared by the
Internet Fraud Complaint Center

"Spoofed" E-mails & Web Sites - A Gateway to Identity Theft and Credit Card Fraud

*E-mail Spoofing - The forgery of an e-mail header so that the message appears to
have originated from someone or somewhere other than the actual source. Spam
distributors and criminals often use spoofing in an attempt to get recipients to
open and possibly even respond to their solicitations.*[i]

*IP Spoofing - A technique used to gain unauthorized access to computers,
whereby the intruder sends messages to a computer with an IP address indicating
that the message is coming from a trusted port.*[ii]

The Internet Fraud Complaint Center (IFCC) is reporting a rise in identity theft, credit card, and
Internet frauds due to the fast growing trend of spoofing popular commerce-related web sites.
This growing trend is in direct correlation to the continuing decrease in home computer prices,
increasing popularity with online auction sites, and the overall lack of technical knowledge of
new individuals online. When this type of fraud is reported to law enforcement, the average
individual is not aware to include the spoofed web site's HTML code or the full header
information from the spoofed e-mail received, thus making the identification and eventual
tracking of the perpetrator more difficult.

Spoofing attacks are based upon the ability to make a user believe that they are securely
connected to a network address, or receiving e-mail from a specific source, when that is not the
case. The problem stems from the fact that the addressing system on the entire Internet is not
secure. This creates problems of spoofing in many areas outside web addresses, including e-
mail.[iii]

The two main spoofing scenarios seen by the IFCC are 'name similarity' and 'link alteration.'

Name Similarity – One of the more common spoofs occurs when the consumer mistypes the
URL they are looking for, or puts the wrong locator at the end. Sometimes the content makes it
obvious to the user that the site is not the one they were expecting, but not always.[iv]
For example, the URL for the White House is www.whitehouse.gov. If the average individual is
not familiar with the .gov locator, they might enter www.whitehouse.com or
www.whitehouse.org. The .com locator will direct the individual to a pornographic web site,
obviously not associated with the White House, although the .org locator directs the
unsuspecting individual to an official looking web site that mocks the current Presidential
administration.

The federal Internet Fraud Complaint Center warned companies and individuals about
an increasing number of bogus e-mails in 2003. (Courtesy of the Internet Fraud
Complaint Center)

For example, consider the "Flaming Fords" Web site. Debra and Edward Gold-
gehn of Marietta, Ga., created the site in protest after their 1985 Ford Ranger sud-

denly caught fire in their driveway. The fire was linked to problems with the truck's ignition. The Web site created widespread publicity and eventually pressured the Ford Motor Company to recall 8.7 million vehicles with faulty ignition switches.[13]

However, Coombs cautioned that "essential to any issues management effort is a firm foundation based on the legitimacy of the issue" and that "without legitimacy, activists are simply annoying latent stakeholders who never find a wider audience for their concerns."[14] And while some Web sites have served as responsible forces for social changes, others have done little more than spread unfounded rumors on the Internet. These tactics fall into the category of what at least one author has called **cybersmears,** the use of the Internet to unfairly attack the integrity of an organization and/or its products and services.[15]

With this environment as a backdrop, monitoring the latest chatter in cyberspace—legitimate criticism and cybersmears—can save organizations from major headaches. "What distinguishes organizations today is the quality of information they retrieve and what they do with it," said Ann Jackson, managing director of New York-based Middleberg & Associates. "The savvy ones incorporate the information into their entire communications program."[16]

Consider the experience of Procter & Gamble. Despite undergoing a rigorous approval process for the federal government, it confronted Internet rumors that one of its household cleaning products was poisonous to pets. Moving quickly, P&G posted information on its own Web site to refute the charges, including supportive statements from the American Society for the Prevention of Cruelty to Animals, the U.S. Humane Society, and the American Veterinary Medical Association.

"It took us about three to four weeks to get on top of it," said Jeff Lane, P&G's executive vice president for state and local affairs. "Once we got the information out there, the calls began to die down."[17]

A popular cybersmear tactic is to establish what are called **gripe sites,** Web sites that focus on grievances—imagined and real—against an organization. One example is "homedepotsucks.com," a Web site established by the Action Resource Center to protest what it believes is Home Depot's contribution to the decline in old-growth rain forests.[18] Legal remedies against gripe sites are few and far between. As long as the posted comments don't cross the line to libel, they are generally treated by the courts as opinions and protected by the First Amendment.

Then there are **blogs,** regularly updated online diaries/news forums that focus on particular areas of interest. Typically, they feature links to news stories and selected sites across the Internet.[19] The fact that they target audiences with specialized interests can be very appealing to public relations practitioners seeking to reach a highly segmented audience. Blogs often have the look and feel of traditional Internet news sites but are administered by an individual or organization with an agenda. Blogs are not necessarily negative—but some clearly are. Before pitching story ideas to a blog webmaster, the first step is to read through the site and determine its true nature.

The best remedy against cybersmears is to monitor the Web regularly, either inhouse or by hiring an Internet monitoring service that keeps track of Web sites and rogue bulletin boards. Some companies make preemptive strikes by purchasing the rights to potentially harmful Web addresses. For example, the *Seattle Times* reported that Chase Manhattan Bank purchased the rights to "Ihatechase.com," "Chasestinks.com" and "Chasesucks.com" after falling victim to a gripe site.[20] Of course, prevention is the best medicine. Having a strong Web presence and emphasizing customer service can stop some cybersmear campaigns before they ever get started.

"Public relations practitioners must counsel management to take a reasoned approach to their online critics," counsels Nicole B. Cásarez, who is both a public relations educator and an attorney. "The time and expense involved in a cyberlibel lawsuit might be better directed to achieving company objectives and generating favorable publicity."[21]

Building a Better Web Site

With the World Wide Web well into its second decade, very few question whether their organization should have a presence on the Internet. But even at this late date, many of these same people have trouble answering the most important question of all: Why should we do this? Like any other public relations tactic, we must first know the purpose—the strategy—behind it. As one public relations executive said, "Avoid the process unless and until you can offer a rationale more sensible than: 'It's way cool.'"[22]

However, the question of purpose is closely linked to another: Who within the organization controls Web site content? After all, marketing professionals and public relations practitioners have different orientations. Some practitioners worry about encroachment, the assignment of non–public relations professionals to manage a public relations function. However, research conducted by Michael Ryan of the University of Houston suggests that encroachment is not as much an issue as it once was. "The biggest organizational problem now seems to lie in teaching others the components of a good site," Ryan wrote.[23]

Here are some basic tips for building a better Web site.

- **Define the Web site's purpose and audience.** What messages do you want to deliver and to whom do you want them delivered? One positive feature of the Internet is that a single Web site can target multiple audiences. However, the message must be relevant to those audiences and in a form they find useful.

- **Focus on content.** While flashing text and spinning graphics may grab a Web surfer's attention, the content keeps it. And if that content is not updated regularly, there's no reason for the surfer to return. Another practical reason exists for letting content rule: Graphics-heavy sites that take a long time to load drive viewers away.

- **Make it user-friendly.** The harder it is for visitors to find what they want, the less successful the site will be in delivering its desired message. Organizing the home page by audience-specific categories is a popular method of simplifying site navigation. Another is to design Web pages that do not require the reader to scroll down for more information.

- **Make it interactive.** Give visitors a chance to contact people within the organization. Some sites solicit opinions on various issues of the day. Other sites feature chat rooms and threaded discussions on matters of specific interest. Remember that the audience is media savvy. Don't ask for feedback unless you plan to use it.

- **Write right.** You are writing for a different medium. According to a study by Sun Microsystems, it takes 50 percent longer to read material on a computer screen than in print. Public relations consultant Sara Means Geigel wrote that "even the most patient people become impatient surfing the Web." She says to use simple words, use active voice, write with active verbs, and "keep sentences short, crisp, and to the point."[24]

- **Create a functional newsroom.** Reporters need easily accessible news releases and media kits. They also want high-quality downloadable photographs and graphics. Create links to stories about your organization. A searchable archive is also desirable.

- **Promote the Web site.** Let people know where you are on the Web. Place its address on all company publications and advertising. Remember: The Internet is a piece of an integrated communications strategy to position or brand your organization.

As your mother probably told you, first impressions are lasting. Often a Web site is the first point of contact between an organization and its stakeholders. In this age of increasing social responsibility, people want to know an organization's mission and values. That's why it is important to post them on the Web. However, once those values have been communicated, the expectation is that the organization will abide by them. Those who do reap the rewards that come with good citizenship. Those who don't are held accountable.

Discussion Questions

1. What is cyber-relations, and how is it different from other forms of public relations?

2. What are key factors in the decision to use the Internet as a public relations tactic?

3. What is a cybersmear, and can you identify any that have happened?

4. How is the Internet involved in the movement toward corporate social responsibility? What steps should companies take in light of this movement?

5. What are some of the first questions one should ask before creating a Web site? What constitutes a good Web site?

Key Terms

blog, p. 325
corporate social
  responsibility, p. 323
cyber-relations, p. 320

cybersmear, p. 325
extranet, p. 323
gripe sites, p. 325

Internet, p. 319
usenet, p. 323
World Wide Web, p. 319

Endnotes

1. Robert H. Zakon, "Hobbe's Internet Timeline." Online: www.zakon.org/robert/internet/timeline.

2. Zakon.

3. Tom Spooner, "Internet Use by Region in the United States," Pew Internet & American Life Project, August 27, 2003. Online: www.pewinternet.org.

4. Spooner.

5. These estimates are based on information in the chart, "Internet Activities," located on the Pew Internet & American Life Web site, www.pewinternet.org.

6. Tracy Cooley, "Interactive Communication—Public Relations on the Web," *Public Relations Quarterly* (Summer 1999), vol. 44, no. 2, 41–42.

7. "The Dumbest Moments in e-Business History," *Public Relations Tactics* (October 2001), 6, 8.

8. Eric C. Newburger, "Home Computers and Internet Use in the United States: August 2000," U.S. Census Bureau, U.S. Department of Commerce.

9. Dirk C. Gibson, "The Cyber-Revolution in Product Recall Public Relations," *Public Relations Quarterly* (Summer 2000), vol. 45, no. 2, 24–26.

10. "Retail E-Commerce Sales in Third Quarter 2003 were $13.3 Billion, Up 27.0 Percent from Third Quarter 2002, Census Bureau Reports," U.S. Department of Commerce news release, November 21, 2003.

11. Randy Bobbitt, "An Internet Primer for Public Relations," *Public Relations Quarterly* (Fall 1995), vol. 40, no. 3, 27–32.

12. W. Timothy Coombs, "The Internet as Potential Equalizer: New Leverage for Confronting Social Irresponsibility," *Public Relations Review* (Fall 1998), vol. 24, no. 3, 289–303.

13. Coombs.

14. Coombs.

15. Nicole B. Cásarez, "Dealing with Cybersmear: How to Protect Your Organization from Online Defamation," *Public Relations Quarterly* (Summer 2002), vol. 47, no. 2, 40–45.

16. Allan Pell Crawford, "When Those Nasty Rumors Start Breeding on the Web, You've Got to Move Fast," *Public Relations Quarterly* (Winter 1999), vol. 44, no. 4, 43–45.

17. Crawford.

18. Cásarez.

19. Lloyd Trufelman and Laura Goldberg, "Pitching Blogs: Latest Type of Online Media Vehicle May Provide Valuable PR Opportunities," *Public Relations Tactics* (August 2002), p. 6.

20. David Segal and Caroline E. Mayer, "Angry Consumers Create Web Sites to Vent against Businesses," *Seattle Times* (March 29, 1999), as cited in Cásarez.

21. Cásarez.

22. Steve Hoechster, "Building a Home Page on the World Wide Web," *Public Relations Tactics* (March 1996), 1.

23. Michael Ryan, "Public Relations and the Web: Organizational Problems, Gender, and Institution Type," *Public Relations Review* (2003), vol. 29, 335–349.

24. Sara Means Geigel, "Web Writing That Wows," *Public Relations Tactics* (February 2003), 15.

case **14.1**

Suing the Customer

The Music Industry Battles Online Piracy

You couldn't blame Wayne Rosso if he fancies himself as the music industry's worst nightmare. Many think that title belongs to Brianna LaHara. In reality, it may belong to someone who loves music and just can't get enough of it. The music industry's worst nightmare may be you.

Don't worry. We are not about to read you your rights. But that is exactly what this case is all about: rights. The music industry has been engaged in a very public struggle to protect the intellectual property rights of singers, composers, musicians, and the recording and publishing companies that sell their work. What has made this struggle extraordinary is that it has pitted the music industry against the very people on whom it depends for its financial support: music consumers very much like you.

The Founding Fathers Meet the Digital Age

The right to protect one's intellectual property dates back to the ratification of the Constitution of the United States in 1788. Article I, Section 8, of the Constitution gives Congress the right "to promote the progress of science and useful arts, by securing for limited times to authors and inventors the exclusive right to their respective writings and discoveries." What makes this right to protect one's intellectual property so special is that the delegates to the Constitutional Convention wrote it into the original draft. They added other rights such as free speech and fair trial later, in the Bill of Rights. Even today, the Constitution does not mention a personal right to privacy—something that exists only through judicial interpretation. All of which goes to say that the Founding Fathers thought intellectual property was something of value.

Of course, the Founding Fathers—and probably your own grandfather—could not have envisioned the Digital Age. The explosion in computer and communications technology has revolutionized the recording industry. Gone are the days of scratchy vinyl records. Crystal-clear CDs and MP3 players have replaced them. Unlike the old analog technology, in which the medium carrying the music eventually wore out, digital music always sounds as good as when it was recorded.

This ability to provide perfect reproductions of recordings may be a blessing for music lovers, but it has also opened the door to music piracy on an unprecedented scale. Law enforcement agencies battled foreign and domestic bootleggers for years. Copyright laws were easier to enforce when the cost of making illegal copies was high. But that changed with the growth of home recording technology and the advent of the Internet. It is now possible for thousands—even millions—of people to download digital music files from the Web at no cost. And that's the rub: To an estimated 43 million Americans, file-sharing is a part of Web culture. However, to the music industry, it is nothing less than theft.

A Three-Tiered Strategy

The Recording Industry Association of America, the music industry's leading trade association, estimates annual losses from piracy at $4.2 billion worldwide. In a statement on its Web site, RIAA likened copyright violators to the legendary Barbary Coast pirates. "Today's pirates operate not on the high seas but on the Internet, in illegal CD factories, distribution centers, and on the street," the statement said. "The pirate's credo is still the same—why pay for it when it's so easy to steal?"

RIAA says everyone—consumers, retailers, record companies, and creative artists—loses to music pirates. To drive home the point, RIAA posted online testimonials featuring artists and composers representing various genres of music. "Music fans cannot expect their favorite musicians to continue to produce quality albums if they are not willing to pay," said singer-songwriter Sheryl Crow. Latino pop artist Shakira noted that making an album is a team effort. "When somebody pirates a record, that not only affects the artist but also the people who worked on it," she said. Country music artist Brad Paisley added, "When you download music illegally, those folks don't get paid."

The music industry took a three-tiered approach to the problem. Nearly two dozen recording companies and music associations formed the MUSIC Coalition, Music United for Strong Internet Copyright. That group launched a multimedia education campaign in fall 2002. The industry also directed its antipiracy message to the corporate and university communities, whose computer networks are often used for illegal downloading. Aggressive enforcement and prosecution was the third—and most controversial—strategy. RIAA announced that it would begin collecting evidence against individual offenders in June 2003. A full-page music industry ad in the *New York Times* warned, "Next time you or your kids 'share' music on the Internet, you may also want to download a list of attorneys."

From Napster to Grokster

The move against individuals was a major shift in strategy. Initially, RIAA had focused its legal challenges against file-sharing services—with some success. The organization successfully sued—and, in effect, shut down—the file-sharing service Napster in 2001. The courts ruled that Napster was guilty of abetting copyright infringement because it operated from a central server that listed the availability of illicit material.

However, just as there are legal loopholes, there are also technical loopholes. In this case, it was the introduction of peer-to-peer (P2P) technology. "P2P architectures utilize a decentralized, distributed model," said network security consultant Mark Thyer. "Utilizing P2P, computers that have traditionally been used only as workstations can act as both clients and servers."

Here's why that is significant: Because of its decentralized nature, companies using P2P technology have no more control over the actions of consumers than do manufacturers of home video recorders. And the latter had been protected from copyright infringement claims since a 1984 U.S. Supreme Court ruling in the so-called Betamax case—hailed by some as the "Magna Carta of the Technology Age." New file-sharing companies, such as Grokster, KaZaA, and Morpheus, emerged using P2P technology. In response to an RIAA lawsuit, a federal judge ruled in April 2003 that Grokster was not guilty of copyright infringement.

"The Court recognized that our file-sharing software has numerous legal and beneficial uses," said Grokster President Wayne Rosso. "This ruling also means that the labels and the studios cannot ban 21st-century technology in defense of their inefficient and outmoded 20th-century distribution models."

Although the industry immediately appealed the ruling, it had no other legal recourse than to turn its enforcement efforts against individual file-sharers.

The Usual Suspects?

Five months after the Grokster ruling, RIAA filed 261 copyright infringement lawsuits against people it claimed were illegally distributing, on average, more than 1,000 music files for millions of other P2P network users. Almost immediately, the action created a national controversy. At the center of the firestorm was 12-year-old Brianna LaHara, an honors student living in public housing on New York's Upper West Side. It was unclear why Brianna and not her mother was listed as a defendant. RIAA said it did not investigate individual backgrounds before filing the lawsuits. Within 48 hours of the lawsuit's being filed, a settlement was hastily arranged. Brianna's mother paid a $2,000 settlement, acknowledged that her daughter had broken copyright laws, and promised that she wouldn't illegally download any more music. Once the news of the settlement was announced, several P2P groups came forward and promised to pay Brianna's fine.

RIAA's lawsuit strategy was ridiculed during a U.S. Senate hearing into Internet copyright infringement. "Are you headed to junior high schools to round up the usual suspects?" asked Sen. Dick Durbin (D-Ill.). Other members of Congress said they were concerned at how RIAA used provisions of the Digital Millennium Copyright Act to obtain the names, addresses, telephone numbers, and e-mail addresses of suspected violators—a practice a U.S. appeals court overturned three months later as a violation of consumer privacy rights. Speaking at the same hearing, William Barr, an attorney for Verizon Communications Inc., accused the music industry of waging a "campaign against 12-year-old girls."

As for Rosso's take on the situation? "Suing a 12-year-old girl—that's child abuse," he said.

"Nobody likes playing the heavy," said RIAA President Cary Sherman. "Yes, there are going to be some kids caught in this, but you'd be surprised at how many adults engaged in this activity."

THE DIGITAL MILLENNIUM COPYRIGHT ACT OF 1998
U.S. Copyright Office Summary

December 1998

INTRODUCTION

The Digital Millennium Copyright Act (DMCA)[1] was signed into law by President Clinton on October 28, 1998. The legislation implements two 1996 World Intellectual Property Organization (WIPO) treaties: the WIPO Copyright Treaty and the WIPO Performances and Phonograms Treaty. The DMCA also addresses a number of other significant copyright-related issues.

The DMCA is divided into five titles:

- Title I, the **"WIPO Copyright and Performances and Phonograms Treaties Implementation Act of 1998,"** implements the WIPO treaties.
- Title II, the **"Online Copyright Infringement Liability Limitation Act,"** creates limitations on the liability of online service providers for copyright infringement when engaging in certain types of activities.
- Title III, the **"Computer Maintenance Competition Assurance Act,"** creates an exemption for making a copy of a computer program by activating a computer for purposes of maintenance or repair.
- Title IV contains six **miscellaneous provisions**, relating to the functions of the Copyright Office, distance education, the exceptions in the Copyright Act for libraries and for making ephemeral recordings, "webcasting" of sound recordings on the Internet, and the applicability of collective bargaining agreement obligations in the case of transfers of rights in motion pictures.
- Title V, the **"Vessel Hull Design Protection Act,"** creates a new form of protection for the design of vessel hulls.

This memorandum summarizes briefly each title of the DMCA. It provides merely an overview of the law's provisions; for purposes of length and readability a significant amount of detail has been omitted. **A complete understanding of any provision of the DMCA requires reference to the text of the legislation itself.**

---

[1]Pub. L. No. 105-304, 112 Stat. 2860 (Oct. 28, 1998).

Copyright Office Summary   *December 1998*   *Page 1*

In an attempt to protect intellectual property in the Digital Age, Congress adopted the Digital Millennium Copyright Act in 1998. The music industry has used these regulations aggressively in an effort to curb music file-sharing. (Courtesy of the U.S. Copyright Office)

Many within the public relations community joined in the chorus of critics. "Why sue the very people you're trying to market to?" asked Kelly O'Neil, president of a Silicon Valley-based firm that had earlier tangled with RIAA. In its online newsletter, the *Measurement Standard,* KD Paine & Partners opined that RIAA officials had severely damaged the organization's reputation, and added, "They are the classic bluff and bluster comic book cops that are all about threats and are totally cut off from 21st century reality."

"Even though we're taking some PR hits, the message is definitely getting out," said Amy Weiss, RIAA's head of communications. Within a few weeks, the organization softened its tactics by first sending out warning letters and giving alleged offenders 10 days to discuss a settlement and avoid litigation.

Looking for Alternatives

RIAA announced that 64 of the 261 lawsuits had been settled out of court less than three weeks after they had been filed. The organization received another 838 affidavits for its "Clean Slate" program, which offered amnesty to P2P users who voluntarily identify themselves and promise to stop illegally sharing music on the Internet.

The controversy also appeared to have the desired effect, with Nielsen/NetRatings reporting that traffic at one of the leading P2P sites had fallen 41 percent. The Pew Internet & American Life Project reported in January 2004 that the percentage of online Americans downloading music files had been cut in half since RIAA began filing lawsuits. That same report said the number of people with P2P file-sharing applications on their computers had dropped significantly and that a growing number of consumers had turned to a new generation of paid online music services.

Even with these successes, many of the music industry's critics believed it needed to look at alternative approaches to combating piracy. Those include imbedded coding that prevents copying, mandated licensing for P2P music sites, and moving away from old media into online distribution. The industry's challenge appears to be giving the public what it wants while preserving the intellectual rights of those who make the music.

"Suing your customers is not a winning business strategy," wrote G. Richard Shell of the Wharton School, University of Pennsylvania. "Industries have a completely different strategic relationship with customers than they do with rivals. And this sort of strategy does not play well in the court of public opinion."

Sources

Alex Adrianson, "Stopping Music Piracy without Breaking the Internet," *Consumers Research* (October 2003), 10–15.

Anti-Piracy Update, Recording Industry Association of America, Undated. Online: www.riaa.com.

Erik Battenberg, "The PR Battle over File-Sharing," *Public Relations Tactics* (November 2003), 1, 11.

"Can This Reputation Be Saved: The Recording Industry Association of America," *The Measurement Standard,* KD Paine & Partners, September 30, 2003. Online: www.themeasurementstandard.com.

The Constitution of the United States, published by the Commission on the Bicentennial of the United States Constitution, 18th ed., 1992.

"Downloading Girl Escapes Lawsuit," Associated Press, as reported on CBSNews.com, September 9, 2003. Online: www.cbsnews.com

Andrew Fano, "The New Internet Cops," *Computerworld* (September 8, 2003), 21.

James Maguire, "File-Sharing Drops as Industry Battles Rage," NewsFactor Network, October 1, 2003. Online: www.newsfactor.com.perl/story/22398.htm.

Roger Parliff, "The Real War over Piracy," *Fortune* (October 27, 2003), 148–156.

"Pew Internet Project and Comscore Media Metrix Data Memo," Pew Internet & American Life Project, January 2004. Online: www.pewinternet.org.

"Recording Industry to Begin Collecting Evidence and Preparing Lawsuits against File 'Sharers' Who Illegally Offer Music Online," Recording Industry Association of America news release, June 25, 2003. Online: www.riaa.com.

G. Richard Shell, "Suing Your Customers: A Winning Business Strategy?" *Knowledge at Wharton,* The Wharton School, University of Pennsylvania, October 22, 2003. Online: http://knowledge.wharton.upenn.edu.

"64 Individuals Agree to Settlements in Copyright Infringement Cases," Recording Industry Association of America news release, September 29, 2003. Online: www.riaa.com.

Mark Thyer, "Understanding and Dealing with Common Peer-to-Peer (P2P) Application Security," *Information Systems Security* (November–December 2003), 42–51.

"U.S. Court Nixes Net Music Subpoenas," Reuters, as posted on CNN.com, December 19, 2003. Online: www.cnn.com.

"United States District Court for the Central District of California Grants Grokster's Request for Summary Judgment and Motion Picture and Recording Industries," Grokster, Ltd. news release, April 25, 2003. Online: www.grokster.com.press.html.

One Cow from Disaster

case 14.2

The Dairy Industry Uses the Web to Prevent Panic

While the year 1929 is best remembered for the stock market crash that launched the Great Depression, farmers in Southern California remember it for an entirely different reason: the last U.S. outbreak of foot-and-mouth disease. And it came on the heels of an even larger outbreak less than five years earlier. During the

1925 outbreak, farmers were required to destroy 110,000 farm animals and 22,000 deer. In today's dollars adjusted for inflation, the economic loss was approximately $14 billion.

Dairy farmer Neil Kasbergen in the Chino Valley clearly understood what the reemergence of foot-and-mouth disease would mean to the U.S. cattle industry when he said, "We're one cow away from a national disaster."

This was the reality in spring 2001, when a European outbreak of foot-and-mouth disease provoked alarm in North America. The problem in Europe had been heightened by poor public communications. The U.S. dairy industry wanted to ensure that the European experience wasn't repeated.

A Crisis without a Plan

That a single infected cow could create a catastrophe for the dairy industry is particularly alarming when one considers that an estimated 9.1 million dairy cattle produced more than 165 billion pounds of milk in the United States during 2001. That includes the production of more than 600,000 tons of butter and 4 million tons of cheese. Those figures represent nearly $25 billion in gross dairy income.

Foot-and-mouth disease is a highly contagious virus that affects cattle, swine, and other hooved animals. FMD can be spread through contact with contaminated animals, their by-products, or contact with contaminated equipment. Although the disease is rarely fatal, it can cause dairy cattle to dry up. There is no known cure, and a widespread outbreak could cause massive economic disruption.

With so much at stake, it is not surprising that the U.S. dairy industry was concerned when an FMD outbreak occurred in Britain in early 2001. Those concerns were heightened by reports that the disease had spread to other nations in the European Union. The U.S. Department of Agriculture immediately ramped up its crisis plans. However, the story in the dairy industry was different. Officials with Dairy Management Inc., a marketing coalition created to build demand for U.S. dairy products, immediately realized that they had no industrywide response to such a crisis. With European government and dairy industry officials under fire for poor public communications, their U.S. counterparts realized the need for immediate action.

Dairy Management Inc. awarded a $2 million issues management contract to Weber Shandwick Worldwide in May 2001. WSW's task was to create an industrywide crisis plan for use in the event the reputation or safety of U.S. dairy products are threatened. Because DMI is a coalition of dairy interests, the agency would need to forge consensus among four national and nearly 30 state and regional associations. This would also require collaboration with federal and state regulatory agencies, animal health and food safety experts, and numerous agricultural and food industries. DMI spokesperson Jean Regalie said the campaign would also take a long-term view of "the way people look at food."

Hard Lessons from Europe

While the European FMD crisis may have been a wake-up call for the U.S. dairy industry, it also provided a roadmap for dealing with such a crisis. Poor media relations had made a bad problem worse. Some of the sharpest criticism came from Britain's battered tourism industry. "As the outbreak spread, the worldwide sensationalist and frequently inaccurate media reporting of its effects started to cause widespread concern on an almost global scale about visiting Britain," reported the *Journal of Vacation Marketing.* Tourism writer Mary Kate O'Riley said, "You only have to look back at the front page of *USA Today* as news of the crisis broke to see the damage done by two simple words: 'Britain closed.'"

Farms Minister Lord Larry Whitty, reacting to a report critical of the British government's handling of the crisis, acknowledged that a national contingency for an FMD outbreak existed but had been known only to ministry staff. "It does raise issues of organization and communication that the government has to take seriously," Whitty said. "That is not criticism of our staff, but we do need to improve communication and be better prepared if this happens again."

Working with a coalition of organizations created its own challenges: learning the roles and responsibilities of each of DMI's member organizations, their management structures, and how they communicated. Weber Shandwick Worldwide also needed an understanding of government crisis plans and the dairy industry's role in them. Focus-group research was used to uncover consumer attitudes toward the dairy industry and the messages it conveyed. It also investigated a variety of technology options for rapid, coordinated dissemination of information.

Web Training

Based on the research findings, planning focused on the overarching goal of giving the dairy industry a unified voice in the event of a crisis. To achieve this end, WSW and DMI created an animal health response plan. It provided guidance for stakeholders at DMI and its member organizations by providing operational guidelines in the event of a crisis, defining individual roles in crisis response, preparing background information for use in a variety of situations, and creating media guidelines for staff.

Another strategy involved the creation of a Web site, the Dairy Response Center. The site would have public areas accessible to all Web users that would include background on a variety of dairy issues, links to related industry and government Web sites, and a feedback page for submitting questions and comments. The plan called for portions of the site relating to specific crisis scenarios to be kept dark for use only as needed. Initially, when the Web site became active, it was seen as a supplement to written crisis planning materials. However, it quickly evolved into the preferred crisis communication channel.

Hand in hand with the development of the crisis plan and the Web site was the crafting of key messages designed to reassure key stakeholders such as con-

---

Keep
Foot-and-Mouth
Disease
OUT
of America

Immediately report any signs of a vesicular condition to your local, State, or Federal animal health official or veterinarian.

Signs include excessive salivation, lameness, weight loss, drop in milk production, and blisters around the mouth and feet.

Early detection is vital to containing and preventing the spread of FMD to protect the Nation's livestock.

For more information on FMD, call 1–800–601–9327.

http://www.aphis.usda.gov

USDA

U.S. Department of Agriculture
Animal and Plant Health Inspection Service

Program Aid No. 1697 • Issued April 2001   *The U.S. Department of Agriculture is an equal opportunity provider and employer.*

Foot-and-mouth disease is one of the greatest threats to the $25 billion U.S. dairy industry. The U.S. Department of Agriculture, working closely with other government and non-government agencies, has engaged in an aggressive public awareness campaign since an FMD outbreak in Europe in 2001. (Courtesy of the U.S. Department of Agriculture) sumers, dairy farmers, producers, distributors, and government regulators. Other important audiences included communicators with DMI member organizations, the media, and foreign markets.

Having plans is one thing. Executing them is another. That is why DMI and WSW engaged in an aggressive stakeholder-training program. Five regional sessions were held in early 2002. Each was conducted online, with voice coaching over the telephone. The purpose of these two-hour sessions was to familiarize the DMI member organization communicators with the Web site's purpose and train them in its use. Five regional crisis and media exercises with mock crisis scenarios were also conducted. Industry communicators were taught about their roles during crises, how crises evolve, and how to interact with other stakeholders—including government, industry organizations, and the media.

Mad Cow Hits the United States

DMI's issues management campaign, crisis plan, and training efforts received high marks from internal and external stakeholders. Training participants gave the sessions high marks. As a result of the positive feedback, DMI budgeted for additional crisis drills and developed individual training modules for local offices. On hearing of the campaign, the Centers for Disease Control and Prevention invited DMI officials to Atlanta in October 2002 to discuss their efforts. DMI and WSW received a Silver Anvil award from the Public Relations Society of America for its crisis communications efforts.

The first real test of the plan came Dec. 22, 2003. U.S. Agriculture Secretary Ann M. Veneman announced at a hurriedly called news conference that a single Holstein cow in Washington State had tested positive for bovine spongiform encephalopathy, commonly referred to as mad cow disease. BSE is a progressive neurological disease among cattle that is always fatal. However, the threat to humans is minimal.

"Despite this finding, we remain confident in the safety of our food supply," Veneman said. "Even though the risks to human health are minimal based on current evidence, we will take all appropriate actions out of an abundance of caution."

Within minutes of the announcement, the Dairy Response Center was online with a statement on BSE, links to affiliated organizations, and background information on the disease. One link was to a Harvard study that said there were sufficient safeguards to deter the spread of mad cow disease. Another link was to a statement from Terry Stokes, chief executive officer of the National Cattlemen's Beef Association, who said, "While this one case is unfortunate, systems have been built over the past 15 years to prevent this disease from spreading and affecting either animal health or public health."

DMI also informed its stakeholders on its Web site that "DMI has participated in industry briefings and at this point will continue to closely monitor the situation and keep you informed."

International reaction to the BSE incident was predictable, with several countries, including Japan, South Korea, and Mexico, temporarily banning the import of U.S. beef. Prices for U.S. cattle futures dropped dramatically after the announcement. Stock prices for restaurant chains such as McDonald's and Outback Steakhouse initially fell sharply, but stabilized after Christmas. "People are thinking maybe there was an overreaction to the mad cow issue," said Edgar Peters of PanAgora Asset Management. To show his belief in the safety of the food chain, a farmer living just down the road from where the infected animal was discovered had hamburgers for lunch.

The long-term effects of the U.S. mad cow incident will take some time to determine. However, early feedback suggests that the U.S. government and dairy industry were much better prepared to communicate than their European counterparts had been. Their job was made easier when tests determined that the infected cow had been born several years earlier in Canada—just months before regulations designed to halt the spread of the disease were enacted.

Sources

Padraic Cassidy, "Beef, Restaurant Stocks Rebound Slightly," CNN/Money, December 26, 2003. Online: http://cnnmoney.com.

Dairy Market Statistics—2002 Annual Summary, U.S. Department of Agriculture, April 5, 2003. Online: www.ams.usda.gov/dairy/mncs/summary.html.

Foot-and-Mouth Disease Factsheet, Animal and Plant Health Inspection Services, U.S. Department of Agriculture (January 2002).

Frank Buckley, "California Recalls Foot-and-Mouth History," CNN, March 29, 2001. Online: www.cnn.com/2001/US/03/29/fmd.hisotry/index.html.

Elliott Frisby, "Communicating in a Crisis: The British Tourist Authority's Responses to the Foot-and-Mouth Outbreak and the 11th September, 2001," *Journal of Vacation Marketing* (December 2002), vol. 9, no. 1, 89–100.

"Maintaining Confidence in Dairy during a Crisis," Dairy Management, Inc., with Weber Shandwick, Silver Anvil Award description, Public Relations Society of America. Online: www.prsa.org/_Awards/silver/search2.asp.

"Minister Defends Disease Strategy," BBC News, October 29, 2001. Online: http://news.bbc.co.uk/hi/england/1626705.stm.

"NCBA Statement Regarding USDA Announcement of Suspect BSE in Dairy Cow in Washington State," National Cattleman's Beef Association, December 23, 2003. Online: www.bseinfo.org/pr1.htm.

Mary Kate O'Riley, "Is There Anybody out There?" *Director* (April 2002), vol. 55, no. 9, 66–70.

"Quick Links," Dairy Response Center, December 26, 2003. Online: www.dairyresponse.com.

Bill Redeker, "Fear Factor: Washington State Farmers Fear Mad Cow Disease Could Affect Business," ABC News.com, December 27, 2003. Online: http://abcnews.com.

"Transcript of News Conference with Agriculture Secretary Ann M. Veneman on BSE," U.S. Department of Agriculture, December 23, 2003. Online: www.usda.gov.

"$2 Million Dairy Management Contract Awarded to Weber Shandwick," *O'Dwyer's PR Daily,* May 21, 2001. Online: www.odwyerpr.com/0521weber.htm.

The Great Firewall of China

case 14.3

Beijing Moves to Control Internet Content

Sixteenth century author Francis Bacon wrote, "The more one knows, the more one will be able to control events." Five hundred years later, Bacon's words are a source of inspiration for many—and of fear for others.

While it seems unlikely that the noted Renaissance author envisioned anything like the Internet, he clearly understood the power of words. Democratic societies are founded on the basis of free expression and an open exchange of ideas. Therefore, it is no surprise that many view the Internet as a liberating force—one that removes information gatekeepers and gives everyone equal access to the marketplace of ideas.

Of course, that is an idealistic view of the Internet. As noted in the introduction to this chapter, not everyone has equal access to the World Wide Web. The introduction of less expensive wireless and computer technology has helped to narrow the gap. However, in some nations—most notably the People's Republic of China—Internet access is less a question of technology than of ideology. Rather than a liberating force, some see the Web as a threat to the controlling authority of nondemocratic governments. That is why, in China, certain uses of the Internet can result in death.

A Balancing Act

For most Westerners, China is as mysterious as it is enormous. Occupying an area comparable in size to the United States, it has four times the population, an estimated 1.3 billion at the start of 2004. As one of the world's oldest civilizations, China was once the leading center of arts and sciences. However, political upheaval in the 19th and 20th centuries brought civil unrest, famines, and foreign occupation. Communists under the leadership of Mao Zedong seized power in 1949 and remain in control to this day. Mao imposed strict controls over everyday life that, according to the U.S. Central Intelligence Agency, cost tens of millions of lives. However, his successor, Deng Xiaoping, introduced market reforms and decentralized economic decision making in 1978. As a result, China's economy has quadrupled during the past quarter-century.

This case focuses on how the Internet has affected the Chinese government's relationships with its key stakeholders. Maintaining tight political controls while loosening economic restrictions has proven to be a difficult balancing act for Chinese leaders. To put it in public relations terms, China must now answer to more stakeholders than it did before Deng's reforms. Having evolved into the world's second-largest economy, China depends on the free flow of foreign goods and services, as well as foreign access to its markets. The more open a nation's markets, the greater the influence of foreign ideas and public opinion.

The difficulty of this balancing act was never more apparent than in the spring of 1989. At that time, most of the world's communist governments were under siege. Soviet Premiere Mikhail Gorbachev had championed *Glasnost,* the politics of openness and reform. In doing so, he unwittingly launched a worldwide pro-democracy revolution that would engulf almost the entire communist bloc, including the Soviet Union.

Gorbachev's visit to China that spring ignited student-led pro-democracy demonstrations in Beijing's Tiananmen Square. Calling the protests "counterrevolutionary turmoil," the government violently suppressed them in what has since become known as the Tiananmen Square Massacre. Although no official count has ever been released, the human rights group Amnesty International estimates that hundreds were killed and tens of thousands were arrested in the government crackdown.

The Tiananmen Square tragedy came just a year before the invention of the World Wide Web. Nevertheless, it gave the world a glimpse of the power of technology in the Information Age. Despite government efforts to restrict the flow of information in and out of the country during the crisis, the emerging new digital technology made that all but impossible. Direct-dial telephones, fax machines, and digital still imaging devices called pixelators subverted communist censorship.

A New Medium for a New China

The phenomenal growth of the Internet has made the Chinese government's balancing act between a free market economy and tight government political control more difficult than ever. One of the greatest challenges facing the Chinese economy is 80–120 million surplus rural workers adrift between the villages and cities. According to the CIA's *World Factbook,* "Beijing says it will intensify efforts to stimulate growth through spending on infrastructure—such as water control and power grids—and poverty relief through rural tax reform aimed at eliminating arbitrary local levies on farmers." All of this requires foreign investment—and the strings that come with it. For example, China's admission into the World Trade Organization in 2001 came only after the government agreed to a series of economic, social, and political reforms.

China has benefited from the growth of the Internet. According to the China Internet Network Information Center, there were an estimated 45.8 million Internet users in China in 2002, a 72.8 percent increase over 2001. There were nearly 300,000 Web sites, with 40 percent of Internet use concentrated in the country's most prosperous cities. This growth is due, in part, to a 1999 campaign called Government on the Net, in which more than three dozen government agencies and bureaucracies established an Internet presence. To promote Internet use, China Telecom, the nation's primary telecommunications provider, launched a program in March 1999 to provide higher-speed data lines and reduce dial-up fees.

China has more than 45 million Internet users, including these two
university students. While the government has encouraged this
growth, it has also acted aggressively to control Web content.
(Courtesy of Robert R. Basow)

"The government sees [Internet technology] as a driver of China's global competitiveness and a key to gaining international recognition," said Jay X. Hu, managing director of the U.S. Information Technology Office in Beijing. Chinese Premier
Zhu Rongji echoed that sentiment during a February 2002 lecture on technology
when he said, "The use of information technology is vital for the world economy
and social development."

The Death Penalty

While hoping to build on the promise of the Internet, Chinese officials have also
dealt with it as a threat. Since 1995, China has passed at least 60 laws in an effort to
control Web content. For example, the State Council issued highly restrictive rules
in September 2000. To promote what it called a "healthy" Internet environment,
the government required Internet service and content providers to supply detailed
records about their subscribers. This included a record of all Web sites visited.

In a second regulation issued the same month, the government prohibited the
posting of nine kinds of information on the Internet. This included "information

that goes against the basic principles set in the Constitution" and "information that is detrimental to the honor and interests of the state." The measure also prohibited "information that undermines the state's policy for religions, or that propagates heretical organizations or feudalistic and superstitious beliefs." That prohibition targeted Falun Gong, a banned spiritual movement that the Chinese government has systematically suppressed.

Chinese efforts at content control also extend to search engines. According to the Harvard Law School's Berkman Center for Internet & Society, the Web sites most often blocked by the Chinese government focus on democracy, Tibet, and Taiwan. (China has been combating an independence movement in Tibet and considers Taiwan part of its territory.) The Web sites of Western universities and news organizations are also routinely blocked. This systematic censorship of foreign Web sites has become known as "the Great Firewall of China."

Amnesty International claims that China has more than 30,000 state security officers who monitor Web sites, chat rooms, and private e-mail. Citing health and safety concerns, the government shut down 150,000 unlicensed Internet cafes in June 2003. Those that remained or reopened with a license were required to install software that filtered out 500,000 banned sites. One such program, the Filter King, sends daily reports about attempted hits on banned sites to local police.

While some Chinese citizens have used technology such as proxy servers— overseas Web sites that allow access to prohibited sites—they do so at great risk. Amnesty International reported in November 2002 that China was holding at least 33 people for offenses related to Internet use. The human rights organization said that two of those detained, members of Falun Gong, died in custody.

"As the Internet industry continues to expand in China, the government continues to tighten controls on on-line information" was the finding of *State Control of the Internet in China,* an Amnesty International white paper. "Internet users are increasingly caught up in a tight web of rules restricting their fundamental human rights."

And just how dangerous is it to Web surf in China? The Supreme People's Court ruled on Jan. 21, 2001, that "in cases of a gross violation of law and where especially serious harm is caused to the state and people, law offenders may be sentenced to death and their properties will be confiscated by the state."

Promises to Keep

Whether China has the will to continue to maintain its delicate balance between economic freedom and political subjugation is one of the great questions at the start of the 21st century. Just as Russia's Gorbachev unleashed forces he couldn't control, many wonder if the Chinese leadership awaits the same fate.

That China won its 15-year battle to enter the World Trade Organization, as well as the right to host the 2008 Olympic games, suggests that the government is gaining much-needed approval on the global stage. Many believe the West should take a more pragmatic view of Chinese reforms. They say that the more China interacts with the rest of the world, the more likely promised reforms will become a reality.

"U.S. companies do not engage with China for the purpose of transforming Chinese society, converting the Chinese people to any particular creed or world view, or, for that matter, remaking Chinese politics in the image of any other country," said Robert Kapp, president of the U.S.–China Business Council. "It is not coincidental that the rapid growth of American business activity in China has corresponded with the rapid growth of China's modern economy, China's plunge into the mainstreams of global commerce and ideas, and the spectacular economic advances that have brought massive benefit to hundreds of millions of Chinese citizens."

However, not everyone is as optimistic. And they cite the Great Firewall of China as their proof. According to San Francisco-based venture consultant David James, "The social consequences of the Internet's open communications could easily spook the government and convince it to slam the door on development."

As for the economic, social, and political reforms promised in exchange for admission to the WTO, "China is a country which keeps its word," Premier Rongji said. "We must earnestly implement our pledges."

Sources

David W. Guth and Charles Marsh, *Public Relations: A Values-Driven Approach* (Boston: Allyn & Bacon, 2000), 374–375.

Alfred Hermida, "Behind China's Internet Red Firewall," BBC News, September 3, 2002. Online: http://news.bbc.co.uk/1/hi/technology/2234154.stm.

E. D. Hirsch, Jr., Joseph F. Kett, and James Trefil, eds., *The New Dictionary of Cultural Literacy*, 3rd ed. (Boston: Houghton Mifflin, 2002). Online: www.bartleby.com/59/3/knowledgeisp.html.

David James, "China's Love–Hate Affair with the Net," *Upside* (August 1999), vol. 11, no. 8, 52–55.

Robert A. Kapp, Testimony before the House International Relations Committee, Subcommittee on International Economy Policy and Trade, June 24, 1998. Online: www.house.gov/international_relations/105th/ep/wsep624983.htm.

"Long Wait over as China Joins the WTO," CNN, December 10, 2001. Online: www.cnn.com.

"State Control of the Internet in China," Amnesty International, AI index: ASA 17/007/2002, November 2002.

"Tiananmen Square: Expanding the Circle of Victims after 11 Years," Amnesty International news release, May 31, 2000. Online: www.amnesty.org/ailib/intcam/china/ns2000.htm.

U.S. Central Intelligence Agency, *The World Factbook*. Online: www.odci.gov/cia/publications/factbook/index.html.

ACT file # 14 . . . .

Creative Thinking

"I'm not creative."

You've either said it or heard it—or both.

Some people, certainly, are more creative than others, but successful public relations practitioners can't plead a lack of the creativity gene. Nor should they.

Creativity is particularly important in Web-based communication, in which an array of media awaits our commands. Fortunately—as you may have guessed—there is a critical thinking process for creativity, known as creative thinking.

In his brief book *A Technique for Producing Ideas,* first published in 1940, James Webb Young, formerly of the J. Walter Thompson advertising agency, detailed a procedure for creative thinking. Young wrote that the process of producing ideas consists of five steps:[1]

1. Gather "raw materials." Not just facts and opinions about the current public relations challenge. Soak up sports trivia, music lyrics, embarrassing limericks, foreign languages—in short, just about everything. Be a perpetual student.
2. "Work over" the raw materials in your mind. Review the situation. Compare it to a painting, a movie, perhaps even a song. Use brainstorming techniques:
   • Shuffle the deck. Write brief ideas, descriptions, or key words—all related loosely or directly to the current situation—on index cards. Mix and match the cards, looking for thought-provoking combinations.
   • Get contrary. What is the opposite of the situation? What communication tactics seem impossible or disastrous in the current situation? Why?
   • Wax poetic. Use similes and metaphors to make unusual comparisons. For example, brainstorming is like eating pizza. Why? Exploring the connection just might lead to something.
3. "Incubate" your unhatched ideas. Quit studying the situation. Move on to something else. Research shows that the subconscious keeps noodling away at challenges even when we sleep. So take a break. On the back burners of your mind, the creative process is warming up.
4. Await the moment of "Eureka! I have it!" Have faith. The idea will come, often when you're doing something completely unrelated—mowing the lawn, taking a shower, or walking the dog.
5. "Shape" the idea into practical usefulness. Creativity is great—but unless you can apply it in the real world, it lands in the scrap heap.

An original idea, Young wrote, "is nothing more than nor less than a new combination of old elements."[2] Young and other theorists recommend that you see operas, visit art galleries, read comic books, window shop—in short, live life, be curious, steep yourself in the liberal arts, and remember what you learn.

The "magic" of new ideas sparks when your research into situations, clients, and stakeholders crashes headlong into your mental storage bin of operatic arias and comic book heroes. And Young believed that this happens when you're not really trying. Immerse yourself in your research, he advised, and focus intensely on your goal—and then forget about it. Let your subconscious do the work for you. At the right moment, generally when you're engaged in another task, your mind will link a key element of your public relations research to some odd memory of, perhaps, a college basketball game—and an idea is born. You can shape it later. Stop for a moment and celebrate.

So go see a good movie tonight and then grab a café latte at that new art gallery. You can tell your friends, "Hey, I'm working."

We told you public relations could be an adventure.

Discussion Questions · · · · · · · · · · · · · · · · · · ·

1. Have you ever had a "Eureka" moment in which your subconscious suddenly delivered a creative idea? What were you doing when that happened?

2. The fusion of different ideas often is easiest to see in advertisements. Have you noticed any ads that feature an unusual combination?

3. What other brainstorming techniques, besides those listed above, have you heard of or used?

4. Do any of the tactics from this book's case studies seem to be the fusion of different ideas?

Endnotes ·

1. James Webb Young, *A Technique for Producing Ideas* (Chicago: Advertising Publications, 1951).

2. Young, 25.

Public Relations Society of America Member Code of Ethics

PRSA Member Statement of Professional Values

This statement presents the core values of PRSA members and, more broadly, of the public relations profession. These values provide the foundation for the Member Code of Ethics and set the industry standard for the professional practice of public relations. These values are the fundamental beliefs that guide our behaviors and decision-making process. We believe our professional values are vital to the integrity of the profession as a whole.

Advocacy   We serve the public interest by acting as responsible advocates for those we represent. We provide a voice in the marketplace of ideas, facts, and viewpoints to aid informed public debate.

Honesty   We adhere to the highest standards of accuracy and truth in advancing the interests of those we represent and in communicating with the public.

Expertise   We acquire and responsibly use specialized knowledge and experience. We advance the profession through continued professional development, research, and education. We build mutual understanding, credibility, and relationships among a wide array of institutions and audiences.

Independence   We provide objective counsel to those we represent. We are accountable for our actions.

Loyalty   We are faithful to those we represent, while honoring our obligation to serve the public interest.

Fairness   We deal fairly with clients, employers, competitors, peers, vendors, the media, and the general public. We respect all opinions and support the right of free expression.

PRSA Code Provisions

Free Flow of Information

Core Principle
Protecting and advancing the free flow of accurate and truthful information is essential to serving the public interest and contributing to informed decision making in a democratic society.

Intent

- To maintain the integrity of relationships with the media, government officials, and the public.
- To aid informed decision-making.

Guidelines
A member shall:

- Preserve the integrity of the process of communication.
- Be honest and accurate in all communications.
- Act promptly to correct erroneous communications for which the practitioner is responsible.
- Preserve the free flow of unprejudiced information when giving or receiving gifts by ensuring that gifts are nominal, legal, and infrequent.

Examples of Improper Conduct under This Provision

- A member representing a ski manufacturer gives a pair of expensive racing skis to a sports magazine columnist, to influence the columnist to write favorable articles about the product.
- A member entertains a government official beyond legal limits and/or in violation of government reporting requirements.

Competition

Core Principle

Promoting healthy and fair competition among professionals preserves an ethical climate while fostering a robust business environment.

Intent

- To promote respect and fair competition among public relations professionals.
- To serve the public interest by providing the widest choice of practitioner options.

Guidelines

A member shall:

- Follow ethical hiring practices designed to respect free and open competition without deliberately undermining a competitor.
- Preserve intellectual property rights in the marketplace.

Examples of Improper Conduct under This Provision

- A member employed by a "client organization" shares helpful information with a counseling firm that is competing with others for the organization's business.
- A member spreads malicious and unfounded rumors about a competitor in order to alienate the competitor's clients and employees in a ploy to recruit people and business.

Disclosure of Information

Core Principle

Open communication fosters informed decision making in a democratic society.

Intent

- To build trust with the public by revealing all information needed for responsible decision making.

Guidelines

A member shall:

- Be honest and accurate in all communications.
- Act promptly to correct erroneous communications for which the member is responsible.

- Investigate the truthfulness and accuracy of information released on behalf of those represented.
- Reveal the sponsors for causes and interests represented.
- Disclose financial interest (such as stock ownership) in a client's organization.
- Avoid deceptive practices.

Examples of Improper Conduct under This Provision

- Front groups: A member implements "grass roots" campaigns or letter-writing campaigns to legislators on behalf of undisclosed interest groups.
- Lying by omission: A practitioner for a corporation knowingly fails to release financial information, giving a misleading impression of the corporation's performance.
- A member discovers inaccurate information disseminated via a Web site or media kit and does not correct the information.
- A member deceives the public by employing people to pose as volunteers to speak at public hearings and participate in "grass roots" campaigns.

Safeguarding Confidences

Core Principle
Client trust requires appropriate protection of confidential and private information.

Intent

- To protect the privacy rights of clients, organizations, and individuals by safeguarding confidential information.

Guidelines
A member shall:

- Safeguard the confidences and privacy rights of present, former, and prospective clients and employees.
- Protect privileged, confidential, or insider information gained from a client or organization.
- Immediately advise an appropriate authority if a member discovers that confidential information is being divulged by an employee of a client company or organization.

Examples of Improper Conduct under This Provision

- A member changes jobs, takes confidential information, and uses that information in the new position to the detriment of the former employer.

- A member intentionally leaks proprietary information to the detriment of some other party.

Conflicts of Interest

Core Principle

Avoiding real, potential or perceived conflicts of interest builds the trust of clients, employers, and the publics.

Intent

- To earn trust and mutual respect with clients or employers.
- To build trust with the public by avoiding or ending situations that put one's personal or professional interests in conflict with society's interests.

Guidelines

A member shall:

- Act in the best interests of the client or employer, even subordinating the member's personal interests.
- Avoid actions and circumstances that may appear to compromise good business judgment or create a conflict between personal and professional interests.
- Disclose promptly any existing or potential conflict of interest to affected clients or organizations.
- Encourage clients and customers to determine if a conflict exists after notifying all affected parties.

Examples of Improper Conduct under This Provision

- The member fails to disclose that he or she has a strong financial interest in a client's chief competitor.
- The member represents a "competitor company" or a "conflicting interest" without informing a prospective client.

Enhancing the Profession

Core Principle

Public relations professionals work constantly to strengthen the public's trust in the profession.

Intent

- To build respect and credibility with the public for the profession of public relations.
- To improve, adapt and expand professional practices.

Guidelines
A member shall:

- Acknowledge that there is an obligation to protect and enhance the profession.
- Keep informed and educated about practices in the profession to ensure ethical conduct.
- Actively pursue personal professional development.
- Decline representation of clients or organizations that urge or require actions contrary to this Code.
- Accurately define what public relations activities can accomplish.
- Counsel subordinates in proper ethical decision making.
- Require that subordinates adhere to the ethical requirements of the Code.
- Report ethical violations, whether committed by PRSA members or not, to the appropriate authority.

Examples of Improper Conduct under This Provision

- A PRSA member declares publicly that a product the client sells is safe, without disclosing evidence to the contrary.
- A member initially assigns some questionable client work to a non-member practitioner to avoid the ethical obligation of PRSA membership.

Glossary

active public opinion Expressed behavioral inclination exhibited when people act—formally and informally—to influence the opinions and actions of others.

actuality feed A public relations tactic that involves providing tape-recorded quotes, news reports, and other information to assist radio reporters in the preparation of news stories.

Acute Crisis Stage According to crisis communications expert Steven Fink, the "point of no return in a crisis," when some damage will be done. How much damage is determined by the crisis response.

ad hoc plan A plan created for a single, short-term purpose.

advertising The process of creating and sending a persuasive message through controlled media, which allow the sender, for a price, to dictate message, placement, and frequency.

after-action report A postcrisis evaluation of a crisis response.

agape A Greek word denoting godlike, compassionate love for one another.

annual meeting A once-a-year informational conference that a publicly held company must, by law, hold for its stockholders.

annual report A once-a-year informational statement that a publicly held company must, by law, issue to its stockholders.

association management companies Organizations hired by associations to provide administrative and management services.

Astroturf lobbying The actions of front organizations created to give the false impression of grass-roots support for a candidate or cause.

aware public opinion Expressed behavioral inclination that occurs when people grow aware of an emerging issue.

backgrounders Documents that supply information to supplement news releases. Written as publishable stories, backgrounders are often included in media kits.

benefits Particular features of a consumer product that appeal to members of a target market.

blogs Regularly updated online diaries/news forums that focus on particular areas of interest.

boundary-spanning role The function of public relations practitioners when they are serving as a bridge or liaison between an organization and its stakeholders.

business-to-business relations The maintenance of mutually beneficial relationships between a business and the other businesses on which it relies to fulfill its goals and values.

categorical imperative A concept created by Immanuel Kant: the idea that individuals ought to make ethical decisions by imagining what would happen if a chosen course of action were to become a universal law, a clear principle that applied to everyone.

channel partners Businesses that assist another business in the distribution of its products to consumers.

Chronic Crisis Stage According to crisis communications expert Steven Fink, the period during which steps are taken to resolve crises.

coalitions Larger groups formed when smaller groups sharing common interests and values combine forces to increase resources and clout in pursuit of common purposes.

commitment In the context of Hon and Grunig's PR Relationship Measurement Scale, the extent to which each party believes and feels that the relationship is worth maintaining and promoting.

communal relationship   In the context of Hon and Grunig's PR Relationship Measurement Scale, an affiliation in which both parties provide benefits to each other because they care for the welfare of the other—even if they expect nothing in return.

communication   The third step in the public relations process, in which tactics developed during planning are executed.

communication audit   A research procedure used to determine whether an organization's relationship-building activities are consistent with its goals and values.

community   A group of people with common attributes. Those attributes may be geographic, demographic, or psychographic.

constituent   When used in the context of political communication, a term used to describe a person represented by public officials. Often used as a synonym for *voter*.

consumer   An individual who purchases and uses products.

contingency plan   A plan created in anticipation of use in a certain set of circumstances.

controlled channels   Media for which the sender determines the timing and content of messages transmitted to targeted publics. Advertising and employee memoranda are examples. An alternate term for controlled media.

controlled media   Communication channels for which the sender determines the timing and content of messages transmitted to targeted publics. Advertising and employee memoranda are examples. An alternate term for controlled channels.

control mutuality   In the context of Hon and Grunig's PR Relationship Measurement Scale, the degree to which parties agree on which has the rightful power to influence the other.

coorientation   A process in which practitioners seek similarities and differences between their organizations' opinions regarding a public and that public's opinion of the practitioners' organizations.

corporate social responsibility   A social movement that holds organizations ethically responsible for how their operations, products, and services affect society.

crisis   A period of personal or organizational stress, the outcome of which is in doubt, is escalating, threatens important values and/or resources, falls under increasing scrutiny of key stakeholders, and threatens to disrupt normal operations.

crisis communications planning   Contingency planning that identifies an organization's or individual's options for managing a crisis response.

Crisis Resolution Stage   According to crisis communications expert Steven Fink, the period following the conclusion of a crisis when things return to normal. However, the definition of normal may have changed.

critical thinking   Reasoned judgment and problem solving driven by research, analysis, and evaluation.

cross-cultural communication   The exchange of messages between members of different cultures.

culture   A collection of distinct publics bound together by shared characteristics such as language, nationality, ethnicity, attitudes, tastes, and religious beliefs.

customer relationship management   A business process in which a company uses a database to help identify, select, and retain individual customers, as well as to predict customer purchasing habits and needs.

cyber-relations   The use of public relations strategies and tactics to deal with publics via, and issues related to, the Internet.

cybersmear   The use of the Internet to attack the integrity of an organization and/or its products and services.

demographic community   A grouping of people with shared nonattitudinal attributes.

denial   An ethics problem in which the decision maker knows the right course of action, but the consequences of that action seem too hard to endure.

digital marketing   The process of promoting products through online media and tactics, including company Web sites, e-mail campaigns, and online advertising.

dilemma   An ethics problem in which important values clash and no solution provides a way to honor all the important values.

disclosure law   Law that governs the full and timely communication of any information relevant to investors' decisions to buy or sell stocks or bonds.

e-commerce   The process of financial transactions using the Internet.

employee relations   The maintenance of mutually beneficial relations between and among an organization and its employees.

ethics   Beliefs about right and wrong that guide the way we think and act.

evaluation   The fourth step in the public relations process, in which results of a public relations program are measured against previously stated goals and organization values.

exchange relationship   In the context of Hon and Grunig's PR Relationship Measurement Scale, one party's giving of benefits to the other only because the other has provided benefits in the past or is expected to do so in the future.

external publics   Groups united by a common interest, value, or values in a particular situation and that are not part of a public relations practitioner's organization. Examples include the news media, government regulators, and securities analysts.

extranet   A controlled-access internal computer network available only to selected external publics (such as customers and vendors) of an organization.

fact sheets   What–who–when–where–why–how breakdowns of news releases. They are included in media kits to assist reporters in the preparation of news stories.

geographic community   A grouping of people with shared location-related attributes.

globalization   The growing economic interdependence of the world's people as a result of technological advances and increasing world trade.

global village   A concept first articulated by communications theorist Marshall McLuhan, suggesting that because of advances in telecommunications technology, we live in a world in which everyone can share simultaneous experiences.

goals   The desired results of a public relations plan.

GOTV   The popular abbreviation for political "get out the vote" efforts.

government relations   The practice of helping organizations build or maintain relationships with government officials and agencies.

grass-roots lobbying   The encouragement of individual stakeholders, often constituents, to petition the government for the purpose of achieving a particular goal.

gripe sites   Internet Web sites that focus on grievances—real and imagined—against an organization.

hard money   Campaign contributions to political candidates and parties that are subject to the limitations of laws governing state and federal election campaign contributions.

ignorance   In ethics, a condition of unawareness that aggravates a problem.

inputs   In terms of public relations practice, the time, energy, and other resources that go into developing strategies and tactics.

insider trading   The illegal and unethical use of information not available to other investors in securities transactions.

institutional investor   A large company or organization that purchases stocks and other securities, usually in large quantities, on behalf of its members.

integrated marketing communications   The coordinated use of public relations, advertising, and marketing strategies and tactics to send well-defined, interactive messages to individual consumers.

internal publics   Groups united by a common interest, value, or values in a particular situation and that are part of a public relations practitioner's organization. Examples include employees, members, and shareholders.

Internet   A global web that links computer networks and allows the sharing of information in a digital format.

intervening publics   Publics with which one communicates in hopes of having them influence the actions of a third party, a primary public.

intranet   A controlled-access internal computer network available only to the employees of an organization.

investor relations   The maintenance of mutually beneficial relations between publicly owned companies and stockholders, potential stockholders, and other publics in the investment community.

inward special publics   Organized groups of stakeholders whose primary focus is to benefit those inside the organization.

iron triangle   The exchange relationship among special interest groups and the legislators and government regulators who oversee programs within their area of special interest.

issue   A topic of interest that arouses public opinion. For something to be considered an issue, it must affect a variety of publics and be evolving.

issues management   A process through which organizations identify and analyze emerging trends and issues for the purpose of preparing timely and appropriate responses.

latent public opinion   A behavioral inclination that exists when people have interest in a topic or issue but are unaware of the similar interests of others.

lobbying   The process of trying to influence governmental legislative and regulatory processes through education and persuasion.

managers   Individuals responsible for the allocation of human and material resources within an organization.

marketing   The process of researching, creating, refining, and promoting a product, and distributing it to targeted consumers.

marketing mix   The combination of marketing tactics used to communicate with targeted consumers. Also, the four traditional aspects of marketing: product, price, place, and promotion.

marketing public relations   The use of the public relations process to promote an organization's products.

media advisories   Documents provided to journalists to inform them of an upcoming event. In addition to the basic facts (what, who, when, where, why, and how), they include logistical information to assist reporters who cover the event.

media kits   Packets of documents designed to assist reporters in covering an organization's events and/or issues. They usually contain a news release, backgrounders, and a fact sheet. They may also include pictures, graphics materials, and other information relevant to the event or issue.

member relations   The maintenance of mutually beneficial relations between and among an organization and its members.

mutual fund manager   Individual responsible for purchasing stock and other securities on behalf of a mutual fund's investors. The investors participate by purchasing shares of the fund.

news   For journalists, timely nonpromotional information of interest to an audience. Its definition will vary, depending on the nature of the audience each journalist serves.

news conferences   Structured meetings between an organization's representative(s) and the news media for the purpose of providing information for news stories.

news judgment   The factors of relevance, scope, proximity, timeliness, and uniqueness with which journalists decide whether an occurrence will be of interest to their audiences.

news releases   Client-related news stories that a public relations practitioner writes and distributes to the news media.

noise   In communication theory, distractions that envelop communication and often inhibit the successful transmission of a message.

nonprofit organizations   Associations that provide educational, professional, and/or charitable services without the expectation or purpose of financial profit.

objectives   Specific milestones that measure progress toward the achievement of a goal.

outcomes   In terms of public relations practice, measures of the effects of a public relations plan.

outputs   In terms of public relations practice, the specific actions taken during the execution of a public relations plan.

outsource   To hire an outside supplier to provide a necessary service, such as a Web site.

outward special publics   Organized groups of stakeholders whose primary focus is to benefit those outside the organization.

partner relationship management   A business process in which a company uses a database to help manage communications and relationship-building activities with partner businesses, such as suppliers and distributors.

pitch letters   Letters sent by public relations practitioners to journalists, often on an exclusive basis, describing newsworthy human interest stories whose publication would generate favorable publicity for organizations.

planning The second step in the public relations process, in which research is translated into a blueprint for achieving desired results.

political action committee An organization, representing a particular special interest, that collects money and distributes it to political candidates. Also known as a *PAC*.

politics A consensus-building process through which public policy is created.

primary publics Publics with whom one communicates in an effort to influence their actions.

proactive media relations The initiation of contact with media organizations in an effort to generate publicity that serves the strategic interests of an organization. This approach allows an organization to set its own agenda.

Prodromal Crisis Stage According to crisis communications expert Steven Fink, the period before the onset of a crisis. Warning signs of a potential crisis appear during this stage.

PR Relationship Measurement Scale An index developed by Linda Hon and James Grunig that measures the strength or health of relationships.

psychographic community A grouping of people with shared attitudinal attributes.

public In a public relations context, any group of people who share a common interest, value, or values in a particular situation.

public affairs The practice of helping government agencies and officials build or maintain relationships with the various constituencies they serve. An ambiguous term, it also is used by corporations to mean government relations or community relations.

public company A company that sells stock in open markets and is owned by its stockholders.

public opinion A public's expressed attitudes on a particular topic at a particular moment in time. It can be fluid, subject to sudden changes in the environment.

public relations The values-driven management of relationships between an organization and the publics important to its success.

reactive media relations Contact with media organizations only in response to a situation that might have beneficially been addressed earlier by proactive media relations.

relational dialectics The forces at play that tend to pull relationships apart.

relationships Ongoing, meaningful interactions between an organization and the various publics that can affect its success.

research The process of gathering information. Research also is the first step in the public relations process.

resource dependency theory The premise that organizations form relationships with publics to acquire the resources they need to fulfill their goals and values.

risk assessment A form of research that identifies potential dangers confronting organizations and individuals.

satisfaction In the context of Hon and Grunig's PR Relationship Measurement Scale, the extent to which each party feels the relationship is one in which the benefits outweigh the costs.

securities analyst An individual who studies and makes recommendations regarding the purchase of specific stocks and bonds.

security A stock or a bond sold in an open market.

shareholder An individual who owns shares, or stock, in a public company or companies.

social exchange theory The premise that people seek to minimize costs and maximize rewards within their relationships.

social responsibility The practice, derived from social contract theories, of believing in and honoring mutual obligations and duties to aid one another and assist the common good.

soft money Campaign contributions to political candidates and parties that are not subject to the limitations of laws governing state and federal election campaign contributions.

special events Planned happenings that serve as public relations tactics.

special interest agencies In the context of the iron triangle, executive branch agencies of government that administer and regulate programs and issues of particular interest to a special interest group.

special interest groups   Organizations of like-minded individuals who come together to lobby government officials and agencies in pursuit of public policy goals.

special interest legislators   In the context of the iron triangle, members of legislative committees that oversee programs and issues of particular interest to a special interest group.

special publics   Organized stakeholder groups formed out of common interests.

stakeholders   People or publics that have an interest in an organization or in an issue potentially involving that organization.

standing plan   An ongoing and long-term plan to nurture a relationship.

stockholder   An individual who owns shares, or stock, in a public company or companies.

systems theory   A management philosophy in which an organization is viewed as a system of interrelated parts interacting with one another and with a larger outside world.

tactics   In a public relations context, specific actions that practitioners take to meet specified objectives.

telecommuting   The act of working at home but communicating frequently with an employer's main office via telephone and computer.

third-party endorsement   Verification of a story's newsworthiness that the news media provide when they publish or broadcast the story. Appearance in an uncontrolled news medium lends credibility to a story because the media are neither the sender nor the receiver but an independent third party.

transparency   A term used to describe open, nonsecretive workings and transactions in governments and other organizations.

trust   In the context of Hon and Grunig's PR Relationship Measurement Scale, one party's level of confidence in and willingness to open up to the other party.

uncontrolled channels   Media, such as newspapers, in which a public relations practitioner cannot control message content, timing, or frequency.

usenet   Online forum for message exchanges in which writers can share information and provide feedback. Usenets are also known as newsgroups, bulletin boards, or chat rooms.

utilitarianism   A philosophy refined by John Stuart Mill that holds that all actions should be directed at producing the greatest good for the greatest number of people.

veil of ignorance   A term and concept created by John Rawls. The veil of ignorance strategy asks decision makers to examine a situation objectively from all points of view, especially from those of the affected publics.

video news releases   Videotaped news stories that an organization produces and distributes to television news media. Video news releases often include interviews and unedited footage of a story or issue of strategic importance.

virtual communities   Collections of people who build relationships and share common interests via the Internet.

Webcast   A video presentation, often live, delivered through a Web site.

white papers   Detailed written reports, often on public policy matters and often containing recommendations for action.

World Wide Web   A graphics-oriented computer network, developed in 1991, that made the Internet more accessible and attractive and helped spur its rapid development.

Index